Principles and Practice of Database Systems

Macmillan Computer Science Series

Consulting Editor
Professor F. H. Sumner, University of Manchester

S. T. Allworth, *Introduction to Real-time Software Design*
Ian O. Angell, *A Practical Introduction to Computer Graphics*
R. E. Berry and B. A. E. Meekings, *A Book on C*
G. M. Birtwistle, *Discrete Event Modelling on Simula*
T. B. Boffey, *Graph Theory in Operations Research*
Richard Bornat, *Understanding and Writing Compilers*
J. K. Buckle, *The ICL 2900 Series*
J. K. Buckle, *Software Configuration Management*
J. C. Cluley, *Interfacing to Microprocessors*
Robert Cole, *Computer Communications*
Derek Coleman, *A Structured Programming Approach to Data*
Andrew J. T. Colin, *Fundamentals of Computer Science*
Andrew J. T. Colin, *Programming and Problem-solving in Algol 68*
S. M. Deen, *Principles and Practice of Database Systems*
P. M. Dew and K. R. James, *Introduction to Numerical Computation in Pascal*
M. R. M. Dunsmuir and G. J. Davies, *Programming the UNIX System*
K. C. E. Gee, *Introduction to Local Area Computer Networks*
J. B. Gosling, *Design of Arithmetic Units for Digital Computers*
Roger Hutty, *Fortran for Students*
Roger Hutty, *Z80 Assembly Language Programming for Students*
Roland N. Ibbett, *The Architecture of High Performance Computers*
P. Jaulent, *The 68000 – Hardware and Software*
M. J. King and J. P. Pardoe, *Program Design Using JSP – A Practical Introduction*
H. Kopetz, *Software Reliability*
E. V. Krishnamurthy, *Introductory Theory of Computer Science*
Graham Lee, *From Hardware to Software: an introduction to computers*
A. M. Lister, *Fundamentals of Operating Systems, third edition*
G. P. McKeown and V. J. Rayward-Smith, *Mathematics for Computing*
Brian Meek, *Fortran, PL/1 and the Algols*
Derrick Morris, *An Introduction to System Programming – Based on the PDP11*
Derrick Morris and Roland N. Ibbett, *The MU5 Computer System*
C. Queinnec, *LISP*
John Race, *Case Studies in Systems Analysis*
W. P Salman, O. Tisserand and B. Toulout, *FORTH*
L. E. Scales, *Introduction to Non-Linear Optimization*
P. S. Sell, *Expert Systems – A Practical Introduction*
Colin J. Theaker and Graham R. Brookes, *A Practical Course on Operating Systems*
M. J. Usher, *Information Theory for Information Technologists*
B. S. Walker, *Understanding Microprocessors*
Peter J. L. Wallis, *Portable Programming*
I. R. Wilson and A. M. Addyman, *A Practical Introduction to Pascal – with BS 6192, second edition*

Principles and Practice of Database Systems

S.M. Deen

Department of Computing Science
University of Aberdeen

MACMILLAN

First published 1985

Published by
Higher and Further Education Division
MACMILLAN PUBLISHERS LTD
Houndmills, Basingstoke, Hampshire RG21 2XS
and London
Companies and representatives
throughout the world

Printed in Great Britain by
The Camelot Press Ltd,
Southampton

British Library Cataloguing in Publication Data
Deen, S. M.
    Principles and practice of database systems.—
    (Macmillan computer science series)
    1. Data base management   2. File organization
    (Computer science)
    I. Title
    001.64'42   QA76.9.D3

ISBN 0-333-37099-6
ISBN 0-333-37100-3 Pbk

Contents

Preface

This book was originally intended as a new edition of my earlier book *Fundamentals of Data Base Systems*, published several years ago. But, in the intervening period, so much has changed in the field of databases that I thought it better to write an entirely new book – with a new framework to incorporate the change. However, like its predecessor, this book also draws heavily from my undergraduate course at Aberdeen, which has now been given for over ten years. A major source of contribution to my course, and more importantly to the contents of this book, has been the deliberations of the *British Database Teachers Conferences*, which I helped to organise in the late seventies and early eighties, with a view to improving the standard of database teaching in the U.K. I have also taken into consideration the comments and suggestions received from the readers of my earlier book. An area to which I have paid special attention is the need of potential research students for an advanced treatment of *some* database issues at the undergraduate level, as part of a general background. This is an open-ended area with considerable scope for disagreements as to what should or should not be included. In this I have been influenced by my involvements in a number of international conferences on database research, and by my experience as a supervisor of research students. Thus the book is intended as a general text on databases for undergraduate students and other interested readers, but has been extended to include some advanced topics for those who need them.

The book deals primarily with the general principles of databases, using the relational and network models as the main vehicle for the realisation of these principles. Its basic objective is to impart a deeper understanding of the issues and problems, rather than to produce database programmers. To reinforce what is learnt, exercises with selected answers are provided at the end of each chapter (except for chapter 1). The references cited can be looked up for further studies.

The book is divided into five parts, with Part I (chapters 1–3) presenting a prerequisite for the appreciation of the main database issues. Part II (chapters 4 and 5) covers the issues and problems, and thus constitutes the kernel of the book. Part III is devoted to the relational and network models and is spread over six chapters (6–11). A rationale of this part could be helpful.

I have presented the first three normal forms and the original relational languages (algebra, calculus, Alpha) as part of a basic (or classical) relational model in chapter 6. Needless to say, a sound knowledge of a relational algebra is essential for a proper understanding of the relational model, and Codd's calculus and Alpha are the principal sources of all subsequent calculus based languages. QUEL is included in chapter 6 as the closest implementation of Alpha. Admittedly SQL is the leading relational language, but I found it more convenient to present it in chapter 8 with QBE, rather than packing it in an already large chapter 6. Chapter 7 on higher normal forms stands on its own.

The Codasyl model is described in chapter 9 in fair detail. In keeping with the objective of this book, I have stressed the semantics more than the syntaxes — syntaxes are given mainly for a more concrete understanding of the concepts involved. An overview of the storage schema in chapter 10 outlines a possible storage model for the Codasyl schema, and also shows where the storage dependent clauses of the earlier schema models have been moved to. The Fortran subschema facility in chapter 10 illustrates the mechanism of supporting a different host language on the Codasyl model. Since the implemented Codasyl packages are based on the earlier models, the section on the past changes provides a link between the latest version and the one that the user may still have in his computer centre.

Obviously the ANSI network model presented in chapter 11 will eventually replace the Codasyl model. Additionally, it offers some new ideas on database/host language interfaces. The same chapter also carries a comparison between the relational and the network models, which attempts to fulfil a need recognised by many teachers.

Part IV (chapters 12 and 13) describes the current state of the art. Chapter 12 reviews user issues, while chapter 13 discusses some special products, including SYSTEM R which demonstrates many of the pioneering implementation techniques of the relational model. The other special products described there represent the earlier data models and hence their coverage highlights their modelling powers, rather than their supporting facilities. Since the hierarchical model (IMS) is regarded by many experts as the third major data model (after the relational and network models), I have described it more fully and also compared its modelling capacity with that of the network model.

The final Part V (chapters 14 and 15) attempts to provide a glimpse of the future, and includes such topics as I thought useful and exciting.

Department of Computing Science   S. M. Deen
University of Aberdeen

Acknowledgements

I wish to thank a number of people who assisted me during the writing of this book. To Ray Carrick, John Edgar, Don Kennedy and Malcolm Taylor of my PRECI research group at Aberdeen, for going through the manuscripts and for suggesting corrections. To David Bell (University of Ulster), Bill Samson (Dundee College of Technology), Stan Blethyn (Bristol Polytechnic) and the publisher's referee for reviewing the material and for their valuable comments. Stan Blethyn also supplied examination questions, some of which are included in the exercises. To Frank Manola (Computer Corporation of America, U.S.A.) for keeping me informed on the latest developments on the ANSI data models.

I am also thankful to Muriel Jones of IBM, Phillip Robling of Cincom and Geoff Stacey of Edinburgh University for reviewing the coverages on IMS, TOTAL and Codasyl DSDL respectively. My special thanks are to my secretary, Sheila Tomlins, for her painstaking typing and retypings of the manuscript. She was a tremendous help.

Finally, I take this opportunity also to express my indebtedness to my family for the support I received. To my wife Rudaina for her patience and encouragement and to two young men, Rami (12) and Alvin (10), for leaving their dad alone even when their computer programs needed debugging.

A Note to Tutors and Readers

As pointed out in the Preface, this book is aimed at undergraduate students and other interested readers such as programmers, systems designers and database administrators. The reader is assumed to possess some knowledge of computers and of Cobol as a general background, within which each topic in the book is developed – starting from a basic level and gradually progressing towards deeper issues. The contents of the book can be logically divided into two parts, basic and advanced. The chapters covering the basic material are

chapter 1
chapter 2
chapter 3
chapter 4
chapter 5 (except section 5.7 which is advanced)
chapter 6
chapter 9
chapter 12

(advanced chapters are marked with an asterisk * in the Contents list).

It should be possible to understand the basic material, by-passing the advanced parts, without any serious loss of continuity. Within each chapter there are issues which are treated in some depth, but a reader not interested in these issues should be able to skip over them, again without any significant loss of understanding of the rest of the material. Every basic chapter is largely self-contained; most of chapters 6 and 9 (the relational and the Codasyl models) can be understood at a preliminary level if – apart from chapters 1 and 2 – only sections 4.1, 4.2 and 4.3 are read beforehand. However, a more thorough understanding of relevant database issues requires the study of both chapters 4 and 5 in full.

For an introductory course on the relational model it should not be necessary to cover functional dependencies and determinants, since both the second and third normal forms have been given alternative definitions. Likewise, quadratic join, outer join and QUEL can also be skipped if so desired. The students can be asked to read relational calculus and DSL Alpha for themselves.

If a briefer coverage is intended for the Codasyl model, then exclude the CALL, CHECK and SOURCE/RESULT clauses, the STRUCTURAL constraint clause and the multimember set types. Also restrict the set order criteria to the DEFAULT option and set selection criteria to the current of set types. Correspondingly, the Alternate clause, the set selection criteria and the subschema working storage section can be dropped from the subschema. Chapter 12 is written mainly for beginners, to give them some notion of the database environments. It is suitable for self-reading by the students.

For advanced studies, chapter 3 should be covered along with other chapters as needed. Much of chapter 10, and the ANSI network and relational models in chapter 11, can be given to the advanced students to read for themselves, with a view to carrying out some of the exercises at the end of those chapters.

Many of the exercises in the book are drawn from Honours degree examination questions. Readers' attention is drawn particularly to exercise 6.9 of chapter 6, which includes a *cyclic* query, exercise 8.8 of chapter 8, which shows a limitation of the relational model, and exercise 9.12 of chapter 9, which illustrates the use of currency indicators. There are also three special case studies presented in exercises 8.7, 8.8 and 8.9 of chapter 8 for relational solutions, and in 9.9, 9.10 and 9.11 of chapter 9 for Codasyl solutions. These case studies help to bring out the comparative features of the two models.

Readers are also asked to have a look at the Preface, which explains the general layout of the book.

PART I: FOUNDATION

1 Introduction

A modern computerised database is essentially a large volume of data stored with its description. Its concept was not a sudden breakthrough in computer technology, it was brought about rather gradually through experience and the pressure of requirements. Many organisations contributed in the development of databases; the list is long and includes computer manufacturers, software houses, user organisations and professional bodies, as described later in this chapter. The chapter also covers some basic concepts, and advantages and disadvantages of databases; but we begin with the history of the evolution of databases.

1.1 History of the evolution of databases

A database may be regarded as the most modern technique of data storage which started with the invention of punched cards by Dr Herman Hollerith (Hollingdale and Tootil, 1970) of the United States Bureau of Census in the 1880s. Dr Hollerith was confronted with the problem of completing the 1880 census of 13 million Americans before 1890 when the next census was due. In 1886 it was clear that the job could not be completed in time using the existing manual means of counting. Necessity was the mother of invention: from his knowledge of the use of punched cards in Jacquard looms, Dr Hollerith invented a method of storing information on them, thus introducing the era of mechanised card files which was to remain the leading information storage medium for the next sixty years.

The first electronic computer ENIAC became operational in 1946. It was designed by Professors Eckert and Mauchley of the University of Pennsylvania for the United States Defense Department, mainly to calculate trajectories and firing tables. In those early days, computers were largely used for scientific calculations where the facility for the storage of data did not feature as an important requirement — the speed of arithmetic calculation was all that was needed. But when their usage was subsequently extended to data processing, the limitations of card files began to be noticed. One of the organisations which became seriously concerned by such limitations was the U.S. Bureau of Census. Faced with the approaching 1950 census, the Bureau became particularly anxious to have a faster storage medium, and this led to the invention of magnetic tape devices. In 1951 a new computer, to be called Univac-1, designed by the same Echert–Mauchley pair, was delivered to the Bureau to cope with the 1950 census data. It had a unique device called

Magnetic Tape System which could read a magnetic tape both forward and backward at high speed (Rosen, 1969). The necessity of the Census Bureau thus
mothered two major inventions in seventy years – the punch card and magnetic
tape files.

The impact of magnetic tape on data storage was overwhelming. Those of us
involved in some early card file processing can still recall the frustration of finding
mispunched, slightly off-punched and screwed up cards scattered in large card files
produced by a computer. The fear of accidentally dropping a box of cards and
getting the cards out of sequence was also considerable. With the advent of the
magnetic tape, all these nightmares were over. It was light, reliable and neat; its
storage capacity and speed were phenomenal compared to a card file. However, the
magnetic tape did not alter the processing mode substantially. The file organisation
was still sequential, although it allowed the representation of variable length records
in a more convenient form. All terminologies of card file systems such as files,
records and fields were carried over to the magnetic tape system. The data-processing
systems used in the 1950s were mostly simple payroll subsystems designed in isolation and independent of other related subsystems. A typical payroll subsystem
would consist of a large number of small programs with many files, each containing
fragmented information. The situation changed when the subsequent attempt to
computerise more complex systems brought in a new breed of experts – the system
analysts. They took a global view and introduced the concept of integrated files to
be shared by a number of programs in more than one subsystem. These shared files
were relatively large and the problem of writing long data descriptions in each program for each file was resolved by the Cobol COPY verb which allowed a program
to copy a pre-written general data description of a file. Conceptually the introduction of the COPY verb represented a major step forward in the separation of data
description from any program. From then on the history of the evolution of database became an account of the progress towards more integrated storage of data
from less integrated storage.

The introduction of magnetic discs in the mid sixties gave a further boost towards this integration. To access a record on a magnetic tape it is necessary to scan
all the intervening records sequentially, but on a disc a record can be accessed
directly, by-passing the other records, and thereby gaining an overall retrieval speed
of 2 to 4 orders of magnitude over magnetic tape. Disc storage, thus, provided the
much needed hardware support for the large integrated files.

By the mid sixties, the concept of Management Information System (MIS) gained
currency. The basic approach was to run the programs of the MIS package on the
files output by all the relevant subsystems, but soon it was found that, for a large
organisation, the number of input files to the MIS package was excessively high
with the attendant problems of extensive sorting and collating. Additionally the
failure of one system could easily wreck the whole operation. The data duplication
in the files resulting in update inconsistencies brought in another problem. Thus
these MIS packages turned out to be unreliable, cumbersome and generally unsatis-

factory. This highlighted the need for greater integration and induced many organisations to favour such a measure.

One of the outstanding products of that time was the Integrated Data Store (IDS) released by General Electric (now owned by Honeywell and called IDS-I) in 1965. As the name suggests, IDS was used to create large integrated files to be shared by a number of applications. It is a forerunner of modern database management systems and is capable of supporting a number of data structures. Its pioneer, Charles W. Bachman subsequently played a very active role in the development of the Codasyl database proposal which incorporates many of the features of IDS.

IDS was soon followed by other MIS packages based on integrated files for major systems. Many organisations invested large sums of money on them only to discover that MIS packages were not as effective as they would like them to be. The problem was the lack of coordination between the files of the major systems. It was soon realised that what was needed was a database containing a generalised integrated collection of data, ideally for all the systems of an organisation serving all application programs. It was recognised that such a database must be both program and language independent if it was to serve all applications; and in particular a change in the data should not require a change in the application program. If a database is to respond efficiently to the conflicting needs of all the application programs then it must provide an adequate data representation facility — supported by a variety of data access techniques. This concept of a database crystallised only in the early seventies although the term database or data bank has been used loosely from the mid sixties to refer to almost any large file.

A number of database management systems, based on diverse data models, appeared on the market in the early seventies. Codasyl became interested in databases in the late sixties and set up a task group to specify a common data model, now known as the *Codasyl* or *network model*. Since the publication of its draft specifications in 1971, there has been a noticeable movement away from the diversity of earlier models, many implementors converging on the Codasyl model.

In parallel with the development of the Codasyl model, other ideas based on mathematical concepts were also pursued by computer scientists. The major outcome of this search was the relational model due to Dr Edgar F. Codd which was first proposed in 1970. The model is simple, elegant and yet very powerful. It caught the imagination of researchers early on, and has been the principal inspiration behind the new area of database research. If Bachman is the father of databases, then Codd is the father of database research. The earlier implementation problems of the relational model have now been resolved, and there now exists a number of relational implementations, including commercial products and research prototypes. Today, the relational model is recognised as the other major model beside the network model. There is however a growing realisation among the proponents of the two models that what is needed is a unified approach where the facilities of both the models, indeed all models, are available within a single framework. This has led to research in data modelling.

The existing principal products of the earlier models (that is, pre-Codasyl and pre-relational) are

IMS (Information Management System) of IBM (Hierarchical model)
ADABAS of Software AG, W. Germany (Inverted structured model)
SYSTEM 2000 of M.R.I., U.S.A. (Inverted structured model)
TOTAL of Cincom, U.S.A. (Net structured model)

In this book the relational and the Codasyl model will be described in Part III, along with ANSI's proposal for the standardisation of the Codasyl model. The earlier models mentioned above will be covered briefly in Part IV followed by discussion of future developments in Part V.

1.2 Institutions involved with database development

We shall briefly describe here the role played by some of the major institutions in the development of databases.

Codasyl

Codasyl or CODASYL (Conference On Data Systems Languages) is an international organisation of computer users, manufacturers, software houses and other interested groups. Its principal objective is the design, development and specification of common user languages. It has produced the Cobol language and is still continuing work on its further development. Codasyl's involvement in databases is a direct consequence of its interest in the extension of the Cobol language facilities. A fuller description of Codasyl and its activities are given in chapter 9.

ANSI

ANSI (American National Standards Institute) is responsible for standardisation of products in the U.S.A. Its subcommittee X3 deals with information-processing systems, in which branch H2 is responsible for database standardisation. The X3 has also a Standard Planning And Requirement Committee (SPARC) which looks at forward planning. SPARC has produced the ANSI/SPARC architecture (chapter 4) and is currently planning for a family of standards for database systems (beyond the scope of this book). X3H2 has undertaken to standardise both the relational and Codasyl models (chapter 11). ANSI, like the British Standards Institution (BSI) is a member of the International Standards Organization (ISO).

BCS, ACM, IEEE, IFIP and others

Both the British Computer Society (BCS) and the Association for Computing Machinery (ACM) have taken an active interest in the Codasyl proposal. The BCS held a conference in October 1971 to discuss the DBTG report of April 1971 and, in October 1974, it arranged a symposium on implementations of the Codasyl proposal. It has a number of working groups in the database area; one of them called DBAWG (see section 9.1) played an active role in enhancing the facilities of the Codasyl model. Between 1980 and 1983 the BCS has sponsored two national and two international research conferences on databases (jointly with the University of Aberdeen) under the chairmanship of this author.

ACM is of course well known for its activities in all aspects of computing, including databases. One of its periodicals called *ACM Transactions On Database Systems (TODS)* is a leading research journal on the subject. ACM's Special Interest Group on the Management Of Data (SIGMOD) represents database experts from all over the world, and it holds annually in the U.S.A. one of the leading database research conferences. Another international series of research conferences, called the Very Large Data Base (VLDB) conferences — originally sponsored by the ACM and IEEE, and now by the VLDB foundation — are held in different countries in different years. David Hsiao (U.S.A.) started both the VLDB series and the *ACM TODS*.

The Institute of Electrical and Electronic Engineers (IEEE) publishes a number of journals, some of which are on databases. It also sponsors international conferences.

ACM, BCS, and other similar national organisations are members of IFIP (International Federation of Information Processing). IFIP has several working groups, one of which, known as WG2.6 (within Technical Committee 2 (TC-2)), deals with data modelling, and organised three special conferences between 1976 and 1979, under the dynamic chairmanship of G. M. Nijssen (then in Belgium, now in Australia). These conferences were very valuable in clarifying ideas on data modelling.

The contributions of the computer manufacturers and software houses in the evolution of the database cannot be exaggerated. Without their keen participation, there would not be a database facility today. IBM in particular has conducted and is still conducting extensive database research. Another commercial organisation in the U.S.A. that has contributed much, particularly to distributed database research, is the Computer Corporation of America, funded largely by research grants from the U.S. Department of Defense. Both the U.S. and Canadian Governments have financed a number of Codasyl publications.

1.3 Concepts and definitions

As indicated earlier, the term database has been used loosely in the past to indicate any large collection of data. In some circles it is still used in this sense, but to a database specialist it means something more specific. Perhaps to emphasise this special meaning, the Codasyl DDLC (see section 9.1) in the late seventies dropped the two-word term 'data base' in favour of a single word 'database'. However, this change of form does not make clearer what a modern database is. We shall try a few definitions below.

A database may be looked upon as

Yesterday's data stored for tomorrow's use.

In this sense, a database can exist without a computer, as long as it can meet future update and retrieval requirements. However, since the subject of this book is computer databases, we may modify the definition as

Yesterday's data stored in a computer for tomorrow's use.

Both these definitions catch the essence of modern databases. A more elaborate definition for computer databases is

A generalised integrated collection of data together with its description, which is managed in such a way that it can fulfil the differing needs of its users.

We can analyse this last definition as follows:

(i) A database is a generalised collection of data.
(ii) The collection is integrated to reduce data replications.
(iii) The collection contains its descriptions called schemas (see below).
(iv) The collection is managed in such a way that it can fulfil the differing needs of its users.

Point (iv) needs further elucidation. To fulfil the differing user requirements, a database has to use flexible data and storage structures. The greater their flexibility, the better is the ability of the database to cope with all user needs for a long time. The flexibility in data structure is achieved by structuring data along their *natural data relationships*. Consider, for instance, parent records and children records in a database. Each parent is related to each of his/her children, and each child to the parent. In addition, each child is also related to the other children of the same parent. A database must represent all such data relationships adequately, along with privacy and integrity constraints, referred to as *usage constraints*, for the protection of data against unauthorised use and undesirable updates. Furthermore, we also need the supporting structures including *access paths* (keys, indexes, pointers) to provide an efficient processing capability. These descriptions of data and storage structures are given in the *schemas*. In order to be useful to all programs, a database must be managed during run-time by an independent piece of software; this software is called the Database Control System (DBCS). Finally, it should be understood that the database users will require both retrieval and update facilities.

From now on, we shall use the term database to imply only computer database unless otherwise indicated. The definition given above outlines the scope of this book. There are of course other ways of defining a database. One such view held by this author defines a database as an extension of the human memory on computers. This and other views will be considered in chapter 14.

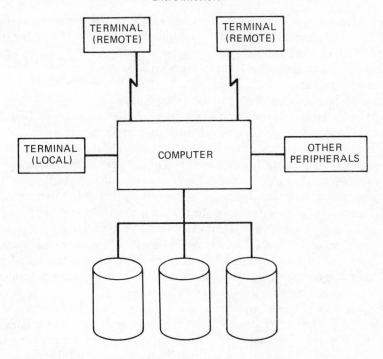

Figure 1.1 A hardware configuration for a database

A diagram of a computer configuration for a database is shown in figure 1.1. A database will normally be stored on direct access devices such as discs. (We shall always assume disc as the storage medium, unless otherwise stated.) The environment may include remote terminals for the database users and can be operated in both batch and online modes as appropriate. The minimum computer memory required for average databases varies from 30K bytes to 160K bytes. A major part of it is occupied by the routines and tables required for the DBCS which acts as an interface between the operating system of the computer and the application programs using the database.

Definitions

We shall define here some of the terms used in the text.

(i) Database Management System (DBMS): A system that generates, runs and maintains databases, and as such the system must include all the software needed for the purpose. Thus IMS of IBM is a DBMS, DMS 1100 of Univac is another.

(ii) Database Control System (DBCS): The software required for run-time control, that is, the run-time management of a database. This is a part of DBMS.

(iii) Database System (DBS): A data-processing system which uses a database. Thus an organisation using a database will have a database system, say for its payroll personnel and sales processing.

(iv) Implementor: An individual or an organisation who implements a specification to produce a DBMS; for instance, Univac is the implementor of the Codasyl proposal on which the DMS 1100 is based.

(v) Manufacturer: A firm that manufactures computers, for example, IBM.

(vi) Data Model: This specifies the rules according to which data are structured and also the associated operations that are permitted. It may also be viewed as a technique for the formal description of data, data relationships and usage constraints. The facilities available vary from one model to another. Some examples of models are: network model, relational model, hierarchical model.

(vii) Transaction: The term means different things to different people. We shall define it as the smallest unit of an application program which extracts a consistent set of data from the database (in the case of a retrieval-only transaction), or which leaves the database in an error-free state (in the case of an update transaction). A transaction is described by one or more programming language instructions (see also section 5.1).

(viii) Application program: A program to process the data of the database for some computer application; it will typically contain one or more transactions described by any permissible *user language*, for example, by a query language, or a host language. The term user program means the same thing. Thus, according to this definition, a single query from an online terminal can also constitute an application program.

(ix) Run-unit: One execution of an application program. This term is typically used in the Codasyl model. An equivalent term is *user process* or just a *process*.

(x) Query language: A very high level language to describe retrieval-only transactions, but recent query languages permit update transactions as well (see section 5.5.1).

(xi) Host language: A language, such as Cobol or Fortran, which is specifically extended to permit database transactions.

(xii) User language: A query or host language in which an application program is written.

(xiii) Database Administrator (DBA): The person responsible for the database in an organisation.

(xiv) User: There are several types of users in a database environment. The application programmer, the systems designer, the DBA are all users. The user department is a user, the organisation as a whole is also a user, but the problem faced by each is different. The term user is employed in this book as a common name for all of them; the meaning will be apparent from the context.

1.4 Facilities and limitations

As indicated earlier, there are a number of Database Management Systems currently available The facilities offered by them vary a great deal, depending on their level of sophistication. In general, however, a good DBMS should provide the following advantages over a conventional system:

(a) *Independence of data and program*
    This is a prime advantage of a database. Both the database and the user program can be altered independently of each other. This saves the time and money that would otherwise be needed in modifying them just to retain consistency.

(b) *Ease in systems design*
    A system designer in a database environment is not concerned with the extensive file design, data duplication, data inconsistency, maintenance, backup facilities, and so on of a conventional system. In a database, data exist in a form suitable for all applications, the designer only has to pick what he needs. The systems design is therefore simpler.

(c) *Ease in programming*
    The programming task is significantly reduced as the programmers are relieved of the details of the file processing, file updates and numerous sorting processes. The level of programming skill required can be lower for a database.

(d) *Multiple host languages*
    A DBMS is expected to support a number of host languages so that a user can choose the one that is most convenient for a particular applications.

(e) *Consistent and up-to-date data*
    A database reduces data duplication and helps to maintain consistent and up-to-date data. In a conventional system data duplication in various files often leads to chaos and inconsistency.

(f) *Concurrent usage*
    A database can permit more than one program to access the database at the same time, thus maximising resource utilisation.

(g) *Data protection*
    In a database, privacy and the integrity of data can be controlled more effectively.

(h) *Query facilities*
    A database is expected to support high level query facilities.

(i) *Evolutionary system*
    Databases are claimed to be evolutionary systems, permitting the user to build his database gradually — and learning from his experience. Facilities for re-organising the database to optimise the overall performance are also expected to be provided. However, the reality is less promising.

The disadvantage of a database is its cost. It is expensive to install, run and maintain. The major cost factors are:

(a) *Large memory*

Databases need large memory to house the DBCS routines, application programs, the database tables, directories, system buffers etc. in addition to the
host operating system.

(b) *Storage devices*

A database requires a large volume of storage, a good part of which is con-
sumed as overheads rather than actual data.

(c) *Channel capacity*

Additional input/output channel capacity may be required to cope with the
increased data traffic between the database on the physical storage devices
and the computer memory.

(d) *Slow processing speed*

The processing speed, particularly the update speed, is very slow in a database,
owing to a heavy overhead (see later).

(e) *Staff overhead*

A database needs additional staff for its administration. Existing staff require
retraining and additional staff may also be needed, depending on the size of
the database.

(f) *Implementation*

The implementation of a database system in a user organisation is a major and
expensive undertaking. Nothing like this happens in conventional data-
processing systems.

(g) *Incompatibility*

The incompatibility of the available data models is a disadvantage for the user;
for once he has installed one DBMS, it becomes very difficult and expensive
for him to change to another.

Increase in programmer productivity and control over data resources are sometimes cited as some of the advantages of databases. In many cases, databases offer
conveniences which are hard to quantify. The value assigned to a convenience
largely depends on what the person is used to. An organisation having installed and
used a database satisfactorily for a while is likely to forget the cost and count the
blessings. The level of justification required to change from a conventionally computerised system to a database system is similar to that required for changing from
a manual to a computerised system. If we regard manual operation as the first
stage in information processing, then the use of a database is the logical third stage.

References

Hollingdale, S. M. and Tootil, G. C. (1970). *Electronic Computers*, Pelican, p. 59
Rosen, S. (1969). *Computing Surveys*, Vol. 1, p. 7

2 Data and File Structure

As a collection of data, a database uses the concepts of data items, records and files in one form or another, and it employs the techniques available for their representations in a computer environment. The knowledge of these concepts and techniques therefore forms a prerequisite for a proper understanding of database technology. This chapter is intended to satisfy this prerequisite.

2.1 Basic concepts

A named collection of *component* types makes up a record type, each component type being either a *data item* or a *data aggregate*. Therefore, a record occurrence (or record for short) is a collection of components. The names given to record types and component types are called record names and component names respectively. Examples explaining these concepts are given in figure 2.1.

Components

A data item is defined as the smallest unit of data type that can take part in processing independently and meaningfully, and hence a data item is *atomic* or *non-decomposable*. In this book, the term *attribute* will be used interchangeably with data item except where indicated otherwise. The name given to a data item is *data item name*, and its value is *data item value*; likewise, we have attribute name and attribute value. In Fortran a data item is often referred to as a field, and in Cobol as an elementary item. Note that following a common practice, we have used the terms data item, data-aggregate and attribute to imply their types, rather than their instances or values. In contrast, the terms record and component mean their instances.

Apart from its indivisibility, a data item value displays a number of other characteristics, some of which are logical or machine independent while others are physical or machine dependent. Every data item value contains a particular value out of a set of possible values, the basic type of a data item being determined by its format, such as numeric or character-string (that is, an alphanumeric). Another way of classification is to look at what we may call its value-type, that is, the meaning of the value it represents, such as a data item for employee numbers. It is possible for several different data items to hold the same value type; for instance,

13

we can use data items named ENO and ENUM both to hold employee numbers. The logical characteristics of a data item imply its size and basic type, whereas the physical characteristics imply storage size in bytes, and other storage properties such as alignment.

A data aggregate (*Codasyl DDLC Journal of Development*, 1981) may consist of a collection of data items and/or other data aggregates. For convenience of discussion, we shall divide it into three subtypes:

(i) *Vector:* A data item repeating a fixed or a variable number of times. If it repeats a fixed number of times, we shall call it a *fixed vector*.

(ii) *Composite item:* A *named* collection of data items which does not repeat. Sometimes the term *composite attribute* is used to imply any collection of attributes, but not necessarily a named or a contiguous collection.

(iii) *Repeating group:* A *collection of data items and/or other data* aggregates, which repeats a fixed or a variable number of times.

Some examples are given below.

Records

To explain some of the terms used above let us consider a customer record type named CUST-REC described in figure 2.1 using Cobol notations. It contains customer number (CNO), customer name (CNAME) subdivided into SURNAME and INITIAL, credit limit (CR-LT), DATE made up of day (DD), month (MM) and year (YY), number of orders (NORD) and for each ORDER the product code (PCODE) and quantity ordered (QTY). In it CNO, SURNAME, INITIAL, CR-LT, NORD, DD, MM, YY, PCOD and QTY are data items, CNAME and DATE are

```
01     CUST-REC.
       03   CNO              PIC X(3).
       03   CNAME.
            05   SURNAME      PIC X(15).
            05   INITIAL      PIC X(55).
       03   CR-LT            PIC 9(4).
       03   BAL              PIC 9(5) OCCURS 3 TIMES.
       03   DATE.
            05   DD           PIC 99.
            05   MM           PIC 99.
            05   YY           PIC 99.
       03   NORD             PIC 99.
       03   ORDER            OCCURS 10 TIMES DEPENDING ON NORD.
            05   PCODE        PIC X(3).
            05   QTY          PIC 9(3).
```

Figure 2.1

composite items, BAL is a fixed vector and ORDER is a repeating group of PCODE and QTY. We should observe that what is or is not a data item is dependent on our requirements. For instance, if we do not subdivide CNAME into SURNAME and INITIAL but declare it as a single string of 20 characters, then CNAME would be a data item. Likewise DATE represented by PIC X(6) without subdivision into DD, MM and YY will also be a data item.

This record type will represent as many records (or record occurrences) as there are customers, one record per customer. Records can be identified by their *key values*, a *record key* (*key* for short) being made up of component types. A key that can identify the records of a given type uniquely is called a *unique key* and the others non-unique keys. *It is sometimes possible for several keys to identify records* uniquely, in such cases usually one of them is selected as the principal key called the *primary key*, all other keys — unique or non-unique — are known as *secondary keys*. If there is only one unique key, it is automatically the primary key. The customer number (CNO) above could act as the primary key if we assume customer numbers to be unique. Customer Name (CNAME) or Credit Limit (CR-LT) or other component types can act as secondary keys. In the example given, more than one customer can have the same name or same credit limit, and hence CNAME and CR-LT cannot act as primary keys. Any key, primary or secondary, can have more than one component type. For instance, (CNAME, CR-LT) concatenated together can be a key. Even a repeating group can be included in a key, as is done in the ADABAS system (section 13.3).

It is possible for a key to have redundant components. For instance, in a key (CNO, CNAME), the CNAME is unnecessary if CNO alone identifies the customer records uniquely. The removal of such redundancies from the primary key is the purpose of the concept of full functional dependency in the relational model, as we shall encounter later.

Files

A file is basically a named collection of records belonging to one or more record type. The term is also used to imply a physical collection of records in one or more areas of a physical device, organised in a specific way to maximise the retrieval and update speed of its records for a particular application. In general we can group files into the following six categories

> serial
> sequential
> indexed
> random
> inverted
> linked

A serial file is simply a collection of records in one physical area without any reference to the key. A sequential file is a sorted serial file, that is, a file where records are stored in ascending or descending order of a key. The update of such a file involves copying the old file and incorporating the new information in the copy. Magnetic tapes can support both serial and sequential files, but not the others, which can be held only by direct access devices, typically discs. These files are discussed below.

2.2 Indexed files

The essential feature of an indexed file is an index table containing a list of the keys and the addresses of the corresponding records on disc. An index table can be constructed in three different ways: implicit, basic and limit. In an implicit index, the table maintains a list of all possible keys, and as a result the keys are always in order. In a 5-digit key we shall have 100,000 (0-99,999) entries in such a table, even if there is a maximum of, say, 1000 records that could be stored. Therefore an implicit index is normally too large for practical purposes. A basic index leads to what is known as an indexed random or an indexed non-sequential file, and a limit index to an indexed sequential file. The former is less commonly used than the latter, which is supported by standard Cobol software.

2.2.1 Indexed random files

The basic index table for these files looks somewhat like this:

Row no.	Key	Record address	Chain (row)
1	1	6	5
2	3	26	0
3	4	15	0
4	5	25	6
5	2	40	2
6	6	100	0

A chain contains the row number in the table for the next higher key. If the next higher key is in the next row, then its chain is traditionally set to zero, all chains being initially at zero. During subsequent amendment runs, when records are deleted or new records are inserted out of sequence, the chains are updated, a deleted record being by-passed by chaining. To find a record directly, the index table is searched by key for the record address, either sequentially or by using some other technique.

2.2.2 Indexed sequential files

The limit index used in indexed sequential files is something of a compromise. Records are grouped into blocks, each block having an exclusive range of keys represented by the highest key, as shown below:

Block no.	Key	Range represented
1	6	1–6
2	12	7–12
3	24	19–24
4	18	13–18

A typical entry for these blocks will be (block number, highest key) pairs, repeated in block number order. Within a block, the records are chained, each chain indicating the location of the next higher record. To access a record, a block with the next higher key is searched. For instance, in this example, to find the key number 14, the block 4, which has the next higher key 18, will be read by the computer. The correct record will be made available by matching the key value. This type of indexing system is very compact and reasonably efficient, and hence popular.

The storage used for an indexed sequential file is divided into three areas which we shall refer to as primary data area (PDA), the cylinder overflow area (COA) and the independent overflow area (IOA), each being divided into blocks. Every cylinder of the disc contains a number of PDA blocks for the original records and a number of COA blocks to accommodate the overflows from these PDA blocks without the necessity of a disc head movement. The overflows from COA are absorbed in IOA. While a PDA block is designed to contain a number of records for efficient storage utilisation, the size of a COA or for that matter an IOA block is usually restricted to holding a single record. If needed for overflows, one or more COA blocks are allocated to a PDA block, all COA blocks belonging to a PDA block being chained. The IOA blocks are also chained. In large files, two levels of indexes are maintained: a cylinder index (giving the highest key on each cylinder) to indicate the cylinder of the record, followed by a block index within each cylinder to locate the block of the record (figure 2.2).

When a file is created, all records within every block are stored in sequential order. It is possible to reserve space in the PDA blocks for new insertions. If a PDA block is full, a record belonging to this block is placed in a COA block, which is chained to the other COA blocks of this PDA block. A PDA block maintains an additional entry showing the address of its first COA block. The actual process can be illustrated by the following example. Suppose a PDA block, capable of holding 6 records has the following 5 records

1	2	3	5	10	

The first IOA cylinder

Cylinder Index Entries
Independent Overflow Area
(All IOA blocks are chained)

Cylinder index occupies
part of the first cylinder
followed by IOA.
More cylinders for IOA
are used if required

A PDA cylinder

Block Index Entries
Cylinder Overflow Area
(All COA block belonging to the same PDA block are chained)
Primary Data Area blocks as specified

As many cylinders as necessary
each containing Block Index,
COA and PDA

Figure 2.2 Indexed sequential file

If in a subsequent run, records 4, 6 and 8 are inserted, the PDA block will be re-organised as

1	2	3	4	5	6

and two COA blocks will be allocated to this PDA block for records 8 and 10. The block index will keep an entry for record 8 and its location in COA, which in turn will have a pointer to the COA block of record 10. If record 9 is inserted in a later run, it would be stored in a COA block; but if COA is full, the record will be placed in an IOA block. In either case, the pointers will be updated as appropriate. To retrieve a record, the appropriate PDA block or COA block is searched as indicated by the index; if the record is not found, the IOA blocks are scanned, following the linkage. Deletions of records are permitted, but the technique varies from flagging the record for subsequent removal by a utility to physically removing it during run-time. As the update is random, it is sometimes possible to have too many new records in a particular block and too few in another, causing a severe overflow in one direction, and underflow in another direction. At this point, the index needs reorganisation. In advanced applications, self-organising indexes such as B-trees (section 3.3.1) are used.

An indexed sequential file can be processed both sequentially and randomly. In sequential processing the chains are used, while in random processing only the wanted records are accessed. Variations in implementation of the indexed sequential technique described are possible.

2.3 Random files

Randomly organised files are held on discs where records are grouped into blocks called *buckets*, with one or more complete buckets per track of a disc. We shall define a *bucket* as the unit of disc input/output, that is, the portion of the disc space that can be retrieved (or written to) by the operating system with a single read (or write) operation. Its size usually varies from 256 bytes in small computers to 4096 bytes in large computers. Instead of using indexes, bucket number (or address) of a record in a random file is found by a calculation on a record key using a formula known as a hashing or an address-generation algorithm (AGA). This formula is supplied by the user in his program. The user must also provide adequate means to deal with the associated overflow problems. Once the address is known, the bucket concerned is accessed directly. The system then produces the wanted record from those in the selected bucket by matching the key value. No pointers or chaining are required. Compared to an indexed sequential file, access is much faster here, since searching through a lengthy index table is avoided. However, it is difficult to design a hashing algorithm which will take care of all future insertions and overflows efficiently. The additional advantage of sequential processing permitted in indexed sequential files is not normally available in random files, but there are a number of applications — such as real-time systems with fast response times — where random files provide the only means of support.

The factors affecting the efficiency of a random file are

> bucket size
> treatment of overflows
> address generation technique

Small buckets tend to increase storage overheads by needing more overflows, and large buckets lead to underflows and long scanning time (to find the appropriate record from the bucket). But given an operating system, the user may not always have any control on bucket size. The most important of these factors — the address generation technique — is discussed below.

Address generation involves the generation of the bucket address from a key value, and it is carried out in three steps. First all non-numeric characters of the keys are converted to numeric form, a convenient method being the replacement of letters A to Z by numbers 10 to 35. In the second step the numeric key values obtained from the first step are transformed into another set of numbers which is evenly distributed over the specified range. In the final step the transformed set of key values is normalised to fit the range of bucket addresses. The most difficult part is the selection of an appropriate key-transformation, known as hashing, technique, for the second step. A number of methods are available (Lum *et al.*, 1971), some of which are more efficient than others, depending on the applications. Some major hashing techniques are given below.

Key organisation

This is a simple method and involves organising the key values into suitable groups which can be used to generate an address. Consider for example a file with 5 groups of key values, each group having 100 records to be distributed over 50 buckets with 10 records per bucket. Suppose the groups are

CB100–CB199, XM300–XM399, LA700–LA799, ZL500–ZL599, MK800–MK899

This set does not need any conversion to numerical values; all that is necessary is simply to use the last two digits 00–99 as the transformed keys, thus giving a range of 100. We calculate the normalisation factor, NF as

$$NF = \frac{\text{total number of buckets}}{\text{range of the transformed key}}$$

$$= \frac{50}{100} = 0.5$$

By multiplying a transformed key by NF and truncating, we find its bucket number. The keys 0 and 1 of each group will go to bucket 0 (10 records), keys 2 and 3 of each group to bucket 1, keys 98 and 99 of each group to bucket 49, and so on.

This method is suitable only if the records are evenly distributed within each group.

Division

Let us assume that we have a maximum TMAX of 1000 records, with 4 digit keys, to be distributed over 50 buckets. (The maximum file size is 1000 records.) Since the keys are 4 digits, the total key range KMAX is 10000 from 000–9999, but representing only 1000 actual keys. Therefore each bucket will have a range of 10000/50 = 200 values, each on average having 20 actual records. In this algorithm, the bucket number is the quotient of the division of the key value by this bucket range of 200. Say the key value is 8557, then the transformed key value

$$\frac{\text{key value}}{\text{bucket range}} = \frac{8557}{200}$$

$$= 43.34$$

$$= 43 \text{ after truncation}$$

The minimum transformed key value is 0/200 = 0 and the maximum transformed key value is 9999/200 = 49, and hence there will be a maximum of 50 transformed key values to be distributed over 50 buckets, which makes the normalisation factor equal to 1. We allocate transformed key value n to bucket $n + 1$ if buckets are counted from 1 to 50. Although the average number of records yielding the same transformed key value is 20, the actual number could vary from 0 to 200, thus causing underflows and overflows in the corresponding bucket (see below).

[Later in the book (section 3.3.2) we shall use the term home hash slot in place of transformed key value, home hash width (HW) in place of average number of records per bucket, and hash divider (HD) in place of bucket range, such that

$$TMAX = HW * HMAX$$
$$KMAX = HD * HMAX$$

where HMAX is the maximum number of hash slots. In this example HMAX = 50, HD = 200 and HW = 20.]

The advantage of the division technique lies in the fact that the resultant distribution retains the original key value order. In this example, key values 0–199 will go in bucket 1, 200–399 to bucket 2, and so on in the key order, if we start with sorted records. If both random access by key and sequential access in key order are needed for the same records (not necessarily by the same application), then the division algorithm would appear to be the best AGA. However, if the key values are clustered (that is, unevenly distributed) in the key range, then some buckets will get too few records (underflows) while others will get too many records (overflows). Underflows waste storage, whereas overflows require an additional overflow management procedure. This problem can be lessened in the following way:

(i) Use a data compression technique to produce a set of compressed key values in the original key sequence, where key values are more uniformly distributed. At the simplest level, this can be done by a procedure which removes the gaps in the original key range. For instance, if we know there will never by any key values in the range of, say, 215–310, then this gap can be eliminated.
(ii) Use a good overflow handling technique.

However, owing to subsequent insertions/deletions, the eventual distribution will be only partially ordered in the key sequence, but it can still provide the random and sequential access to a set of records most efficiently (see also section 3.3.2). Instead of using the division technique with data compression, if we divide the records into groups defined by upper and lower keys, then we shall have an indexed sequential file. Some experts are reluctant to call the division technique a true hashing technique, as it produces a sequential, rather than a random, key distribution.

Remainder

We shall use the previous example of maximum of 1000 records, with 4 digits key values to be distributed over 50 buckets. The transformed key value is taken as the remainder of the division of the original key value by the number of buckets. For the key value 8668

$$\frac{\text{key value}}{\text{total no. of buckets}} = \frac{8668}{50} \text{ , remainder} = 18$$

The range of the transformed key values is 0–49 as before, and hence the normalisation factor is 1. Therefore this key value 8668 will be allocated to bucket number [18 + 1] = 19, counting the first bucket as number 1.

This hashing technique randomises the original key value distribution; for instance, key values 0, 50, 100, 150, . . ., 9950 yield bucket 1; values 1, 51, 101, 151, . . ., 9951 yield bucket 2, and so on. It is obvious that a sequential access to these records in the key order will be most inefficient, since a different bucket has to be accessed for every next key.

As in the case of the division technique, every transformed key value will on average have 20 records, the actual number varying from 0 to 200. However, this technique is more effective against clustered distribution; for instance, there will be no problem if all the 1000 key values lie in the range 0–999 (a check for the reader). On the other hand if the values are clustered in groups 0–24, 50–74, 100–124, and so on (at equal divisor distance) then records will overflow in buckets 1–25, underflowing in the rest; but this kind of clustering is generally considered to be less likely. Therefore the remainder technique provides a better protection against clustering, but slows down the speed of sequential access by the same key. It has been used in many database implementations.

Radix transformation

In this method the key is changed into a number base other than its own. For example, 52419 can be transformed to, say, base 11 as

$$5 \times 11^4 + 2 \times 11^3 + 4 \times 11^2 + 1 \times 11^1 + 9 \times 11^0 = 76371$$

Buckets numbers can be found by multiplying this transformed key 76371 by the appropriate normalisation factor. This method can be used to break down clusters and produce an evenly distributed set.

Midsquare method

Here the value of the key is squared and the central digits of the square are used as the transformed key. Assume that we have a 5-digit key for a file with 2000 buckets. Then, if the key under consideration is 25312, we have

$$25312 \times 25312 = 0640697344$$

Selecting the central 4 digits 0697 as the transformed key, then the bucket number for this key is

$$\frac{\text{total number of buckets}}{\text{the range of the transformed key}} \times 697 = \frac{2000}{10000} \times 697 = 139.4$$

Therefore 139 is the bucket number.

Shifting

Let us assume that the key is 64012418. Now split the key in the middle into two parts, 6401 and 2418. We can now add these to the middle of the key to yield the transformed key as follows:

$$
\begin{array}{rr}
6401 & 2418 \\
64 & 01 \\
24 & 18 \\
\hline
\end{array}
$$

$$\text{transformed key} = \quad 89 \quad 43$$

Now we can normalise the value of the transformed key to give the address.

Folding

In this technique the key is partitioned into a number of parts, each equal to the address length, and then folded over along the partition boundary like a piece of paper. The digits falling into the same position are added. Assume, for example, an 8-digit key with 3-digit address length. Then

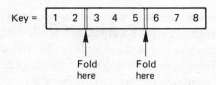

So we have the situation shown in figure 2.3.

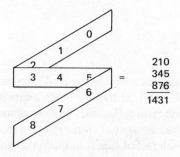

$$
\begin{array}{r}
210 \\
345 \\
876 \\
\hline
1431
\end{array}
$$

Figure 2.3 Folding

Now take 431 as the three-digit transformed key and adjust as necessary to fit the range of the addresses. Note that the last part of the fold has only two significant digits since the key is 8 digits long. The folding and shifting methods are useful for large keys.

Polynomial method

In this method, each digit of the key is expressed as the coefficient of a polynomial. The key 25312 therefore becomes

$$2x^4 + 5x^3 + 3x^2 + x + 2$$

The polynomial is divided by another invariant polynomial and the remainder is
taken as the transformed key.

Investigation (Lum *et al*., 1971) shows that the remainder method gives best
overall performance as a randomiser, with the polynomial and the midsquare
methods coming next. Other complex hashing methods such as digit analysis or
Lin's method (Lum *et al*., 1971) are found to be poor in performance, and hence
are not described above. As pointed out earlier, the division algorithm can sometimes be used to advantage where true randomisation is not needed.

2.4 Inverted files

The files discussed so far are commonly used in data processing and are referred to
as the *regular files*. Their organisation is simple, each record being characterised by
a single key by means of which any of the records can be related. Departure from
this concept involves a complex organisation where a record can be accessed either
through multiple keys or through pointers linking the related records. The first of
these is the inverted file organisation which permits multiple keys per record.
Essentially there are two ways of organising an inverted file, as follows.

Fully inverted file

In a fully inverted file, every data item of a record is represented as a key, and an
index table is maintained for all their values. Since a data item value could be
common to more than one record, the index table consists of entries for every data
item value followed by the addresses of all the relevant records. Similarly, since all
the data item values of each record appear in the index table, there is no need to
store data records in the conventional sense; hence the file is inverted. However, the
file maintains for each record a location which, instead of holding data item values
of the record, contains pointers, one for each data item value, indicating their
positions in the inverted index. A record can be reconstructed following these
pointers. Although this method provides storage economy, it makes retrievals and
updates both cumbersome and costly; hence fully inverted files are not popular.

Partially inverted file

In a partially inverted file, data records are stored explicitly in addition to index tables for the keys. It is not necessary to represent all the data items as keys. It can be viewed as a file supporting multiple keys as against a single key of an indexed sequential file, and as such it can be implemented as a collection of indexes, one for each key.

However, there are two methods of creating index tables. In the traditional technique no distinction is made between primary and secondary keys, each entry of an index table containing a key value followed by the addresses of the relevant records. In a more modern technique, sometimes called *secondary indexing technique*, one key is declared as primary which identifies the records uniquely; the other keys are secondary. In the primary index (that is, the index table for the primary key), an entry contains a key value and the physical address of the record concerned, but in the secondary indexes (that is, the index tables for the secondary keys), the physical locations are replaced by the primary key values, thus providing a level of indirection from the physical storage. Therefore if the physical addresses of the records change − as they would be in a reorganisation − only the primary index is affected. However, it makes the access by secondary key slightly slower. Figure 2.4 shows a primary index for customer number (CNO) and a secondary index for credit limit (CR-LT) for the customer record mentioned earlier. To retrieve the customers with credit limit £1000, we must first access the secondary index table for the key CR-LT to get the relevant customer numbers (A30, A40 and A51), and then the primary index to get the physical locations, 11, 12, 13 of the records. In the older technique the index table for the key CR-LT will keep the physical locations instead of customer numbers, and therefore need less disc accesses; but in that case, in the event of a physical reorganisation, the physical locations must be changed in every single index table. This inconvenience of re-

Row No.	CNO	Physical Location	Chain (Row No.)	Row No.	CR-LT	Primary Key Values	Chain (Row No.)
1	A20	11	0	1	1000	A30, A40, A51	0
2	A30	11	0	2	5000	A50	0
3	A40	12	0	3	7000	A55	0
4	A44	12	0	4	8000	A20, A44	END
5	A50	13	0				
6	A51	13	0				
7	A55	14	END				

Primary Index   Secondary Index

Figure 2.4 Partially inverted files for two types of indexes. The content of chain is assumed to be the same as in indexed sequential file

organisation is usually traded off against the disadvantage of slightly slower access. In complex queries involving a number of secondary keys, the wanted records are first selected from the secondary index tables, and then the selected records are retrieved by the primary index table. In these cases the overhead of this extra access to the primary index is considered to be acceptable.

In all indexing, there are two main problems: one is to locate the entry of a given key in the correct table and the other is to update and maintain the tables. If the index tables for inverted files (one table for each key) are implemented and maintained as in index sequential files, then given a key value the system would first locate, through a master table, the appropriate index table for that key, and then the entry of the key value would be found, following the cylinder and block indexes of the index table. If a record is inserted or deleted, appropriate alterations must be made in all the index tables; it will involve a corresponding insertion or deletion of a row in the primary index table. However its effects on the secondary index tables *could* be limited to only an addition/deletion of a column containing the primary key value. For instance, if in figure 2.4 two customer records with

(i) CNO = A25 CR-LT = 5000, physical location 15
(ii) CNO = A48 CR-LT = 6000, physical location 20

are inserted and are followed by the deletion of two others A30 and A55, then the result will be as shown in figure 2.5.

Row No.	CNO	Physical Location	Chain
1	A20	11	8
2	A30	11	–
3	A40	12	0
4	A44	12	9
5	A50	13	0
6	A51	13	END
7	A55	14	–
8	A25	15	3
9	A48	20	5

Row No.	CR-LT	Primary Key Values	Chain
1	1000	A40, A51	0
2	5000	A25, A50	5
3	7000	A55	–
4	8000	A20, A44	END
5	6000	A48	4

Figure 2.5 Partially inverted files of figure 2.4, after insertion of two records and deletion of two others. A subsequent garbage collection run is needed to remove the by-passed rows (denoted by a hyphen in the chain column). An actual implementation will be more complex

The partially inverted files or multikey record types are used in the **ADABAS** and SYSTEM 2000 database systems, with additional facilities for linking related records.

2.5 Linked structures

In linked structures (Martin, 1975; Wiederhold, 1983) records may be related by pointers, which can support a variety of logical sequences of records, independently of their physical locations. The pointers themselves can be logical, physical or of other types, as will be discussed in the next chapter. Some of the basic structures used to link records are *open list* or *chain* and *closed list* or *ring*. In a chain, the end record does not point back to the header record, but in a ring it does. We shall discuss both of these shortly, but first we note the conventions used in the illustrations (figure 2.6).

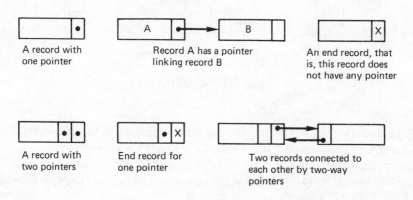

Figure 2.6

2.5.1 Chains and rings

It is possible to construct chain structures by linking the records in a number of ways. A few of the more important structures are discussed below.

One-way chains

A one-way chain is a list of records connected by pointers either in the forward (that is, the ascending) or in the backward (that is, the descending) direction of a desired sequence (figure 2.7) whereas, in a two-way chain, records are connected in both forward and backward directions. This facilitates bidirectional search (figure 2.8).

In the index tables of section 2.2.1 and figures 2.4 and 2.5, only the forward chain is shown. Addition of an extra column in those tables for a backward chain

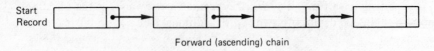

Forward (ascending) chain

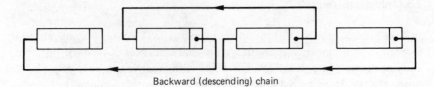

Backward (descending) chain

Figure 2.7

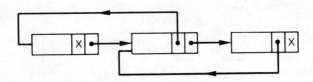

Figure 2.8 Two-way chain

will produce two-way chains, so providing bidirectional search capabilities.

Rings are extensions of chains, where the last record is allowed to possess a pointer to the first, thus forming a closed configuration. Processing can start at any record and continue through the ring. One-way and two-way rings are shown in figure 2.9.

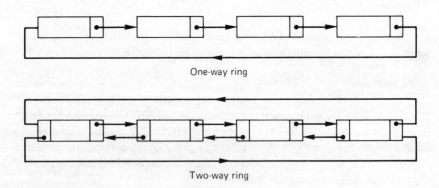

One-way ring

Two-way ring

Figure 2.9

2.5.2 Tree and net

A tree structure may be regarded as an example of the structures supported by complex files. It is used to represent a hierarchical data structure in the form of nodes and branches, a node or a branch being a record. A branch may become a node, generating further branches and thus giving rise to successive levels of hierarchy. A node is often known as the owner or the parent and the branches from it as its members or children. A tree is identified by its topmost node (or root node) which is also known as the *root record*. An example of a tree is given in figure 2.10. The nodes in the tree could be the components and subcomponents of a product A which is made up of part numbers B1, B2 and B3. Part number B1 is made up of part number C1 which is composed of D1 and D2, and likewise part number B3 is composed of C2, C3 and C4, C3 itself being constructed from D3, D4 and D5. We have thus got a tree showing four levels of hierarchy.

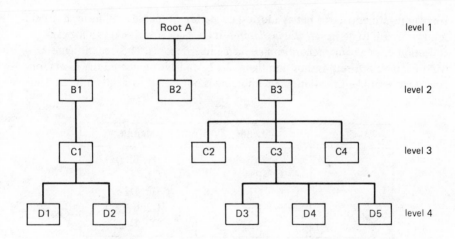

Figure 2.10 A tree structure with four levels of hierarchy

In a tree, a branch cannot belong to two different nodes, but in a *net* it can, as shown in figure 2.11 where part C is a direct subordinate component of both sub-assembly A and part B. A net structure is therefore more flexible.

The tree of figure 2.10 can be stored by chaining the records in any desired order. A depth first or *hierarchical* order would have the following sequence

A, B1, C1, D1, D2, B2, B3, C2, C3, D3, D4, D5, C4

The records can be linked both backward and forward in direction by chaining. There are other ways of representing a tree, some of which are discussed in sections 3.3 and 13.2 (IMS).

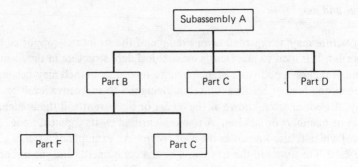

Figure 2.11 A net structure

2.5.3 Atomic dataset

We may regard a tree or a net as a logical collection of records and hence as a data-set. It is useful to define an *atomic dataset* or an *A-set* (for short) as a logical collection of one owner record and all its member records. The tree of figure 2.10 will then have 5 A-sets as shown in figure 2.12. We have numbered the A-sets for convenience of identification; the numbering is not meant to signify any particular ordering.

A-sets	Owner	Members
1	A	B1, B2, B3
2	B1	C1
3	C1	D1, D2
4	B3	C2, C3, C4
5	C3	D3, D4, D5

Figure 2.12

The concept of A-set is very important, as it can be used to implement data relationships of interest in this book, including complex data structures such as tree and net structures, and therefore we shall examine below the ways in which an A-set can be supported.

To begin with, an A-set can be represented by a physical collection of records headed by its owner record and followed by its member records. This is rather a rigid structure, and cannot be applied generally without a heavy record replication, since the same record could participate in many A-sets. A more flexible structure is a physical collection of identifiers headed by the owner's primary key value and followed by the members' primary key values. This structure may be considered to be a basic technique for representing A-sets; it is illustrated in figure 2.13.

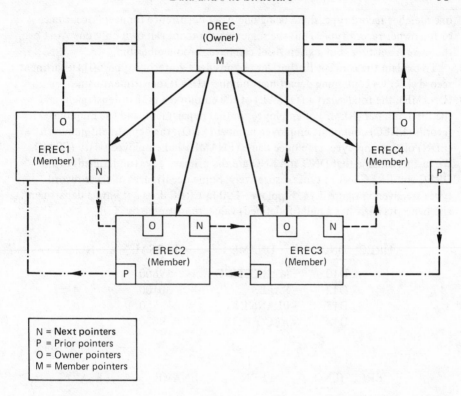

Figure 2.13 A-set with two-way links, owner and member pointers. EREC1 and EREC4 do not have prior pointer and next pointer respectively

Let us consider an A-set containing a department record (DREC) as owner, and 4 employee records (EREC1–EREC4) as members. The members can be chained to each other in the forward direction by next (N) pointers, and in the backward direction by prior (P) pointers. Each member can also have an owner (O) pointer to indicate its owner, and the owner may have a set of member (M) pointers, one for each member. This is shown in figure 2.13 which provides a powerful access facility. Given an owner, any member can be accessed directly, and given a member the owner of the A-set can be found directly. The members themselves can also be traversed in both forward and backward directions. (Note that the members are linked here by a two-way chain, not a ring, since the last member does not point to the first member.)

2.5.4 A-set type

It is convenient to regard an A-set as an instance or occurrence of a named *A-set type* which is a logical data structure characterised by one owner record type and one member record type, there being one A-set occurrence for every occurrence of the owner record type. Thus the same owner record can own only one A-set of the same A-set type, but a given A-set can have zero membership.

To explain the concept further, let us consider two record types: (i) Department record (DREC) containing department number (DNO), department name (DNAME), the total salary (TOTSAL) of the employees in that department and the total number (NEMP) of employees in that department; and (ii) Employee records (EREC) containing employee number (ENO), the department number (EDN) of the employee, employee name (ENAME) and employee salary (ESAL). We further assume that DNO and ENO are the primary keys (underlined) of the DREC and EREC record types respectively. Some occurrences of these record types are given in figure 2.14. Employee E90 in EREC does not have a department, and hence its EDN has a null (undefined) value, represented by X.

DREC (DNO	DNAME	TOTSAL	NEMP)
D10	MARKETING	19600	3
D12	SALES	30100	4
D15	PLANNING	0	0
D18	ACCOUNTS	9000	1

(a)

EREC (ENO	EDN	ENAME	ESAL)
E10	D12	NOBLE	8800
E14	D12	SMITH	8000
E15	D10	NICHOLS	7000
E60	D10	SMITH	7600
E62	D18	STUART	9000
E72	D10	SMITH	5000
E75	D12	BLYTH	6600
E80	D12	FORD	6700
E90	X	HUTT	9000

(b)

X means absence of any department.

Figure 2.14

We can now construct an A-set type called WORKER as

A-set name	WORKER
Owner name	DREC
Member name	EREC

and represented diagrammatically by figure 2.15(a) or (b).

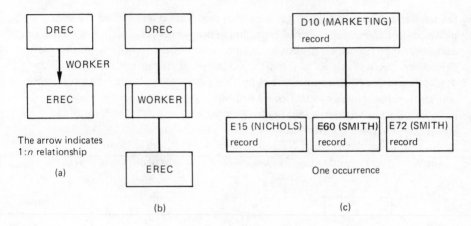

Figure 2.15

Figure 2.15(a) is known as Bachman's diagram, following its introduction by Charles Bachman to represent Codasyl set types (see chapter 9). Figure 2.15(b) is a variation of Bachman's diagram to be used in this book. Figure 2.15(c) shows an A-set owned by the Marketing Department. The four A-sets of this A-set type are shown in figure 2.16, where owner and member records are represented by their respective primary key values.

Owner	Members	Number of Members
D10 (MARKETING)	E15, E60, E72	3
D12 (SALES)	E10, E14, E75, E80	4
D15 (PLANNING)		0
D18 (ACCOUNTS)	E62	1

Figure 2.16 The occurrences of A-set type WORKER

The A-set owned by D15 is an *empty A-set* as it has zero members. The others are *non-empty*. As owner records are inserted or deleted, the number of A-sets in this A-set type will change. The membership in each A-set will also change when employees are inserted or deleted. However, some employees may not belong to any A-set; we assume employee E90 is such an employee who does not have a department.

A-set name

Sometimes we may need to define more than one A-set type between the same pair of owner and member record types and hence we need a unique A-set name for each A-set type. Consider, for instance, Tutor and Student records of some universities where some tutors act as regents and advisors of students. A regent is an academic guardian of his students, but he leaves it to the advisor to suggest suitable courses to them. The same tutor could be both regent and advisor, but not necessarily of the same student; additionally the same advisor may not advise all the students of the same regent. We can represent these relationships by two A-set types, with A-set names REGENT and ADVISOR, as shown in figure 2.17.

Clearly we need A-set names to distinguish them. In general, every A-set can be

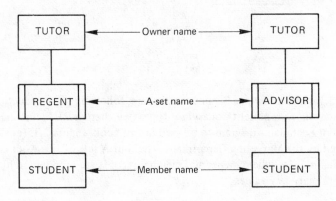

Figure 2.17

identified by its A-set name plus its owner identifier. The owner identifier can be the primary key value of the owner, or some other unique identifier, including its internal identifier.

Recursive A-set types

As A-set types are logical data structures, the same record type can participate in many different A-set types, sometimes as owner and sometimes as members. The same record type can even be the owner and member in the same A-set type. For instance, let us assume (figure 2.18) that EREC had an additional attribute MNO for manager numbers, managers being also employees.

Now we can create an A-set type called EMSET as shown in figure 2.19 (the creation of a new set type does not affect other set types such as WORKER). This type of A-set type may be called *recursive* as the owners and members belong to the same record type, and it permits the same record to be both owner and member even in the same A-set. Here, we have nine A-sets, one for each employee record

EREC (ENO	EDN	ENAME	ESAL	MNO)
E10	D12	NOBLE	8800	E90
E14	D12	SMITH	8000	E90
E15	D10	NICHOLS	7000	E15
E60	D10	SMITH	7600	E15
E62	D18	STUART	9000	E62
E72	D10	SMITH	5000	E15
E75	D12	BLYTH	6600	E90
E80	D12	FORD	6700	E90
E90	X	HUTT	9000	E90

Figure 2.18

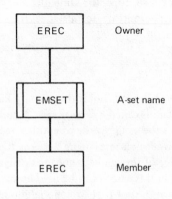

Figure 2.19

as owner; but only three of them are non-empty (figure 2.20) and the other six empty.

OWNER	MEMBERS
E90 (HUTT)	E10, E14, E75, E80, E90
E15 (NICHOLS)	E15, E60, E72
E62 (STUART	E62

Figure 2.20 The non-empty A-sets of EMSET

Extension of A-set types

The concept of A-set type can be extended to include ownerless A-sets and conditional A-sets. Any suitable collection of records, say employees of grade x, could be defined as an A-set without any particular owner. The corresponding A-set type can be called an *ownerless* or *singular* A-set type, singular because there will be only a single A-set of that A-set type. Such an A-set type can be used to define groups of records of the same type for specific purposes. Conditions can be used in the declaration of an A-set type to specify which owner/member record qualifies to be owner/member; for instance, we can prevent the creation of unnecessary empty sets from a recursive set type by specifying the qualifying owner records. Likewise we can define by an appropriate membership condition in a singular A-set type, say, all employees who do not belong to department E80 and whose salaries are higher than £7000.

An A-set type can be *disjoint* or *non-disjoint*. In a *disjoint A-set type* we do not permit the same member record to appear in more than one A-set of the A-set type; in this case each A-set has a disjoint (that is, non-overlapping) collection of members. In a non-disjoint A-set type, the same member can belong to more than one A-set of this type, thus permitting, for instance, the same employee to work in more than one department.

Formation of A-set types

Attribute EDN in Employee Records holds the primary key values (DNO values) of the Department records, and is called a *foreign key*. A component type in a record type is a foreign key if it is the primary key of another record type. Foreign key values essentially act as owner pointers (figure 2.13) as they identify the owners of each member. The presence of foreign keys automatically defines A-set types (the foreign key name – EDN in this case – can be used as an A-set name if needed; see section 11.3.2 for further discussion). The relational models, ADABAS and TOTAL, use essentially this foreign key concept to define A-set types (under different title, style and restrictions). The Codasyl model ignores the presence of foreign keys and builds explicit pointers/indexes of various types to link the member records to each owner. IMS supports net structures where each node can be assumed to be an A-set type, and all records can be connected in a hierarchical order. These models, except for ADABAS, permit only disjoint A-set types. More detailed discussions will be given in the appropriate chapters.

We summarise below some of the characteristics of A-set types:

(i) There is at most one A-set of a given type for each owner record.
(ii) An ownerless A-set type is permissible.
(iii) A given A-set can have zero, one or many members.
(iv) All occurrences of a member record type need not belong to an A-set occurrence (see Employee E90).
(v) Conditions may be imposed to restrict ownerships and memberships.
(vi) Recursive A-set types are permissible.
(vii) The same record can be both owner and member in the same A-set.
(viii) The same record type may participate in many different A-set types either as owner, member or both, without any restriction.

(ix) An A-set type can be disjoint or non-disjoint.

(x) An A-set can be identified by the A-set name plus its owner identifier.

We have shown above some of the techniques used to support advanced files. In the next chapter, we shall examine their implementation techniques, including those of A-set types, in greater depth.

Exercises

2.1 Discuss the relative advantages of indexed sequential and randomly organised files in data processing.

2.2 Explain the concept of inverted files, and describe a modern technique for their implementation, with comments on the performance efficiency of the technique.

2.3 What is a Bachman diagram? Discuss the concept of A-sets and their basic implementation technique for random and sequential access to member records.

References

Codasyl DDLC Journal of Development (1981)

Lum, V. Y. *et al.* (1971). *Communications of the ACM*, Vol. 14, p. 228

Martin, J. (1975). *Computer Data-base Organisation*, Prentice-Hall

Wiederhold, G. (1983). *Database Design*, second edition, McGraw-Hill

The last two books are recommended for advanced reading.

3 Pointers and Advanced Indexes

In the previous chapter we have discussed some well-known techniques used to support simple and complex files. It was quite clear that complex data structures, permitting a record to participate in a number of A-sets, can be implemented only by the extensive use of pointers. In this chapter we wish to examine the implementation techniques of such pointers, including advanced indexes at a depth adequate for an understanding of the efficiency-related issues of databases as discussed later in this book. With this end in view, we shall cover here the types of pointers, methods of organising them, and some advanced indexing techniques.

3.1 Pointer types

We are using the term pointer in a very generalised sense — as a value that provides a link to another record. Therefore we can have the following four categories of object that can act as pointer

> Absolute and relative addresses
> Algorithmic address
> External identifier
> Internal identifier

3.1.1 Absolute and relative addresses

An absolute address is, as the name suggests, the absolute physical address of a record, while relative address is the relative physical address. If absolute addresses are used as pointers, then access to the target record is faster, but such pointers are most unstable, since the absolute physical addresses of records are changed quite frequently. Such changes might occur if a prior record in storage is deleted, if a new record is inserted at a prior point or if records expand or contract. There could be other reasons as well, such as changeover to new disc storage medium with a different track capacity. Because of this instability, absolute addresses are not generally used as pointers. The relative addresses are relative to a given start position, and are partly device dependent, permitting records to move up or down the storage space. As long as the relative positions are retained, they remain stable. Relative addresses are often used in chaining, as in the index table of index sequential files. The row numbers in the index table of section 2.2.1 are relative addresses and are held in the column for Chain. They are not, however, very convenient for the implementation of logical collections of records such as A-sets, since the relative stored positions of ordinary records, unlike the rows of the index table, can change frequently owing to updates.

3.1.2 Algorithmic address

An algorithmic address is the value of address generated by a hashing algorithm, and is used to provide fast random access, as in random files. The advantage lies in the fact these addresses not only provide fast accesses, but also do not require any storage space except for overflow-handling.

The main limitation of algorithmic addresses is their inability to generate a set of unique, contiguous addresses for a set of essentially non-contiguous primary key values. This point will be clearer if we examine the examples of the hashing algorithm given in section 2.2 The addresses (bucket numbers) produced there are not unique, since several key values yield the same address. One possible way of guaranteeing uniqueness is to increase the range of addresses to match the range of potential primary key values. If we do so, for instance, in the example for the remainder algorithm (section 2.3), we need to use 10000 buckets for 10000 possible key values, thereby wasting 90 per cent of space, since there are only 1000 actual records. This means that we have failed to produce a set of unique, contiguous addresses for the actual keys, and hence have produced the wastage. Such wastage of course is not acceptable.

The second drawback with hashing algorithms is the underflow and overflow problems mentioned earlier. Within these limitations, they are used to generate relative physical addresses, such as bucket numbers.

3.1.3 External identifier

By external identifiers, we mean record key values which can be used to relate two records, as is done in figure 2.14 which shows which employees work for which departments, with EDN as the foreign key holding its key values for the external identifiers. They are called external pointers since they are not internal to the database control system, but visible to the user as part of the records. They are also logical as they do not give physical addresses.

3.1.4 Internal identifier

Internal identifiers are codes or values used to identify records uniquely for the internal use of the database control systems. These identifiers do not normally change their values during the lifetime of the records concerned. They are also referred to as logical pointers, logical addresses, or internal pointers: in ADABAS they are Internal Sequence Numbers (ISN), and in the *old* Codasyl model they are database keys. Internal pointers are preferred over absolute and relative pointers as they provide some storage independence. The term *surrogate* used in recent literature implies a unique permanent record identifier which never changes: it is storage independent and can be the primary key but should ideally be a pure pointer which is never re-allocated to another record, *even after the deletion of its former record*. This concept is particularly important in a historical database (chapter 14) where all past database records are retained for possible future use.

The main disadvantage of the use of primary keys (external identifiers) as unique pointers is that the key size varies from one record type to another, which is inconvenient. Therefore most DBMSs use compact and fixed-size internal identifiers instead. Even in the relational model, where internal identifiers are not explicitly recognised, foreign keys can be replaced in storage by internal identifiers.

The generation and maintenance of internal identifiers along with the need to find the corresponding physical addresses raise some interesting database issues concerned with convenience and efficiency; these discussions have been deferred to section 4.4 of the next chapter.

3.2 Pointer organisation

Internal identifiers are used as pointers in constructing data structures. If these pointers are stored as part of the records themselves, then they are embedded, otherwise they are non-embedded, that is, they are held away from the records as separate index tables.

3.2.1 Embedded pointer

As an example, let us assume that figure 2.13 represents the SALES department and its employees, as shown in figure 2.14. Then the affected DREC and EREC of figure 2.14 will be changed as shown in figure 3.1. In this figure we have used primary key values as pointers, but in practice some internal identifiers will be more likely. There will probably be pointers also for other departments and their members.

The advantage of embedded pointers is the ability to find the related records from any given record without needing further disc accesses to index tables. This works very well so long as there are only a small number of records in the structure, and so long as the structure is not too complex. The main disadvantages are:

DREC(DNO	DNAME	TOTSAL	NEMP	POINTER TYPE	POINTERS)
D10	MARKETING	19600	3		
D12	SALES	30100	4	M	E10 E14 E75 E80
D15	PLANNING	0	0		
D18	ACCOUNTS	9000	1		

EREC(ENO	EDN	ENAME	ESAL	POINTER TYPE	POINTERS)
E10	D12	NOBLE	8800	O/N/P	D12 E14 X
E14	D12	SMITH	8000	O/N/P	D12 E75 E14
E15	D10	NICHOLS	7000		
E60	D10	SMITH	7600		
E62	D18	STUART	9000		
E72	D10	SMITH	5000		
E75	D12	BLYTH	6600	O/N/P	D12 E14 E80
E80	D12	FORD	6700	O/N/P	D12 E75 X

Figure 3.1 Embedded pointers for SALES department and its members. X indicates absence of a pointer. The column for pointers shows: Member (M), Owner (O), Next (N) and Prior (P)

(i) If there is a large number of member records, then the space required to store the owner record along with its pointer space will be large. If the member pointers are dropped, then the member record cannot be accessed randomly, which will slow down access speed.

(ii) The structure can become very entangled if the same record participates, as it may do, in many A-sets and/or as owner and/or member, and particularly if there are different pointer options in different A-set types — such as one-way links in some A-set types, and bidirectional links in some others, while there are member or owner pointers in others. The differentiation of the pointers of different A-set types then becomes tricky.

To illustrate some of the problems, we have represented in figure 3.2 the A-sets of the tree in figure 2.10, each A-set having four types of pointer — member, owner, next and prior. This is clearly a messy and confusing technique. There are other representational techniques that can be used, but the points to be stressed are the variable size of pointer space and the attendant differentiation problem of which pointers belongs to which A-sets. This problem becomes more acute if all the four types of pointer (prior, next, owner, member) are not required for all the A-sets.

The problem of the variable size of pointer space can be overcome by using a number of fixed-length pointer segments, as shown in figure 3.3. It is possible, of

Data	Pointers							
Data of record A	M	IB1	IB2	IB3				
Data of record B1	M	IC1	O/N/P	IA	X	IB2		
Data of record B2	O/N/P	IA	IB1	IB3				
Data of record B3	M	IC2	IC3	IC4	O/N/P	IA	IB2	X
Data of record C1	M	ID1	ID2	O/N/P	IB1	X	X	
Data of record C2	O/N/P	IB3	X	IC3				
Data of record C3	. M	ID3	ID4	ID5	O/N/P	IB3	IC2	IC4
Data of record C4	O/N/P	IB3	IC3	X				
Data of record D1	O/N/P	IC1	X	ID2				
Data of record D2	O/N/P	IC1	ID1	X				
Data of record D3	O/N/P	IC3	X	ID4				
Data of record D4	O/N/P	IC3	ID3	ID5				
Data of record D5	O/N/P	IC3	ID4	X				

Figure 3.2 Member (M), owner, next, prior (O/N/P) pointers for the five data sets of the tree in figure 2.10 (a messy representation)

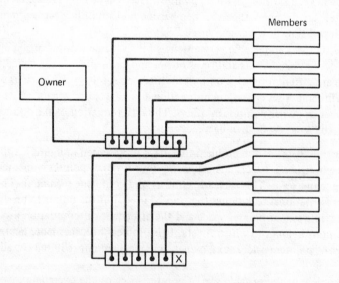

Figure 3.3 Multisegment pointer array for member pointers

course, to use these segments selectively for different types of pointer and different A-sets, but this will require an elaborate technique for pointer and A-set identification, and will also make updates particularly difficult.

3.2.2 Non-embedded pointer

It should be clear from the foregoing discussion that embedded pointers have serious limitations in constructing data structures which are of interest. Here we shall examine non-embedded pointers, which can be supported by three types of index. unsorted, partially sorted and sorted.

Unsorted index: An unsorted index is a simple list of internal identifiers without any particular order. For instance, the member pointers of A-sets can be an un-sorted list of member identifiers, with one list per A-set, held on some disc space that is independent of the records. This is useful if the intention is to process the member records of a given A-set one by one in no particular order, as it might be in the case of the employees of a particular department for monthly salary pay-ment, where the order in which the employees are processed is not important.

Partially sorted index: In this case, the pointers are held in sorted order of either internal identifiers or of other specified keys, with one such set of pointers for each A-set. New insertions are simply appended at the end, rather than sorting the whole list for each insertion during the run-time. The deletions are flagged, but not necessarily removed during run-time. Periodically, the list, including the insertions is re-sorted by either a utility or the DBCS, which also removes the previously flag-ged deletions. Sequential access in sort order is fairly fast, as long as the unsorted part is small. If the incidence of insertions is low, then this type of partially sorted listing is a cheap way of providing most of the sorted facility. Three examples of partially sorted lists are given in figure 3.4. Note that, if the partial sort is expected to be in a particular key order, then a (key value, internal identifier) pair instead of an internal identifier alone has to be present in the list in the key value order — since, in the absence of key values, future insertions cannot be made in the right place.

Figure 3.4(a) gives a partially ordered list of internal identifiers I_i, for one A-set, the Home and Overflow areas starting with the total number of entries (10 and 3 respectively) in each. 'A-set Id' contains A-set identifier, and 'Total size' gives the size of the index for this A-set, whereas 'Start of overflow' yields the start byte of the Overflow area in this index. Figure 3.4(b) shows the list in partial primary key order, each entry being a pair of primary key P_i and internal identifier I_i values. The number of entries in the Home and Overflow slots (4 and 2 respectively) are also shown. In figure 3.4(c) the order is in the secondary key sequence and hence the representation is more complex, since there can be more than one internal identifier for the same secondary key value S_i. The Home and Overflow areas start with the number of S_i entries in each area, in this case 3 for Home area and 2 for

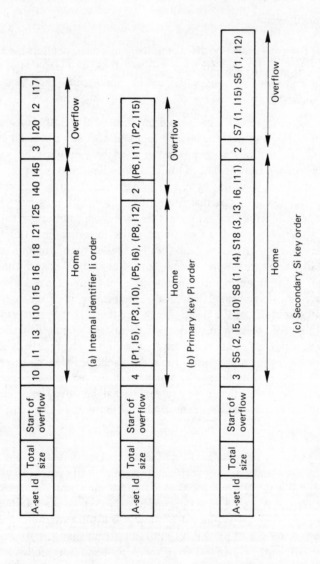

Figure 3.4 Partially ordered pointers – see the text for explanation

Overflow area. The entries in the brackets after each Si show: [Si (N, list of N internal identifiers Ii matching this Si)] . New records matching an existing Si can be inserted using the Overflow area if needed.

Sorted index: In this case internal identifiers are held in their own sequence, or in sequence of a specified key (primary or secondary), essentially as shown in the sorted part of figure 3.4(a), (b) and (c). However, the need to maintain the pointers always in the correct sequence in spite of insertions and deletions calls for a more elaborate organisation for the index. We shall discuss some of the relevant techniques in the next section.

3.3 Advanced indexing techniques

The indexing technique used for index sequential files as discussed in section 2.2.2 is quite satisfactory so long as there are not too many insertions and deletions. Since the size of the overflow area is limited and pre-declared, sometimes the independent overflow area can become full, while some primary data area and some cylinder overflow area are still empty. This happens because of the random nature of updates, which may result in having too many overflow records for some primary data area and too many underflow records in others. Thus the index becomes un-balanced, growing haphazardly in some directions, and shrinking in others. This leads to storage wastage and inefficiency, requiring periodic reorganisation of the index by a utility program. Such indexes require careful monitoring and mainten-ance, and therefore are not favoured in databases. The most widely used indexes are Balanced trees (B-trees) (Knuth, 1973; Comer, 1979) which we shall discuss below, along with two other recent ideas, one based on what is called a Hash tree (H-tree) and the other based on data-page splitting.

The efficiencies of indexes are usually measured in terms of a disc access, which is the average time needed to retrieve a bucket (section 2.3) from a disc, and is derived from an average of the head movement time and latency of the disc con-cerned. In database operations the CPU time is usually considered to be insignificant compared to the input/output (I/O) time, and hence the tendency to use the num-ber of disc accesses as a measure of efficiency. In common with database literature, we shall use the term *page* instead of bucket as the unit of disc access.

3.3.1 Balanced tree

In a binary tree each node divides into two other nodes, whereas in a balanced tree a node breaks into many nodes, but unfortunately the abbreviation B-tree is used for both. Sometimes the term B∗tree is preferred for balanced tree, but on the other hand Knuth employed it to mean a special type of balanced tree. In the circumstances, we have arbitrarily opted for B-tree as the shortened name of balanced tree in this book, but this choice will not raise any confusion as we shall not discuss any binary trees here. The type of B-tree described here is sometimes known as a B+ tree.

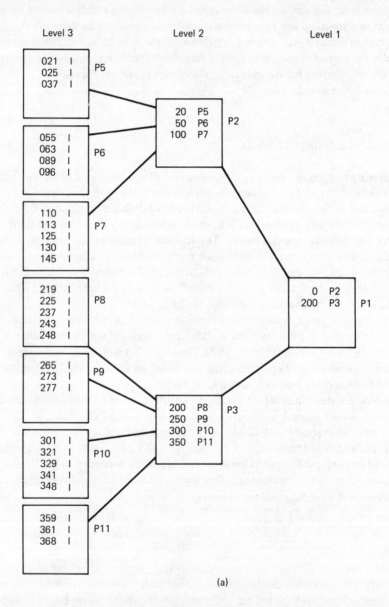

(a)

Figure 3.5 (a) A B-tree of height 3. If keys 212 and 345 are added, both two lower and one upper boxes are broken. The upper pages are shown to contain the page numbers of the lower pages

A balanced tree is basically a self-reorganising indexing technique, in which no distinction is made between home and overflow areas. The index is divided into a number of fixed-size pages linked in a hierarchical fashion in order of a specified key. Each page contains a range of key values stored in the strict key sequence. Any new entry on the page must be inserted in the correct sequential position; if the page overflows, a new page is added which takes either the lower or upper half of the entries, as indicated in figure 3.5(a) which shows a B-tree of height 3, its three levels spreading over pages P1 to P11.

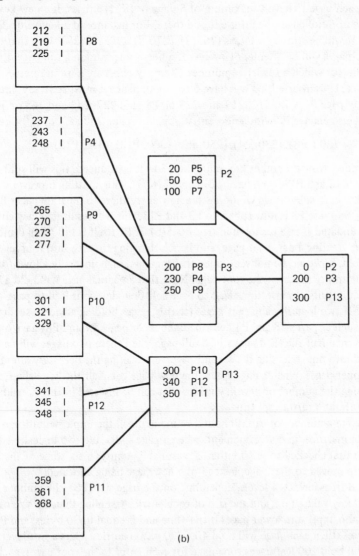

(b)

(b) Updated B-tree, pages P5, P6 and P7 are not shown

Each entry on a leaf page contains a pair of (K, I) values in order of K, where K is the key value (shown as a number in figure 3.5) and I is the internal identifier (values are not specified in the figure). The upper pages are assumed to contain their lower page numbers in place of I, and hence it is a B+ tree. If this index is simply required to be organised in order of internal identifiers, then key values would be irrelevant and would not be in the index. At the highest level of the B-tree we have the root page or root node (page P1), and at the lowest level leaf pages or leaves (P5 to P11), with other nodes (pages P2 and P3) in between. In the figure, we assume each page to have a maximum of 5 pairs of (K, I) entries. If a new key value falls on a non-full page, then it is entered there. For instance, if a key value 270 is inserted it will be stored on P9, as (265, I), (270, I), (273, I) (277, I) in that order; no other pages will be affected. However if a new value falls on a full page, the page must split, for which a sufficient number of empty pages are kept in reserve. If a key value 212 is inserted, P8 will have 6 pairs and hence it must split, say, into P8 and a new page P4, with 212, 219 and 225 on P8, and 237, 243 and 248 on P4. This will also change P3 with a new entry, say, key value 230 as

$$(200, P8), (230, P4), (250, P9), (300, P10), (350, P11)$$

in that order. Now if another key value, say, 345 is introduced, this will split P10 into, say, P10 and P12, each having 3 pairs of (K, I). This splitting however will cause P3 also to split, as we would need a new entry there to separate pages P10 and P12. Suppose P3 is now split into P3 and P13, this will result in a new entry in P1. The updated B-tree is shown in figure 3.5(b). If P1 itself is full, then it must also split, creating a new root page, and hence changing the tree into four level. This would, however, be unusual, since the original design normally allows for sufficient empty space on the root page. Note that an actual page will hold a lot more than 5 pairs. As insertions lead to page splitting, deletions lead to page collapse. If two logically adjacent pages (that is, pages holding adjacent sequences of pairs such as pages P8 and P4 described above, or pages P7 and P8) have on each page less than half the (K, I) pairs of a full page, then these two pages will be consolidated into one, releasing the second page, and making the necessary alterations in the upper pages. When a page splits, the new page gets half the key values, thus maximising the number of new key values that can be inserted in the old and new pages, without a further splitting.

There are a number of variations and refinements in the implementation of B-trees. For instance, in one refinement, when a page splits, the two logically adjacent pages are first checked to see if either is reasonably empty; if so, some of the entries are moved to that page, instead of a new page being allocated.

Most B-trees have 2–4 levels, depending on the page size (PS), the number of expected key values (W), and the size of each entry. Assuming that the size of each entry in the upper and lower pages is the same and is equal to 20 bytes, and PS = 4096 bytes, then each page will hold 4096/20 = 200 entries. Thus a two-level B-tree will hold 200 leaf pages (one page for each entry in the root page), each leaf page having 200 (K, I) entries, with a total of about 40K key values. By the same token, a three-level B-tree will hold up to 800K key values. However, since page size varies between 256 and 4096 bytes, depending on machine size, the smaller machines will be able to handle fewer (K, I) pairs per page.

To retrieve an internal identifier of a key value from an n-level B-tree directly, we need n disc accesses, with one disc access for each level. However, normally the root page is kept in the memory, and hence we need $(n-1)$ disc accesses. Thus to get the internal identifier for K = 243 of figure 3.5(a), with root in the memory, we require 2 disc accesses: 1 access to retrieve page P3 and then another access to retrieve page P8. On each page accessed, we may use a binary chop technique to find either the page number to the lower node, or the required (K, I) pair. (If we have a set of records in the memory, then in a *binary chop* first the middle record is matched against the wanted record to determine if the wanted record is in the lower or upper half of this set. The qualifying half then becomes the new set whose middle record is again checked. Thus, applying binary chops on the successive qualifying sets, the wanted record is found. This technique is faster than a sequential scan.) We ignore the CPU time. In subsequent discussion we shall always assume that there are $(n-1)$ disc accesses for an n-level B-tree (with root in the memory).

B-trees can be used as indexes for primary or secondary keys or for supporting A-sets. If the (K, I) pairs in figure 3.5(a) represent member records of a given A-set, then the member records can be searched sequentially in both forward and backward directions in the key order and also randomly by key values, taking $(n-1)$ disc accesses to find the internal identifier by random access. Thus a B-tree can support the equivalent of next, prior and member pointers of figure 2.13. However, the internal identifier I may not give the actual physical address, and in that case further disc accesses, say, m disc accesses, will be needed to retrieve the wanted record, thus requiring $\{(n-1) + m\}$ disc accesses altogether for direct access. Another B-tree can be used to hold the (I, physical address) pairs; but this will normally be considered inefficient (see section 4.3). Note that if the B-tree of figure 3.5(a) contains (K, physical address) rather than (K, I) entries, then we shall have reorganisation problems, as discussed in section 3.1.1 earlier.

B-trees guarantee a balanced index, which is self-reorganising, and therefore extensively used in database implementation. It is also sometimes referred to as a dynamic indexing facility. Although we have concentrated above mainly on random access, it should be quite obvious from figure 3.5 that all the internal identifiers can be accessed quickly in key order in both forward and backward directions.

3.3.2 Hash tree

In a Hash tree or H-tree (Deen, 1985), an attempt is made to replace the upper nodes of an n-level B-tree by a division hashing (section 2.3) so that the number of disc accesses is reduced to nearly 1 compared to $(n-1)$ in the B-tree. We shall give below first the hash-tree technique and then an example.

In this technique the key values are first compressed by an order-preserving compression algorithm to remove permanent gaps (that is, the value range that will never be filled) in such a way that the resultant compressed key values still retain the original key order. A division hashing algorithm (section 2.3) is then applied which yields transformed key values called home hash slots (figure 3.6). Each home hash slot has a fixed number of entries of (K, I) pairs. This number is the average number of key values per bucket, and is called home hash width (HW). In a given hash slot all entries are kept in strict key order as in a B-tree. Overflow hash slots may be given a smaller overflow hash width (OW) to reduce wastage, and they are allocated dynamically as and when required. An overflow hash slot can be assigned to any overflowing (home or another overflow) hash slot, but a given overflow hash slot can belong to only one prior (overflowing) hash slot. When an overflow hash slot is released, as a result of deletions, it can be re-allocated to any needy over-flowing hash slot. The basic organisation of a hash slot is shown in figure 3.6(b) where

C = current number of entries of (K, I) pairs in the hash slot i
N/P = Next/Prior hash slots in key order
$(Ki1, Ii1)$ = first (K, I) pair currently in this i^{th} hash slot
(KiC, IiC) = last (K, I) pair currently in this i^{th} hash slot

The index pages containing hash slots are divided into home pages and global overflow pages, but all pages are of the same size. Home hash slots are held on home pages, with one hash slot per page. If the page can take H entries, then HW is designed to be smaller than H, such that some space is left for future insertions on the same page as local overflow. Typically HW/H would be 70-75 per cent, leaving 25 to 30 per cent space for local overflows. Global overflow pages have only overflow slots with typically several slots per page, each slot holding the spill over from a home slot or from another global overflow slot. The structure of the index given in figure 3.6(b) is also used for global overflows, except that the number of entries per slot would be fewer, if OW < HW.

As an example, let us consider a file having 1000 employee records, with a 5-character key field as follows

A1001–A4000 weekly paid employees
B1001–B3000 monthly paid employees

Assume that the other numbers are not used by the company. The compression algorithm will allocate compressed key values 1–3000 for the employee numbers A1001–A4000 in the correct order, 1 being the compressed key value for A1001 and 3000 for A4000. Similarly the compressed key value for B1001 will be 3001 and that for B3000 will be 5000.

The maximum compressed key value is KMAX = 5000. The maximum number of keys is TMAX = 1000 distributed, say, over HMAX = 125 home hash slots, with

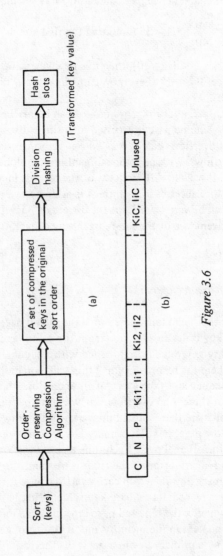

Figure 3.6

HW = 8, H = 10 and OW = 5. We generate hash slot h by dividing a compressed key value k by hash divider HD = KMAX/HMAX = 40. Then h = k/HD.

Given an original key value, we find its compressed key value by applying the compression technique. For instance, if the original key value is A2505 its compressed equivalent is 1500, and hence its home hash slot is calculated as

$$\frac{1505}{40} + 1 = 38 \text{ (counting the first slot as 1)}$$

If in the 38th hash slot $C < H$ (= 10), then this new key value will be inserted in the appropriate place. If C = H then an overflow hash slot will be allocated as shown in figure 3.7.

This technique ensures that the required slot can be reached in a minimal number of disc accesses. A home page is accessed by a single disc access. By choosing HW with care, most overflows can be located on the home page, thus reducing the need for global overflows. With periodic reorganisations, global overflows can be kept under control. If we allow 10 per cent of the records in global overflows, then we would need 1.1 disc accesses in hash trees as against $(n-1)$ disc accesses in a B-tree. The saving can be very significant for B-trees of 3 levels and higher. As against this, the convenience of the self-reorganising capabilities of B-trees has to be considered.

3.3.3 Data-page splitting technique

We outline here another technique, based on hashing and page splitting, for storing records in primary key order so as to provide fast random and sequential access by that key. The primary key value is first hashed with a suitable algorithm, to determine a data page where the records yielding that value on hashing are stored in strict primary key sequence. In the event of an underflow, the unused space on the page is wasted but, if there is an overflow, a new empty page is attached as an overflow page. The records are then redistributed over to these two pages (the original page and this overflow page) in strict primary key sequence, each page receiving half the records of the original page. Each time a page overflows, such a split takes place followed by a redistribution of the records. A small *overflow index* holding the range of the primary key values on each overflow page is maintained for each hash value. To place a record, its primary key value is first hashed, and with the help of the overflow index the required page is found. The index is expected to be small so that it can be kept in the memory and, if this is so, a record can be retrieved randomly by a primary key in a single disc access.

The technique therefore stores records in primary key order and provides a very fast access in that order. As in most things, there are other overheads which might not always be acceptable. Firstly storage utilisation is likely to be somewhat low, probably around 70 per cent though this may not be considered unreasonable,

| 10 | N | P | (1500, I), (1510, I), (1514, I), (1520, I), (1530, I) (1535, I), (1540, I), (1542, I), (1545, I), (1552, I) |

Full hash slot

As a result of inserting the new key value 1505 the home slot will have

| 10 | N | P | (1500, I), (1505, I), (1510, I), (1514, I), (1520, I), (1530, I), (1535, I), (1540, I), (1542, I), (1545, I) |

Assuming that the overflow slot previously had key value 1565, it will now be

| 2 | N | P | (1552, I) | (1565, I) | ←——— unused ———→ |

Figure 3.7

particularly in view of its access efficiency. Secondly in a large file of many pages and overflows, the overflow index could be too large for memory. The third problem arises from secondary keys. To access records by a secondary key we need an index that gives either the storage location(s) or the primary key value(s) for a given secondary key value. If a (secondary key, storage location) index is supported, this index will need substantial reorganisation after every page splitting. This will probably be unacceptable, particularly if there are several secondary keys (and hence several such indexes). The second option with a (secondary key, primary key) index would be preferable, unless the size of the primary key is large. A large primary key will tend to make the secondary key indexes large and consequently inefficient. In practice, primary keys can be large.

In fairness, data-page splitting is an interesting technique and can be used effectively in a relatively small file when the primary key is short or access by a secondary key is less important. For more advanced techniques, see Date (1985).

Exercises

3.1 Discuss the different types of pointer and their use in database implementation.
3.2 Describe an algorithm in a pseudo-code to implement a B-tree for a key made up of department number and employee name, where employee names are not unique.

References

Comer, D. (1979). The ubiquitous B-tree. *ACM Computing Surveys*, Vol. (11:2), June, p. 121

Date, C. J. (1985). *Introduction to Database Systems, Vol. 1*, 4th edition, Addison-Wesley (this discusses some advanced tuple placement techniques)

Deen, S. M. (1985). A tuple placement technique for databases. *Computer Journal*, Vol. (28:3), July

Knuth, D. E. (1973). *The Art of Computer Programming, Vol. 3, Sorting and Searching*, Addison-Wesley, section 6.2.4, pp. 471-9

PART II: DESIGN ISSUES

4 Architectural Issues

The architecture of a database determines its capability of meeting user requirements reliably, effectively and efficiently. Our present understanding of it owes much to the experimental and theoretical studies of the past decade, with contributions from many sources — among them database researchers, database practitioners and a number of committees such as ANSI/SPARC (1975, 1978), BCS/DBAWG (section 9.1), BCS/DDSWP (1975), IFIP/WG 2.6 and ISO/TC97/ SC5/WG3 (ISO, 1981). In this chapter we wish to discuss some of the relevant issues and present a basic architecture.

4.1 Three basic levels

The information that we wish to store in a database exists in the realm of our interest, as *perceived* by us. This realm may be assumed to be populated with things or *entities*, and their static and dynamic characteristics. The entity characteristics, which include data, data relationships and usage constraints, constitute the content of our databases. Therefore the first major step in the design of a database is to analyse these characteristics with a view to their classification into types for deeper understanding, and to transform this understanding into a formal description based on types and associated rules.

This process of formalisation usually involves many steps and even an element of moving in circles, but the end product is a description of entity characteristics, which is logically complete. This formal description is referred to as the logical data description or a *conceptual schema* (figure 4.1) which represents the information model of interest.

At the next level of our description, the relevant computer storage structures and operational efficiencies are considered; here the designer concerns himself with the problem of organising and storing entity characteristics (described in the conceptual schema) efficiently in computers which have fixed-structured hardware (usually

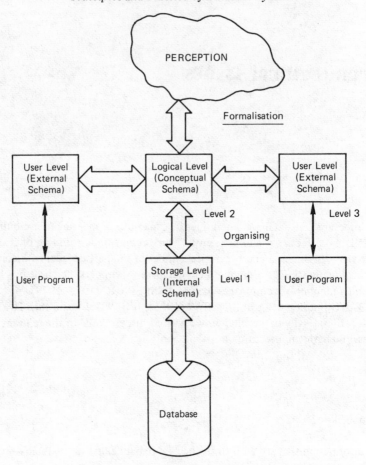

Figure 4.1 A basic three-level data description

discs). The end result of this exercise is a description referred to as the *storage* or *internal schema*, which maps the content of the conceptual schema on to the realities of computers. Much of the storage schema is equivalent to file descriptions of a Cobol program, and is treated as such by the operating system.

So far we have described how objects in the conceptual schema can be organised and stored in a computer in accordance with an internal schema, but we have not specified how user programs can enter the database. This is done by introducing 'doors' through a third level of descriptions, called *user views* or *external schemas*. This user level is needed to interface the user programs to the database, since the other two schemas are written in independent languages which do not provide the required facility. An external schema describes the data needed for a specific application (all the data of the database may not be needed) in a form most convenient to that application.

These three levels — conceptual, internal and external — form the basic of modern database architecture. While there is only one conceptual schema and one internal schema, there can be many external schemas, one for each type of requirement. The ANSI/SPARC architecture described in section 4.5 is based on these concepts.

4.2 Entity characteristics

A conceptual schema may be viewed as an instance of the data model to be used in a given database. The richness of a data model and hence the effectiveness of a conceptual schema depends on the facilities that it can provide for the representation of entity characteristics. We wish to examine below some of these characteristics at an elementary level, starting with the following four basic concepts:

> Entity
> Property
> Association
> Type or Class

The fifth basic concept is usage constraint which will be discussed in chapter 5, as part of the data protection facility. It should perhaps be mentioned that there is no general agreement among the experts about these concepts, or indeed the terms to be used to express them — which is thus an ideal breeding ground for more data-modelling researchers. However, the discussion given below represents a broad middle ground, and is particularly useful for the understanding of other related issues (see also section 14.1 for further discussion).

Entity

An entity is an object about which we store data. A person, book, place, event, an idea or even a relationship can be an entity. Similar entities together form a type of entity. For instance, the entity type person refers to all persons, whereas a person entity implies a particular individual such as the person with the name Smith (see also below). What it or is not an entity depends on our subjective human judgement and perception. For instance, a colour can be an entity if we are interested in its properties, or it can be the property of another entity.

Entities can be dependent on each other. If in an organisation every employee is required to belong to a department, then the existence of an entity employee is conditional on the prior existence of an entity department. On the other hand, a relationship entity, such as the one between a student and a course, can exist only if both the related entities exist. The former is an instance of *extrinsic dependence*, since the entity employee *can* exist without a department if the company rules are suitably changed; but the latter is an instance of *intrinsic dependence*, since the relationship entity cannot exist without the presence of both the related entities, whatever the rules. Entities can also show hierarchies, for example, entities pencil, rubber, pen, etc. can be grouped together as an entity stationery.

Property

The data which we collect about an entity are its *properties*, each property being
a value of a property type. For an entity type person, person name, department
number, employee number, driver's licence number, salary, job title can all be
property types described by their respective property names. For a particular entity
person, the corresponding properties (or property values) can be Smith, Dept10,
E10, SMT3812314001, 6000 and programmer, but the person-name Smith (or
for that matter employee number E10) is not the entity, the entity is the person
whose name is Smith and whose employee number is E10. Thus Smith and E10 are
properties which describe the entity. We cannot store entities, we can only store
their properties such as person's name and employee number. One or more of these
properties, sometimes in combination, can identify the entity uniquely. Both
employee number and driver's licence number are likely to be unique identities,
but a person's name usually is not, since several persons can have the same name.
If employee numbers are unique only within a department, then (department
number, employee number) in combination will be a unique identifier, but not
employee number alone. Of several possible unique identifiers, we may select for
convenience one of them to represent that entity. This identifier, which can be
composite, is called an *entity identifier*. We may define an entity record as the
collection of the properties of an entity.

When an entity record is represented in a computer, we may sometimes give different attribute names to the same property name. For instance, the property name
'employee number' can be named in one record type as ENO, in another EMPNO
and in yet another as ENUM. Thus property names show one to many relationships with attribute names. A property can show a hierarchical structure such as
in 'Date', which can be constructed from three other properties, namely, day, month
and year, or from two other properties such as day number and year. This implies
that a given higher level property can sometimes be decomposed into different
sets of lower level properties.

Association

An association represents one to one (1:1), one to many (1:n) and many to many
($m:n$) relationships among entities, such as between father and mother (1:1), department and employees (1:n) and students and courses ($m:n$). An association shows a
logical relationship in the sense that an entity can enter into many associations. A
hierarchy of associations among entities also exists; although such a hierarchy can be
looked on as a set of related associations. Examples of such a hierarchy are the
associations between divisions and departments (1:n), and departments and employees (1:n), assuming each organisation has a set of divisions, with each division having
a set of departments.

Type or class

As mentioned earlier, entities and properties are categorised into types or classes such as employees, departments, employee numbers, department numbers, salary and so on. All entity records describing entities of the same type are entity records of the same type. Correspondingly there can also be association types between entity types as we shall see in the next section. The classification scheme also requires each type of object to be named uniquely by a type name for the purpose of identification. We thus have an entity record name for the entity records of the same type, and an association name for the associations of the same type. All items of a given type are its population and any single item is a *value, instance* or *occurrence* of that type.

Further characteristics

There exist $m:n$ relationships between entity types and property types. Entity type person can be characterised by the property types name, age, salary and weight; with age and weight also shared by entity type car. What constitutes an entity, property or association is perception dependent; for example, male and female persons can be represented as two distinct entities, or as the values of property type sex for entity person. Even an association can be perceived as a property with the help of a repeating group. For instance, in an association between departments and employees, the employee records for a department can be treated as a repeating group of that department record, and thus a property of that department.

4.3 Data representation

The concepts of entity record and association types are well known and have been supported by all major data models in one form or another. In this section, we wish to examine them further, showing how and to what extent they can be represented by the ordinary record and A-sets introduced in chapter 2.

4.3.1 Entity records and associations

The differences between an entity record and an ordinary record are:

(i) In an entity record type a deliberate decision is made (although it is perception dependent) about an entity type, its property types and its identifier before the record type is specified. In an ordinary record type such a deliberate decision is not necessarily made.

(ii) In an entity record type there is a relationship between the property name and attribute name as defined earlier. In an ordinary record type, this relationship is generally ignored.

There is no basic representational difference as regards (i) above; after all we can assume all records to be entity records but (ii) indicates a limitation of ordinary record types. None of the major commercially available data models recognises this relationship between property names and attribute names, although in some cases a data dictionary can be used to support it (section 5.4). This relationship could be represented by creating a special record type, each record occurrence yielding the different attribute names for the same property type. However, subject to this limitation, we may assume that an entity record is identical with an 'ordinary' record.

We may define an identity component (alternatively a primary key) as the component of an entity record type that yields entity identifiers. If declared as part of the record description either in the conceptual schema or in a data dictionary, these can be used as the permanent identifiers of entity records. However many data models, including the network model, do not recognise the concept of identity component or primary key, and this can sometimes create an identification problem. The concept of surrogates can also be used as permanent identifiers.

We discussed earlier two types of entity relationships, one leading to relationship entities and the other to associations. We examine the distinction in greater detail below.

(i) *Relationship entity*

A relationship between two or more individual entities can be viewed as a new entity if we are interested in its properties. Such an entity is intrinsically dependent, as explained earlier, on those related entities. The properties of the relationship entity should be such that they are exclusive to the relationship but not to any of the related entities. A common example is the relationship between a course and a student, where an exclusive property of interest is the performance of the student in that course, say the examination marks. This is an example of what is sometimes called an *information-bearing* relationship, the information it bears being the properties of the relationship. It is possible to have a relationship entity dependent on more than two related entities as explained in section 4.3.3.

The need to define an intrinsically dependent entity (and hence relationship entity) arises in the event of an $m{:}n$ association between entity types. In a $1{:}n$ association, say between entities departments and employees, we do not need any relationship entity, since the properties of the relationship between an employee and his department, such as employee's date of joining the department, can be represented as an exclusive property of the entity employee. However, if the employee works for several departments (with potentially different joining dates), then the joining dates cannot be viewed as being independent of the entity department, and hence cannot be represented as the exclusive properties of the entity employee; obviously we need to invoke a relationship entity to represent this adequately. But by allowing an employee to work in several departments we change the original $1{:}n$ association to an $m{:}n$ association, confirming that a relationship entity is required only in $m{:}n$ associations.

There appears to be a certain amount of arbitrariness in invoking relation-ship entities for $m:n$ associations, but not in $1:n$ associations, although a $1:n$ association can easily become an $m:n$ association as indicated above. This is why some experts such as Chen do not recognise this separation between $1:n$ and $m:n$ relationships — their ideas are briefly mentioned in chapter 14. In the meantime we shall continue to use the concept of relationship entities, as developed above, at least as an expedient.

(ii) *Associations*
In contrast to a relationship entity, an association indicates the existence of a $1:n$ or $m:n$ relationship among entities, and hence among their entity records.

4.3.2 1:n association

We may regard a $1:n$ association as an instance of a named $1:n$ association type bet-ween an owner and a member entity type. It is similar to a *disjoint A-set type*, the difference being that an association is a conceptual object expressing a relationship between entities, whereas an A-set is an atomic dataset representing a logical coll-ection of owner and member records. A $1:n$ association between the entities of the same type is termed a $1:n$ loop or as a $1:n$ recursive association type, and may diagrammatically be represented in the form of a loop (figure 4.2) where figure 4.2(a) shows the $1:n$ relationships between managers and other employees of figure 2.19, while figure 4.2(b) shows a family tree where one person as parent is related to other persons as children. Another example of a loop structure is the relationship between the head-teacher and other teachers (figure 4.2(c)). A Member of Parliament (MP) represents all voters in his constituency, including himself if he is a voter there, and hence the relationship between MPs and voters also forms a $1:n$ loop. An example of $1:n$ association among entities of the same type is given in figure 2.15(a).

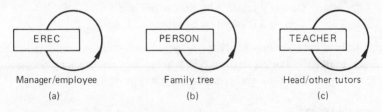

| Manager/employee | Family tree | Head/other tutors |
| (a) | (b) | (c) |

Figure 4.2

The characteristics of $1:n$ association type can be restated as:

> *A given entity can be participate at most once as owner and at most*
> *once as member in the same 1:n association type.*

We shall refer to this rule as the *1:n association restriction rule*. It allows recursive relationships, including the appearance of the same entity in the same association occurrence, both as owner and member. This rule is obeyed by disjoint A-set types.

4.3.3 m:n association

This is the most general form of association that can exist among the occurrences of the same or different entity types, to be referred to as *m:n* loop or *network* respectively. We shall begin with a network.

Network

To show the representation of a network, we consider the *m:n* association between courses and students mentioned earlier. The association is diagrammatically represented below where the double arrow indicates that each occurrence of one type can own many occurrences of the other type.

m : *n* association

Suppose that the explicit relationships among the entities courses and students are:

> Student 1 takes the Courses 1 and 3
> Student 2 takes the Courses 1, 2 and 3
> Student 3 takes the Courses 1 and 2
> Student 4 takes the Courses 1 and 3
> Course 1 is taken by Students 1, 2, 3 and 4
> Course 2 is taken by Students 2 and 3
> Course 3 is taken by Students 1, 2 and 4

Although defined between two entity types there is only one *m:n* association between them, unlike the 1:*n* association type where there can be many occurrences. In fact in all *m:n* associations, each association is a type of its own.

Direct representation

To represent the above association directly, we may define two A-set types, say T1 and T2, T1 owned by courses and T2 by students (figure 4.3). Obviously, these A-set types are non-disjoint, since the same member entity participates in more than one A-set of the same type. However, since the same member entity can have as many owners as there are owner records in the same A-set type, the maintenance of the required A-set indexes is cumbersome and expensive. Many data models, including the network model, do not permit such a direct representation.

A-set types	A-sets	Owner	Members
T1	1	Course 1	Student 1, Student 2, Student 3, Student 4
	2	Course 2	Student 2, Student 3
	3	Course 3	Student 1, Student 2, Student 4
T2	1	Student 1	Course 1, Course 3
	2	Student 2	Course 1, Course 2, Course 3
	3	Student 3	Course 1, Course 2
	4	Student 4	Course 1, Course 3

Figure 4.3

Indirect representation

In an indirect representation, we invoke the relationship entity and resolve an $m{:}n$ relationship into two $1{:}n$ association types (more correctly one $1{:}m$ and one $1{:}n$ association type).

Let us then assume that there exists a relationship entity for each pair of related course and student, each entity to be represented by CiSj, where Ci is the entity identifier of course i and Sj is the entity identifier of student j. We then have the following relationship entities

	Student 1	Student 2	Student 3	Student 4
Course 1	C1S1	C1S2	C1S3	C1S4
Course 2		C2S2	C2S3	
Course 3	C3S1	C3S2		C3S4

to be referred to as CSL (short for Course Student Link) entities, the corresponding entity records being CSL records. The $m{:}n$ associations can now be resolved as

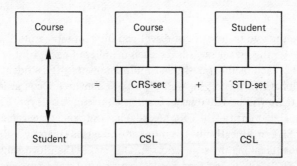

where each CSL entity CiSj is owned by course i in one $1{:}n$ association type and by student j in the other $1{:}n$ association type as

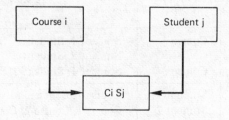

This technique makes the Course and Student records independent of each other. We can now represent the relationship by disjoint A-set types, say CRS-SET and STD-SET owned by the Course records and Student records respectively. The CSL records are members in both the A-set types, but the same CSL record appears only once in A-sets of the same type as shown in figure 4.4, unlike the A-set types T1 and T2.

A-set type	A-sets	Owners	Members (link records)
CRS-set	1	Course 1	C1S1, C1S2, C1S3, C1S4
CRS-set	2	Course 2	C2S2, C2S3
CRS-set	3	Course 3	C3S1, C3S2, C3S4
STD-set	1	Student 1	C1S1, C3S1
STD-set	2	Student 2	C1S2, C2S2, C3S2
STD-set	3	Student 3	C1S3, C2S3
STD-set	4	Student 4	C1S4, C3S4

Figure 4.4 Representation of the network of figure 4.2 by CSL records. Note that a CSL record is represented by a pair of keys

To compare the two techniques of direct and indirect representation, we have listed in figure 4.5 the owner records for each member of each A-set.

In T1 and T2, each member entity has multiple owners. If a student takes 10 courses, he will have 10 owners in A-set type T1. Likewise if a course is taken by 100 students, there will be 100 owners for that course in A-set type T2. In contrast, the member entity (the CSL records) has only one owner in each of CRS-SET and STD-SET, irrespective of the number of courses taken by a student or the number of students taking the same courses. This makes the processing of the CRS-SET and STD-SET simpler; in other words disjoint A-set types are generally simpler and easier to process and maintain.

Member	A-set type	Owner records
Student 1	T1	C1, C3
Student 2	T1	C1, C2, C3
Student 3	T1	C1, C2
Student 4	T1	C1, C3
Course 1	T2	S1, S2, S3, S4
Course 2	T2	S2, S3
Course 3	T2	S1, S2, S4

(a)

Member	A-set type	Owner record
C1S1	CRS-SET	C1
C1S2	CRS-SET	C1
C1S3	CRS-SET	C1
C1S4	CRS-SET	C1
C2S2	CRS-SET	C2
C2S3	CRS-SET	C2
C3S1	CRS-SET	C3
C3S2	CRS-SET	C3
C3S4	CRS-SET	C3
C1S1	STD-SET	S1
C1S2	STD-SET	S2
C1S3	STD-SET	S3
C1S4	STD-SET	S4
C2S2	STD-SET	S2
C2S3	STD-SET	S3
C3S1	STD-SET	S1
C3S2	STD-SET	S2
C3S4	STD-SET	S4

(b)

Figure 4.5 (a) Direct representation. (b) Indirect representation

A network can also exist among the entities of more than two types. Consider, for instance, the relationship among patient, doctor and drug. Each patient can have many doctors and take many drugs, each doctor can treat many patients and prescribe many drugs; and each drug can be taken by many patients and prescribed by many doctors.

If we wish to consider the details of each drug (such as date, dosage, effect) prescribed to each patient by each doctor, then we have a triangular *m:n* association among patient, doctor and drug. This cannot be directly represented by A-set types since three record types are involved, but it can be resolved into three 1:*n* association types, each to be represented by a disjoint A-set type as shown

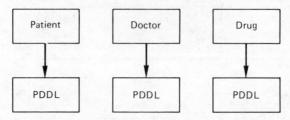

where PDDL represents the relationship entities for patient–doctor–drug link. There would be one relationship entity for each triplet, the corresponding entity record holding information exclusively on the relationship of the triplet. Another example of a similar triangular relationship is the one among employees, projects and machines, each having an *m:n* association with the other two.

m:n loop

In an *m:n* loop, as against a 1:*n* loop, the records of the same type show many to many associations among themselves. An example is a relationship among parts, where each part is related to a number of other parts as superior and/or subordinate parts, leading to part explosion problems. The direct representation of an *m:n* loop is generally too cumbersome. The standard practice is to recognise the relationships as entities through link records and thus resolve the *m:n* loop into two 1:*n* associations, as discussed below.

Suppose there are four part records A, B, C and D, all belonging to the same record type PART but A is made up of 2 Bs and 6 Ds, and B is made up of 4 Cs and 3 Ds, as displayed in figure 4.6.

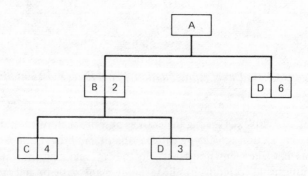

Figure 4.6

Given a part, we may wish to find all its subordinate parts with quantities (that is, the number of the subordinate parts in its immediate superior part) right up to the lowest level subordinate parts. This is the downward search, where at each level a part explodes into a number of subordinate parts. The reverse process is the upward search, where all the superior parts of a given subordinate part are extracted.

This twin processing is also known as the 'bill of material processing', following the name of an IBM package called Bill of Material Processor (BOMP) designed for the purpose. To represent the problem, consider two entity types, part records and part relationship records with the following entity records:

(i) Part Records (PART), one record for every part, each containing information such as part code (PC), part description, re-order level and so on. Assume that part codes A,B,C and D are the values of the primary key (entity identifiers) of these part records.

(ii) Relationship Records (PLINK), one record for each superior/subordinate pair. Each PLINK record contains the identifier of the superior part (SUP), the identifier of the subordinate part (SUB) and quantity (QTY) of the subordinate part used in that superior part. The unique key for PLINK record is (SUP, SUB).

The records are shown in figure 4.7.

PC	Other data
A	Other information
B	Other information
C	Other information
D	Other information

PART records
Key: PC

SUP	SUB	QTY
A	B	2
A	D	6
B	C	4
B	D	3

PLINK records
Key: SUP + SUB

Figure 4.7

We form two 1:n association types and hence disjoint A-set types to be called SUBSET and SUPSET (figure 4.8), the SUBSET to find the subordinate parts and SUPSET to find the superior parts for a given part. The owners and members of the two A-set types are displayed in figure 4.9. In each A-set type there are four A-sets, owned by A,B,C and D respectively (figure 4.9). The members are represented by their key values which are the concatenated values of attributes (SUP, SUB) in record type PLINK. In SUBSET, the members of each owner are those PLINK records where the owner is the superior part (the attribute SUP of PLINK records). Conversely in SUPSET the members of each owner are those PLINK records where this owner is the subordinate part. The A-sets owned by C and D in SUBSET and

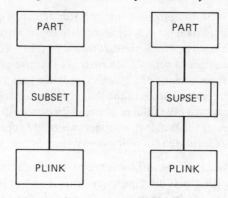

Part Explosion Problem

Figure 4.8

Owners	Members	Owners	Members
A	AB, AD	A	–
B	BC, BD	B	AB
C	–	C	BC
D	–	D	AD, BD
SUBSET		SUPSET	

Figure 4.9

by A in SUPSET are empty, indicating that C and D do not have any subordinate parts, and that A does not have any superior part.

It should now be easy to see how SUBSET can be used for downward and SUPSET for upward search. To find the subordinate parts of, say, part A, we get the PLINK records AB and AD via the respective A-set owned by part A in SUBSET. The two PLINK records give the subordinate parts B and D which now can be used as identifiers to retrieve the other information on parts B and D from PART records. On the other hand, to find the superior parts of, say, D, we get their identifiers and quantities from PLINK records AD and BD through the respective A-set owned by part D in SUPSET. The process can thus be repeated until the lowest parts in the case of downward, and the highest parts in the case of upward, search are found.

4.4 Data placement and access

In the previous section we took a top level view of two fundamental concepts — namely entity record and association — examining their representation techniques in the conceptual schema. In this section we shall again look at them, but from the lower level — as seen from the internal schema — reviewing how entity records and associations are physically placed in storage and what access facilities can be supported for them. In general, a data placement strategy is aimed at providing a fast update and retrieval facility and at the same time allowing for some storage independence. By update we mean insertion, deletion and amendment. Often there is a conflict between update and retrieval efficiency as one can be gained at the expense of the other, and therefore trade-offs are necessary. Some of these issues will also be covered in this section.

4.4.1 Data placement

There is only one physical sequence in which records can be stored and therefore it is important to make the best use of that sequence. For instance, if records are stored with key values 1, 11, 21, 31, ... in the first bucket of a disc, 2, 12, 22, 32, ... in the second bucket and so on, then no amount of indexing is going to give a very fast retrieval in that key sequence, as one disc access will be needed for each record, the same bucket being accessed over and over again. It will probably be more efficient in this case to access each bucket only once, and sort the records. Therefore, it is very important to store records in the most advantageous sequence. Some of the commonly used sequences are as follows.

(i) *Time sequence*: The records can be stored in order of their insertion, that is, *insertion time sequence*. The first record inserted will be in the first location, the second record inserted in the second location and so on. If the records to be inserted are sorted on a particular key before insertion, then this key order will be preserved except for subsequent unordered insertions. In other words, if records are inserted in time sequence they can be made to reflect a key order only for the records inserted during the first loading. Nevertheless records are sometimes inserted in time sequence — as in a Codasyl option — with a view to accessing them in their placement order, such as Find the First/Next/Prior/Nth/Last record. It is also possible to store the record in reverse time order, storing the first record in the last location of the available space.

(ii) *Key sequence*: In this case an attempt is made to store records in a specified key sequence to provide fast access in that key order. As with the time sequence, only the first set of records can be physically stored in the key order, the subsequent insertions will generally be unordered. A chaining technique (embedded pointers) can be used to indicate the correct order.

(iii) *Random access*: If fast random access is the aim, then the records can be stored either in the *direct* or *calc* mode (both are old Codasyl terms). In the direct mode the value of a specified key is taken as the physical location, but a problem arises if the location is already full. In the calc mode records are stored via a hashing technique, usually the remainder technique.

(iv) *Fast random and sequential access by a key*: An attempt is made to store the records as in (ii) but, instead of chaining, a B-tree or H-tree is implemented.

(v) *Page splitting*: In this all records are always kept in primary key order, reorganising the records within a page in the event of new insertions. If a page is full, a new page is attached. The records of the original page are redistributed in the primary key order over the original page and the new page, each page getting half the number of records (see section 3.3.3 for comments on its efficiency).

(vi) *Clustered*: If the records of one type are mostly accessed in conjunction with the records of another type, then they can be stored together. This can be best illustrated by considering the department and employee records of figure 2.14. If the employee's records are most frequently accessed within a department, then they should be physically stored in that clustered fashion, effectively treating the employee records as a repeating group. Its clustered placement is shown in figure 4.10 (we have ignored employee HUTT as he does not belong to any known department).

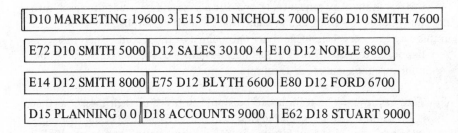

Figure 4.10 Clustered placement

The main headache in such a sequence comes from updates. Insertions of new employees can only be handled by storing them elsewhere and linking them with chains; but deletions leave gaps. Since two record types are mixed together, the subsequent reorganisation of the database is harder in a clustered placement. However, in a retrieval dominated system the clustered sequence can be advantageous. In the Codasyl model this sequence is available for storing set owner and members together (section 10.1).

(vii) *Hybrid*: There can be other placement techniques, particularly involving combinations of those given above.

It is often possible to provide better performance at the cost of storage space. For instance, if every data page is only partially filled, then the existing records can easily expand (if new data items or repeating groups are added) if need be without overflowing. Moreoever if each page is expected to receive a stipulated group of records (as in the Calc mode), then again a low density distribution helps. Indeed in many commercial database implementations data pages are not allowed to exceed some 70 per cent load factor during the first loading of the database, leaving the remaining 30 per cent reserved for future insertions.

4.4.2 Generation of internal identifiers

As mentioned in section 3.2, internal identifiers are used for internal references to records in a database, and they should have the following characteristics

> A compact fixed size
> Storage independence
> Fast access to storage

It is easy to design an internal identifier with a compact fixed size, but the last two characteristics are contradictory and hence difficult to achieve. A trade-off is therefore needed. There are essentially four ways of generating internal identifiers:

> Primary key
> Physical location
> Independent values
> Functions of primary keys

As mentioned in chapter 3, primary keys fail on compact size, but are nevertheless used as internal identifiers in some small systems.

Many implementations ignore storage independence and simply take the physical address as the internal identifiers, while others — as in SYSTEM R and some Codasyl implementations — allow some flexibility. In the latter case, an internal identifier is taken as the physical page number appended by the position of a location in the page header. This location gives the start byte of the record on that page. For instance, an identifier 1002 could imply page 10 and location 2. Figure 4.11 for page 10 gives a value 351 at location 2, implying that this record starts at byte 351 of this page as indicated by the arrow. This technique allows a record to be moved up or down the page. If the original record expands (say owing to addition of new attributes), and if the page is full, then the entire record is moved to a non-full page, keeping a pointer in the home page (the original page) which gives the new location; but the internal identifier is not changed. In this case, two disc accesses are necessary to find the record by internal identifiers, one to get to the home page by the internal identifier and the other to get the required page. If the record has to be moved again to another page, the pointer in the home page is changed accordingly to indicate the new page, so that no more than two disc accesses are ever needed.

If independent identifiers (unrelated to storage locations) are used, then we need an extra index to link these identifiers to storage locations and hence access by internal identifiers becomes rather slow. The fourth technique is a compromise which generates an internal identifier by applying a division hashing on the primary key value and stores records in the internal identifier sequence. If the records are of fixed length L, then the start byte of the record with internal identifier N is

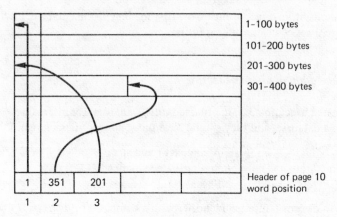

Figure 4.11 Data page

$L * (N-1) + 1$ irrespective of page size, since space is reserved for all records from identifier 1 to NMAX (where NMAX is the highest internal identifier), even if some records do not exist. Knowing the page size, the actual position on a page can be found. The technique provides fast random and sequential access by both internal identifiers and primary key, and has been implemented in the PRECI system (Deen, 1982). It gives a good performance when the distribution of the primary key values is not highly clustered.

4.4.3 Implementation of associations

Associations are implemented in the internal schema by A-sets, and therefore the distinction of an association as a pure entity relationship, divorced from the consideration of access paths, loses in implementation, since A-sets are means to support related records. Some A-set implementation techniques are:

(1) *Foreign keys*: Foreign keys in the member records can support A-set types, as pointed out in chapter 2. For non-disjoint A-set types a repeating group of foreign keys may be allowed, as is done in ADABAS. This technique may also be referred to as the embedded owner pointer technique where pointers are primary key values. In storage of the member records, these key values can be replaced by internal identifiers of the owners (section 2.6.4).

(2) *Physical placement*: Member records can be physically placed close to owner records, as in the clustered record placement technique discussed earlier. Since records are physically stored in only one place, this technique can be used in only one A-set type for a given member record type.

(3) *Embedded pointers*: Next or Prior pointers can be attached to member records, or member pointers can be attached to the owner record (see section 3.2.1).

(4) *Non-embedded identifiers*: For each occurrence of a given A-set type, we can maintain a list headed by the owner identifier and followed by its member ident-

ifiers. Ideally these identifiers should be internal identifiers, although they can be unordered, partially ordered or fully ordered (section 3.2.2).

(5) *Member keys*: If the internal pointers of the member records in (4) above are sorted in a specified member key order, then we get this option. Strictly speaking, this may be regarded as an ordered access facility rather than a basic implementation technique, particularly since it is equivalent to the secondary key indexing of record types where the foreign key forms the first part of that secondary key. To explain the technique, we return to DREC and EREC of figure 2.14.

Suppose we wish to use ENO as member key for A-set type WORKER. In implementation we can use K = (DNO, ENO) as the key and store each K value with the internal identifier I of each member record in K value order. The resultant A-set index is

> (D10E15,I), (D10E60,I), (D10E72,I),
> (D12E10,I), (D12E14,I), (D12E75,I), (D12E80,I)
> (D18E62,I)

The DNO values identify the A-sets within this A-set type. In actual implementation, 'I' will be replaced by a value. Since ENO is the primary key of EREC, each ENO value has a distinct internal identifier. However if we use ENAME as the member key, then this uniqueness will be lost; in this case, the representation has to be changed to (K,n,I) in each group as follows (n giving the number of internal identifiers for this K value):

> (D10 NICHOLS, 1,I), (D10 SMITH,2,I,I)
> (D12 BLYTH, 1,I), (D12 FORD, 1,I) (D12, NOBLE, 1,I), (D12 SMITH,1,I)
> (D18 STUART,1,I)

If we design a secondary key for EREC made up of (EDN, ENO) or (EDN, ENAME) then we get the same indexes as given above (we shall ignore Employee record E90 as it does not have a proper EDN value). Thus the A-set indexes become identical with secondary key indexes if the owner identifier (or foreign key) is used as the first part of that key. The additional access paths to A-sets, such as those shown in figure 2.13 can be implemented by a combination of the above techniques.

4.4.4 Data redundancy

Data integration is generally regarded as an important characteristic of a database. There is no doubt that the avoidance of redundancy should be an aim, but the vigour with which this aim should be pursued is open to question.

Redundancy is direct if a value is a copy of another, and indirect if the value can be derived from one or more other values; they usually occur in the form of replicated and derived attribute values respectively. Both direct and indirect redundancies simplify retrieval but complicate updates; and conversely integration makes retrieval slow and updates easier. Consider, for instance, the employee records of figure 2.14. Since DNO is part of the employee records, we can print employee details with department numbers without accessing the department records, but to update DNO we must update both the record types simultaneously, so that other users accessing the database at the same time cannot get inconsistent values in between the two updates. On the other hand, if DNO did not appear in employee records then update of department records would be easier, but it would slow down the retrieval of employee details with department numbers. Therefore there is a trade-off, and it depends on expected usage — favouring redundancy for low update and high retrieval rate.

An example of indirect redundancy is the total department salary TOTSAL as the sum of individual employee salary ESAL (figure 2.14), or age from date of birth. Some indirect redundancies are essential for data validations (for example, use of control totals) while others such as age have retrieval conveniences. Therefore, while attempts should be made to avoid unnecessary redundancies, we cannot eliminate them altogether.

4.4.5 Access paths

Access paths required for databases can be approximated to those required for the underlying data structures. We shall assume records as the units of access and A-sets as the building blocks of $1:n$ and $m:n$ associations, since they appear to be the common denominators of the basic data structures in most major data models.

Access paths for records:

- Random access by one or more user defined keys
- Sequential access by one or more user defined keys
- Random and sequential access by internal identifiers

Access paths for A-sets:

- Random access to A-sets of a given type by owner identifier
- Random access to an A-set of a given type by a member identifier
- Sequential access to the A-sets of a given type by owner identifiers
- Random access to a member by one or more user defined keys
- Sequential access to a member by one or more user defined keys or by internal identifiers

By identifiers above we imply unique identifiers which can be primary key or internal identifiers; the term key means any key which could be primary or secondary. Sequential access to the A-sets of a given type is often equivalent to accessing the owner records in the desired sequence and then accessing the A-sets directly by each owner identifier in turn. If there is more than one type of member record (as in the Codasyl model), the sequential access can be required either exclusively for the members of a given record type or for all members irrespective of their record types. Many of these access facilities have been discussed earlier at file level and some of these are diagrammatically represented in figure 2.13.

If the data model supports larger data sets, as in IMS, then in addition we need:

- Random access to each dataset of a given type by dataset identifiers
- Sequential access to each dataset of a given type by dataset identifiers

Sequential access to records, A-sets, members and datasets should basically permit retrieval by positions such as first, last, next or prior occurrence of that type in the defined key or identifier order. The key may consist of one or more attributes.

Flexibility and efficiency

It should be possible to define some or all of these access paths for a record type or A-set type as the case may be. More access paths make retrievals easier, but updates very expensive. If a record is a member of, say five A-set types, each supported by two member keys, then there would be 10 member key indexes for this record. If these indexes are B-trees, each taking about two disc accesses to locate a position, then any update of this record might involve 20 disc accesses for the indexes alone. This is a reason why we must strike a balance between access paths and update require-ments. In an ideal situation the DBA should be able to change access paths periodic-ally, depending on past or predicted performance (section 5.3). When there is a multiplicity of access paths (as is usual in databases), the run-time system has to decide on the best access path for a given transaction. This leads to interesting research problems in access path optimisation, as mentioned in section 5.3.3.

In the next section we shall consider a database architecture and show how it can support the facilities discussed above, without burdening application programmers with the details.

4.5 Database architecture

Early databases were developed as the direct extension of large files, with a simple architecture based on a single level description of data which did not make any distinctions between various levels. IDS-I and TOTAL are products of that period. The Codasyl DBTG report of 1971 recognised the need for a two-level approach — with a system view called schema and a user view called subschema — as a means to provide greater data independence. A similar two-level approach is also used in IMS. As experience grew, the need for further stratification became apparent, culminating in the ANSI/SPARC proposal of a three-level schema architecture and a data dictionary. Broadly speaking, with this architecture, we have probably reached a relatively stable state, at least in so far as the schema levels are concerned. Future refinements are most likely to be in the form of sublevels within those three levels, rather than new levels (see also section 14.1).

This architecture is reviewed in this section, beginning with a brief overview in subsection 4.5.1, and followed by discussions on the three schemas in the next three subsections. The last subsection describes issues in data manipulation.

4.5.1   The ANSI–SPARC model

The origin of the ANSI-SPARC model goes back to November 1972 when the Standards Planning and Requirement Committee (SPARC) of ANSI-X3 set up a study group called ANSI-X3-SPARC/DBMS study group — more cryptically ANSI/SPARC or just ANSI study group — to specify a model for database standardisation. Although it was independent of the relevant Codasyl committees (DDLC and PLC — see chapter 9) there was some co-ordination between them.

ANSI/SPARC produced its interim report in February 1975 followed by its final report in 1977, in which a database architecture (figure 4.12) based on a three-level schema — conceptual, external and internal — and an integrated data dictionary was proposed. The committee was not created to, and did not, produce any

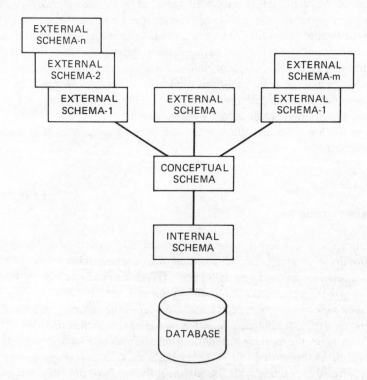

Figure 4.12 ANSI/SPARC architecture

language specification, but it introduced a number of important concepts. Its main finding on the architecture received a wide level of acceptance and formed the foundation of the current thinking on architecture.

The ANSI/SPARC study group divided the system view of databases into the conceptual and the internal schema, and upgraded the old user view into a hierarchy of external schemas (figure 4.12). The basic notions of these schemas have been presented earlier, and some more details will now follow.

The lowest level external schema is mapped to the internal schema either *indirectly* via the conceptual schema or *directly*, by-passing the conceptual schema. The former provides greater data independence (see next section).

A key feature of the ANSI/SPARC architecture is the recognition of an integrated data dictionary to hold data about the schemas and directories. The dictionary is expected to service both the users of the database and the run-time system by supplying the necessary information. It is discussed in section 5.4.

4.5.2 Conceptual schema

As indicated in section 4.1, a conceptual schema is meant to be a formal description of data, independent of any storage consideration. The ANSI/SPARC report has not formally specified any structure or content of the conceptual schema; however, most experts will probably expect it to contain minimally the descriptions of

Entity record types
Association types
Usage constraints

A point that should be stressed here is that a conceptual schema must not contain any storage dependent clauses; for instance, when an entity record is described in a conceptual schema, this description should contain only data types of attributes (for example, integer, real, character etc.) and their length (such as the maximum number of digits or characters), but not any storage characteristics such as bytes occupied. Most present-day implementations do not have a pure conceptual schema; they usually include some storage characteristics of one sort or another. Therefore we shall use the term *database schema* as a common name for both pure and impure conceptual schemas, reserving the term conceptual schema only for its pure form.

4.5.3 Internal schema

The internal schema describes the storage strategy for the data of the database with a view to achieving optimal run-time performance and optimal storage space utilisation. Access path optimisation, storage optimisation, optimal buffer management and better indexing techniques are some of the interesting research issues relevant to the internal schema. (We shall use the terms internal schema and storage schema synonymously, as we have done earlier.) The basic contents of an internal schema are as follows.

Storage strategy
Storage space allocation for data and indexes;
record descriptions for storage (with stored sizes for data items);
control of data redundancy;
record placement and a strategy for generating internal identifiers;
association implementation technique;
overflow management strategy.

Access paths
Specification of keys (primary and secondary);
indexes and hashing techniques for keys and pointers for chaining records in specific sequence.

Miscellaneous
Data compression techniques, if any;
data encryption techniques if any;
mapping of the storage schema to the conceptual schema.

An internal schema may specify storage space in terms of operating system pages for better efficiency.

Given a conceptual record type (that is, a record type in the conceptual schema) it could be that some of its data items and record occurrences are more frequently used than others. If so, the internal schema designer could split a conceptual record type in a number of storage record types (called *vertical fragmentation*); and if it improves the overall access performance, then he can store only some specified occurrences (*horizontal fragmentation*) rather than all the original occurrences, on a particular storage area, in accordance with a record placement strategy (see later). If fragmentation is used, the system must link the different fragments to recreate each original record when needed. In a more advanced placement technique, fragments can be allowed to be replicated if this enhances the overall performance (see section 10.1.1).

Data compression techniques are sometimes used to minimise storage requirement, as in ADABAS. Encryption provides extra confidentiality over and above passwords. By mapping, we mean a declaration stating the correspondence between conceptual and storage objects. For instance, if a conceptual record type is given a different name in the storage schema or if it is represented by several storage record types, then we have to stipulate the counterparts of a conceptual record type in the storage schema. This correspondence is the mapping. The conceptual/ storage schema mapping should be declared in the storage schema so that the conceptual schema does not require any change in the event of a storage reorganisation.

The content of the conceptual schema is assumed to be more stable than that of the internal schema, since the latter deals with performance-related topics. Given a conceptual schema, there could be several possible internal schemas, one of which is likely to be more suited to a specific performance requirement (see section 5.3).

4.5.4 External schema

A given user program can invoke only one external schema, which is normally designed to cater for a specific application, possibly involving several user programs. An external schema serves the following principal functions:

(i) It selects a logical subset of the data of the database as needed for the intended application, but the subset chosen can overlap with another external schema.

(ii) The subset is presented in the form most convenient to the intended user language. For instance, record description with level numbers may be ideal for Cobol users but not for Fortran users. There can be other, more substantial variations.

(iii) By restricting the access of the user to the necessary subset of the data, rather than allowing access unnecessarily to the whole database, it contributes towards the privacy protection of data.

As mentioned earlier, the ANSI model permits a hierarchy of external schemas to be defined. Therefore, starting from a language-independent external schema, we can have one Cobol dependent and another Fortran dependent external schema. Likewise, an external schema may present a relational view which in turn might support other external schemas for specific applications. However, we shall ignore this type of hierarchy in subsequent discussions in this book, and assume a single-level external schema except where qualified otherwise.

Normally an external schema will map on to the conceptual schema which will in turn map on to the internal schema. This two-stage mapping is less efficient, but provides greater data independence in the sense that the external and internal schemas can be altered independently of each other. However, for more efficient mapping the ANSI model permits, as an alternative, the direct mapping of external schemas on to the internal schema, thus by-passing the conceptual schema (figure 4.13) as mentioned earlier. This, of course, curtails data independence, since in this case every time the internal schema is changed, the external schema along with the dependent application programs might also have to be changed. Such a situation would arise if an application program uses data structure, keys and indexes which are subsequently dropped from the internal schema. However, in the rest of this book we shall assume only two-stage mappings (see also section 4.6) which make the internal schema invisible or transparent to the external schema and conversely the external schema transparent to the internal schema.

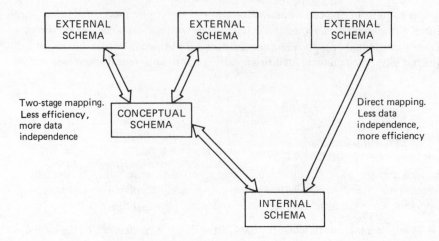

Figure 4.13 Mappings and data independence

The ANSI report does not specify in any detail the content of an external schema; but if we accept the minimal content of the conceptual schema listed earlier, then a corresponding external schema may contain the descriptions of

(i) entity record types (only those needed)
(ii) association types (only those needed)
(iii) additional usage constraints, if necessary, on top of those specified in the conceptual schema, and
(iv) entries for external to conceptual schema mapping if relevant but no storage schema dependent clauses.

However, depending on the intended user language, this subset of data can be described in different types of data structures. The likely variation between the conceptual and external schema will be discussed in the next section.

If the objects in the external schema are different from those in the conceptual schema, then we require some mapping declarations. A common example is the mapping between different data names; this is essential if the conceptual data names are illegal in the external schema — such as variable names longer than six characters or variable names with hyphens in a Fortran external schema. In that event, we must define alternative variable names for the Fortran external schema and state which external name corresponds to which conceptual name. Finally, the inclusion of the mapping in the external schema makes the conceptual schema independent of the external schemas.

As indicated earlier, an external schema can be independent of user languages, but in that case it has to support a higher level external schema, or some mechanism to interact with the allowed data structure of that user language. For simplicity, we shall assume all external schemas are not only single-level but also user-language dependent; this user language can be a host language or a high level language.

The external schema represents an important area of research covering user facilities. There are many research projects aimed at designing application-specific external schemas (and query languages) such as for airline reservation systems, banking systems and so on, using data structures which are not necessarily supported by the underlying conceptual schema. This leads to interesting mapping and optimisation problems. Intelligent query processing is another challenging topic with impact on the external schema (see chapter 14 for more detail).

4.5.5 Data manipulation

A database can be accessed either from a purpose-built non-procedural language (such as the relational languages) or from a host language (such as Cobol, Fortran, PL/I and so on), but in both cases through an external schema. The language that interfaces user programs and the database is called the data manipulation language (DML) and, as the name suggests, it permits the manipulation of the data in the database. Any user language that uses the database has to include the necessary data manipulation (DM) commands as part of its language constructs, *as done in all non-procedural languages* (see section 5.5).

The standard input/output commands of a host language normally operate on its own files, but not on a database; and hence there is a need for special DM commands. Whereas the DM commands in a non-procedural language tend to be high level, those in a host language are usually lower level, *record-at-a-time* commands, sometimes called *navigational* commands, as they seem to navigate through the database, examining one record at a time. They are also called procedural commands. The main functions of these navigational DM commands are

- to select a record from the database, subject to stipulated conditions being satisfied
- to present the record to the application program via the external schema
- to insert new records and associations into the database
- to modify existing records and associations of the database
- to delete existing records and associations from the database

The syntaxes of these commands are often slightly adjusted to suit different host languages, although the semantics usually remain the same (see section 10.2 for the Codasyl model). The non-procedural commands usually operate on a group of records at a time, particularly for the retrieval of data, as we shall see in chapter 6.

A good DML should provide what is called *access transparency* to application programmers who should be able to access any record of the database using any of the access procedures of the DML, irrespective of whether or not the relevant access paths are specified in the storage schema. For instance, in a navigational language he should be able to process any record by any key randomly or sequentially or in any desired order, even if that key or that order is not implemented. Likewise, he should be able to access the owner record, the prior record or the next record from a member record, or a member record from an owner record, even if these access paths are not specified in the storage schema. Naturally access will be faster if relevant access paths are specified; but if they are not specified, the DBCS will have to do extra work, including sequential scanning and sorting, to locate the wanted record if needed. This access transparency is essential if the application programs are to be independent of the storage schema. The relational model provides total access transparency, while other models vary in this regard.

4.6　Data independence

Data independence in the context of a database implies the independence of one view of data with respect to others. This permits the DBA to make changes in one view, to improve certain aspects of database performance, without disturbing the other views. The main areas of interest are as follows.

(i) Conceptual Schema (CS): In principle, the conceptual schema is independent of other views. In is specified, (at least in theory) before other views, and is compiled independently.

(ii) Internal Schema (IS): This view cannot be independent of the conceptual schema, as its purpose is to organise the storage of entity characteristics described in the conceptual schema. It is compiled against the conceptual schema and it would normally require redesign after every change of conceptual schema. However, the internal schema is independent of the external schema, and can become independent of the characteristics of physical devices if storage allocation is made in terms of pages rather than tracks and cylinders, and if logical pointers rather than physical addresses are used for the internal reference of the records.

(iii) External Schema (ES): Although an external schema is a logical description of a subset of the entity characteristics, it is not meant to be a subset of the actual descriptions in the conceptual schema; some variations can be permitted between these two views. The external schema independence refers to the ability to define an external schema differently from the conceptual schema and, once compiled, its stability against changes in the conceptual and internal schema with respect to recompilation. These two aspects are described as logical data independence and logical binding in sections 4.6.1 and 4.6.2 respectively.

(iv) Application Program (AP): Since the application program processes data described in the external schema, it is naturally dependent on the latter, and also on the internal schema if the DM commands do not provide access path transparency. However, since modern DBMSs are expected to provide access transparency, we shall assume an application program to be independent of internal schema. Another associated question is: once compiled, how stable is the application program against the subsequent alterations in the external and internal schema? This question will also be answered under logical binding in section 4.6.2.

4.6.1 Logical data independence

Since the external schema is meant to provide an application oriented view, its data structures should reflect the requirement of that application. The more powerful the data structures, the easier is the programming for that application. Likewise an external schema for a very high level user language normally supports very high level data structures which are constructed from the relatively simpler conceptual data structures, through a complex mapping hidden from the user. Therefore the variations that should ideally be permitted between external and conceptual data structures are endless. However, at the very lowest level the following variations should be permitted.

(i) *Component:* The external schema definitions of formats of components should be permitted to be different from those of the conceptual schema. For instance, it should be possible to declare a numeric item in the conceptual schema as an alphanumeric item in the external schema.

(ii) *Record types:* It should be possible to define an external record type with only a subset of the components of a conceptual record type. It should not be necessary to include all conceptual record types in the external schema.

(iii) *Associations:* It should be possible to declare only the necessary associations in the external schema.

4.6.2 Logical binding

An application program or an external schema may be said to be stable if it does not require any recompilation in the event of changes in the other views. Recompilations are usually messy and laborious, and particularly unwelcome when a large number of application programs and external schemas are involved. Therefore a reduction in the number of recompilations is considered to be an important feature of a database architecture, and this depends on the time of linking the different schemas for the execution of an application program.

If the schemas are linked together at the time of the compilation of the application program, then recompilations will be needed if any schema changes subsequently. On the other hand, if the linking is carried out at the execution time of each DM command, then recompilations are not needed. This linking is called *binding*, which is defined as a process of converting one view of data into another so that the elements of one view can be obtained in the frame of reference of the other. We shall now elaborate this process.

Binding is a term used in the implementations of programming languages and it links the programmer's view of data to that of the machine. In the context of databases there are five views, giving the following four stages of conversion:

(i) application program/external schema (AP/ES)
(ii) external schema/conceptual schema (ES/CS)

(iii) conceptual schema/internal schema (CS/IS)
(iv) internal schema/physical storage device.

The first three stages together constitute what is termed a logical binding, and links the programmer's view with the internal schema view. The last stage is the physical binding, which lies in the domain of the operating system that binds the internal schema to the physical device, and hence it is outside the scope of this book.

The binding in each stage represents a conversion directory which contains a set of conversion tables including, in some cases, procedures. For the execution of an application program, we need to produce an AP/IS conversion directory by consolidating AP/ES, ES/CS and CS/IS conversion directories. However, if a view changes after the production of the combined AP/IS directory, then the consolidation process has to be redone, since the directory of the changed view (AP/ES, ES/CS or CS/IS) would be altered by the change. Therefore, in general, the longer the directories of these three stages are kept separate, the less redoing is needed in the event of a change. We discuss below some possible options and current practices.

The compilation of the storage schema against the conceptual schema may be assumed to precede that of any other view. This compilation generates the CS/IS directory which yields the storage references for conceptual objects. Likewise the ES/CS directory is produced from the compilation of the external schema against the conceptual schema, but at this stage ES/CS and CS/IS directories *can* be converted into a combined ES/IS directory; but it is not advisable to do so, as it would require the external schema to be recompiled each time the storage schema is changed. Ideally the changes in the conceptual schema *should not* cause any recompilation of the external schema, except where changes involve deletion or alteration of conceptual objects referenced in the external schema.

Next should come the compilation of the application program against the compiled external schema. Ignoring the compilation of the host language and syntax checking, the compilation of the application program will produce (i) a User Work Area (UWA) and (ii) conversion of DM commands. The UWA is the program buffer to hold the data described in the external schema (section 9.4) and it is bound to the conceptual schema by the ES/CS directory. Therefore the application program should not really require any recompilation in the event of external schema change if the external schema objects in the application program are not deleted or altered.

The conversion of DM commands is trickier. During the compilation, at one extreme, a command can be replaced by a general Call statement (or equivalent) and at the other by an optimised Call statement where the command can be bound with the storage schema by transforming ES/CS and CS/IS directories into a combined AP/IS directory. In the latter case, which is known as *compilation time* binding, the system checks what access paths are actually available in the storage schema, and how best (thus optimising) the DM command can be executed in terms of the available access paths. Once bound, the application program will require recompilation if the storage schema (more correctly CS/IS directory) changes subsequently.

However, if the command is replaced by a general Call statement (or equivalent) then it can be bound to the storage-schema access paths later, either at load time or at execution time. In a *load time binding*, the command is converted each time that the program is loaded for running, while in an *execution time binding*, which is also known as *dynamic binding*, the command is converted at the time of its execution. The execution time binding allows maximum data independence, but it is also most expensive in terms of CPU time. In very high level languages when complex mapping (and hence lengthier binding) is involved, execution time binding would be inadvisable except for infrequently used programs. Compilation time binding is the least flexible and also the least expensive. However, it is possible to implement compilation time binding in such a way that if any relevant object is changed, the DBCS recompiles the program automatically; this is convenient but not necessarily cheap. The binding process can also be spread over the compilation, load and execution time, with part of the binding being done at each occasion.

If an application program is used only once, then execution time binding can be more efficient, but most programs, including those for queries, are usually run repeatedly. Therefore most implementors prefer compilation time binding, although it causes recompilation problems. The automatic recompilation facility mentioned above is not yet available on commercial products.

Exercises

4.1 Describe the entity characteristics that should be represented in a conceptual schema.

4.2 Explain the following, with examples:
 (a) Relationship entity
 (b) Information-bearing relationships
 (c) Evolution of $1:n$ relationships to $m:n$ relationships.

4.3 Explain, with a diagram, the ANSI/SPARC architecture for databases, with special emphasis on the mappings between different levels. Assess the model critically.

4.4 Describe, giving justification, the basic content of the external, conceptual and internal schemas.

4.5 Explain, with an example, the technique of representing an $m:n$ relationship by link records, and compare its advantages with those of a more direct representation.

4.6 Given a set of cousins, show how you can represent their relationships. Discuss alternative techniques if any.

4.7 Describe the various record placement and set implementation techniques, with an assessment of their relative merits.

4.8 "Implementation of A-sets is equivalent to providing access paths by secondary keys". Verify this statement with examples.

4.9   Describe the storage and access strategy in databases under the following headings, and comment on their impact on performance:

> Data placement
> Surrogate generation
> Access paths
> Pointers and indexes.

4.10   Non-disjointed A-set types represent *m:n* relationships directly and yet they are not used in the Codasyl or relational models. Discuss the implementation problems of non-disjointed A-set types and explain why they are avoided in many data models.

4.11   Explain the concept of binding and discuss the various types of binding available for databases with particular reference to data independence.

References

ANSI/SPARC DBMS Study Group Report (1975). *ACM SIGFIDET*, Vol. (7:2), (Interim report)

ANSI/X3/SPARC (1978). DBMS Framework — Report of the Study Group on DBMS. *Information Systems*, Vol. 3 (Final report)

BCS/DDSWP (1975). *Report on Data Dictionary System*, BCS, 13 Mansfield Street, London W1M 0BP

Deen, S. M. (1982). An implementation of impure surrogates. *Proceedings of the 8th VLDB Conference, 1982*, p. 245

ISO (1981). *Concepts and Terminology for the Conceptual Schema*, edited by J. J. van Griethuysen *et al.*, ISO Report ISO/TC97/SC5/WGB, February

5 Supporting Facilities

In the previous chapter we discussed the database architecture which provides a skeleton to support entity characteristics, user languages, storage structure and data independence. The additional facilities which are needed to build a proper DBMS around that skeleton are as follows.

(i) Concurrent usage: The usage of the database by more than one program at the same time.
(ii) Data protection: The protection of data against error, loss and damage, and the protection of confidentiality. The specification of usage constraints in the conceptual schema is a prerequisite for this protection.
(iii) Database modification and optimisation: The ability to reorganise a database through alterations in conceptual and storage schemas and to optimise runtime performance.
(iv) Data dictionary: A meta data facility to assist the users and the system.
(v) Languages and utilities: These are needed for operations and maintenance.
(vi) Database control system.

These features together with those examined in the previous chapter determine the quality of a DBMS and hence they can be used as the main basis in its critical evaluation. We devote below one section to each of the features listed above, with a seventh section on the details of database recovery, as an advanced topic, an outline of which is included under data protection.

5.1 Concurrent usage

Concurrent usage implies the use of the database by several processes, or more correctly several transactions, at the same time. If this facility is not available, then only one transaction can be allowed in the database at any one time, resulting in an under-utilisation of the database. On the other hand, if concurrent usage is permitted, the DBCS can run into several problems, mainly concerning concurrent updates as illustrated below. But first we shall explain what we mean by a transaction, since the term is often used by different people to mean different things.

A transaction is a basic unit of a user process in a database, typically having:

- a read-phase to read one or more related data values, called *read-set*, from one or more records belonging to one or more record types in the database

- a computer-phase to compute on the read-set and possibly on other data to produce a *write-set*, consisting of one or more data values for one or more records belonging to one or more record types
- a write-phase to write the write-set into the database

To some extent, these phases can overlap. The read-phase is absent in an insertion-only transaction, whereas the write-phase is absent in a retrieval-only transaction, but both the phases may be present in an amendment. The read-set of a retrieval-only transaction should be such that it provides a consistent set of data for a specific requirement. For instance, if a user is interested in the latest amount credited to his bank account (credit record), and his balance (balance record), then his read-set should include both the records so that he gets a consistent picture. If he retrieves the balance record in a different transaction, he might get a different balance, as there can be further deposits made in between. Likewise, the read/write sets of an update transaction should contain the records needed for a consistent update which will leave the database in an error-free and consistent state (see also commit unit in section 5.1.5).

In a very high level language a single program instruction can describe all three phases of a transaction, whereas in a not so high level language (such as Cobol or Fortran) there can be many instructions for each of the three phases of a transaction.

From the user's point of view, a transaction is considered as *atomic*, implying that it either succeeds or fails without anything in between, although it may consist of many input, output and computation instructions. If it fails, the system must undo everything done in it and return to the pre-transaction state of the database as if nothing has happened. The principle of atomicity implies that transactions in a process (that is, in a program) cannot be nested (that is, a transaction cannot have another transaction inside it).

A process can have several transactions (none nested), but in the following discussion we shall ignore the distinction between a process and a transaction, on the assumption that only one transaction can be issued by a process at any one time.

5.1.1 Concurrent update

Let us consider two transactions tA and tB from concurrent process A and B respectively, both updating accumulated sales to a customer in the following record

D715	SMITH	588 7333	180

where D715 is the customer's account number, Smith is the customer, 588 7333 is the telephone number and 180 is the total sales. The following sequence of events may take place:

(i) Process A reads the original record as given above (read-phase of tA).

(ii) Process B also reads the original record as given above (read-phase of tB).

(iii) Process A updates the total sales by adding 50 to it (write-phase of tA) and writes the record back to the database as

D715	SMITH	588 7333	230

(iv) Process B updates the sales by adding 270 to it (write-phase of tB) in the original record that it read, and returns the record to the database as

D715	SMITH	588 7333	450

overwriting the updated version generated by process A.

The final version is incorrect since the update of A is lost; the correct version should have been

D715	SMITH	588 7333	500

To prevent this loss of an update transaction, the process B must be forced to read/re-read the record after it was modified by process A. This is called '*forcing a serialisation*' of the *interleaved* transactions. To understand this let us look again at the sequence of events leading to the lost update in

tA (read)
tB (read)
tA (write)
tB (write)

The two transactions are interleaved; they can be serialised as

either tA (read), tA (write), tB (read), tB (write)
or   tB (read), tB (write), tA (read), tA (write)

Either of these two serial sequences of transactions will prevent the loss of the update. Thus a serialisation removes the update anomaly and it can be achieved by introducing a system of locking and unlocking records, where a record is locked during its update so that the other processes cannot access it until it is unlocked or released by the first process. If this scheme is used, process A and B in the above example will be required to declare their intention to lock the record on reading, whereupon the record will be locked as soon as it is read by any one of them, say by A. The process B, and others, if any, wishing to access this record must then wait in a queue until it is released by A.

Locking at record level as discussed above is very effective for controlling concurrent updates. But owing to the large overheads involved in providing a locking mechanism for individual records, many DBMSs permit locking only for larger units of data such as a page or a file. In subsequent discussions the term data resource will generally be used to denote the unit of data where locking is allowed, although at times we may give the example of records for convenience. The term *granularity of locking* refers to the size of such data resources.

The lost update shown above occurs only because one update is dependent on the outcome of the other update, for if process A does not add but changes the total sales to 370, and likewise process B changes it to 500, independently of the previous sales value, then there will be no conflict, assuming that the latest update represents the latest value. Perhaps a clearer example would be the modification of the telephone number by process A and B, to 580 7730 and 678 1225 respectively. In step 3 above, tA updates the telephone number to 580 7730 and in step 4 tB updates the telephone number to 678 1225, without any conflict, since the new values do not depend on each other's update. We may conclude that an update loss occurs only when more than one process attempts to make a dependent alteration to the same data value at the same time. The standard solution, as pointed out earlier, is the forced serialisation of these concurrent processes, usually by means of locking. However, there is a fly in the ointment, as discussed below.

5.1.2 Deadlock and rollback

The basic system of locking and unlocking illustrated above can lead to what is known as *deadlock* or *deadly embrace*. Deadlock is a general logical problem which can arise whenever two or more contending processes wish to exercise exclusive controls over common resources. Consider two update transactions tA and tB from processes A and B respectively, each requiring data resource 1 and 2 for its update. The following sequence of events might take place:

   (i) Process A gets exclusive control of resource 1.
  (ii) Process B gets exclusive control of resource 2.
 (iii) Process A requests for resource 2, but A must wait in a queue until B releases resource 2.
 (iv) Process B requests for resource 1, but B must wait in a queue until A releases resource 1.

We have now reached a deadlock as neither transaction tA nor transaction tB can proceed, since process A will not succeed in getting resource 2 nor will B succeed in getting resource 1.

Deadlocks are not peculiar to databases alone; in fact deadlock in resource allocation is recognised in all multiprogramming operating systems although its occurrence there seems to be very rare. There are fundamental differences between the data and non-data resources: first a data resource or a record can change with time as a record is updated and secondly it does not have duplicates in the sense that, if a process needs a particular record, no other record in the database can fulfil this need. But a non-data resource such as a line printer does not change, and any one of several line printers may meet the need. These differences probably make databases with a large number of data resources more vulnerable to deadlock. We do not intend to discuss here the deadlocks involving non-data resources as they are specific to operating systems.

Returning to the above example of deadlock, if processes A and B are deadlocked then all the processes waiting in the queue for resource 1 and resource 2 will be caught up, and in turn other processes might also be affected if they are waiting for resources to be released by those in the queue for resource 1 and 2. This may eventually bring the whole database to a halt. Prevention is certainly better than cure, but if a fail-safe prevention proves impossible, the system should provide means of detecting and resolving deadlocks once they occur. This process of resolution is known as *rollback* as it involves rolling back to a previous state and allowing one of the contending processes, selected on the basis of some pre-defined priority scheme, to proceed after releasing the necessary resources. The priority scheme can, for instance, be built on the number of locked records in a transaction or on other desirable preferences. The major problem associated with the use of rollback mechanism lies in the efficient detection of a deadlock as we shall see below.

The general conditions for deadlock are laid down by Coffman *et al.* (1974). We present them here with some modifications:

(i) *Concurrency condition*
Processes claim exclusive control of more than one resource.
(ii) *Hold condition*
A process continues to hold exclusively controlled resources until its need is satisfied.
(iii) *Wait condition*
Processes wait in queues for additional resources while holding resources already allocated to them.
(iv) *Cycle condition*
A circular chain of processes exists such that each process holds one or more resources that are being requested by the next process in the chain.

The fourth condition *cycle* defines the state of a deadlock provided that the other three conditions are true. Consider figure 5.1(a), (b), to be referred to hereafter as *stategraphs*, where each process has an exclusive control of one or more resources and requests the control of an additional resource held by another process pointed by the arrow. In figure 5.1(a) there is no deadlock as the process A can wait for the resource to be released by B, but figure 5.1(b) displays a deadlock involving three processes.

In more formal terms the stategraph of figure 5.1(a) does not contain a cycle, but that of figure 5.1(b) does, indicating the existence of a deadlock. To detect a deadlock, the system must maintain some form of stategraphs to be updated each time that a resource is allocated, requested or released. After every unsuccessful request, the stategraph must be examined for cycles and, if found, the rollback mechanism must be invoked. In its simplest form, the system may maintain for

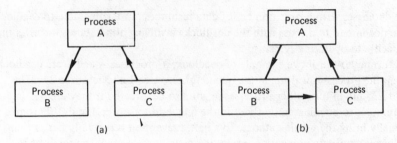

Figure 5.1 Stategraphs. The process at the head of an arrow is holding a resource
    wanted by the process at the tail of the arrow. (b) constitutes a dead-
    lock, but (a) does not

each process a list of exclusively allocated resources and one requested resource
for which the process concerned is waiting in a queue, assuming that a process may
not queue for more than one resource at a time. Starting from the last requested
resource, we can scan through the lists to determine the existence of a cycle. To
illustrate the technique, let us consider lists of resources for four processes A, B, C
and D, where the numerical entries in figure 5.2 represent the resources, the last
entry in each case being the requested resource, which if zero indicates the absence
of a request. Suppose that the processes A and B are waiting for resources 8 and 10
respectively, and process D has just made a request for resource 15 as shown in the
figure 5.2.

Scanning through the list, we find that B is holding resource 15; we now check
its requested resource which is 10. Again by scanning we find process A holding
resource 10. We scan again and find that its requested resource 8 is being held by
the original process D which needs 15. Thus a cycle is formed. If the requested
resource for A was 2 instead of 8, we would not have had any cycle. Since the
resource list will normally be kept in the memory, the CPU time for scanning and
updating the resource list can be considered to be negligible. This type of technique
is used in the IMS of IBM. The DMS1100 of Univac also employs a similar detec-

Processes	Resource list
A	1 10 ➞ 8
B	4 ➞ 15 ⤬ 3 ➞ 10
C	2 0
D	8 ➞ 6 ➞ 15

Figure 5.2 Resource list for processes A, B, C and D, showing the formation of a
cycle as process D requests for resource 15

tion and rollback strategy. Some other DBMSs base their strategy on prevention rather than resolution of deadlocks, with a variable degree of efficiency.

5.1.3 Prevention of deadlock

In order to avoid deadlocks, we shall examine below the concurrency conditions laid down earlier. If any of the conditions can be relaxed, then deadlock can be avoided (Everest, 1974).

Concurrency condition

If we limit the exclusive control of resources to one per process at any one time, deadlock can be eliminated. Every process must then release its locked data resource if it wishes to lock another data resource. But this will disallow an update transaction whose read or write-set contains several records. We therefore cannot relax the concurrency condition.

Hold condition

We may force a process to release all its locked resources and rollback to a previous state if it subsequently fails to gain exclusive control of a resource. This is known as the *pre-emption* strategy. But a return to a previous intermediate state in the update is unsafe for a data resource, since such a state cannot usually be well defined owing to the changes that can occur in the data. The best recourse is to fall back to the original state before the transaction started. This can be accomplished by delaying the writing of any part of the update in the database until after the successful completion of the whole update.

Wait condition

To offset this condition, we may insist that a process must declare and gain exclusive control of all the resources it needs exclusively for a particular transaction before it uses any of them. This technique is known as the *preclaim* strategy. If a process fails to acquire the exclusive control of any single resource of the declared list, it must release all its locked resources and try again later. While holding some resources exclusively, a process may not request for additional resources except those previously declared. This technique can be used satisfactorily for both data and non-data resources so long as the resources required are known at the beginning. But if the need for a resource is known only dynamically — say by checking on their values, as is done sometimes — then this technique would fail, and hence the preclaim technique is not very satisfactory. However, although a particular record occurrence required might not be known, the record type concerned is generally known at the beginning and, therefore, by enlarging the size of a data resource to accommodate all the occurrences of a record type, the problem can be overcome. But large units of data resources may lead to inefficiency in processing, as more processes are likely to wait in queues for records in those resources.

The situation could be improved if variable-size data resources are permitted so that the application programmer can lock individual records when the need is known, and record types otherwise.

Cycle

It can be shown that a cycle will not form in a stategraph if all the resources are requested in a specified linear order. Consider, for instance, the previous example where transaction tA and tB both need resource 1 and 2. Now if process A has locked resource 1 and requests for resource 2, it will get the resource, since process B cannot lock resource 2 and request for resource 1, as this is in the wrong order of resources. Thus a deadlock is avoided. However the implementation of this technique requires the ordering of all resources and the forcing of the application programs to request them in the correct order. Obviously, it cannot work if the requirement of a resource is known only dynamically. And also if the programmer makes an error in the order, then deadlock can occur. Nevertheless, the technique is used in ADABAS with a backup facility for rollback in the event of a deadlock.

5.1.4 Comparison of the techniques

It is clear from the above that three techniques, namely detection followed by rollback, preclaim and pre-emption, appear to be good candidates for adoption. We shall show their relative merits below by an example. Let us consider two processes A and B, each wishing to carry out a consistent series of updates, transaction tA requiring the data resources R1, R2 and R3, and transaction tB requiring data resources R1, R3 and R4 with the sequence of events as given below for each case:

Deadlock and rollback

  (i) A reads and locks R1 and R2, and modifies them into R1' and R2'.
 (ii) B reads and locks R3 and R4, and modifies them into R3" and R4".
(iii) A wishes to read and lock R3 which is held by B.
 (iv) The DBCS checks for a deadlock.
  (v) B wishes to read and lock R1 held by A.
 (vi) The DBCS recognises a deadlock.
(vii) The DBCS invokes the priority routines and decides to rollback A.
(viii) A undoes its update work done so far, returning R1' and R2' to their original states R1 and R2, and then releases R1.

(ix) B reads and locks R1 and completes its updates, producing R1″, R3″ and R4″ which are then released.

(x) A now reads and locks R1″ and R3″, and completes its update, subsequently releasing them.

Note that in step (viii), R1′ and R2′ are returned to R1 and R2 for preserving consistency, as B wants R1 and not R1′, and R2′ produced by A in step (i) is not necessarily consistent with R1″ and R3″ produced by B in step (ix); but R2 forms a consistent set with these R1″ and R3″ by definition.

Pre-emption

(i) A reads and locks R1 and R2, and modifies them into R1′ and R2′.

(ii) B reads and locks R3 and R4, and modifies them into R3″ and R4″.

(iii) A attempts, but fails to read and lock R3 held by B.

(iv) A undoes its update work done so far, returning R1′ and R2′ to their original states R1 and R2, and releases them both.

(v) B reads and locks R1 and completes its update producing R1″, R3″ and R4″ which are then released.

(vi) A now reads R1″, R2 and R3″, and completes its update, subsequently releasing them.

Preclaim

(i) A reads and locks R1, R2 and R3.

(ii) B requests for R4, R3 and R1, but it must wait.

(iii) A completes its update producing R1′, R2′ and R3′ which are then released.

(iv) B reads and locks R4, R3′ and R1′, and completes its update, the resources being then released.

This example shows clearly the simplicity of the preclaim strategy. The simplicity would be more striking if larger read/write sets were involved. But this advantage must be contrasted with the inefficiency of using large units of data resources (see also the next subsection). The main disadvantage of the pre-emption strategy compared to preclaim is that in the former all updates carried out up to the point of pre-emption are wasted. The deadlock and rollback technique appears far worse, involving four extra steps, (iv), (v), (vi) and (vii), compared to the pre-emption strategy. However, its performance can be improved by reducing the number of stategraphs to be maintained, which can be done by a *time out* mechanism, where the application programmer sets an upper limit on time for which his program may queue for a particular data resource. If the exclusive control of the resource is not gained within the time limit, a process may leave the queue and rollback to a suitable previous state.

From the discussions above, the pre-emption strategy and probably the preclaim strategy with variable-size data resources would be the better bet, although we might envisage a situation where other techniques could be more efficient. Ideally the DBMS would cater for a number of techniques from which the application programmer could select the one that suited him best, such as the preclaim strategy when the wanted records are known beforehand, and the pre-emption strategy otherwise, but the processing overhead would be very heavy.

5.1.5 Commit

As indicated earlier, an update transaction changes the database from one error-free or consistent state to the next. The relevant sequence of steps necessary to change the database from one consistent state to the next, corresponding to an update transaction, is called a *commit unit*. In fact an update transaction is a user view or an abstract form, whereas a commit unit is the system view, or a less abstract form, of the same process. In describing an update transaction, we concentrate only on its read-set, write-set and the computations necessary to derive the write-set from the read-set, without describing the *actions* required to preserve the consistency of the database; these *actions* are part of a commit unit.

The write-set of an update transaction may contain one or more records, depending on the requirements of consistency. If we change an employee name of EREC in figure 2.14, then the write-set has one record; on the other hand if we change an employee's salary it must contain two records, his record and his DEPT record which contains salary totals. A commit unit begins when the first action such as locking starts, and its ends when the update is successfully completed or failed with all locks released. The database may be momentarily inconsistent inside a commit unit (such as after the update of the employee salary but before adjusting the total salary in the Department record), but not outside it. Since no concurrent processes can enter the data in the read/write-set of a transaction within the commit unit, and since the commit unit leaves the database consistent after its completion, it provides a formal mechanism to prevent update loss by concurrent processes, and also to preserve database consistency. It can be implemented, as mentioned earlier, by exclusive update locks which prevents the read/write sets of a given update transaction being retrieved or modified by other concurrent transactions.

As stated before, sometimes it is necessary to read a consistent set of records even in a retrieval-only transaction (that is, multirecord read-set) such that no other concurrent processes can make them inconsistent during the execution of the retrieval transaction. This can be ensured by retrieval locks, permitting concurrent retrieval but not update (Hawley *et al.*, 1975). Thus we have two types of locks for a resource, a LOCKR for protected retrieval when no update can take place and LOCKU for exclusive updates. The disadvantage of this scheme is that long transactions will produce long queues for LOCKR, and long exclusive reading processes such as those required to produce a backup file will hold up updates. The efficiency can be improved if we delay the consolidation, that is, the writing of the write-set back into the database proper, until a transaction is wholly complete. This would imply the division of a commit unit into two phases, a long update phase under LOCKU where the records concerned will be modified, but not written into the database itself, and a short consolidation phase, say under a new lock LOCKC, when the updated version generated in the previous phase will be copied or committed into the database. The beginning and end of a transaction are usually indicated in an application program by statements such as BEGIN TRANSACTION ... END TRANSACTION or alternatively by BEGIN COMMIT ... END COMMIT. Therefore the DBCS can identify the beginning and end of a transaction. In this scheme, as the database remains unaltered in the update phase, a protected retrieval with LOCKR can be permitted simultaneously with a LOCKU, but not during the short consolidation phase under LOCKC. A locking system based on these concepts is described in the next subsection.

5.1.6 Synchronisation protocol

The process of ensuring that a transaction begins and ends in an error-free state of a database in a concurrent environment is called concurrency *synchronisation*. A *synchronisation protocol* is a set of agreed procedures to achieve such a synchronisation, a *protocol* being *a set of agreed procedures to do something*. It follows from above that a good synchronisation protocol based on locking needs three types of locks, which are listed more explicitly below.

(i) A LOCKR to allow reading of data resources so that they are protected against changes during the reading process. An unlimited number of transactions should be able to issue LOCKR for the same data resource. A LOCKU should not prevent the simultaneous applications of one or more LOCKRs, but if a LOCKC exists either on a data resource or is waiting in a queue for that resource, a LOCKR may not be applied.

(ii) A LOCKU to permit the update of a data resource but not its consolidation into the database. Only one process may issue a LOCKU for a data resource and the others wishing to update the same data resource must wait in a queue, although a LOCKU may co-exist with a number of LOCKRs.

(iii) A LOCKC to allow the copying of the updates into the database itself to the exclusion of any LOCKR or LOCKU. LOCKC should be transparent to the application programmer, being automatically invoked by the DBCS at the end of a transaction on behalf of the updating process. If a LOCKR exists on a data resource, the process with LOCKC should wait at the head of the queue for this data resource, disallowing any new LOCKR or LOCKU.

This suggested locking system will provide four modes of access.

(i) No-lock mode to read any number of records without any locks. A LOCKR or a LOCKU on a data resource may not inhibit it from being read in this mode. A process wishing to read unrelated single records should normally use this mode.

(ii) LOCKR mode to read a consistent set of records under LOCKR. A LOCKR will be held back only if there is a LOCKC on the data resource or if a LOCKC is waiting at the head of the queue for the data resource.

(iii) LOCKU mode to read a data resource for update. It must wait in a queue if a LOCKU or LOCKC is already there on the data resource.

(iv) LOCKC mode for altering the actual database when no other process can get access, LOCKC having priorities over other locks.

A list of the locked resources can be maintained in a database buffer for checking when needed. The solution of the concurrency problem and the locking system suggested here is mainly for the purpose of elucidating the issues involved; an actual implementation is more complex.

An alternative synchronisation protocol based on *timestamps* rather than locks, is possible. It requires all data resources to show the time of their last update (data timestamp) and each transaction to include its start time (transaction timestamp). The content of a timestamp need not be the actual time (from a physical clock), since an incremental count giving the time sequence (from a logical clock) should be adequate. Indeed the data timestamp need not be permanently stored but can be generated starting from zero each time that the database is loaded for running, as done in SDD-1 (Bernstein and Shipman, 1980). The data timestamp provides an integrity check for lost updates which would be apparent if the timestamp of an update transaction is lower than the data timestamps of the data item values in its write-set. The transaction timestamps can be used to serialise all interleaved update transactions in time sequence (that is, to execute all conflicting update transactions in transaction timestamp order) and thus avoid conflicts. Note that only the conflicting update transactions are serialised, but not the non-conflicting ones which should be executed concurrently. If *all* transactions are serialised, then there is no concurrency at all, since only one transaction will be executed at a time. But to serialise only the conflicting transactions we need to identify them before they begin. This can be achieved if all transactions are analysed (called *pre-analysis*) for conflicts beforehand, but it is complex — beyond the scope of this book. However this techniques has been used with some success in SDD-1 (see also chapter 15).

5.2 Data protection

The protection of data involves three types of security:

Physical
Operational
Authorisational

The physical security relates to the physical loss or damage of storage devices and communications equipment which must be protected against natural disaster, theft, fire, accident, dust and so on. The installation management is responsible for such protection of all the physical devices used in the installation, and therefore we shall not discuss it in this book. The operational security has two aspects, one known as *integrity protection* implies the protection of data against errors, and the other known as *reliability* concerns the maintenance of a correct and whole database, despite loss and damage of data. The authorisational security refers to the *confidentiality* or *privacy protection* of data against unauthorised use. These will be considered in this section.

5.2.1 Integrity protection

The integrity constraints can be viewed as a set of assertions to be obeyed during the update of a database for the preservation of an error-free state. A state is invalid or erroneous if it violates stipulated rules. As pointed out by Schmidt (1977), some of the constraints can be more conveniently incorporated as part of the data structure such as in component type, record type, and association type entries of the conceptual schema, while others — the more complex ones — require special constructs, which can be specified separately, say in a Constraint Section of the conceptual schema. In some cases, the specification might include a pre-written procedure.

Integrity requirements

We discuss below some of the important integrity checks on data items, record types, association types and placement keys.

(a) Data items
The integrity checks on data items can be divided into four groups:

  (i) Type check: The DBCS should be intelligent enough to carry out type check on data item values automatically, without requiring a special integrity specification.
 (ii) Redundancy check: This can be of two types — direct and indirect (section 4.4.4), both of which must be checked.

(iii) Range check: This ensures that a single data item value or a set of values in combination as target(s) belongs to specified range(s) of permissible values (sources). An example of targets in combination is a date such as February 29, 1981, which is invalid, although individually, day = 29, month = February and year = 1981 are valid.

(iv) Comparison check: In this check, a function of a set of data item values (target or source) is compared against a function of another set of data item values (source or target). The function can be multi-valued and a set can be single-valued. Examples of this kind of constraint could be the requirements that the average and standard deviation of some values must not exceed some pre-set limits, or that the average salary-rise of a group of workers must be equal to that of another group of workers. Both targets and source data item values may span over several records of one or more types, as in the case of total quantity withdrawn from stock (stock record) which is the sum of quantities sold to customers (customer records) and quantities sent out for rework (rework records).

(b) Records

A record type may have constraints on the total number of its occurrences, or on the insertions and deletions of records. Many of the constraints are on individual records, for example, the records of employees who have resigned cannot be deleted until the financial year has ended; but there are other constraints which apply to groups of records, for example, not more than three employees can be on leave at the same time (assuming that the employee records contain start leave and end leave dates).

(c) Associations

One of the interesting questions about associations is whether or not an owner record can be deleted in the presence of member records. It appears that there are at least three cases when an owner can be deleted:

 (i) When an owner of an association is replaced by another.

(ii) When the owner's entity identifier is changed (see below).

(iii) When an owner does not exist any longer — the affected members will not then belong to any association.

To safeguard against an inadvertent deletion, the DBCS should issue a warning message and ask for reconfirmation before deleting the owner. The following integrity requirements seem relevant for associations, particularly if we allow conditional ownerships and memberships.

 (i) Owner record — conditions for insertion, deletion, modification of owner record in an A-set type — criteria to be an owner of a given member (for example, matching key values or other conditions).

(ii) Member record — criteria to be member record of a given owner (again it could be matching key values or other conditions) — conditions for entry, exit and change of membership (for example, Codasyl Automatic, Manual, Fixed etc. classes) from an A-set type.

The conditions can be described by a predicate or other suitable means

(d) Placement keys
If the record placement technique is based on a key, then any subsequent change in the value of that key will make it impossible for the record by that key to be found. Many data models including the Codasyl suffer from this vanishing trick. However, placement keys are meant to be specified in the internal schema, and therefore the system should automatically re-insert records with new keys if old values are modified by the user. Alternatively the user should be warned about the undesirable consequences of alterations.

Classes of integrity controls

From the processing point of view, we may distinguish three classes of integrity controls (Deen, 1982):

Semantic integrity
Interprocess integrity
Internodal integrity

By *semantic integrity* we imply the preservation of a meaningful database as perceived by the DBA, against inadvertent, erroneous or malicious updates. To preserve this integrity the DBA may specify constraints such as that the date February 29, 1981 is invalid, or that an employee's salary must not exceed his manager's salary. All integrity issues discussed earlier fall under the semantic category, except the loss of placement key, which is really an inconvenience rather than an integrity problem.

Interprocess integrity relates to protection against lost update and momentary inconsistency caused by concurrent processes discussed in the previous section. The definition of semantic integrity can arguably be extended to include interprocess integrity as well, but we will make a distinction following current practice, which does not regard loss of an update transaction by a concurrent process or the momentary inconsistency viewed by another concurrent process as jeopardising the meaning of data. Also the solutions are different in the two cases.

The third class is *internodal integrity* which is similar to interprocess integrity, except that it applies to a distributed database where data are dispersed, sometimes with replication, over several nodes (each node can be an independent database). Errors similar to those in interprocess integrity are encountered, although their solutions are usually more complex owing to the presence of communications links. The subject will be touched upon in chapter 15, and hence will not be discussed here any further.

An aim of the research in data modelling is to stipulate all possible integrity constraints in the conceptual schema so that the DBCS can automatically ensure an integral database at all times. It would seem that at least in principle we can specify all semantic integrity constraints in the conceptual schema, but automatic enforcement of these constraints is prohibitively expensive since the DBCS will have to invoke generalised procedures. The alternative of programmers carrying out the necessary integrity checking is cheaper, but less reliable. Therefore a mixed approach, with some checks by the programmer and some by the DBCS is currently practised. The programmer can be aided by providing pre-written procedures which he can invoke as necessary for integrity checks. In time, as the computing cost comes down, we shall probably see a gradual shift of the task of integrity preservation from the programmer to the DBCS.

The interprocess integrity is preserved by declaring commit units for transactions in the application programs as discussed in the previous section. This, however, does not prevent a programmer from using an incomplete or inconsistent set of records in the transaction, for instance, updating only the employee salary but not the total department salary. Such a transaction will leave the database inconsistent. Is there any way of preventing such errors by letting the DBCS exercise more control? If we could pre-define all possible update transactions in the database, for every attribute value and every set of attribute values, then such definitions could be stored as part of the conceptual schema. In that case, whenever an attribute value is updated all its related attribute values everywhere in the database could also be automatically updated by the DBCS, thus making the task of programming easier. Such a general facility is possible in principle, but its implementation is not yet feasible, except in limited instances. Just the definition of all possible transactions will be a major problem, let alone the implementation overheads. There are also transactions that cannot be predicted at all. Consider for instance the following transaction

withdraw money from employer A
and distribute it to employee B
supplier C
and agent D
all records being in the same database.

The database will not be consistent until all the receiving records are updated, but there is no way of predicting this write-set, since the employer could have distributed the money on a different set of records belonging to different record types. The alternative is to view all the money records in the database as a *write-set*. This will make the locking granularity large, and thus reduce concurrency.

5.2.2 Reliability

A database can be lost or damaged owing to system malfunction, or through loss or physical damage of the storage devices. (It can also be damaged by erroneous concurrent updates as discussed in the last section — but this is not considered here.) The normal protection against such damage is the retention of the previous copies of the database, made periodically by dumping a copy on to magnetic tapes. In an *n tape* cycle, *n* number of copies are maintained at any given time, copy 1 being the current (period 1) database while others are the successive copies from the previous periods. In the event of a failure, the database is recreated from the most recent copy available. The protection system will fail only if all *n* copies are damaged or destroyed. However, dumps are time-consuming and cannot be attempted too frequently. Therefore, to cover the interval between successive dumpings, we need an *incremental dump*, to be referred to as a *log file*. Several types of log files are possible, but we shall describe only one form below. In addition to a log file we also need a so-called *checkpoint* to enable the DBCS to initiate automatic recovery after a processor failure. We therefore need the following backup files:

(i) *Dump*. Dumps are taken periodically, usually when the database is not active.
(ii) *Log file*. A log file consists of a set of log records, each log record containing the values of database items before and after a change, there being no before values for insertions, and no after values for deletions. These values could be the values of the data items of the affected database record(s) and the values of the affected index and directory entries, including the associated page numbers and page offset positions. Alternatively they could be the copies (images) of the affected database pages, a *before image* being the copy of a page before the change, and an *after image* being a copy of the same page after the change. In some systems, the term 'look' or 'journal' is preferred to 'image'.

   This file is usually used for recovery purposes (see section 5.7 for more detail).
(iii) *Checkpoint*. A checkpoint is the copying of the content of some database buffers and associated information, often at pre-determined intervals, say every five minutes, into the log file. It is needed in a recovery. However, the definition of checkpoint varies; a version is given in the section 5.7.

Restarting facilities

Restarting of a database may be required if an application program, the database or the processor fails. This must first be recovered into an error-free state before it can be restarted, and as far as possible recovery/restart should be automatic (see section 5.7).

(i) Program failure
   Since an updated transaction is not written into the database until after the successful completion of the commit unit, the new values are simply dropped from the log file in the event of a transaction failure. This is called *undoing* of a transaction. If a transaction failed during the consolidation phase then the system has to use checkpoints to find the state of its execution, and *redo* the transaction (section 5.7).

(ii) Database failure

If a part of the database fails, the programs not accessing that part should continue uninterrupted. The affected programs should be held at their last checkpoint and restart automatically as soon as the error is removed.

(iii) Processor failure

Processor failure can be avoided by using a multiprocessing configuration as in some real-time systems requiring high reliability. The load is distributed over all the processors in such a way that if one fails the others take over its function automatically by sharing, thus giving reduced but unimpaired performance. Such a system is said to possess a *failsoft* mechanism that provides a 'graceful degradation of services' and thus makes the system *failsafe*. Recovery from processor failure is described in section 5.7.

5.2.3 Privacy protection

The confidentiality of information in a database is of utmost importance. Information is power which can be used to harm others, and therefore rigorous control must be instituted to protect the interests of all concerned. There are also legal requirements as regards confidentiality of information, but the laws vary widely from one country to another, and also with time. These are beyond the scope of this book, but the interested reader should consult Lane (1985). We concentrate here on the computer techniques of privacy protection. Access to a database can be sought to extract data, to modify data or to alter the access control codes. No programs should be permitted to use the database for any of these functions without specific authorisation from the DBA, who should have the facility to exercise control at several levels by means of specific access codes or passwords as indicated below.

Access control

(i) Access to terminals

In addition to keeping the terminals locked to unauthorised users, special access cards or passwords could be instituted for the DBCS to examine before granting access to a terminal.

(ii) Access to storage device

Access to each physical device, such as a disc, could be controlled by special codes.

(iii) Access to conceptual-schema objects

Once a storage device is accessed, further codes could be provided to access the successive hierarchy of data such as record types, associations and so on. Whether access control should be extended to the data item level appears debatable, owing to heavy overheads.

(iv) Access to external-schema objects

There is a good case for extending access codes to external schema as well. In a database installation the DBA would normally be responsible for the generation of external schemas; controls in their usage can be exercised by privacy locks.

(v) Access to special programs

Confidential data should be accessible by special programs only. Codes should be instituted not only to access these confidential data, but also to access the relevant application programs.

All access control assertions could be described in the conceptual/external schema as necessary. It is also possible to make additional assertions giving or denying selective rights to specified users for insertion/deletion/amendment of stipulated data items, records, record types, associations and so on. Sensitive data may be divided into several datasets in the conceptual schema in such a way that individually they do not mean much, but jointly they may reveal explosive information. Consider, for instance, a medical database where patient records containing name, address, age etc. are in one record type, and the medical history but not the patient's name is in another. Unless the patients' names are related to the medical histories, the confidentiality will not be breached. The DBA may, therefore, like to permit a user to access either record types singly, but not both jointly. Unfortunately there is no effective protection purely against joint extraction of information; we can at best just make it more difficult, for instance, by devising a multilevel access system for such a group of record types, the first level codes permitting access to the record types singly, and the second level codes for accessing a second record type of the group by the same application program. But if an application programmer has authorisation to access the record types singly, he can use two programs to extract the information needed and a third program, or himself manually, to relate them. Therefore there is no special solution to this problem, except to impose rigorous control on each record type individually. For highly sensitive data, sometimes data encryption techniques are used.

Access code

The codes to be employed for controlling access require careful consideration. An access code has two parts. The first part can be described as a lock residing on a special area of the database and the second part as the key (or the password) needed, as it were, to open the lock to access the relevant data unit. The DBCS compares the key with the lock and if a match is obtained access is granted.

At an elementary level the value of the key could be the same as that of the lock, in which case the DBCS would simply match the two before allowing an access. The success of this scheme will rather depend on keeping the locks secret from a potential intruder. The DBA is bound to have the list of all the locks and hence the keys which, for highly sensitive information, may not be desirable for him to know. However, the protection against such disclosure of keys from locks can be guaranteed if the lock L is made a complex function of the key K such that L = f(K). The DBCS will evaluate the function f(K), granting access if L = f(K). It is possible to design the function f(K) in such a way that it is practically impossible to invert it, even if the intruder knows all the mathematical expressions involved. Therefore if such a scheme is adopted, the locks and the mathematical expressions involved need not be kept secret (Evans and Weiss, 1974).

Access-control schema

One argument for the creation of a separate storage schema has been the need to isolate the more frequently varying objects from the conceptual schema so that they can be changed as necessary without affecting the stabler parts. If this argument for stability is applied to the present conceptual schema, then we can identify four sublevels, as shown in figure 5.3, each sublevel being a candidate for a separate schema. At the moment there appears to be a strong case for isolating privacy assertions into a separate access-control schema, as explained below.

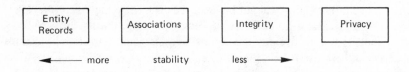

Figure 5.3 Conceptual schema stability

The facilities required for privacy protection vary widely, and sometimes can be very complex. For instance, a doctor could permit a consultant to read, but not to update, some data on a patient over a stipulated period. Sometimes he might also grant the consultant permission to authorise a second consultant to view the same or parts of the same data, all the while he, the original doctor, retaining the right to revoke all such permissions. The doctor cannot give his own password to the consultant, as this will be equivalent to permitting the consultant access to all his data. He must therefore creat a special password for that purpose alone. It is difficult to foresee all such access-control requirements at the time of creating the conceptual schema; on the other hand we do not wish to change the conceptual schema every time such a need arises. The solution therefore lies in the creation of a separate, more modifiable, access-control schema.

5.3 Modification and optimisation

Once a database is constructed, it is very difficult to modify it, short of generating a new database; yet such modifications are needed on a periodic basis in order to

(i) tune it for improved performance as data usage changes

(ii) add new systems as requirements grow

(iii) alter the conceptual schema as the enterprisal perception of data changes.

We therefore need facilities to modify a database with minimum inconvenience. The issues involved can be viewed from the following angles:

> Performance monitoring
> Database reorganisation
> Database restructuring

By performance monitoring we mean collection of usage statistics on the database performance and their analysis. Reorganisation implies changes at the physical storage level whereas restructuring refers to the changes at the logical level. In this book, we shall use the term reorganisation to include changes in the storage schema (or its equivalent) as well as the subsequent physical reorganisation of data. The storage structure is related to data usage and concerns the run-time efficiency, whereas a conceptual schema is supposed to mirror the enterprisal perception of data, ideally unrelated to the run-time efficiency. In the current implementations we have database schemas rather than conceptual schemas and hence efficiency requirements often dictate changes at that schema, although less frequently. The external schemas need to be restructured as well, but we have not considered them here as they do not normally affect the physical database, binding being usually achieved through recompilations. We shall address these issues in greater detail below, and conclude this section with comments on run-time optimisation.

5.3.1 Performance monitoring

Statistics necessary for performance optimisation generally fall into two categories: static and dynamic statistics (BCS/DBAWG, 1980). The static statistics refer to the general state of the database and can be collected by a monitoring program when the database is inactive. They might include:

> number of records per record type
> population of data items
> distribution of records over storage space
> overflow utilisation for data and indexes
> distribution of association members over storage space

The dynamic statistics relate to the run-time characteristics and can be collected only when the database is running in a normal or in another desired mode. The statistics collected could be:

(i) Data usage: frequency of access to and update of each data item value,

> record and A-set

(ii) Use of each type of DM command and response time.
(iii) Use of keys and type of access (sequential/random).
(iv) Frequency of disc accesses for type of use.
(v) Access to indexes and overflows.
(vi) Use of buffer space.

Since the presence of a monitor program slows down the database processing, dynamic monitoring is not popular. Sometimes it is possible to study specific characteristics by using a good simulation model instead.

Database reorganisation

Reorganisation of the database will in theory be attempted after the usage statistics are collected and analysed, although in practice it could be based on an intuitive evaluation. The task involved can be simple or complex, depending on the alterations contemplated. If the intention is only to add or delete a key or to change an index, then this could be done relatively easily through a storage schema. On the other hand, if all the original record types are changed into new types on a many to many basis, the resultant modifications will be drastic — and consequently time-consuming and expensive. In this case a new storage schema must be designed and old data converted into a new form.

Ideally, of course, a database should be self-reorganising, the storage schema and stored data changing dynamically as usage changes — always giving the optimal performance (Hammer and Chan, 1976; Stocker, 1977). In general, this will involve an automatic redesign of a storage schema followed by an automatic conversion of the old database into a new one. It is difficult to see how these tasks can be completely automated, since human decisions are required in the design of storage schema and often in the conversion of the database from one form to another. It is not therefore surprising that the research prototypes on self-reorganising databases are based on very simple data structures with limited objectives.

Assuming that the redesign of a storage schema is a human function, we can think of at least three different approaches in the reorganisation of one database into another (Sockut and Goldberg, 1979).

1. Direct reorganisation: In this case the new database is recreated from the old one by a single, if long, step. However, the normal update processing of the old database cannot be continued once the conversion begins. Many large users find this hibernation period too long.
2. Selective reorganisation: A selective reorganisation, such as on a single record type, is possible so long as changes are straightforward and can be localised. Such reorganisation could be carried out in quick bursts, without halting the normal processing for too long.

3. Phased reorganisation: This refers to complex reorganisations being carried out in phases. A first phase could be the creation and storage of new record types from the old ones, followed by subsequent steps where keys and indexes are generated. Normal processing should be possible after each stage, although it will be non-optimal until all the phases are complete.

The success of these approaches will depend on the architecture and the associated facilities of a DBMS.

The principal obstacle of a gradual reorganisation is paradoxically also a main virtue of a database, namely data integration. A database is usually so well integrated that if anything is altered many other things are affected. If we split a storage schema record type, then not only the occurrences of this record type, but also those of other record types sharing the same data pages are affected, as they would probably require re-allocation which might affect their internal identifiers and hence all their indexes. Therefore the alterations involved are much more extensive than might seem at first sight.

Theoretical aspirations on reorganisation facilities are very high. A few years ago a Codasyl Group (SDDTTG, 1977) produced a report outlining the problems of reorganisation and database portability. It has proposed a model with three modules: a *reader*, a *restructurer* and a *writer*. The reader converts the source database into a canonical form, the restructurer changes the data definition in accordance with a specification, whereupon the writer produces the target database. The model recognises many to many relationships between sources and target databases, and allows reorganisation into a different type of database — for example, from a Codasyl to an IMS database. The model is too ambitious even as a research vehicle and has not been implemented anywhere as far as this author knows. However, there are a number of less ambitious research models (Sockut and Goldberg, 1979).

The current commercial products do not provide an adequate reorganisation facility. Part of the blame lies with the current designs which virtually ignore the reorganisation requirement. Improved products based on the ANSI/SPARC architecture should provide better facilities in the future.

5.3.2 Database restructuring

The restructuring of a conceptual schema implies changes in its contents, such as

    Insertion/deletion of data items
    Insertion/deletion of record types
    Splitting and recombination of record types
    Insertion/deletion/modification of associations
    Insertion/deletion/modification of usage constraints

A restructured conceptual schema will normally be followed by the reorganisation of the database involving a new storage schema.

In a good data model, the restructuring should not necessarily require changes or recompilation in the existing external schemas.

5.3.3 Run-time performance

The performance of a database depends not only on an optimised storage schema but also on the ability of a database control system to select an optimal run-time strategy, using techniques such as query optimisation, access path selection and buffer management.

The concept of query optimisation owes its origin to the relational queries. A given query can be formulated in many different ways, some being more efficient than others. Therefore the first step is the generation of an optimal code, largely with the help of a pre-processor, to be followed by the second step of selecting an optimal execution strategy (see also section 8.4). The access path selection concerns the selection of the best access paths for the execution of a query optimisation, as used in SYSTEM R (section 13.1).

An optimal strategy in buffer management (Sherman and Brice, 1976; Smith, 1978) seeks to minimise disc accesses by the best use of buffer space which has to hold control tables, indexes and data during the run-time. A page-swapping strategy based on anticipated usage should allow the more frequently accessed pages to stay in the buffer longer, thus reducing the need for disc accesses. The success depends on correct anticipation. However, progress in this area has been slow, lacking in both theoretical work and practical implementation. The operating system also acts as a handicap as it may swap the pages out, being totally oblivious of the best strategy so laboriously worked out by the DBCS! Therefore, there is a need to improve the functions of the operating systems for databases.

5.4 Data dictionary

The key to effective use of the data in a database is its proper documentation, without which a user is bound to get lost. The concept of a data dictionary was originally introduced as a means of providing this documentation, but it has now been extended to imply a holder of all the necessary information for the users and the DBCS. In this 'holder' we might store the definitions of data, their meanings, usage constraints and authorisation status, source and object codes of schemas and programs, utilities, design tools, database procedures, administrative and run-time control information, usage statistics, backup facilities and so on. As a 'holder' the title data dictionary appears to have been misnamed, but the more appropriate term *meta* (data about data) database somehow failed to capture the popular imagination.

Apart from the ANSI/SPARC study group which recognised the data dictionary as an integral part of a database architecture, the BCS/DDSWP and DBAWG also helped to define its scope and functions. However, this unanimity on its need has not yet crystallised into any generalised model for implementation. Most major implementors support some data dictionary facility, but the services they provide vary. Some possible contents of a data dictionary are listed below.

(1) *Users:* Permitted user numbers and authorisation status.

(2) *Data description:* Description of data and the explanation of their meanings and usage, including integrity requirements. Typical information on data items and record types could be

Data items	*Record types*
Property name	Name
Format (both logical and physical)	A-set types that it owns
Validation requirements	A-set type that it belongs to
Its meaning and usage	Its properties
Record types where it appears	Its entity type
Its attribute name in different record types	Its meaning and usage
Access control requirements	Validation requirements
Its cardinality	Access control requirements
Its duplicates	Its cardinality
	Its size
	Its storage characteristics

The list could easily be made longer. Some of the information can be held in textual form, but the rest would need special meta record type and meta association, such that all kinds of user questions about data, their meaning and their usage constraints can be answered.

(3) *Programs and schemas:* The source and object codes of programs and schemas, with various version numbers and registration status — for example, each user program can be registered for retrieval, update or test, with a list of its users. Similarly, there can be several versions of conceptual, storage and external schemas, some being developed, others being in use. This registration could also facilitate automatic recompilation (for rebinding when necessary) in the event of a change in one schema which affects other schemas and application programs.

(4) *System support facilities:* Database procedures, utilities (see later) and design tools. The database procedures are invoked during the run-time as necessary.

(5) *Performance data:* All usage statistics, their analysis and evaluation reports.

(6) *Backup information:* Backup files, systems logs and recovery information.

(7) *JCL and run-time parameters:* Job Control Language for running the database and the relevant run-time parameters in each case — for example, buffer size, recovery strategy, operation mode (production or development), page-swapping strategy and so on.

The data description facility, usually supported in all implemented data dictionaries, helps in data analysis and also as a documentation aid. Newer data models recognise the importance of meaningful data descriptions, by attempting to include them in the conceptual schema, rather than in a data dictionary (see also section 5.5.2).

5.5 Languages and utilities

A database management system requires data manipulation facilities for users, system languages for data descriptions, and controls and utilities for database maintenance. We shall describe these below:

5.5.1 Data manipulation facility

We have discussed the basic functions of a data manipulation language in section 4.5.5, where the concepts of procedural and non-procedural languages have also been introduced; but here we wish to examine them a little further.

A procedural language is one in which the user has full control over the logical flow of his programs. Procedural DMLs are normally used within a host language. The advantage of such a DML lies in its flexibility and processing efficiency, since an expert programmer can normally use it very effectively for optimal performance; but the disadvantage is the time and effort needed to write such an application program.

In a non-procedural language, the user does not spell out the detailed logical procedures, instead he employs high level commands, as is done when using a report generator or a sort program. The term query language is often used as a synonym for a non-procedural DML, although like a procedural DML it can also provide both retrieval and update facilities. The origin of this synonym goes back to the days when non-procedural DMLs were predominantly retrieval (query) oriented; the situation has now changed but the old term has remained. Thus we see SQL (Structured Query Language), providing both retrieval and update commands (see section 8.1). Non-procedural DMLs are particularly suitable for inexperienced users, sometimes referred to as non-expert or non-programmer users. Non-procedural languages are often used in an interactive mode.

One of the serious drawbacks of a non-procedural DML is its inflexibility; it would be impossible to carry out a complex calculation in such a language. However, this limitation can be overcome by allowing a non-procedural DML to be used both in a stand alone and host language mode; in the latter mode the non-procedural DM commands are embedded in the host language program, as can be done with SQL. The second limitation of a non-procedural DML is supposed to be its relative processing inefficiency, but this is probably not true any longer for a large number of queries, owing to the use of sophisticated query optimisation techniques. Thus the non-procedural DMLs have come a long way from being a simple facility for inexperienced users and are now a very sophisticated tool for experts and non-experts alike.

Some languages are more procedural than others. A highly non-procedural language is usually highly problem oriented, the level of procedurality being dependent on the generalisation that can be achieved in defining the problems. Since constructs supported in an external schema are language dependent, a highly procedural DML requires problem oriented data structures to be declared in the external schema. Such data structures along with their complex mappings to the conceptual schema can be supported by so-called *abstract data types*, which can be viewed as a mixture of data structures and the necessary DM commands for their derivation from lower level structures. We are likely to see an increasing use of this concept in the future (see also section 14.2.3).

5.5.2 Systems languages

Languages used in databases are sometimes called sublanguages as they serve only specific functions. DML of the sort described earlier is also a sublanguage unless it provides the full range of other functions such as those provided by a host language. We shall identify below sublanguages needed for the creation and maintenance of the database; their compilation with a data dictionary is shown in figure 5.4.

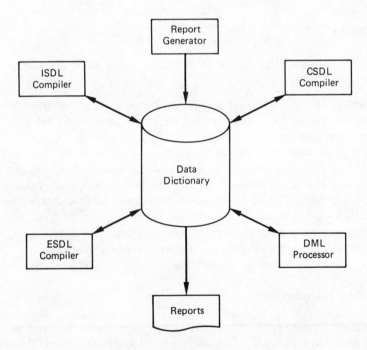

Figure 5.4 Data dictionary

(1) *Conceptual Schema Description Language (CSDL)*

This is the language in which the conceptual schema is written. Its compilation produces a number of tables and possibly procedures of various kinds, including a symbol table which maintains a list of conceptual objects and their internal codes.

(2) *External Schema Description Language (ESDL)*

There could be a separate ESDL for each type of DML. Since an ESDL and its DML are interdependent, some experts are against their division into two separate sublanguages. An ESDL is compiled against the compiled version of CSDL.

(3) *Internal Schema Description Language (ISDL)*

This language describes the internal schema or storage schema, and is compiled against the compiled version of a CSDL. Its compiled version might include a list of conceptual-schema objects in internal codes, their storage characteristics, key specifications, indexing techniques and so on.

(4) *Modification Languages*

Two modification languages, one for CSDL and the other for ISDL, are necessary for changing the conceptual and the internal schema respectively. Instead of separate languages, modification functions can be provided as part of CSDL and ISDL.

(5) *Database Control Language (DBCL)*

This is equivalent to a job control language for a database, to be used by the DBA to initiate compilations, modifications of schemas, and to specify run-time parameters such as internal buffers, priority scheme for concurrent usage and so on.

5.5.3 Utilities

To operate a database a large number of utilities are required. We have listed below some of them.

(1) *Dump, print and edit entries:* to dump selected parts or the whole database, to print selected parts in a prescribed format, and to edit errors in the tables/ directories/page headers and so on, of the database.

(2) *Garbage collection and re-allocation routine:* to remove deleted records physically from the storage devices, to consolidate the space released and to re-allocate it to where it is needed. Some DBCS may do such a task automatically.

(3) *Index reorganisation routine:* to reorganise indexes and their overflows – this is difficult and is part of database reorganisation.

(5) *Monitoring and analysis routines:* to collect statistics on the database operations and to analyse them for the reorganisation of the database.

5.6 Database control system

In this section we shall briefly discuss the design philosophy of the Database Control System, its operational functions, its operational concepts and the role of the DBCS in the basic operation of a database.

5.6.1 Design strategy

The design of a database control system could in theory be based on any one of the following three strategies:

  (i) As an integrated part of the application.
 (ii) As an integrated part of the operating system.
(iii) As an independent system acting as interface to the operating system.

As an integrated part of an application, the DBCS would be more or less a tailor-made system generated by an extended host language providing faster data transfer than would otherwise be available. However, a major disadvantage is the cost of developing so many tailor-made systems, each application having its own exclusive DBCS. Secondly, data protection would be problematic as it would be difficult to ensure the absence of incompatibility among these systems. Finally concurrent usage would also be difficult to achieve as one system would not know what the other is doing and, if concurrent usage is allowed, memory required to accommodate so many exclusive Database Control Systems will be very large. The first strategy therefore cannot be used.

The second approach could represent an ideal solution from the user's point of view if it retains a centralised control and yet provides efficient access to the database. However, the problem is the design of an operating system which, in addition to its normal function, can manipulate structured information involving hierarchies, cross links, access codes etc. as required for a database. The feasibility of this approach has yet to be ascertained.

The third possibility is a compromise between the first two approaches where the DBCS acts as an interface between the application program and the operating system. But this is rather inefficient as the application program cannot directly communicate with the operating system. For the present, however, only this approach offers a viable solution. Research is currently being conducted to improve operating systems to provide, among other things, a better environment for database control systems (Traiger, 1983).

5.6.2 Operational functions

A large number of routines are required for the creation and execution of a database. The details of these routines depend on implementations, and are hence beyond the scope of this book. However, for an appreciation of the complexities of database operations, we shall present below a typical top-level view of these routines (Deen *et al.*, 1982), highlighting the principal operational functions (figure 5.5).

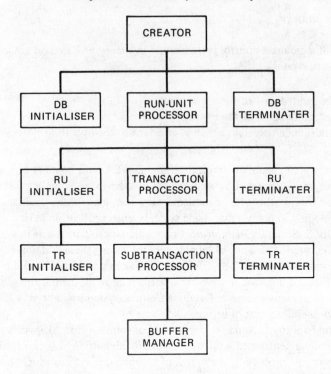

Figure 5.5 Some database operational functions

(1) *Creation*
Its function is to create a database in accordance with a storage schema, and to populate it with data. The process includes creations, initialisations and population of a large number of data files, index files and database directories.

(2) *Database (DB) initialiser/terminater*
A database has to be initialised at the beginning of each session, and terminated at the end of each session. A session is the period when transactions are processed against the database. Initialisation involves setting up system buffers, system parameters, backup files, run-time tables and so on. At the termination of each session the relevant files and tables have to be updated from current buffers, all locks released and all files closed, making sure that the database is in an integral and self-consistent state, with nothing left loose.

(3) *Run-unit (RU) initialiser/terminater*
Before a run-unit can be executed, it has to be logged with the database, and the necessary external schema tables loaded and initialised. At the termination of each process, these tables have to be updated and closed.

(4) *Transaction (TR) processor*

For each transaction the necessary data files (for record types) and index files have to be opened, read, interpreted and updated, concurrency control procedures invoked and backup data generated. Execution-time query optimisation and access path selection, if any, will also take place here. Privacy checks are normally carried out during the compilation, but further checks can be made at the beginning or during the execution of the transaction. Some integrity checks on data validation will be made on the read-set at the beginning of the transaction, and further integrity checks on the write-set during or towards the end of the transaction. At the beginning of each transaction, a commit unit is invoked where specified, and the necessary retrieval and update locks applied. At the end of the transaction all locks must be released. The transaction must either succeed, or fail in which case the database must be returned to the previous state, with the help of a recovery manager (section 5.7).

(5) *Subtransaction processor*

A transaction could be made up of one or more subtransactions and each subtransaction made up of one or more database input/output and computation operations. A relational query (a transaction) for instance can be made up of several other relational operations such as join, union and so on. Each of these operations would be a subtransaction requiring a number of database input/output and computation operations (see also the next section).

(6) *Buffer manager*

Ideally all buffers should be managed optimally to reduce disc accesses.

(7) *Miscellaneous*

An error handling and analysis routine is needed to report errors at any stage. Many of the routines need to be written in *re-entrant code* such that the same piece of code can be used by several processes simultaneously. This is also called *multithreading*. In the absence of this facility, the routines for a given command such as 'to store record' can be entered by only one subtransaction at a time, the other subtransactions must wait in a queue even if they wish to store different records. Therefore a multithreading facility is essential for an efficient concurrent processing.

5.6.3 Operational concepts

The operations involved during the running of a database are shown in figure 5.7. Although the diagram is partly based on the Codasyl approach, it illustrates the general problem well. We have assumed that there is a three-level schema architecture with execution time binding for the application and internal schema, the ES/CS and CS/IS binding being done during the compilations of the external and internal schemas. Therefore the presence of the compiled version of the conceptual schema (that is, object conceptual schema) is not needed during the run-time. The database is held on secondary memory which we assume to be discs. The primary memory is the computer memory, containing

(i) The operating system of the computer.

(ii) DBCS.

(iii) Object internal schema (including CS/IS Directory).

(iv) Object external schema (including ES/CS Directory).

(v) Object application program (including AP/ES Directory).

(vi) User Working Area (UWA). As introduced in section 4.6.2, this acts as a loading and unloading zone between the DBCS and the application program.

(vii) Error status indicator. This indicates the outcome of a DM command, and should hold an error code, with different codes for different errors. If it is zero, we assume the command to have been successful.

(viii) System buffer. System buffers are designated areas in the computer memory for holding specific information. For a database, at least two types of system buffers can be used, an input/output (I/O) buffer to serve as the loading and unloading area for the operating system and the DBCS, and a reserved area to hold the most frequently used parts of the database so that the number of physical input/output operations is minimised (figure 5.6). The data transfer between the database and the I/O buffer is carried out by the operating system and that between the I/O buffer and the various UWAs by the DBCS.

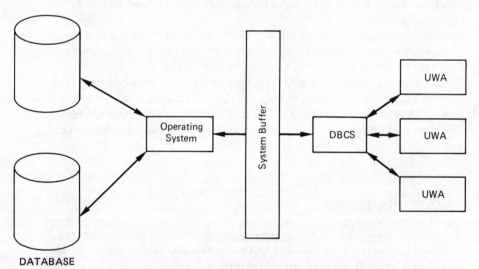

Figure 5.6 Interface of the UWA with the database

When a process requests a record from the database, the following operations take place (the numbers in the brackets indicate the links on figure 5.7).

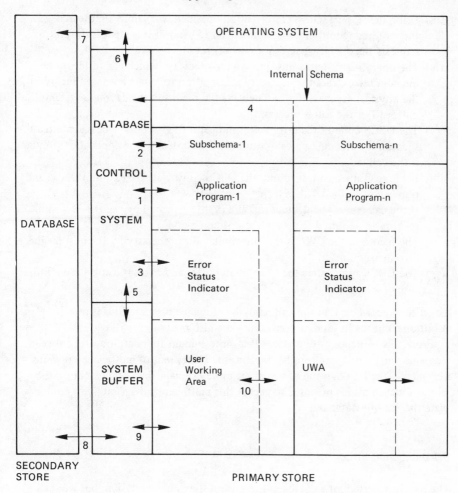

Figure 5.7 A conceptual diagram of database operations

(i) The application program using the DM command makes a call for one or more external schema (ES) records to the DBCS specifying the required arguments for selection (1).

(ii) The DBCS analyses the calls against the information present in the object ES (unless this has been done earlier during the compilation of the program) (2), returning the control to the program for invalid calls, after setting the error status indicator. Once the validity is ensured, the DBCS searches through the AP/ES, ES/CS, CS/ES directories to find the storage schema information and to select an access path.

(iii) Using the storage schema information obtained, the DBCS first searches for the required record in the system buffer (5) and, if it is absent, the DBCS requests the operating system to deliver it (6).

(iv) The operating system scans through its directory (which can reside in the memory) to extract the necessary information to locate a wanted record in the physical database (7), and delivers the record in the database system buffer (8) if the call is successful.

(v) The DBCS updates the error status indicator (3) for both successful and unsuccessful outcome of a call, returning the control to the application program if the call fails.

(vi) If the relevant record is found, the DBCS constructs the external record and transfers it to the UWA (9).

(vii) If the call is successful, steps (iv) and (v) are repeated by the DBCS if more records are required to satisfy the DM command.

(viii) The record in the UWA is then manipulated as necessary by the host language (10) instructions in the program.

(ix) The DBCS administers the I/O system buffer and takes specific action in the case of buffer overflows.

To write a record back to the database, the sequence of operations is reversed. Additional checks for update consistency are also made.

From this sequence of operations it is quite evident that data transfer between a database and a program is rather inefficient. The extent of inefficiency obviously depends on the DBCS, some of which are more efficient than others, but on the whole, unless a user is prepared to accept this inefficiency, he should not contemplate the use of a database.

5.7 Database recovery

The recovery system of a database depends on the implementation, but we shall present below a simplified technique, based on more recent concepts, mainly for an understanding of the principal issues. We shall assume recovery is carried out by a Recovery Manager, from a log file on disc in the event of a processor failure which destroyed the database buffers, but not the database itself. The Recovery Manager (RM) is a component of the DBCS responsible for database recovery.

In the above context, we can consider three categories of update transactions at the time of the processor failure.

(i) *Completed transactions: these transactions are completed and also consolidated* (that is, completely written) into the database, with all the relevant locks released. They do not need any recovery.

(ii) *Committed transaction: these transactions are completed, but not yet consolidated into the database itself — they were being consolidated or about to be consolidated into the database under LOCKC (section 5.1.6) at the time of the failure. The RM must *redo* these transactions, implying that it must write/ rewrite them from the log file into the database, under LOCKC correctly. A primitive RM will probably consolidate them from scratch, rewriting every-thing even if some parts were correctly consolidated before, whereas a good RM will rewrite only selectively.

(iii) *Incomplete transactions: these transactions have failed or only partly com-pleted* during the processor failure, and they must be *undone*, returning the database to a previous state as if nothing has happened. Again a primitive RM might correct each affected database page by replacing the new values by the old ones from the log file, whereas a clever RM may arrange things in such a way that database pages are not involved.

5.7.1 Log file

What an RM can or cannot do also depends, among other things, on the content of the log file and checkpoint record. In our case, we shall assume a log file to contain the following log records for each transaction

> one BEGIN COMMIT record
> one or more detail records
> one END COMMIT record
> one COMPLETE record

each log record being qualified by its transaction number. If a transaction involves only one database record, even then there could be several detailed records contain-ing old values, new values, index/directory data, and so on, irrespective of whether data item values or whole pages (images) are held in those log records. Since a transaction could involve several database records in its write-set, we shall in general expect a fair number of detailed records in the log file for each transaction. The END COMMIT record is written on the log file *after* a transaction is success-fully completed, *but before* it is consolidated into the database. The COMPLETE record is written *after* a transaction is successfully consolidated into the database with all locks released. Clearly a COMPLETE record cannot be written in the log file unless there is already an END COMMIT record in it for that transaction. Therefore a committed transaction will end on an END COMMIT, and a completed transaction on a COMPLETE record in the log file.

Each log record is given a log record number (LRN) in the time sequence of writing the log record in the log file. In a concurrent environment the log records of different transactions get interleaved in time sequence, and therefore the log records of a given transaction may not get a contiguous sequence of LRNs as shown in figure 5.8 for transaction T1 to T5. The Prior pointers contain the LRN values of the prior log record of the same transaction, which is useful in a backward search of log records.

LRN	Data	Prior (LRN)
1	BEGIN COMMIT (T1)	0
2	BEGIN COMMIT (T2)	0
3	BEGIN COMMIT (T3)	0
4	Old values (T1)	1
5	Old values (T2)	2
6	New values (T1)	4
7	BEGIN COMMIT (T4)	0
8	END COMMIT (T1)	6
9	Old values (T3)	3
10	New values (T2)	5
11	BEGIN COMMIT (T5)	0
12	COMPLETE (T1)	8
13	. . .	. . .

Figure 5.8

We now make three important assumptions:

(1) *Write-ahead log:* For each database update, we have two write operations, writing on the log file and consolidation into the database. The question is which one should be done first? If the database is first updated and if the system crashes before the corresponding log records are written out, then the RM will not know about this consolidation, which will cause recovery problems. Therefore the log file must be written first. This is called write-ahead log.

(2) *Consolidation:* As stated above, we assume that an updated transaction will not be consolidated in the database until it is successfully completed. Then an END COMMIT record will be written on the log file, and only after this action will the transaction be consolidated into the database, under LOCKC. Therefore if a transaction fails before the END COMMIT record is written out on the log file, it cannot have any effect on the database itself, and hence the *undoing* operation will involve only the discarding of the relevant log records from the log file, without requiring any *undoing* on the database itself. The *redoing* will be required if the processor fails in the consolidation phase under LOCKC after the END COMMIT but before the COMPLETE record is written in the log file.

(3) *Database pages:* we assume that each database page header maintains one entry for each committed transaction which is active on that page, each entry containing transaction number (T#) and the LRN of the previous log record of this transaction (LL) that has been consolidated on to this page. Assuming that log records of the same transaction are consolidated in ascending order of their LRNs, the LL will also be the highest log record of this committed transaction so far consolidated on

this database page. The pair (T#, LL) of a transaction can be inserted on a page when LOCKC is established on this page for this transaction, and can be deleted from the page when the LOCKC concerned is released. Depending on locking granularity, there could be more than one LOCKC and hence more than one committed transaction on the same page at the same time. For instance, if a page is the unit of locking then there will be only one transaction at a time, whereas if a record is the unit, then there could be many. In either case, a given committed transaction could appear on several pages at the same time, since an update involving even one record will have a data page and possibly several indexes and directories to update. However, these details do not concern us here; all we need is one (T#, LL) pair on the page (data, index or directory page) for each committed transaction of the page. LL helps to reduce the *redo* work.

5.7.2 Checkpoint

If the processor fails, it is possible to find the offending record by searching the log file, but a log file is usually very large, and hence a checkpoint is used to reduce the search area. A checkpoint, we shall assume, does the following:

(i) First it writes the content of the log buffers out to the log file. Normally the log buffers will be written out only when they are full, but a checkpoint will *force* them out at the time of the checkpoint, even if the buffers are not full.

(ii) Then it creates a special *checkpoint record* (including an LRN for it) on the log file, the record containing a triplet (T#, HL, HD) for each transaction active at the time of the checkpoint. T# is the transaction number, HL is the highest LRN of its log records (that is, the LRN of the most recent log record of this transaction in the log file), and HD is the LRN of the highest log record of this transaction so far consolidated in the database. Note that log buffer will hold this triplet for each active transaction. Obviously HD ≤ HL; HD is initially set to null and remains so until after the END COMMIT record of this transaction is written out to the log file, since the consolidation phase cannot begin before this is done. For a committed transaction at checkpoint time, HD on the checkpoint record is equal to LL on the database page header, since both HD and LL yield the highest log record of this transaction so far consolidated in the database; but after the checkpoint the LL would be greater than HD if more log records are consolidated in the database.

5.7.3 Recovery process

To understand how the recovery mechanism works, let us consider the eight transactions numbered T1 to T8 of figure 5.9 where a checkpoint is taken at time tc.

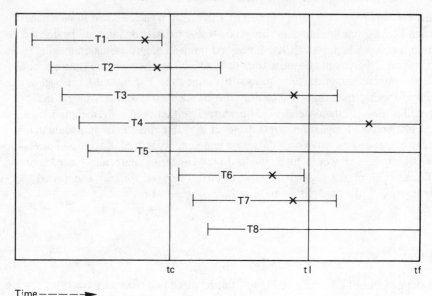

*Figure 5.9 tc = checkpoint time, tl = last time log file was updated, tf = time
        system failed. X on a transaction indicates the point in time when the
        END COMMIT record is written*

Assume that the last log buffers were written out to the log file at time tl and the
processor has failed at time tf, where tc < tl < tf.

The starting positions of the transactions are as follows.

(i)   T1 starts before tc and finishes with COMPLETE record written before tc,
      and hence it does not enter the recovery process. X in the diagram indicates
      the time when the END COMMIT record is written.

(ii) T2, T3, T4 and T5 start before tc and continue after it, and hence are listed
      in the checkpoint record, with their HL and HD. Only T2 has an END COM-
      MIT record, as indicated by the position of X, written before tc.

(iii) T6, T7 and T8 start after tc and hence are not listed in the checkpoint record.

   The end positions of the transactions are

(iv) T2 and T6 are completed with COMPLETE records written before time tl,
      and hence the RM does not have to *undo/redo* them.

(v)   T3 and T7 have END COMMIT records, as indicated by X (but not COM-
      PLETE records), written before time tl. They have to be redone.

(vi) The END COMMIT record of T4 was written into the log buffer but not into
      the log file before the crash. Since the log buffer is destroyed, the RM cannot

know about this commitment and hence T4 must be *undone*. (Such records can be saved if the DBCS always writes the END COMMIT and COMPLETE records in the log file as soon as the relevant update is finished, without waiting for the log buffers to be full. This is a reasonable strategy, but not considered here.)

(vii) T5 and T8 were only partially done at the time of the crash, and hence they must be *undone* as well.

In fact, in our scenario, the RM cannot make any distinction between T4, T5 and T8; all of them will have to be *undone*; however, note that none of them are written into the database as they are not committed transactions.

To recover in our scheme, the RM must search the log file backward (backward trace) from the end, scanning every log record until the most recent checkpoint record is reached. During this backward search, the RM will produce two lists, list A for the completed transactions and list B for the committed transactions, adding each transaction with a COMPLETE record to A, and each transaction with an END COMMIT record to B. When the checkpoint record is reached, it will remove from B those transactions that are in A, thus leaving in B only the transactions that were committed but not completed after the checkpoint. In addition to transaction number T#, list B will also contain HL and HD; HL in this case will be the LRN of the END COMMIT record, and HD will be assumed null until the checkpoint record is reached. If we take our earlier example, we shall end up with T6 and T2 in list A, and T7 and T3 in list B, before the checkpoint record is read.

From the values in the checkpoint record the HDs in list B will be updated. In our example, HD of T3 is null in the checkpoint record, and T7 does not appear in the checkpoint record, and hence list B will remain unchanged by this update. It is possible to have transactions where the END COMMIT records are written just before time tc but their consolidation did not begin until after time tl when the last buffers are written out; these transactions will not have any log records in the log file after the checkpoint record, and hence they will not appear in list A or B until the checkpoint record is encountered in the backward trace. To include these transactions in list B, we select those transactions of the checkpoint record that are not in list A or B, and examine the log record (as identified by the highest LRN held in HL of each transaction in the checkpoint record) of each such transaction, to ascertain if any of them are committed transactions. If any of them are, then we add them to list B, with HL and HD (HD will be null). In the above example there is no such transaction.

The list B is the *redo* list, its contents being used for *redoing*. List A is used only as an aid to create B, and hence can be discarded after B is complete. For each transaction in the *redo* list, the RM will examine each database page for LRN > HD, but carrying out the *redoing* only where LRN > LL. The presence of HDs in the checkpoint record helps to reduce the LRNs to be processed, and hence reduces database pages to be accessed. This *redo* may be called *roll forward* as against an *undo* which will be *roll back*.

If the processor fails immediately after the checkpoint but before any further log records are written out, then the technique outlined above will still work. In that case when the checkpoint record is read by RM, the content of list A and B will remain zero. In the above example, if the processor failed immediately after the checkpoint, transactions T6 to T8 will not take place, and T2 will be the only committed transaction to be redone.

This technique does not require any *undo* or roll back (except abortions of the incomplete transactions), since the database pages are not altered. Restart of the system can begin only when the recovery process is complete. However the recovery can fail, requiring restart of the recovery itself. Therefore it is necessary *to ensure that redoing of a transaction (or a log) a given number of times is the same as doing it only once*. That is, the redo of a redo of a redo . . . of, say, x is equal to the redo of x. Gray (1979) calls this an *idempotent* redo.

5.7.4 Gray's protocols

Gray has formalised the recovery process for the general case of a distributed database by four protocols, sometimes referred to as Gray's recovery protocols (Gray, 1979; Gray *et al.*, 1981), as given below:

(1)   consistency locks
(2)   Do/Undo/Redo log
(3)   Write ahead log
(4)   Two-phase commit (for distributed databases only – and hence not discussed here, but see chapter 15).

We can adopt this formalism for non-distributed databases if we interpret locks to mean concurrency locks (section 5.1.6) instead of internodal consistency locks, and if we drop the two-phase commit protocol. Clearly we need locks, since without them a database cannot be updated consistently.

We can assume a DBCS to have three update components – Insert, Delete and Modify – corresponding to the insert, delete and modify actions of DM commands for record updates. According to Gray, each of these DBCS components should incorporate three further operations, a *Do operation*, an *Undo operation* and a *Redo operation*, as described below.

Do: carries out the update action, and also creates the necessary log records in the log file for *Undo/Redo* of that action.
Undo: undoes the action, using the log records created by the *Do operation*.
Redo: redoes the action, using the log records created by the *Do operation*.

Gray further suggests an optional *Display* option to be incorporated in each of those DBCS components for presenting the log in a human readable format. He also underlines the need for write-ahead log and *idempotent* Undo/Redo, discussed earlier. If new DBMS are designed in this way, each update component having

Do/Undo/Redo and optional display operations, then the task of the RM will be much easier. It will then invoke the Redo routines of the appropriate update component each time that it encounters a relevant log record in the redoing process.

Gray investigated the size problem of on-line log files. According to his estimate, a large operational database could generate up to 200 million bytes of log data every day, so requiring a new disc for log to be mounted every day. To ensure that the recovery can always be made from the same disc, it is necessary to have some overlaps between two successive discs; this overlap can be achieved by removing incomplete transactions by the *Do operation* from the old to the new file at the start of a new file.

5.8 Conclusion

We have looked into a number of facilities that are essential for the proper functioning of a modern database. The concurrency control facility allows parallel updates of the database by several users by serialising the conflicting updates. The main problem there is the resolution/prevention of deadlocks arising out of protocols based on locking, since the efficiencies of the available techniques vary. The automatic preservation of a meaningful database (semantic integrity), against inadvertent and malicious errors is unlikely to materialise in the near future, mainly owing to high processing overheads. We must therefore rely on programmers, as we must do for the preservation of interprocess integrity. Recovery and restart facilities are needed to recover from an erroneous state and to restart the database from the previous error-free state. The protection of the data from unauthorised users is another key issue; the privacy requirements seem very complex and can be best supported by a separate access-control schema which the user can change more easily as and when required.

Modifications of schemas and databases are necessary to improve performance and to add new systems but the facilities available at the moment are inadequate, although the ANSI/SPARC model, postulating a separate internal schema, has given a lead in the right direction. The performance of a database can also be improved by query optimisation, optimal selection of access paths and efficient buffer management. A data dictionary is expected to service both the user and the DBCS by holding all the necessary information as meta data. Although everyone wants a data dictionary, there is no agreement on what its content should be. A number of products with varying facilities are available, but a very generalised facility is probably a long way off.

Both procedural and non-procedural languages are necessary for database users. The present trend to provide more non-procedural languages, some with general purpose and some with problem-oriented functions, is likely to continue. There is a need for supporting further languages and utilities for database operations. The processing efficiency of databases is poor, owing to the heavy overheads needed to support their facilities, which include concurrent processing and an error-free and reliable service.

Exercises

5.1   List and explain the causes of deadlocks in concurrent updates. Discuss the solutions available, including their implementation techniques, and give a brief critical assessment of their relative effectiveness.

5.2   A technique of serialisation is used to achieve concurrency in databases and yet, if all updates are serialised, there will not be any concurrency left. Discuss the issues involved.

5.3   Discuss the issues in the performance optimisation of databases with particular reference to the types of statistics that should be collected for this purpose. Specify, giving justification, a multilevel database architecture that will facilitate performance optimisation.

5.4   Describe the three types of integrity problems in databases along with the controls that can be exercised to resolve them.

5.5   Explain the issues of privacy protection in databases and discuss the solutions available.

5.6   Describe, with a conceptual diagram, the run-time operations of a database to execute a data manipulation command in a non-concurrent environment. You may assume execution time binding and hence the presence of the compiled versions of internal, conceptual and external schemas in the run-time system.

5.7   Describe, with a diagram, the components of a Data Base Control System.

5.8   Discuss critically the languages and compilers that are needed to be supported for a database.

5.9   Discuss Gray's four protocols and describe a recovery system based on those protocols.

5.10 Describe, with a suitable diagram, how a database can be recovered after a processor failure.

5.11 Discuss the possible functions of an integrated data dictionary in a database.

5.12 Explain the following terms:
  (a) Atomicity of transactions
  (b) Interleaved transactions
  (c) Synchronisation protocols
  (d) Commit unit
  (e) Checkpoint record
  (f) Write-ahead log.

References

BCS/DBAWG (1980). *Standing Paper SPO9 on Database Control functions*, BCS, 13 Mansfield Street, London W1M 0BP

Bernstein, P. A. and Shipman, D. W. (1980). Concurrency control in a system for distributed databases. *ACM TODS*, Vol. (5:1), March, p. 18

Coffman, E. G. *et al.* (1974). *ACM Computing Surveys*, Vol. 3, p. 67

Deen, S. M. (1982). Distributed Databases — an introduction. *Distribution Databases*, edited by H. J. Schneider, North-Holland

Deen, S. M. *et al.* (1982). Run-time management in a canonical DBMS (PRECI). *Proceedings of the Second British National Conference on Databases*, edited by S. M. Deen and P. Hammersley (BCS) (the run-time system described in section 5.6.2 is based on this PRECI architecture)

Evans, A. and Weiss, E. (1974). *Communications of the ACM*, Vol. 17, p. 437

Everest, G. G. (1974). *Data Base Management* (IFIP), North-Holland, p. 241

Gray, J. N. (1979). Notes on database operating systems. *Operating Systems: An Advanced Course*, edited by R. Bayer *et al.*, Springer-Verlag, New York, pp. 393–481

Gray, J. N. *et al.* (1981). The recovery manager of the SYSTEM R database manager. *ACM Computing Surveys*, Vol. (13:2), June, p. 223

Hammer, M. M. and Chan, A. (1976). Index selection in a self-adaptive DBMS. *Proceedings ACM SIGMOD Conference 1976*

Hawley, D. *et al.* (1975). *Computer Journal*, Vol. 18, p. 206

Lane, V. P. (1985). *Security of Computer-based Information Systems*, Macmillan, 1985

Schmidt, H. A. (1977). An analysis of some constructs for conceptual modelling. *Architecture and Models in DBMS*, edited by G. M. Nijssen, North-Holland

SDDTTG (1977). Stored data description and data translation: a model and a language. *Information Systems*, Vol. (2:3)

Sherman, S. W. and Brice, R. S. (1976). Performance of a database manager in a virtual memory system. *ACM TODS*, Vol. (1:4), December, p. 317

Smith, A. J. (1978). Sequentiality and prefetching in database system. *ACM TODS*, Vol. (3:3), September, p. 223

Sockut, G. H. and Goldberg, R. P. (1979). Database re-organisation — principles and practice. *ACM Computing Surveys*, Vol. (11:4), December, p. 371

Stocker, P. M. (1977). Storage utilisation in a self-organising database. *Proceedings of AFIPS NCC Conference*, Vol. 46

Traiger, I. L. (1983). Trends in system aspects of database management. *Proceedings of ICOD-2*, edited by S. M. Deen and P. Hammersley, John Wiley

PART III: RELATIONAL AND NETWORK APPROACHES

6 Basic Relational Model

A *relation* is a mathematical term for a two-dimensional table such as a collection of records (for example, see figure 2.14). It is characterised by rows and columns, each entry there being an attribute value. The reason for calling this a relation rather than a matrix lies in the lack of homogeneity in its entries — the entries are homogeneous in the columns but not in the rows. A relational database consists of such relations which can be stored on a physical device in a variety of ways.

From the late sixties, a number of people toyed with the idea of constructing databases with relations as the basic building blocks, but the breakthrough came in 1970 when Dr Edgar F. Codd of IBM proposed a generalised relational model, chiefly to provide data independence (Codd, 1970). The model was subsequently improved and expanded by Codd, and very quickly it became the main focus of all research activities on databases. The basic model specifies only a data structure in the form of relations for the conceptual schema and several versions of a high level language to manipulate relations. The absence of internal and external schemas has led to a wide variation in implementations, as we shall see later. In this chapter we shall cover the basic relational model, leaving the advanced features to chapters 7 and 8.

In section 6.1 we shall describe some relational concepts, to be followed by a discussion of normalisation in section 6.2. The data manipulation languages — relational algebra, calculus and DSL Alpha — will be covered in the next section, followed by the implementation issues in section 6.4.

6.1 Basic concepts

An attractice feature of the relational model is its simplicity. A relation is a table of data and may consist of only one row and one column, thus providing the simplest possible data structure which can be used as the common denominator of all data structures. It simplifies the design of the conceptual schema as there is only one logical data structure, that is, the relation, to consider. Furthermore the relational model provides an unparallelled freedom to the application programmer by enabling him to access any attribute value in the database directly; the access mechanism, being associative or content addressable as an attribute, is accessed apparently by its value rather than by its position or a pointer. This freedom of access is achieved firstly by expressing relations in what Codd defines as first normal form and secondly by using a powerful data manipulation language known as relational algebra. The basic operations on relations, such as those required to extract an attribute value or to combine parts of two relations to form a third relation, are carried out by relational algebra. Codd has also developed a predicate calculus known as relational calculus which he subsequently used to construct a high level data manipulation language named Data Sub-Language (DSL) Alpha.

Some definitions

Each column of a relation contains the values of a named attribute, and each row is called a *tuple*. The word tuple is taken from the description of groups, such as quintuple, sextuple etc. Thus a group of n elements is an *n-tuple*. In a relation of n columns, each tuple, that is, each row, is an n-tuple. The number of rows or tuples in a relation is its *cardinality*, and the number of columns is its *degree*. The individual elements in a relation are attribute values. If we consider an m by n relation (m rows and n columns), we have

a relation of degree n and cardinality m, that is, a relation containing n columns and m tuples, each tuple being an n-tuple. There are $m \times n$ attribute values, each tuple having n attribute values.

A relation of degree 1 is called *unary*, degree 2 *binary*, degree 3 *ternary* and degree n *n-ary*. The characteristics of a relation are

(i) All entries in a column are of the same kind.
(ii) Columns are assigned distinct names called attribute names.
(iii) The ordering of the columns is immaterial.
(iv) Each tuple is distinct, that is, duplicate tuples are not allowed.
(v) The ordering of tuples is immaterial.

The *extension* of a relation is the set of tuples in the relation at any given time, and therefore it varies with time, as tuples are inserted or deleted. Another associated term is *intension* which refers to the permanent characteristics of a relation, such as relation name and attribute names, including all the relevant integrity constraints. The intension of a relation can be found in the conceptual schema of the database and the extension in the data of the database, the intension defining all permissible extensions.

The term domain means a collection of values of the same property type. Although in some cases columns and domains have one to one correspondence, in other cases they have not. For instance, a domain for part numbers, where a given part number can be both a superior and a subordinate part number, can form two distinct columns as shown in relation COMP of figure 6.1.

Likewise columns DNO and EDN of relations DREC and EREC (figure 2.14) respectively belong to a single domain of department numbers. Therefore the same domain can be shared by different columns each with possibly different attribute names, in the same or different relations. In the same relation the

COMP (SUP-PART	SUB-PART	QUANTITY)
A180	C240	7
C240	H100	3
C240	D120	7
E110	B153	10
E120	E110	2

Figure 6.1 A relation of degree 3

attribute names have to be different for identification, as in figure 6.1. Just as a relation cannot have duplicate tuples, *a domain cannot have duplicate values either*. Strictly speaking, column is not a relational term, but it is increasingly used to indicate *all the values* of a given attribute of a relation.

Keys and attributes

The tuples of a relation can be uniquely identified by one or more keys, each key containing one or more non-redundant attributes. These keys are called *candidate keys*. One of these keys can be arbitrarily selected to identify the tuples; this key is known as the *primary key*. If there is only one candidate key for a relation, then this key must be the primary key. Each relation in principle must have a primary key. Consider relations DREC and EREC of figure 2.14. There both DNO and DNAME are unique identifiers of relation DREC and hence candidate keys. We may select DNO as the primary key. In relation EREC, ENO is the only candidate key and hence it is also the primary key. Since DNO is a unique identifier of DREC, DNO concatenated with any other attribute of DREC will also be a unique identifer, but the second attribute will be redundant. A candidate key must not include any redundant attribute. Another constraint of the relational model is that a primary key cannot have null values, since a null value cannot identify a tuple. Date (1981) calls this *entity integrity*.

If an attribute (or a collection of attributes) of a relation holds the primary key value of another relation, then this attribute (or this collection) is called the *foreign key*. Thus EDN is a foreign key of relation EREC. A foreign key can have only two possible values, either the relevant primary key value or a null value (the foreign key of record E90 in figure 2.14 is a null value). No other values are permitted. This is known an *referential integrity* — since values are obtained by reference to the owner's primary key values.

A foreign key may or may not form part of a member's primary key, depending on the situation. For instance, if employee numbers are unique only within a department, then (EDN, ENO) will be the primary key of EREC, instead of ENO alone.

Comparison with standard data-processing concepts

In data-processing terms we may approximate a relation to the occurrences of
a record type, a tuple to a record occurrence, an attribute to a data item, and a
column to the collection of all values for a single data item. Degree is the number
of data items in the record and cardinality is the total number of records in the
record type. A unary relation is a record type consisting of a single data item,
a binary relation is a record type of two data items, and so on.

However, a record type can have data aggregates which are not permitted in
relations; a record type is thus equivalent to an unnormalised relation (see later).
In a relation, the ordering of tuples and attributes is not recognised, as they are
addressed individually; that is, the next tuple or the next attribute does not make
any sense in the strict relational model, but in a record type the ordering of
records or the relative position of attributes is meaningful. Finally by definition
a relation cannot have a duplicate tuple, but there is no such conceptual restriction
on the existence of a duplicate record in a record type. These discussions are
summarised in figure 6.2(a), (b).

Relational terms	Data-processing terms
Relation	All the occurrences of a record type
Tuple	Record
Attribute	Data item
Column	All the values of a data item
Degree	Number of data items in the record type
Cardinality	Total number of records in the record type
Primary key	Unique key

(a)

Figure 6.2 (a) Equivalence of relational terms with data-processing concepts.

Item	Relation	Record type
Data aggregate	Not allowed in normalised relations	Allowed
Ordering of data items	Immaterial	Can be important
Ordering of tuples or records	Immaterial	Important
Duplicate tuple or record	Not allowed	Immaterial
Primary key	Important	Immaterial

(b) Difference between relational and data-processing concepts

6.2 Normalisation

Codd has identified certain structural features in relations which create retrieval and update problems. These undesirable features can be removed by breaking a relation into other relations of desirable structures. This process is known as normalisation, which may be defined as a step by step reversible process of transforming an unnormalised relation into relations of progressively simpler structure. Since the process is reversible, no information is lost during the transformation. Originally Codd defined three types of undesirable properties − data aggregates, partial key dependency and indirect key dependency − which can be removed in three stages of normalisation known as first (1NF), second (2NF) and third (3NF) normal forms. We now have also a fourth (4NF) and even a fifth (5NF) normal form. In this chapter we shall describe only the first three forms, deferring the higher forms to the next chapter.

A relation is unnormalised if it contains data aggregates. In the first normal form, data aggregates are removed, by breaking the unnormalised relation if necessary into several other relations. The second and the third normal forms remove partial and indirect dependencies of attributes on candidate keys, as will be explained below. At each stage of normalisation a relation is broken down into several others; however, it is possible for a relation to be in third or even in a higher form to start with. Since the process of normalisation is successive (figure 6.3) a relation in the nth normal form is also in the $(n-1)^{th}$ normal form.

6.2.1 First normal form

The purpose of the first normal form is to simplify the structure of a relation by ensuring that it contains only data items and no data aggregates. More formally

A relation is in first normal form if every component in it is atomic.

Since this is a very simple structure, a relation in first normal form is said to be *normalised*. To understand how data aggregates can be resolved, let us examine the three subtypes of data aggregates introduced in section 2.1 with the help of CUST-REC of figure 2.1.

(i) *Vectors*: If a vector occurs a maximum of n times, then it can be replaced by n explicitly named and independent data items; for instance, BAL of CUST-REC can be replaced by BAL1, BAL2 and BAL3.

(ii) *Composite items*: Composite items can be replaced by their constituent data items; for instance, we can drop CNAME and DATE from CUST-REC, retaining only their subordinate items.

(iii) *Repeating group*: A repeating group can be eliminated only by converting it into a separate relation, for instance, a separate relation for PCODE and QTY of CUST-REC.

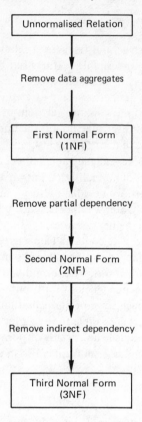

Figure 6.3 Three levels of normalisation

If we apply these normalisation principles to CUST-REC then we have the following two relations, say CR1 and CR2.

CR1 (<u>CNO</u> SURNAME INITIAL CR-LT BAL1 BAL2 BAL3 NORD DD MMYY)
CR2 (<u>CNO</u> <u>PCODE</u> QTY)

where the primary keys are underlined. In CR1, there is one tuple for each customer, with CNO as the primary key. In CR2, there is one tuple for each CNO and PCODE value pair with (CNO, PCODE) as the primary key. The presence of CNO as foreign key in CR2 in essential, as otherwise product code and quantity cannot be related to the customers. We shall not return this example any further, but the reader should be able to convince himself later that both CR1 and CR2 are in 3NF.

It should be clear from the above that vectors and composite items can be resolved into atomic components quite easily without creating new relations, but this is not so with a repeating group which requires a drastic action, that is, the creation of new relations by splitting the original unnormalised relation. Therefore the removal of repeating groups is usually seen as the main target of the first normal form, and as such we shall use it as the rough definition of first normal form from now on, assuming that vectors and composite items, if present, are already resolved. Before proceeding further, we give an example of such an unnormalised relation called CUSTORD (figure 6.4) for customer orders.

```
CUSTORD (O# C#   NI  IC  UP QO IC  UP QO IC  UP QO IC  UP QO...)
         1  241  3   A10 5  10 C13 3  20 P15 7  18
         2  250  4   A10 5  15 B16 12 2  B20 8  1  C13 3  5
         3  241  2   B16 12 11 B21 2  15
```

Figure 6.4 An unnormalised relation

It contains order number (O#), customer number (C#), number of items ordered (NI), quantity ordered (QO), with (IC, UP, QO) repeating NI times, once for each item ordered in a given customer order. It is assumed that unit price of an item does not depend on customer orders. We can normalise CUSTORD by splitting it into two normalised relations CORD and CORD2 as given in figure 6.5. Both relations have one candidate key each, O# and (O#, IC) respectively, as underlined.

We have shown above how an unnormalised relation can be normalised. However by definition, as given in section 6.1, relations are supposed to be normalised, since the orderings of columns in a relation can be immaterial only if every component

CORD (O#	C#	NI)	
1	241	3	
2	250	4	
3	241	2	
CORD2(O#	IC	UP	QO)
1	A10	5	10
1	C13	3	20
1	P15	7	18
2	A10	5	15
2	B16	12	2
2	B20	8	1
2	C13	3	5
3	B16	12	11
3	B21	2	15

Figure 6.5 Relations in 1NF. The unnormalised relation of figure 6.4 is split into two relations

is atomic (the ordering of columns in a data aggregate is not immaterial — the relative order is important there). *Therefore we shall drop the superfluous prefix 'normalised', and will always assume a relation to be normalised (that is, in first normal form) unless it carries the prefix 'unnormalised'.* Consequently the term relation to be used in all subsequent definitions of normal form will mean normalised relation. However we may still, on occasions, employ the term 'normalised relation' to emphasise the atomicity of its components.

6.2.2 Second normal form

As noted earlier (O#, IC) is the sole candidate key and hence the primary key of relation CORD2. In this relation the order number or item code alone cannot uniquely identify quantity ordered, we need both order number and item code for this identification. On the other hand, item code alone can uniquely identify unit price which is independent of order numbers.

In relational terminology, QO is *fully functionally dependent* on (O#, IC), implying that the full key (O#, IC) is needed for the unique identification of QO; in contrast, UP is only partially functionally dependent on (O#, IC) since only part of the key (O#, IC), namely IC, is sufficient for the unique identification of UP. Both QO and UP are non-key attributes (that is, they are not part of any candidate key) whereas O# and IC are key attributes (that is, they are part of candidate keys). The partial dependence on candidate keys causes the following update anomalies.

(i)   Insertion: If we wish to introduce a new item in relation C2 with specific unit price, we cannot do so unless a customer places an order, as we need an order number, thus we are prevented from storing data about a new item. (Since the O# is part of the primary key, it cannot have null values by definition, and hence we need a genuine order number.)

(ii) Deletion: If the data about a customer order is deleted, the information (price in this case) about the item is also deleted. If this happens to the last order for that item, the information about that item will be lost from the database. (Again we cannot use a null value for primary key to retain information on price.)

(iii) Amendment: As the data about an item, say price, appears as many times as there are orders for it, amendment on that data of the item would be cumbersome.

These problems are avoided by eliminating the partial dependence in favour of full dependence (we drop the word *functional* for economy) by splitting relation CORD2 into two others as shown in figure 6.6. Note that relation CORD has no such problem, and hence it is in 2NF; in fact it is in 3NF.

IORD (O#	IC	QO	PRICE (IC	UP)
1	A10	10	A10	5
1	C13	20	C13	3
1	P15	18	P15	7
2	A10	15	B16	12
2	B16	2	B20	8
2	B20	1	B21	2
2	C13	5		
3	B16	11		
3	B21	15		

Figure 6.6 The normalised relations of figure 6.5 in 2NF. The partial dependence of unit price (UP) on the key (O#, IC) is now removed

Determinant

Before we present a more formal definition of the second normal form, we must explain the concept of *determinant* and *functional dependency*.

A *determinant* is an attribute or a set of non-redundant attributes which can act as a unique identifier of another attribute (or another set of attributes) of a given relation.

In other words, a determinant is a non-redundant unique key for one or more attributes of a relation. If attribute (or a set of attributes) A is a determinant of attribute B, then B is said to be *fully functionally dependent* on A. This is written as A → B which can be read as

A determines B (that is, A is a determinant of B), or,
B is fully functionally dependent on A.

The converse notation B ↛ A, can be read as: B does not determine A (meaning B is not a determinant of A) or B is not fully functionally dependent on A.

In relation CORD2, IC → UP, and (O#, IC) → QB since the values of IC can uniquely identify the values of UP, and likewise the values of (O#, IC) can uniquely identify the values of QB. However (OH#, IC) ↛ UP, since IC → UP; that is, although the values of (O#, IC) can identify the values of UP uniquely, the presence of O# values is redundant since IC alone can uniquely identify UP. Equivalently, QB is fully dependent (again dropping the term functional) on (O#, IC); but UP is only partially dependent on (O#, IC), since it is fully dependent on IC which is a part of (O#, IC).

The concept of determinant is very important for the understanding of normalisation, as it is used also in the definition of 3rd, even in 4th, normal form. Therefore we now give a further example. Consider a relation EMPLOYEE (figure 6.7) for

EMPLOYEE (E#   S#   EN)

12	A21	ALVIN
15	C23	RAMI
20	A18	RAMI
23	B44	ALVIN
27	D15	ADNAN

Figure 6.7

employee number (E#), social security number (S#) and employee name (EN) where E# and S# are unique, but EN is not.

Here, E# can uniquely identify both S# and EN, and S# can also uniquely identify both E# and EN; but EN cannot uniquely identify any attribute as it has duplicate values. Therefore

E# → S#, E# → EN (to be written as E# → S#, EN)
(Note, in contrast, A → (B, C) will mean A determines the composite
attribute made up of B and C).
S# → E#, EN

but   (E#, S#) ↛ EN, since one of them in (E#, S#) is redundant.

This shows again that a determinant is a non-redundant unique key for one or more attributes of a relation. We shall now define a second normal form as

A relation is in second normal form if every non-key attribute is fully dependent on each candidate key.

If we now examine relation CORD2 again, non-key attribute UP is only partially dependent on (O#, IC) which is a candidate key. Therefore relation CORD2 is not in second normal form. We resolve relation CORD2 into two others, IORD and PRICE, which are in 2NF (figure 6.6). In fact relations IORD and PRICE, and also relation CORD, are 3NF.

6.2.3 Third normal form

A relation in 2NF can also show update anomalies of the type discussed earlier. As an example, consider a relation STOCK (figure 6.8), containing bin number (B#), part number (P#), the quantity of a part number in a bin (QB), and the lead time (LT) and re-order level (RL) of each part number.

We assume that the parts of a given part number may be stored in several bins, but the same bin does not hold parts of more than one part number; we further assume that the lead time and re-order level are fixed for each part number. The candidate key for this relation is B#, on which all attributes are

STOCK (B#	P#	QB	LT	RL)
210	30	5	10	5
211	30	10	10	5
225	50	7	7	6
231	81	3	15	10
232	81	12	15	10

Figure 6.8 A relation in 2NF, showing indirect dependence of lead time (LT) and reorder level (RL) on the bin number (B#) through the part number (P#)

fully dependent (B# → P#, QB, LT, RL); since the B# is a single attribute, the question of partial dependence does not arise. Yet some attribute values are repeated in relation STOCK, showing signs of update anomalies. For instance, we cannot store LT and RL information of a new expected part number in the database unless we actually have a bin number allocated to it (since a null value is not permitted in a primary key). If we run out of stock, and allocate the bin number to some other part number, then we cannot hold LT and RL information for the out of stock part numbers. If the LT and RL information of a part number is altered, we have to update in many different tuples, as this information repeats itself.

We need a third normal form to eliminate these anomalies. The original third normal form defined by Codd (1971a) was later improved by Boyce, and hence this new version, given here, is sometimes called Boyce-Codd normal form (BCNF) (Codd, 1974). We shall give two definitions.

Definition 1

A relation is in third normal form if, and only if, for each candidate key, every attribute not in that key is fully and directly dependent on that key.

This implies that if a relation is in 2NF if every attribute not in a particular candidate key is *directly dependent* on that key, then this relation is in 3NF. If we apply this definition to relation STOCK, we find that the attributes LT and RL, although fully dependent on B# (B# → LT, RL), are not directly dependent on it, since they are fully dependent on P# (P# → LT, RL) which is in turn fully dependent on B# (B# → P#). We observe that the statement A → B guarantees only the full dependency of B on A, but not its direct dependency on A. The indirect dependency can be removed by splitting relation STOCK into STOCK1 and STOCK2 as shown in figure 6.9.

STOCK1 (B#	P#	QB)
210	30	5
211	30	10
225	50	7
231	81	3
232	81	12

STOCK2 (P#	LT	RL)
30	10	5
50	7	6
81	15	10

Figure 6.9 The relations of figure 6.8 in 3NF, the indirect dependence being removed

Definition 2

A relation is in third normal form if every determinant is a candidate key.

This definition is due to Sharman (1975). Its elegance lies in its simplicity and directness. It is independent of second normal form — we no longer need a relation to be in 2NF before it could be in 3NF. Indeed we can forget about 2NF, direct dependency, key attribute and non-key attribute altogether, and arrive at a 3NF directly. The application of this definition is also easier, as shown below.

In relation STOCK, $P\# \to LT$ (also $P\# \to RL$) and hence $P\#$ is a determinant, but it is not a candidate key and hence this relation is not in 3NF (the second determinant is B# which determines P#, QB, LT and RL, and is a candidate key). The resolved relations STOCK1 and STOCK2 are in 3NF since the determinants there are candidate keys. Applying the above definition directly to relation CORD2, by-passing 2NF, we find: $IC \to UP$, but IC is not a candidate key and hence CORD2 is not in 3NF. The relations CORD, IORD and PRICE are in 3NF. In relation EMPLOYEE (figure 6.7), $E\# \to S\#$, $S\# \to E\#$, and hence it has two determinants; since both are candidate keys, EMPLOYEE is in 3NF.

Let us consider another relation, say a relation ADVICE holding data of a consultancy company which has a number of experts to advise clients on subjects such as insurance, investment and taxation. We assume that there can be more than one expert on the same subject, but the same expert cannot deal with more than one subject, and that a client receives advice on a subject from only one expert although he may receive advice on another subject from another expert. Their data are shown in relation ADVICE containing CLIENT, SUBJECT and EXPERT, given in figure 6.10.

Here $EXPERT \to SUBJECT$ but EXPERT is not a candidate key, and therefore this relation is not in 3NF. We can also arrive at the same conclusion by applying the

ADVICE (CLIENT	SUBJECT	EXPERT)
JAMES	INSURANCE	PHELAN
JAMES	TAXATION	HOLT
HARRIS	INSURANCE	ACKER
MARX	INVESTMENT	BRAGG
MARX	TAXATION	HOLT

Figure 6.10

first definition of 3NF given above, but the process is more tortuous — we leave
it to the reader to try. This relation is resolved into AD1 and AD2 which are in
3NF (Figure 6.11). Relation AD1 is an *all-key* relation, that is, there is no non-
key attribute, (CLIENT, EXPERT) being the primary key. In relation AD2, the
key is EXPERT. The reader might be interested to know that, according to Codd's
original definition, relation ADVICE would have been in 3NF, although it shows
update anomalies as some attribute values are repeated.

A useful corollary of the definition of 3NF is

An *all-key* relation with a single candidate key is in 3NF.

As there is only one candidate key, there is no attribute outside it to be fully/directly
dependent on it. Hence the relation is in 3NF. We can also prove this corollary
in terms of the second definition of 3NF, as follows. In a composite candidate
key, if part A is a determinant of another part B of the same candidate key, then
B is redundant; but this is not possible since a candidate key contains only non-
redundant attributes. Therefore part of a candidate cannot be a determinant of
another part. As there is no other attribute in the relation, there is no determinant
which is not a candidate key; hence the relation is in 3NF.

AD1(CLIENT	EXPERT)
JAMES	PHELAN
JAMES	HOLT
HARRIS	ACKER
MARX	BRAGG
MARX	HOLT

AD2(SUBJECT	EXPERT)
INSURANCE	PHELAN
INSURANCE	ACKER
INVESTMENT	BRAGG
TAXATION	HOLT

Figure 6.11

An *optimal nth* normal form is defined as the minimum number of relations in that normal form for the original unnormalised relation.

The concept of third normal form had a great impact on areas of data processing beyond the relational model, particularly in data analysis. The principal advantages of 3NF are seen as the easy identification of entities and keys, and the resolution of complex data structures into simpler forms. We therefore conclude this subsection with a rule-of-thumb definition of a third normal form outside the strict relational model. A record type, shorn of repeating groups, but having a unique key, is in 3NF if every data item outside the key is identifiable

> by the key
> by the whole key
> and by nothing but the key.

Its updated version for 4NF is given later. This definition is the modified form of the one first given by Robinson (1978).

Although the concept of normalisation is important, what is or is not a deter-minant depends on human judgement and interpretation. For instance, in relation CORD2, if we assume the unit price to depend on the size of the order as well as on item code, then $(QO, IC) \twoheadrightarrow UP, IC \rightarrow UP$. This will produce a relation PRICE (QO, IC, UP) rather than PRICE (IC, UP). If some customers are favoured, UP could depend also on C#. The database management system cannot automatically know these considerations. Moreover what is true at the time of database creation may not remain valid later, owing to a change in, say, company policy. For these reasons, normalisation cannot be automatically enforced or checked by a system; human intervention is required, unless of course all that detail consideration is also input to the system. It should also be stated that the relational languages do not require relations to be in any higher normal from than the first, as we shall see in the next section.

A normalised relation is a mathematical concept imposed on the real world to produce a clean and simple structure, but in the normalisation process we usually resolve an entity record into several tuples. A tuple therefore does not generally hold all the properties of an entity, but only some, as allowed by the normalisation. Consequently, a tuple identifier (say primary key value) is not necessarily an entity identifier. These restrictions are trivial, since we can represent an entity record by a set of tuples. However, there are some other limitations of the relational model which will be considered later (see section 14.1.4).

6.2.4 Data representation

The one to many relationship in the relational model is achieved by including the owner's primary key in the member relation as a foreign key. This technique permits us to support all $1:n$ associations discussed in section 4.3.2, with the foreign key name as the association name, as shown in figure 6.12.

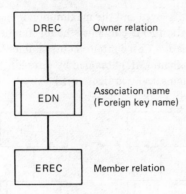

Figure 6.12

An *m:n* relationship can be represented only indirectly, by resolving it into two
1:*n* relationships, as done with the course (CRS), student (STD) and link (CSL)
records of section 4.3.3. Their relational equivalent is shown in figure 6.13, where
relation CRS contains course number (C#), course name (CN), the university year

CRS (C#	CN	YR	MX)
C1	COMPUTER SCIENCE	1	25
C2	MATHEMATICS	2	20
C3	ACCOUNTANCY	1	30

STD (S#	SN	AGE)
S1	ADAMS	21
S2	WARD	25
S3	REMUS	20
S4	BENN	22

CSL (CC	SS	MK)
C1	S1	50
C3	S1	65
C1	S2	40
C2	S2	70
C3	S2	48
C1	S3	82
C2	S3	51
C1	S4	67
C3	S4	77

Figure 6.13

(YR) in which the course is given and the maximum number (MX) of students who can take the course; relation STD contains student number (S#), student name (SN) and age (AGE). Relation CSL contains course number (CC), student number (SS) and an examination mark (MK) obtained by a student in a course. The relationship is shown diagrammatically in figure 6.14.

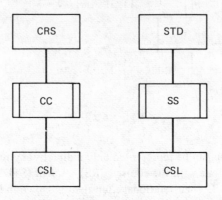

Figure 6.14 m:n *relationship between courses and students*

Representation of loop structures does not present any problems. A 1:*n* loop showing Head-teacher relationship (figure 4.2), can, for instance, be represented by a relation TCH(T# TN H#) containing teacher number (T#), teacher name (TN) and the teacher number of the head of the department (H#). There, each teacher tuple will contain the teacher number of his head of the department as if it is a foreign key in the attribute H#. For the head of the department himself, the values of T# and H# will be the same unless he has a different teacher as his head (figure 6.15).

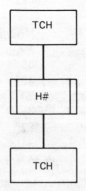

Figure 6.15 A loop

An *m:n* loop must be resolved into two 1:*n* loops as we did with the part explosion problem of figure 4.7. If we assume PART and PLINK as relations, the relational equivalents of their 1:*n* association types would be figure 6.16, where SUB and SUP are foreign keys and hence association names.

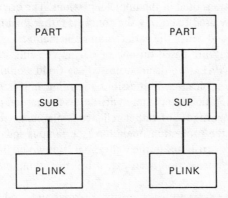

Figure 6.16 m:n *loop resolved into two loops*

The proliferation of foreign keys required to sustain relationships does not necessarily lead to data redundancy, since they (the foreign keys) can be replaced by indexes in implementation.

6.3 Data manipulation

Relational algebra, based on the operations of the set theory, provides a powerful technique of retrieval in a relational database. DSL Alpha is equivalent in retrieval power, but relatively easier to use.

In this section we shall present the basic facilities of the relational algebra, relational calculus and DSL Alpha, mainly to indicate their retrieval power. Although there exist a number of implementations of relational algebra, Alpha has never been implemented. Its closest equivalent is QUEL which we shall briefly describe later in this section. Apart from QUEL, there are a number of other relational languages available to-day; two of them — SQL and QBE — will be covered in chapter 8. We should observe that none of the relational languages uses the concepts of primary/candidate keys of normalisation, beyond the require-ment that relations must be in 1NF. Attributes are referenced by names and tuples by matching attribute values. Furthermore a relational operation does not guarantee the preservation of higher normal forms — an operation on relations in 3NF can produce a result relation which is not in 3NF. The only guarantee is that the result relation will be in 1NF.

6.3.1 *Relational algebra*

Following Codd's original definition of the relational algebra, many papers and
books have been written on the subject to explain it further. While there is no
disagreement on the definitions of the basic relational operations, there is a wide
variation in the notations used in the implementations. The original notations of
Codd were principally used to convey the concepts rather than to provide a syntax
for implementation, and hence the variation in implementations. In this subsection
we shall present an algebra based on one of our implementations called PRECI
Algebraic Language (PAL). We decided not to use Codd's original notations as
they sometimes give misleading impressions regarding implementability. For
instance, in Codd's notation the common attributes for natural join and division
operations are not identifed, but rather reliance is placed on the indiscriminate
and frequent use of the projection operation (the famous square brackets) to
produce the necessary attributes in the right order; this would be unusual in an
implementation, since projection is an expensive operation, and should be used
sparingly.

Relational algebra operates on one or two relations and produces a new relation
as the result. The operations are expressed in a system of notation and can be used
to retrieve information from one or more relations or to update a tuple of a relation.
We shall describe here seven operations of which the first three, *union, intersection*
and *difference*, are traditional set operations, and the other four, *projection,
selection, join* and *division*, are less common. In describing these operations, we shall
also introduce the concepts of temporary and virtual relations.

Operations in the relational algebra presented here are evaluated from left to
right with the following order of precedence:

1. The right-hand side of comparison operators $= \; < \; \geqslant \; \leqslant \; > \; \neq$
2. Comparison operators
3. Logical operators ⎫   NOT
    (in order of precedence)⎰   AND
                                     OR
4. Selection   :
5. Division   /
6. Join   *
7. Projection   %
8. Intersection   !
9. Union and difference   ++ ——
10. Assignment   := (not a relational operation)

The symbols given above are those used in PAL. Brackets may be used to indicate
a different order of priority. In the text, we shall use the symbol ⇒ to indicate
the result of an operation; for example, A − − B ⇒ R implies that 'A difference B'
yields relation R as the result. This symbol (⇒) is not part of the relational algebra,

but is used in this book as a convenience to explain examples to the readers. In common with other relational languages, PAL also uses the notation R.A to mean attribute A of relation R; R is called the qualifier of attribute A. PAL supports a number of other operations and functions, but these are not presented in this book (Deen *et al.*, 1981, 1985).

Union

The union of relation A with relation B, denoted as A ++ B is the set of all tuples without repetition. This can be used to add a new tuple to a relation in the memory. For example

CRS ++ {"C4" "PHYSICS" 3 20}

will add the tuple {C4 PHYSICS 3 20} to relation CRS of figure 6.13.
In these examples alphanumeric values are represented within double quotes.
Note that two relations can be 'unioned' only if they have identical sets of attributes. Such relations are said to be *union-compatible*.

Intersection

The intersection of relation A with relation B, denoted as A ! B, is the set of all tuples belonging to both A and B. This can be used to find a common set of tuples between two relations.

Difference

The difference of relation B from relation A, denoted as A −− B, is the set of all tuples belonging to A but not to B. This can be applied to remove a tuple; for instance

CRS −− {"C3" "ACCOUNTANCY" 1 30}

Like union, a difference operation can be applied only if the relations are union-compatible. In a relational algebra, the union and difference operations are normally used to manipulate relations in the User Work Area (section 5.6.3), but not to update relations in the database proper which is usually done by specific Insert/Delete/Replace commands (not discussed here).

Projection

Projection is the extraction of one or more named columns from a relation in a specified order. Strictly speaking, in all relational operations, duplicate tuples are meant to be eliminated from the resultant relation, since a relation is not supposed to have duplicate tuples. However the removal of duplicates involves extra processing (see section 8.4), but sometimes the presence of duplicates in the answer does not matter. Therefore two types of projection are generally used; one is called *projection* denoted in PAL by % (single percentage sign) and the other *project unique,* denoted in PAL by %% (double percentage sign). Duplicates are removed from project unique, but not from projection.

We use the notation R:=(A, B, C) % P to denote R as the resultant relation containing the columns A, B and C projected from relation P in that column order. The bracket is unnecessary if only a single column is projected, for example A % P. The sign % may be read as 'projected from' or simply 'from'.

We give below some examples of project unique and projection from the relations of figures 6.8 and 6.13.

(P#, LT, RL) %% STOCK			S# % STD ⇒ R(S#)
⇒ R(P# LT RL)			S1
30	10	5	S2
50	10	6	S3
81	15	10	S4

(YR, CN, MX) % CRS

⇒ R (YR	CN	MX)
1	COMPUTER SCIENCE	25
2	MATHEMATICS	20
1	ACCOUNTANCY	30

Although the ordering of columns is immaterial in a relation, nevertheless sometimes we need columns in a particular order, say for printing the values. Projection is the only relational operator which yields this ordering facility. The actual order of the columns in a relation produced by the other relational operations is implementor-defined and is immaterial to the operation. In theory, no relational operators, including projection, require the columns in the operand relation(s) to be in any particular order.

Finally, always use projection in preference to the more expensive project unique unless the removal of duplicates is really needed.

Selection

Selection is used to extract tuples from a relation, subject to conditions specified in a predicate, and is therefore somewhat complementary to projection which extracts columns. The form of the operation is

Relation: Predicate

to be interpreted as 'select tuples where the predicate is true'. The colon : means 'where' or 'such that'.

The predicate may contain a series of conditions connected by AND, OR; each condition is made up of relational expressions involving this and other relations and *one* comparison operator — like an IF statement of ordinary programming languages. The result of selection is another relation, say R, which contains all the original columns, usually in the original order, but is populated with only the selected tuples. Some examples of selection are given below.

Query (1). Extract the tuple(s) of student WARD from relation STD (figure 6.13)

$$STD : SN = \text{“WARD”}$$

to be read as select STD tuples where SN = "WARD".

The result is

S#	SN	AGE
S2	WARD	25

Query (2). Find the student number of WARD

$$S\#\%STD : SN = \text{“WARD”}$$

to be read as get S# from STD where SN = "WARD".

The result is

S#
S2

In accordance with the precedence rule defined earlier, the selection will be carried out before projection. Observe that the use of project unique in place of projection above will yield the same result, since student numbers are unique in relation STD. As it happens, the result relations of the queries in this subsection do not produce any duplicate tuples, and hence we have used projection rather than project unique.

Query (3). Find from relation CSL the student numbers of those students who scored more than 55 in course C1

$$SS\% CSL : CC = \text{“C1”} \text{ AND } MK > 55$$

The result is

SS
S3
S4

Temporary and virtual relations

The result of a relational operation can be stored in a temporary relation (defined by the user in the User Work Area as part of data declaration) by an assignment command; for example

$$R := CRS -- \{\text{``C3'' ``ACCOUNTANCY'' 1 30}\}$$

where R is declared previously as a temporary relation with attributes for course number, course name, year and maximum capacity. R will now hold two tuples of CRS. A temporary relation can be treated by relational operations like any other relation, its tuples being available for subsequent processing. However, if the symbol := is replaced by ==, then we have the definition of a virtual relation; for example

$$V == CRS -- (\text{``C3'' ACCOUNTANCY 1 30})$$

where V is a *virtual* relation which does not exist as a relation, but acts as a symbol for the expression on the right-hand side. Therefore virtual relations are very handy as symbols to represent long expressions or to break a long query into smaller parts, as will be shown shortly. Note that a variable can be reused to represent a different virtual relation later. Query (3) above can be reformulated as

$$V == CSL : CC = C1 \text{ and } MK > 55$$
$$SS \% V$$

The compiler will replace SS % V by SS % CSL: CC = "C1" AND MK > 55, and hence no extra processing is involved during the execution time. However, if we write (assuming R is appropriately pre-declared)

$$R := CSL : CC = \text{``C1'' and } MK > 55$$
$$SS \% R$$

then R will be evaluated, and SS projected from R. This is inefficient since the result of selection is unnecessarily stored in R. Further examples of the use of virtual relations are given later, showing how they can be used in PAL to break up a long single query into a series of simpler queries (multi-step query).

Join

A join is a combination of two relations sharing a common domain. If column A1 of relation A and column B1 of relation B are common columns (that is, they belong to the same domain), then the join of A and B over these common columns is denoted as A(A1) * (B1)B which produces a relation, say R, as the result. Relation

R consists of all the tuples obtained by concatenating each tuple of A with all tuples of B that have the matching value under the common column; a tuple of a relation is excluded from the resultant relation if it does not have a matching value in the common column of the other relation. The resultant relation contains all the columns of both the original relations, but the common column appears only once. Consider two relations A (DOCTOR PATIENT) and B (PATIENT DRUG), and their join R, as given below.

A(DOCTOR	PATIENT)	B(PATIENT	DRUG)
DARWIN	EINSTEIN	EINSTEIN	A17
KELVIN	NEWTON	EINSTEIN	B18
MAXWELL	EINSTEIN	FERMI	S13
DALTON	FERMI	LIEBNITZ	K25

Their join R: = A(PATIENT) * (PATIENT)B is

R(DOCTOR	PATIENT	DRUG)
DARWIN	EINSTEIN	A17
DARWIN	EINSTEIN	B18
MAXWELL	EINSTEIN	A17
MAXWELL	EINSTEIN	B18
DALTON	FERMI	S13

To take another example, the join of STD and CSL, = R: = STD (S#) * (SS) CSL, is

R(S#	SN	AGE	C#	MK)
S1	ADAMS	21	C1	50
S1	ADAMS	21	C3	65
S2	WARD	25	C1	40
S2	WARD	25	C2	70
S2	WARD	25	C3	48
S3	REMUS	20	C1	82
S3	REMUS	20	C2	51
S4	BENN	22	C1	67
S4	BENN	22	C3	77

Figure 6.17

Although relations STD and CSL are in 3NF, their join R is not. Likewise relations A and B are in 3NF but their join is not. We give below examples of more join operations.

Query (4). Find the names and exam marks of the students who took course C1. In a multi-step answer, we may write it as

$$V == CSL : CC = \text{``C1''}$$
$$W == STD (S\#) * (SS)V$$
$$(SN, MK) \% W$$

which the compiler will transform into the following single-step answer (which the user can write directly)

$$(SN, MK) \% STD(S\#) * (SS) CSL : CC = \text{``C1''}$$

According to the precedence rule the selection will be evaluated first. The result of CSL : CC = "C1" is

```
(SS  CC  MK)
 S1  C1  50
 S2  C1  •40
 S3  C1  82
 S4  C1  67
```

This when joined with STD over S# and SS, yields

(S#	SN	AGE	C#	MK)
S1	ADAMS	21	C1	50
S2	WARD	25	C1	40
S3	REMUS	20	C1	82
S4	BENN	22	C1	67

These are really the C1 tuples of figure 6.17. The effect of projecting (SN,MK) is

SN	MK
ADAMS	50
WARD	40
REMUS	82
BENN	67

which is the result.

If we are interested only in student names but not in their marks, then selection can be used in place of join; for example SN % STD(S#) * (SS)CSL : CC = "C1" can be equivalently rewritten as

SN % STD : S# = SS % CSL : CC= "C1"
                inner block

outer block

Selection is possible because we wanted only SN which belongs to STD alone, whereas previously we wanted SN and MK belonging to STD and CSL. Thus *a join is needed whenever resultant columns belong to more than one operand relation.* The join produces a combined relation, from which the desired columns can be extracted. From now on we shall normally use join only when the wanted columns belong to more than one relation, otherwise selection will be used.

The selection shown above is called a *nested* selection (paralleling the nested IF statements of programming languages) where the selection on S# of STD (*outer block*), depends on the selection on CC of CSL (*inner block*). The selection operation can be nested to any arbitrary depth; the precedence of operations in PAL ensures that the right-hand side of any comparison operator in the selection predicate, and hence the inner block, is always evaluated before its left-hand side in the outer block.

Query (5). Find the names and course numbers of students who scored more than 70 in their examinations

$$(SN, C\#) \% STD (S\#) * (SS) CSL : MK > 70$$

The selection will be done before join, with the final result

SN	C#
REMUS	C1
BENN	C3

Query (6). Find the names and marks of students who took computer science

$$(SN, MK) \% STD (S\#) * (SS) CSL : CC = C\# \% CRS : CN = \text{"COMPUTER SCIENCE"}$$

The inner block of selection is first evaluated, yielding C1 as the result. The query then becomes equivalent to $(SN, MK) \% STD(S\#) * (SS)CSL : CC = \text{"C1"}$ which is the same as Query (4). This query looks less daunting if it is broken down by using virtual relations

$$V == CRS : CN = \text{"COMPUTER SCIENCE"}$$
$$W == CSL : CC = C\# \% V$$
$$Z == STD (S\#) * (SS)W$$
$$(SN,MK) \% Z$$

The reader might have observed that the projection operation can be used to decompose a relation and the join operation to recreate the original relation from the decomposed relations. Indeed the whole process of normalisation can be viewed as a series of projections, whose resultant relations can be joined to re-create the original relation. Some examples of the last section are reconsidered below:

$$(B\#, P\#, QB) \% STOCK \Rightarrow STOCK1 (B\# P\# QB)$$
$$(P\#, LT, RL) \% STOCK \Rightarrow STOCK2 (P\# LT RL)$$

STOCK1 (P#) * (P#) STOCK2 ⇒ STOCK (B# P# QB LT RL)
(O#, IC, QO) % CORD2 ⇒ IORD (O# IC QO)
(IC, UP) % CORD2 ⇒ PRICE (IC UP)
IORD (IC) * (IC) PRICE ⇒ CORD2 (O# IC UP QO)
CORD (O#) * (O#) CORD2 ⇒ REL (O# C# NI IC UP QO)

The content of REL above is

REL(O#	C#	NI	IC	UP	QO)
1	241	3	A10	5	10
1	241	3	C13	3	20
1	241	3	P15	7	18
2	250	4	A10	5	15
2	250	4	B16	12	2
2	250	4	B20	8	1
2	250	4	C13	3	5
3	241	2	B16	12	11
3	241	2	B21	2	15

This is the relational equivalent CUSTORD (figure 6.4) but normalised (though not in 3NF), with candidate key (O#, C#, IC).

The correct name of the join operation discussed above is *natural join*, although it is usually called *join*, without the prefix. There are also other forms of joins, one of which is called a *quadratic join* or *Cartesian product*. It is represented here by **
without common columns, where each tuple of the first relation is concatenated with each tuple of the second relation, as shown in figure 6.18 for relations R1 and R2.

R1 (NAME	DEPT)	R2 (DRINK	PRICE)
JOHN	D30	COKE	40
HARRY	K30	PEPSI	50
DON	B10		

R1 ** R2 ⩾ R3 (NAME	DEPT	DRINK	PRICE)
JOHN	D30	COKE	40
JOHN	D30	PEPSI	50
HARRY	K30	COKE	40
HARRY	K30	PEPSI	50
DON	B10	COKE	40
DON	B10	PEPSI	50

Figure 6.18 R3 as the quadratic join of R1 and R2

A quadratic join is useful in queries where every possible combination of tuples of the two relations is required.

One of the problems with a natural join is that it can lose information since the result relation does not contain the unmatched tuples of the operand relations. Such information-losing joins are generically known as *inner joins*. There is another type of join, called *outer join* (Date, 1983), where information is not lost. It operates like a natural join, except that the unmatched tuples are retained in the result relation with null values replacing the missing attribute values. For instance, an outer join of relations A and B (page 157) to be represented as A(PATIENT) *? (PATIENT)B, with common columns inside the brackets, and *? as the symbol for the outer join operation, is

T(DOCTOR	PATIENT	DRUG)
DARWIN	EINSTEIN	A17
DARWIN	EINSTEIN	B18
KELVIN	NEWTON	?
MAXWELL	EINSTEIN	A17
MAXWELL	EINSTEIN	B18
DALTON	FERMI	S13
?	LIEBNITZ	K25

where ? represents null values. Strictly speaking, this is an *outer natural join*, although commonly called an outer join. No information is lost in this join, unlike relation R of page 157. There are queries which require outer joins (Date, 1983).

Division

We may divide a binary relation by a unary relation if the column of the unary relation shares the same domain with a column (referred to as the common column) of the binary relation. The result of such a division is a unary relation containing the other column (that is, the uncommon column) of the binary relation. An attribute value of the uncommon column of the binary relation is selected for the resultant relation if its associated entries in the common column contain all the values of the unary relation. We denote a division R:= B(B1 |B2)/(U1)U where B is the binary relation with B1 as the uncommon and B2 the common column, whereas U is the unary relation with column U1; columns B1 and B2 are separated by | (vertical bar). Now consider a binary relation DT and three unary relations DI, DJ and DK as given in figure 6.19. Dividing DT by DI, DJ and DK, we have

DT (S#|C#)/ (C#) DI ⇒ R(S#)	DT(S#|C#) / (C#)DJ ⇒ R(S#)	DT(S#|C#) / (C#)DK ⇒ R(S#)
S1	S1	S1
S2	S3	
S3		

DT(S#	C#)	DI(C#)	DJ(C#)	DK(C#)
S1	C1	C1	C1	C1
S1	C2		C2	C2
S1	C3			C3
S1	C4			
S2	C1			
S2	C3			
S2	C4			
S3	C1			
S3	C2			

Figure 6.19

The advantage of the explicit inclusion of column names in the division notation is that, if the relations have other columns not participating in the division process, then those other columns would be ignored in the division. For example

CSL (SS⏐CC) / (C#)CRS

will be equivalent to the projection of (SS, CC) from CSL and C# from CRS before the division is carried out. The projections are

(SS	CC)	and	(C#)
S1	C1		C1
S1	C3		C2
S2	C1		C3
S2	C2		
S2	C3		
S3	C1		
S3	C2		
S4	C1		
S4	C3		

The result of the division is S2. The user of course can use projections explicitly before the division if he wishes to.

Division is most profitably used to answer questions like 'find the student numbers of the students who took *all* the courses'. This 'all' is sometimes referred to as the *universal quantifier* (see section 6.3.2). The division CSL (SS⏐CC) / (C#) CRS does just that.

Query (7). Find the names of the students who took *all* the courses

SN % STD : S# = SS % CSL (SS⏐CC) / (C#)CRS

The result is

SN
WARD

Query (8). Find the names of the students who took *all* the courses C1, C2 and C3

SN % STD : S# = SS % CSL (SS I CC) / ("C1", "C2", "C3")

"C1", "C2", "C3" are treated as three tuples of a unary relation. Alternatively this query can be formulated by intersection operations, by first creating one temporary relation for each course and then intersecting them as shown below.

R1:= SN % STD : S# = SS % CSL : CC = "C1"
R2:= SN % STD : S# = SS % CSL : CC = "C2"
R3:= SN % STD : S# = SS % CSL : CC = "C3"
R:= R ! R2 ! R3

Obviously the intersection operation is clumsy and long-winded. It will be very difficult to answer Query (7) by an intersection operation. Both Queries (7) and (8) are 'all' type query, asking for only those students who took all the courses available, not just any course. In such cases the division operation is preferable to the intersection operation. We summarise below the usage of operators:

- Use selection whenever possible
- Use join only when the wanted attributes belong to more than one relation
- Use division in 'all' type queries
- Use projection sparingly

A further discussion on efficiency is given in chapter 8. A number of other relational operations have also been defined by Codd, but those given here are commonly used. The above examples show the power of a relational algebra; however, in general, the construction of algebraic expressions can sometimes be tedious even if the technique can be learnt quickly. The relational calculus is meant to be easier.

6.3.2 Relational calculus

In a relational algebra the user specifies the detailed operations for extracting information, whereas in Codd's relational calculus the user defines what he wants, and leaves it to the system to work out the operations required. The expression of this relational calculus has two parts, a target list which consists of a list of the wanted elements separated by commas and a predicate which qualifies the wanted elements. It is written in the form

Target list: Predicate

to be interpreted as: extract the elements in the target list where (or such that) the predicate is true. The target list may contain relation name or a list of attribute names in the form R.A for attribute A of relation R.

The following notations are used in constructing a predicate

> $\exists$ there exists (a tuple) (existential quantifier)
> $\forall$ for all (tuples) (universal quantifier)
> $\neg$ logical NOT
> $\wedge$ logical AND
> $\vee$ logical OR

along with standard comparison symbols, as in PAL.

The quantifiers $\exists$ and $\forall$ are used for relations which are in the predicate but not in the target list. We shall now construct relational calculus expressions for some queries including those expressed earlier in relational algebra.

Query (1). Extract the tuple containing information on WARD (from the relations on figure 6.13)

$$STD : STD.SN = \{\text{"WARD"}\}$$

Query (2). Find the names of the students who scored more than 70 in their course examination

$$STD.SN : \exists \, CSL \, (CSL.SS = STD.S\# \wedge CSL.MK > 70)$$

This is to be read as: extract the column SN of relation STD such that relation CSL has a common column SS with S# of relation STD and has a column MK with a value greater than 70. The presence of the existential qualifier $\exists$ can be viewed as: given an STD tuple, does *there exist* a CSL tuple such that its SS value is equal to the S# value of that STD tuple and its MK > 70? If the answer is yes (true), then extract SN value of the STD tuple. If the answer is no (false), do not extract the SN value. This question is repeated for each STD tuple, until all STD tuples are processed.

Query (3). Find the names of the students who took the course COMPUTER SCIENCE

$$STD.SN : \exists \, CSL \, \exists \, CRS(CSL.SS = STD.S\# \wedge CSL.CC = CRS.C\# \wedge CRS.CN = \{\text{"COMPUTER SCIENCE"}\})$$

Query (4). Find the student numbers of the students who took *all* the courses

$$CSL.SS : \, \forall \, CRS \, (CSL.CC = CRS.C\#)$$

Universal quantifier $\forall$ refers to all the courses. The query says: given a set of CSL tuples with the same SS value, if the condition CSL.CC = CRS.C#

is satisfied for *all* CRS tuples, then retrieve that SS value. The query is repeated for each set of CSL tuples with different SS value. If we replace $\forall$ by $\exists$ and rewrite the query as

$$\text{CLS.SS} : \exists \text{ CRS (CSL.CC = CRS.C\#)}$$

it will be equivalent to finding every student who has taken *any* course, rather than *all* the courses. Therefore the distinction between $\forall$ and $\exists$ is very important. In a relational algebra where such symbols are not used, the operation with universal quantifier is replaced by division, and those with existential quantifier are replaced by join and selection, as appropriate.

Query (5). Find the names of the students who took all the courses

$$\text{STD.SN} : \forall \text{ CRS } \exists \text{ CSL (CRS.C\# = CSL.CC } \wedge \text{ CSL.SS = STD.S\#)}$$

The symbol $\forall$ again refers to *all* the courses. It, along with $\exists$, can be viewed as: given an STD tuple, does there exist a CSL tuple whose SS value is equal to the S# value of that STD tuple and whose CC value is equal to the C# value of a CRS tuple? If the answer is yes and holds for *all* CRS tuples, given the same STD tuple, then extract the SN value of that STD tuple.

Note that any relation not in the target list must be quantified in the predicate with symbol $\exists$ or $\forall$ as appropriate. The relations in the predicate, which must include the target relation(s), are linked together through common columns, each link being expressed by an equality sign between two column names; therefore they may be assumed to be *joined* together on those common columns. The predicate may include other conditions that specify the characteristics of some columns or tuples of the relations in the predicate.

6.3.3 Data sub-language Alpha

DSL Alpha (Codd, 1971b) as noted earlier, is directly based on the relational calculus. An Alpha command has the following structure:

Command   Workspace name   (Target list) :   Predicate

The workspace is a user-defined working relation with appropriate attributes. The target list and the predicates are formed exactly the same way as in relational calculus, except that a few additional facilities can be included in the form of qualifiers on predicates or library functions (see later). The following commands have been proposed:

GET   Construct the defined relation in a workspace from the database.
PUT   Insert tuples into the database from the workspace.
DELETE Delete all the tuples of a relation from the database, but retain its entry in the database directory.

DROP   Drop all information about this relation from the database including its entry in the directory.

UPDATE   Modify a relation or a tuple of the database to reflect the changes already made in the workspace.

HOLD   Warning to the system for concurrent users that a relation or a tuple will be modified.

RELEASE   Cancellation of HOLD.

OPEN   Begin transmission of one tuple at a time rather than a whole relation at a time.

CLOSE   Close transmission of tuples (terminates OPEN).

We shall consider a few examples of the use of DSL Alpha using a workspace WS, which we assume is appropriately defined by the user.

Retrieve relation STD (figure 6.13) from the database to the workspace

$$\text{GET WS (STD)}$$

The result would be all the tuples of relation STD. The user can also retrieve only the selected attribute in a given order; for instance he may specify

$$\text{GET WS (STD.SN, STD.S\#)}$$

which will retrieve only the columns SN and S# in that order.

Queries (1) to (5) of the relational calculus, discussed earlier, can be formulated in DSL Alpha by adding just GET WS before those calculus expressions and by enclosing their target lists in brackets ( ).

A relation already retrieved can be amended by using HOLD and UPDATE commands; for example

> HOLD WS (STD.AGE) : STD.SN = {"BENN"}
> Add say 2 to AGE by a host language statement, and then
> UPDATE WS

Qualifiers on predicate

Information can be extracted in ascending or descending order of selected attribute values by specifying an UP or DOWN qualifier in the predicate; for example, to get the names of the students who got more than 45 marks in course C1 in ascending order of their age

$$\text{GET WS(STD.SN)} : \exists \text{ CSL(CSL.SS = STD.SC} \wedge \text{CSL.C\# = \{"C1"\}} \wedge \text{CSL.MK} > 45) \text{ UP STD.AGE}$$

Library functions

The following library functions are proposed for DSL Alpha:

COUNT   – to count the number of tuples

TOTAL   — to sum the values of an attribute

MAX ⎫
MIN ⎭   — to find the maximum or minimum value of an attribute

AVERAGE — to find the average of the values of an attribute

TOP (N,A) ⎫

             — logical variable set up to indicate whether a specific value of an
BOTTOM   attribute A is the Nth largest or Nth smallest
(N,A) ⎭

We take here a few examples:

(i) Find the number of students in relation STD

$$\text{GET WS(COUNT(STD.S\#))}$$

(ii) Find the total marks obtained from relation CSL

$$\text{GET WS(TOTAL(CSL.MK))}$$

Tuple variable

In many languages, such as Cobol, the record name is used as a variable
to hold a record occurrence during the processing. For instance, for a record
name EMP-REC in Cobol, we would write: MOVE SPACES TO EMP-REC,
or READ EMP-REC, thus using record name as a record variable. Analogously,
we also use relation name as tuple variable, that is, to hold a tuple of that
relation. We have done this in all the relational queries given earlier. However,
in DSL Alpha it is possible to declare one or more variables, in addition to the
relation name, as tuple variables of the relation. This is done by a so-called
Range declaration, with one entry for each tuple variable, called range variable.
For instance

$$\text{RANGE STD R}$$
$$\text{GET WS (R.SN, R.S\#)}$$

where R is a range variable which ranges over the tuples of STD, that is, R holds
one tuple of STD at a time. The compiler will automatically define appropriate
attributes for R. However, the same variable R can be used in another query by
another RANGE declaration for another relation (irrespective of the number of
attributes that relation has); but until another RANGE declaration is encountered,
R above will legally accept only the tuples of STD. In DSL Alpha, a range variable
can be used as an alias (say to shorten a long relation name) or to provide a reference to a second tuple of the same relation, as done by the label declaration in
SQL (section 8.1). In QUEL, presented in the next subsection, only range variables
and not relation names are permitted as legal tuple variables.

6.3.4 QUEL

QUEL (Query Language) was implemented by Stonebraker *et al.* (1976) for INGRES relational database systems (see also chapter 13). In design, it is close to DSL Alpha, with some of the unfriendly aspects removed. We offer here a brief overview of this language.

QUEL allows four commands – RETRIEVE, REPLACE, DELETE and APPEND – with the following structure

COMMAND result-name (Target list) WHERE condition

Result-name is the equivalent of workspace in Alpha, and can be the screen. QUEL does not use any existential or universal quantifiers, but all queries are assumed to be existentially quantified. As noted earlier, relation names are not allowed as tuple variables which must be declared by a RANGE declaration. Below, we shall first show the QUEL equivalents of Queries 1 to 4 of relational calculus, assuming WS to be the user-defined workspace – where the result is saved.

Query (1).

> RANGE OF S IS STD
> RETRIEVE INTO WS (S.S#, S.SN, S.AGE) WHERE S.SN = 'WARD'

QUEL does not seem to allow tuple as a default unit of retrieval, and hence attribute names are listed in this query.

Query (2).

> RANGE OF S IS STD
> RANGE OF L IS CSL
> RETRIEVE INTO WS (S.SN) WHERE L.SS = S.S#
>   AND L.MK > 70

Query (3).

> RANGE OF S IS STD
> RANGE OF L IS CSL
> RANGE OF C IS CRS
> RETRIEVE INTO WS (S.SN) WHERE L.SS = S.S#
>   AND L.CC = C.C# AND
>   C.CN = 'COMPUTER SCIENCE'

'INTO workspace' in the above queries is an option which is used to save the result into the named workspace. If it is omitted the result is displayed at the terminal, and not saved. The duplicate tuples are removed from the result only if the INTO option is used.

Query (4).

Since QUEL does not use any universal quantifier, queries involving 'all' can be formulated only indirectly, for instance, by using a COUNT function and negation. The query to find the student numbers of the students who took *all* the courses can be equivalently (if tortuously) restated as: find the student number of each student where the number of courses *not taken by the student is zero* (that is, he has taken all the courses). This query is expressed as

> RANGE OF C IS CRS
> RANGE OF L IS CSL
> RETRIEVE INTO WS (L.SS) WHERE COUNT (L.CC WHERE
> NOT (L.CC = C.C#)) = 0

Some other examples

Delete the tuple on student S1 from STD

> RANGE OF S IS STD
> DELETE S WHERE S.S# = 'S1'

Increase the maximum number of students allowed in course C1 by 10 per cent

> RANGE OF C IS CRS
> REPLACE C (MX = 1.1 * MX) WHERE C.C# = 'C1'

To increase the value by, say 10, we would write MX = MX + 10 instead of MX = 1.1 * MX above. To insert a new student in STD (with values as given)

> APPEND STD (S# = 'S5', SN = 'JONES', AGE = 21)

In DELETE and REPLACE the result-name must be a tuple variable, whereas in APPEND it must be the name of the relation. As in DSL Alpha, QUEL also supports a number of functions, such as COUNT, SUM, AVG, MIN and MAX. The expressions given above demonstrate the closeness of DSL Alpha and QUEL. In execution, a QUEL query is optimally decomposed by the system into a set of simpler queries (however, its earlier versions are less efficient compared to SQL (section 8.1)). The language also supports some integrity constraints.

6.4 Implementation issues

The relational model provides a technique to describe data logically along with a set of powerful high level languages to manipulate the data, but without specifying any architecture or storage strategy. As such the model can be viewed at two levels: firstly as a relational language facility with a relational external schema on the top of other data models, and secondly as an independent data model with an implementor-defined architecture and attendant facilities. The first is sometimes referred to as a relational interface or a relational view, and has been implemented on the top of the Codasyl model (Mercz, 1979; Zaniolo, 1979). Implementation there must address two issues

(i) Mapping of a relational external schema on the databases schema of the supporting model

(ii) Mapping of the relevant relational language on the DM commands of the underlying model.

The performance efficiency of a relational interface depends on the mapping efficiency and also on the performance efficiency of the underlying DBCS. Some of the 'interfacing' issues will be considered in section 11.3.4. Here we wish to concentrate on the second issue — implementation as an independent model, which we shall assume to be based on ANSI/SPARC 3-level schemas.

6.4.1 Architectural issues

We have shown earlier (section 6.2.4) that the relational model can be made to support entity records and associations for a conceptual schema. However the original model did not include any technique for privacy and integrity assertions and although subsequent research has produced some effective constructs, there is no single coherent specification which can be described as *the* relational approach. Privacy constraints as developed for SYSTEM R (see section 8.1) are very powerful, but integrity constraints are less satisfactory. Basically, integrity constraints are specified in the form of a predicate against selected columns.

Since the relational model does not specify any storage schema, such a schema is implementor-defined, along with its associated facilities such as data placement, overflow management, primary and secondary keys, pointers and indexes. An efficient implementation matching the power of a relational language requires a solution of a series of problems related to optimisation. Some of these have been mentioned earlier, and will be discussed further in chapter 8.

While the original relational model made no distinction between a conceptual schema and an external schema, the more recent works have produced some application facilities, usually known as 'views'; we shall encounter them in chapter 8. One particular attraction of the relation model is the data independence it provides by separating relations and relational languages from the storage structures. Although the purity of such concepts was later enshrined in the ANSI/SPARC model by specifying separate conceptual and external schemas, the relational model started it.

6.4.2 Supporting facilities

None of the functional issues discussed in the previous chapter has been specified for the relational model. It is therefore meaningless to say whether the relational model provides data protection, concurrency control, data modification or a data dictionary facility. They are entirely implementation dependent. It is, however, sometimes argued that the restructuring of the conceptual schema would be easier in the relational model owing to the inherently simpler structure of relations. A relation can be easily split into several relations, and conversely several relations can be easily restructured into one. This decomposition/recomposition is certainly easier in the relational model, but the restructuring of the conceptual schema is only the first, perhaps the easiest, step in the total process of restructuring and reorganisation. Other factors such as the facilities of the storage schema could be more important.

6.4.3 Remarks

The early expectation of the relational model was very high, some believing it to be the last word on data modelling. There were many anguished debates on the relative merits of the relational and the network models, each side with its band of the faithful, usually with the researchers favouring the relational model. These debates have clarified some of the underlying issues and have resulted in a greater understanding of the problems in data modelling.

Part of the early expectation was also based on naivety. Many were dazzled by the power of the relational languages and the crispness of the third normal form (the fourth and the fifth forms came later), and believed the days of messy keys, pointers and indexes were over. It is like being mesmerised by the elegance of a swan swimming gracefully over the calm water, without realising the existence of an ugly pair of feet paddling furiously underneath to maintain that elegance. Once people started implementing relational prototypes, the ugly feet appeared in the form of those messy keys, pointers and indexes, which the DBA still has to worry about just as in other models. The magic spell was broken.

Let us not, however, minimise the importance of the relational model. If as a data model it turned out to be less than perfect (see also section 14.1.4), it is still an outstanding model; its contributions, particularly as the initiator of new ideas and as the carrier of new research, are unparalleled. We list some of them:

- it showed for the first time that data modelling can be based on a sound theoretical framework rather than only on *ad hoc* hunches
- it gave impetus to research on the whole area of data modelling, including some on integrity and privacy constraints
- it provided an important tool for data analysis in the form of third and subsequent normal forms

- it opened up a whole range of research on non-procedural languages and 'view' facilities
- it paved the way for research in query optimisation and access path optimisation
- it emphasised the need for data independence by separating the logical data description from the access-efficiency related concepts
- it has provided a basis for a standard data structure and language, as needed in distributed databases for intermodel data conversion and communication

Many of these points will be further examined later in this book, particularly in chapters 7, 8, 11 and 12.

Exercises

6.1   Explain, with examples, the following relational concepts:

    (a) Intension and extension
    (b) Entity integrity and referential integrity
    (c) Primary, candidate and foreign keys
    (d) Attribute, column and domain.

6.2   Explain, with examples, the concepts of full functional dependency and determinants, and discuss their roles in the normalisation theory. Can you define the third normal forms without them, and if so, how?

6.3   Normalisation is a reversible process in which no information is lost during the transformation. Starting with an unnormalised relation, show that the higher normal forms are produced by projection, and the original relation can be obtained by a suitable join of the projected relations.

6.4   "It is not possible for a system to ensure that any input relation is in 3NF." Discuss the reasons and state why relational queries do not require relations in 3NF. Also assess the impact of 3NF on data analysis.

6.5   "Normalisation is an aid to capturing the semantics of the real world." Illustrate and justify the process of obtaining a set of relations in third normal form from the relation R represented below, and outline the advantages of the method.

RELATION R

ENO	SECTION	NI	CNO	TOPIC	SHN
			Course attended		
628	1432	YH947621A	B28	Welding	628
719	872	HL954327A	B28	Welding	833
			A43	Fitting	
			A47	Plumbing	
833	872	ZR618946A	A43	Fitting	833

ENO	SECTION	NI	Course attended		SHN
			CNO	TOPIC	
941	1432	YL249164A	B28	Welding	628
			A37	Carpentry	

where ENO is employee number, NI National Insurance number, CNO course number and SHN section head number. Each section has only one head.

6.6 Describe with an example, how an $m:n$ loop can be represented in a relational model.

6.7 Explain, with examples, the following four relational operations:

> Selection
> Projection
> Division
> Join

Also show their use in relational query expressions, with one example for each. You may use the following relations in your examples. (Primary keys are underlined)

> STUDENT (<u>SNO</u> SNAME AGE DNO)
> COURSE (<u>CNO</u> CNAME)
> LINK (<u>CNO</u> SNO)
> DEPT (<u>DNO</u> DNAME)

6.8 Given below are four relations used by a library information system:

> BOOK (<u>B#</u> BN A#)   for all the books of a library
> LOAN (<u>B#</u> R#)   for all the books on loan to the readers
> AUTHOR (<u>A#</u> AN)   for the authors of the books
> READER (<u>R#</u> RN)   for the readers of the library

where B# is book number,   BN book name
       R# is reader number,   RN reader name
       A# is author number,   AN author name.

Answer the following four queries using PAL, DSL Alpha and QUEL.

(i) What are the names of the books written by Dickens?

(ii) What are the names of the Dickens' books on loan?

(iii) Where are the names of the readers who have borrowed Dickens' books?

(iv) What are the book numbers of the books not on loan?

6.9 Given below are three relations, with primary keys underlined

> DEPT (<u>DNO</u> HDN DNAME BUDGET)
> TUTOR (<u>TNO</u> HNO TNAME SAL)
> STUDENT (<u>SNO</u> SNAME SDN REGENT AGE)

where DNO is the department number and both HDN and HNO are the tutor number of the head of the department. The head of the department also acts as a tutor whose head is himself. A student's department number is given by SDN, each student having a regent with tutor number held in REGENT. Answer the following queries using PAL and QUEL.

(i) What are the student numbers of the students over 21 who are looked after by a regent named Smith or Murray?

(ii) What are the student numbers of the students looked after by regents who are not heads of departments?

(iii) What is the student number of each student whose regent belongs to his (student's) own department? (This is a cyclic query; note its difference from the query below.)

(iv) What is the student number of each student whose regent belongs to any student's department (assuming that there are departments without students)?

(v) What are the names of the physics tutors who are not regents?

References

Codd, E. F. (1970). A relational model of data for large shared data banks. *Communications of the ACM*, Vol. (13:6), June

Codd, E. F. (1971a). Further normalisation of the database relational model. *IBM Research Report RJ909*, August

Codd, E. F. (1971b). A database sublanguage founded on the relational calculus. *IBM Research Report RJ893*, July

Codd, E. F. (1974). Recent investigations in relational database systems. *Proceedings of the 1974 IFIP Congress*, North-Holland, p. 1017

Date, C. J. (1981). *Introduction to Database Systems. Vol. 1*, 3rd edition, Addison-Wesley

Date, C. J. (1983). The outer join. *Proceedings of ICOD-2*, edited by S. M. Deen and P. Hammersley, Wiley, p. 76

Deen, S. M. *et al.* (1981). Design of a canonical database system (PRECI). *Computer Journal*, Vol. (24:3), August

Deen, S. M. *et al.* (1985). Data integration in distributed databases. Department of Computing Science, University of Aberdeen, Aberdeen (to be published)

Mercz, I. (1979). Issues in building a relational interface on a Codasyl DBMS. *Data Base Architecture*, edited by G. Bracchi and G. M. Nijssen, North-Holland, p. 191

Robinson, K. (1978). *The Computer Weekly*

Sharman, G. C. H. (1975). *Technical Report TR12.136*, IBM Laboratory, Hursley, Winchester

Stonebraker, M. R. *et al*. (1976). Design and Implementation INGRES. *ACM TODS*, Vol. (1:3), September

Zaniolo, C. (1979). Design of relational views over network schemas. *Proceedings ACM SIGMOD Conference* 1979

7 Higher Normal Forms

Although relational languages do not require higher normal forms, they are nevertheless useful as tools for analysis of data and for the imposition of constraints which protect data from some update anomalies. As the first to the third normal forms have been covered before, we shall devote this chapter to the other normal forms, in particular the fourth normal form. We shall also attempt to answer questions such as "is there an ultimate normal form?" and make some comments on the practical usefulness of some of the more exotic theoretical work on normalisation.

7.1 Fourth normal form (4NF)

As we stated in section 6.2.1, normalisation requires the isolation of repeating groups of an unnormalised relation into a separate relation. The question is: should we really make a single relation for all the repeating groups, or should we make a separate relation for each repeating group? The correct answer to this question depends on the nature of a repeating group. If it is what is called an *independent* repeating group, then it must be separated into another relation. In some cases the third normal form forces such independent repeating groups into separate relations but, in others, a further normalisation in the form of fourth normal form is needed. R. Fagin at IBM (Fagin, 1977) and C. Zaniolo at the University of California discovered fourth normal form independently, although Fagin's comprehensive paper (Fagin, 1977), rather than Zaniolo's Ph.D. thesis, is usually quoted in this connection.

The definition and use of 4NF is quite straightforward. However, for a clearer understanding we shall first explain what we mean by *independent* repeating groups and the conditions where 3NF can remove them.

7.1.1 Independent implied repeating groups

Let us consider an unnormalised relation containing employee name, a repeating group of his children's names and a repeating group of his projects. We assume the employee name and children names to be unique, and a child not to have both parents among the employees. The children's names and projects are repeating groups, but they are independent of each other since we assume that the projects on which the employee works do not depend on his children, and vice versa. This relation in normalised form is shown in figure 7.1.

ECP (EMP	CHILD	PROJ)
ROSS	PAUL	PJ1
ROSS	PAUL	PJ4
KENT	SALLY	PJ1
KENT	SALLY	PJ6
KENT	AMY	PJ1
KENT	AMY	PJ6
HARDY	JACK	PJ4
HARDY	JILL	PJ4

Figure 7.1

We shall call the columns CHILD and PROJ *independent implied repeating groups* (IIRG) because they are independent of each other, and because they represent repeating groups of the original unnormalised relation. Another way of looking at it is that, given an employee, all the possible pairs of his child and project appear. This means the pairings do not contain any 'information'; they would carry information only if some pairings can be absent, that is, if an employee with a particular child cannot work in some projects. Since this is not so, child and project are independent of each other. It is quite obvious that this relation has considerable redundancy which leads to update anomalies. Here employees and children have a $1:n$ relationship (whereas employees and projects have an $m:n$ relationship).

Since child names are unique, CHILD → EMP, and therefore CHILD should be a candidate key according to 3NF, but this is not so. Therefore, relation ECP is not in 3NF; we may resolve ECP into relations EC and EP as shown in figure 7.2.

EC (EMP	CHILD)	EP (EMP	PROJ)
ROSS	PAUL	ROSS	PJ1
KENT	SALLY	ROSS	PJ4
KENT	AMY	KENT	PJ1
HARDY	JACK	KENT	PJ2
HARDY	JILL	HARDY	PJ4

Figure 7.2

As against an independent implied repeating group, there are also dependent implied repeating groups. Consider an unnormalised relation containing for each customer

Customer number (C#), the set of his order numbers (O#), the set of item codes (IC) in each order number)

We can represent them by a relation, say SALES, as shown in figure 7.3. Each customer has a repeating group of his orders, each order being made up of a repeating group of item codes. Therefore, order number and item code for a given customer number are *not* independent of each other (that is, all possible combinations of (O#, IC) pairings do not occur). The only determinant is (C#, O#, IC) which is the candidate key. (Note that, although O# and IC are dependent on each other, their ordering (that is, their relative position) is immaterial; for instance, we could have written the relation as SALES (IC O# C#) without any loss of information.)

SALES (C#	O#	IC)
250	11	P10
250	11	P15
250	15	P10
250	15	P60
380	11	P10
380	12	P30
380	12	P60

Figure 7.3

7.1.2 Definition and application of 4NF

We have explained above the concept of IIRG, and shown that in some cases 3NF forces such an IIRG into a separate relation. However, there are other cases where a relation with an IIRG can be in 3NF. In those cases a 4NF is needed, as discussed here.

In relation ECP, employees and children have $1:n$ relationships; if this was not so, CHILD could not have been the determinant of EMP, and relation ECP would have been in 3NF. To see this, let us consider a slightly different relation EHP, where the children's column is replaced by a column of hobbies (HOB), as shown in figure 7.4. We assume the following:

(a) Each employee can have many hobbies and the same hobby can be taken up by many employees; that is, the relationship between employees and hobbies is many to many. Unlike CHILD → EMP in relation ECP, here HOB ↦ EMP (owing to the $m:n$ relationship).

(b) Each employee can have many projects and many employees can work in the same project; that is, the relationship between employees and projects is also many to many.

(c) The hobbies of an employee have no bearing on the projects in which he works, that is, hobbies and projects are independent of each other.

```
EHP  (EMP              HOB              PROJ)
       ROSS            CHESS            PJ1
       ROSS            CHESS            PJ4
       ROSS            GO               PJ1
       ROSS            GO               PJ4
       KENT            BRIDGE           PJ1
       KENT            BRIDGE           PJ6
       HARDY           CHESS            PJ4
       HARDY           BRIDGE           PJ4
```

Figure 7.4 Candidate key is (EMP HOB PROJ) and hence the relation is in 3NF

Because of the presence of many to many relationships between employees and hobbies, and between employees and projects, none of these attributes are determinants. The single determinant of this relation is (EMP HOB PROJ) which is the candidate key, and hence EHP is in 3NF. Nevertheless the relation is littered with redundancies which cause update anomalies. Information about an employee's project will be lost if he does not have a hobby or if he gives up his previous hobby (the reader may recall that we are not allowed to have null values for any part of a primary key). Likewise, information on the hobbies of an employee will be lost if he does not have a project. Owing to redundancy, the amendment of hobbies and projects will also be cumbersome. As we shall soon see, this relation is not in 4NF; we may remove these anomalies by decomposing the relation into two others EH and EP, as shown in figure 7.5.

```
EH  (EMP         HOB)        EP  (EMP          PROJ)
      ROSS       CHESS             ROSS        PJ1
      ROSS       GO                ROSS        PJ4
      KENT       BRIDGE            KENT        PJ1
      HARDY      CHESS             KENT        PJ6
      HARDY      BRIDGE            HARDY       PJ4
```

Figure 7.5 Relations in 4NF. Relation EP is identical with its namesake in figure 7.2

We shall give below two definitions of 4NF, the first definition is based on the foregoing discussion and can be stated as follows.

Definition 1

A relation in third normal form is in fourth normal form if it does not contain any implied repeating group *that is independent of other attributes of the relation.*

According to this definition, relations ECP and EHP are not in 4NF, and hence they must be decomposed as done earlier. Relation SALES is in 4NF.

We shall develop below the second definition, based on the concept of *multi-determinant* which is a generalised version of *determinant*. If we examine relation EHP closely we find that, although an employee does not determine (that is, uniquely identify) a hobby, he nevertheless determines completely a set of hobbies *independently of projects*; that is, an employee *multidetermines* hobbies (independently of projects), to be denoted as EMP $\rightarrow \rightarrow$ HOB. So we say, employee is a *multideterminant* of hobbies. Conversely, we can say that HOB is *multi-valued dependent on EMP*. Likewise *EMP is also a multideterminant of PROJ*, that is, EMP $\rightarrow \rightarrow$ PROJ (independently of hobbies this time). Returning to relation ECP, we again find EMP $\rightarrow \rightarrow$ CHILD, EMP $\rightarrow \rightarrow$ PROJ; however, the converse is not true, that is, CHILD (or PROJ) does *not* multidetermine EMP, since EMP and PROJ (or CHILD) are not independent of each other. Similarly in relation EHP, HOB (or PROJ) does not multidetermine EMP. The essential condition of multi-valued dependency is

> Attribute A is a multideterminant of attribute B in presence of attribute C if each A-value can act as a unique identifier of a set of B-values independently of the values of C in the relation.

Observe that if A $\rightarrow \rightarrow$ B independently of C, then A and C are not independent of each other (all possible pairings do not occur), and hence the converse B $\rightarrow \rightarrow$ A independently of C cannot hold. Whenever we say A $\rightarrow \rightarrow$ B we shall mean that there is at least another attribute C present in the relation where B and C are independent of each other, although we may not always mention C explicitly. Attributes A, B and C can be composite and the set of B-values identified by an A-value could overlap with other such sets. For instance, in relation EHP, the set of hobbies identified by an employee overlaps with the similar hobby sets of other employees, because of the *m:n* relationship between EMP and HOB; but in relation ECP where EMP $\rightarrow \rightarrow$ CHILD, the children's names do not overlap, because of the 1:*n* relationship between employees and children. Therefore, the definition of multideterminant A $\rightarrow \rightarrow$ B holds, irrespective of whether A and B have 1:*n* or *m:n* relationships.

If the set identified in B is single-valued, which it can be, then each A-value identifies a single B-value; that is, A becomes a determinant of B (A $\rightarrow$ B) or equivalently B becomes fully functionally dependent on A. Therefore, full functional dependency is a special case of multi-valued dependency. If A is a determinant of B, A is also a multideterminant of B, to be expressed as

$$\text{if } A \rightarrow B, \text{ then } A \rightarrow \rightarrow B$$

but the converse is not necessarily true. In relation EHP, if each employee is allowed to have only one hobby (or only one project), then EMP $\rightarrow$ HOB (or EMP $\rightarrow$ PROJ) as a special case of multi-valued dependency. However, in relations ECP and EHP we have the following dependencies (independent of the third attribute):

$$\text{Relation ECP: EMP} \rightarrow \rightarrow \text{CHILD (but EMP} \nrightarrow \text{CHILD)}$$
$$\text{CHILD} \rightarrow \rightarrow \text{EMP (also CHILD} \rightarrow \text{EMP)}$$

$$\begin{array}{ll}
\text{EMP} \rightarrow\rightarrow \text{PROJ} & (\text{but EMP} \nrightarrow \text{PROJ}) \\
\text{PROJ} \rightarrow\rightarrow \text{EMP} & (\text{but PROJ} \nrightarrow \text{EMP}) \\
\text{Relation EHP: EMP} \rightarrow\rightarrow \text{HOB} & (\text{but EMP} \nrightarrow \text{HOB}) \\
\text{HOB} \rightarrow\rightarrow \text{EMP} & (\text{but HOB} \nrightarrow \text{EMP}) \\
\text{EMP} \rightarrow\rightarrow \text{PROJ} & (\text{but EMP} \nrightarrow \text{PROJ}) \\
\text{PROJ} \rightarrow\rightarrow \text{EMP} & (\text{but PROJ} \nrightarrow \text{EMP})
\end{array}$$

We give below the alternative definition of 4NF.

Definition 2

A relation is in fourth normal form if every multideterminant is a candidate key.

This definition is a simple extension of Sharman's definition of 3NF (Deen, 1980). It allows a direct application of 4NF without requiring 2NF or 3NF as intermediary. We shall give below some examples of its use.

In relation EHP, EMP $\rightarrow\rightarrow$ HOB but EMP is not a candidate key, and hence EHP is not in 4NF. We decompose it to EH and EP which are binary relations and are in 4NF (see later). In relation ECP, EMP $\rightarrow\rightarrow$ CHILD, but EMP is not a candidate key. We resolve it into EC and EP as in figure 7.2. In relation SALES, O# and IC are *not* independent of each other; a customer number cannot identify a set of item codes without their order numbers. There is no multideterminant which is not the candidate key. Hence its relation SALES is in 4NF.

To convince the reader that we do not need to concern ourselves with second and third normal forms any longer, we shall apply the definitions of 4NF to some of the relations of section 6.2. Note that if A $\rightarrow$ B, then A $\rightarrow\rightarrow$ B. In relation CORD2, of figure 6.2, IC $\rightarrow\rightarrow$ UP which is independent of other attributes there (since IC $\rightarrow$ UP), but IC is not a candidate key; we therefore resolve CORD2 into IORD and PRICE of figure 6.7. In relation EMPLOYEE (figure 6.6), E# $\rightarrow\rightarrow$ S#, E# $\rightarrow\rightarrow$ EN, S# $\rightarrow\rightarrow$ E#, S# $\rightarrow\rightarrow$ EN, but both E# and S# are candidate keys and hence relation EMPLOYEE is in 4NF. (The third attribute in each of the multi-valued dependencies is obvious.) In relation STOCK of figure 6.8, P# $\rightarrow\rightarrow$ LT (and also RL), but P# is not a candidate key, and therefore we resolve it into STOCK1 and STOCK2. In relation ADVICE (figure 6.10) EN $\rightarrow\rightarrow$ SN and hence it must be resolved, as is done in figure 6.11.

Although there are two independent implied repeating groups in both relations EHP and ECP, these relations would violate the constraints of 4NF, even if the second repeating group becomes non-repeating. Let us assume that an employee in EHP is allowed only one project, as shown in relation EHP1 (figure 7.6).

According to the first definition of 4NF, HOB is an implied repeating group that is independent of PROJ, and hence EHP1 is not in 4NF. According to the second definition of 4NF, EMP multidetermines HOB which is independent of PROJ, but EMP is not a candidate key, and hence relation EHP1 must be resolved into EH1 (EMP, HOB) and EP1 (EMP, PROJ) as shown in figure 7.7.

EHP	(EMP	HOB	PROJ)
	ROSS	CHESS	PJ1
	ROSS	GO	PJ1
	KENT	BRIDGE	PJ1
	HARDY	CHESS	PJ4
	HARDY	BRIDGE	PJ4

Figure 7.6

EH1	(EMP	HOB)	EP1	(EMP	PROJ)
	ROSS	CHESS		ROSS	PJ1
	ROSS	GO		KENT	PJ1
	KENT	BRIDGE		HARDY	PJ4
	HARDY	CHESS			
	HARDY	BRIDGE			

Figure 7.7

However, if we assume that an employee is allowed only one hobby and only one project, as shown in relation EHP2 (figure 7.8) then this relation is in 4NF, since EMP $\rightarrow \rightarrow$ HOB, EMP $\rightarrow \rightarrow$ PROJ, and EMP is a candidate key. In other words, neither HOB nor PROJ are implied repeating groups. Therefore, more than one independent attribute can appear in the same relation in 4NF, as long as none is an IIRG.

EHP2	(EMP	HOB	PROJ)
	ROSS	CHESS	PJ1
	KENT	BRIDGE	PJ1
	HARDY	CHESS	PJ4

Figure 7.8

7.1.3 Side effects of 4NF

In the definition of multideterminant, and of 4NF, we have implicitly assumed a relation to have at least three attributes. Since a binary relation has only two attributes, it is treated as a special case. A binary relation is always assumed to be in 4NF unless it is a quadratic join of two unary relations. Fagin (1977) has given a mathematical explanation of this special case, which is beyond the scope of this book.

There is another type of relation, called *irreducible* relation, which is assumed to be in 4NF. A relation is *irreducible* if it cannot be decomposed into two or more relations without losing information (Biller, 1979). Therefore it follows that, if we can decompose a relation into a set of projections and if the original relation can be recreated from these projections by a suitable join, then the original relation is reducible. Consider two possible projections R1 and R2 of relation COMP (figure 6.1) and their join R3:=R1(QTY) * (QTY)R3 in figure 7.9. Clearly R3 is not identical to COMP, as it has two extra tuples marked by the rectangles. Therefore

R1 (SUP-PART	QTY)		R2 (SUB-PART	QTY)
A180	7		C240	7
C240	3		H100	3
C240	7		D120	7
E110	10		B153	10
E120	2		E110	2
(a)			(b)	

R3 (SUP-PART	SUB-PART	QTY)
A180	C240	7
A180	D120	7
C240	H100	3
C240	C240	7
C240	D120	7
E110	B153	10
E120	E110	2

(c) R3 = R1 (QTY) * (QTY) R2

Figure 7.9

COMP is irreducible, and so is relation SALES. However, relations ECP and EHP are reducible, but their projections EC, EP and EH are not. Another example of a reducible relation is a relation holding person-identifier and birth date, which can be resolved into three irreducible relations containing (person-id, day-number), (person-id, month number) and (person-id, year number) respectively.

We shall conclude this subsection with simple-minded criteria for 4NF:

- separate each independent repeating group into a separate record type with its key

- ensure that each record type has at least one unique key
- ensure that each data item of the record type outside the key is uniquely identifiable

> by the key
> by the whole key, and
> by nothing but the key (except by other
>   unique keys if present)

7.2 An ultimate normal form

The definition of an ultimate normal form depends on the type of operations permitted in the decomposition of relations into other relations. Normalisations discussed so far are based on the following ground rules:

(i) When a relation is decomposed into a set of relations, each new relation is a projection of the original relation.
(ii) The original relation must be the join of the set of the new relations.

Therefore, we have used projections and joins as our operators. Fagin (1979) has introduced a new normal form, referred to as the fifth normal form, as the 'ultimate' normal form, if projection and joins are the only legal operators, as we have assumed so far. He favours the term projection-join normal form (PJ/NF), instead of fifth normal form (5NF) to emphasise its finality with respect to the projection and join operators, and also to underline the allowed operations. As the earlier normal forms are based on full functional dependency (FFD) or multi-valued dependency (MVD), so this new normal form is based on a so-called *join dependency* (JD). Fagin showed that MVD, and hence FFD, is a special case of JD, and that a relation in 5NF is also in 4NF. These proofs are, however, beyond the scope of this book.

7.2.1 Fifth normal form (5NF)

In section 6.1 we defined normalisation to be a reversible process, implying that the original relation can always be recreated. In the previous examples we have simply assumed that an offending relation can be split into two others to create higher normal forms without any loss of information. The fifth normal form questions this assumption and shows that some relations in 4NF could be decomposed without losing any information into, say, three but not two projections.

In fact FFD and MVD used in the earlier normal forms correspond to 2-way decompositions. A join dependency is more general, and can require decomposition into more than two new relations at the same stage of normalisation, as we shall see later. Whereas each FFD and MVD is determined by a single candidate key (leading to definitions such as 'every multideterminant is a candidate key') a JD could be determined by one or more keys, which makes its intuitive understanding more difficult. We shall attempt to explain below the concepts of 5NF in simpler terms, without the mathematical rigour (Kent, 1983).

Join dependency

If a relation R is decomposed (by projection) directly into a set (not necessarily disjoint) of relations R1, R2 . . . Rn, then R obeys join dependency if R is a suitable join of R1, R2 . . . Rn. In that case no information is lost by the decomposition of R into R1, R2 . . . Rn. This is called *non-loss* decomposition. A relation does not obey any join dependency if it cannot be non-loss decomposed into any set of projections.

We can separate join dependencies into two types: (i) those where projections are based on candidate keys and (ii) those where projections are not so based. If a relation R has n attributes, including, say, at least one candidate key, then clearly R can be decomposed into $(n-1)$ binary relations R1, R2 . . . $R(n-1)$, each containing the candidate key and one other attribute, such that R is a suitable join of these relations. Thus relation STOCK1 (figure 6.9) can be decomposed into STOCK11 (B# P#), STOCK12 (B# QB), with STOCK1 : = STOCK11 (B#) $*$ (B#) STOCK12. It is easy to see that a relation R will obey a join dependency if each of the projections R1, R2 . . . Rn contains a candidate key of R. Such key-based join dependencies are not relevant to normalisation, and hence will be referred to here as trivial join dependencies.

The second type of join dependency is non-trivial and determines normalisation. A fifth normal form is achieved when a relation cannot be non-loss decomposed any further by non-trivial projections (that is, projections *not* based on candidate keys). This rule can be formally restated as

A relation is in 5NF if it does not display any non-trivial join dependency.

Intuitively, therefore, a 5NF must be the ultimate normal form where projections and joins are the legal operators, since all further decompositions that can be made are based on candidate keys. Observe also that 5NF does not necessary produce irreducible relations, but unrestricted projections, including those based on candidate keys, will produce irreducible relations; furthermore, if the candidate key is a single attribute, then these irreducible relations will be binary.

3NF is achieved by non-loss decomposition on determinants whereas 4NF is achieved by non-loss decomposition on multideterminants. The ultimate position is reached when a relation cannot be non-loss decomposed any further except by projections based on candidate keys. This implies that 5NF is not only the ultimate normal form, but it is also a superset of 3rd and 4th NF, since in 5NF there cannot be any determinant or multideterminant which is not a candidate key. Thus a relation in 5NF is in 4NF and in 3NF. However, two questions remain:

1. What does 5NF 'buy', except giving us a feeling of the completeness?
2. How do we recognise that nothing else is left for non-loss decomposition?

We discuss these below.

7.2.2 An example of 5NF

Let us consider below a relation AGENT for agents (A#) selling products (P#) of companies (C#), as given in figure 7.10(a). This relation is an all key relation and does not show any multi-valued dependency; therefore this is in 4NF, but not necessarily in 5NF.

Now suppose that there is a symmetric rule which must be obeyed and which says: if an agent A sells a product P and if agent A represents a company C, and if company C makes that product P, then this agent A sells product P made by company C. (He can also sell product P made by another company if he represents that company.) In that case we non-loss decompose relation AGENT non-trivially into three projections AP, PC and CA, as shown in figure 7.10(b). Therefore, relation AGENT shows non-trivial join dependency and hence is not in 5NF, but its projections are. The projections implement the rule stated above. If there was no such rule, for instance, if an agent was allowed to sell any product irrespective of whether or not he represents that company, then relation AGENT would have been in 5NF.

The fact that we need three projections, rather than two, can be verified by reconstructing the original relation AGENT from the join of AP, PC and CA. First take any two of these, say AP and PC; their join APPC: = AP (P#) $*$ (P#)PC is shown in figure 7.10(c) which contains an extra tuple, namely {A2, P1, C2}. This is removed by the final join APPC(A#, C#) $*$ (A#, C#)CA which yields relation AGENT. The reader can try this reconstruction by joining any two of the three projections AP, PC and CA; there will always be an extra tuple to be removed by the final join. All decompositions that we have done up to 4NF were two-way decompositions at each stage; but here for the first time we encounter a three-way decomposition. This is typical of relations in 4NF but not in 5NF.

What is wrong with relation AGENT? It potentially includes data redundancy. For instance, if A2 were to sell P2 of C1, we need only to add A2 P2 as a tuple in relation AP, rather than tuple A2 P2 C1 in AGENT where C1 would be redundant. This may appear trivial but, as more tuples are added, the reduction does become significant. This can be demonstrated by constructing an example with a larger number of tuples. Therefore, we conclude that 5NF, like other normal forms, helps to remove data redundancy.

A relation in 4NF is always in 5NF except where there exist symmetric rules such as the one stated earlier, on agent, product and company, which pairs the attributes into (agent, product), (product, company) and (company, agent). This leads to a three-way decomposition in 5NF. In both 3NF and 4NF we can identify determinants and multideterminants, and decompose the offending relation accord-

```
AGENT (A#        P#      C#)

            A1      P1      C2
            A1      P2      C1
            A2      P1      C1
            A1      P1      C1

                    (a)
```

```
AP  (A#     P#)     PC(P#      C#)     CA  (C#     A#)

        A1      P1          P1      C2          C2      A1
        A1      P2          P2      C1          C1      A1
        A2      P1          P1      C1          C1      A2

                    (b)
```

```
APPC(A#          P#          C#)

        A1          P1          C2
        A1          P1          C1
        A1          P2          C1

        A2          P1          C2

        A2          P1          C1

                    (c)
```

Figure 7.10 (a) A relation in 4NF, but not 5NF. (b) Relations in 5NF. (c) The join APPC: =AP (P#) * (P#) PC

ingly; but there is no such straightforward technique in 5NF, where we must look for the presence of symmetry constraints.

Finally, although the process of normalisation is meant to remove data redundancy, it does not eliminate it completely, particularly when redundancies are dependent, such as in figure 7.3 where (C#, O#) repeats for each IC. There are also many other instances (Kent, 1983).

7.2.3 Other forms of normalisation

So far we have considered normalisation based on projection and join operations. The next important operators to consider are union and a corresponding, inverse operator which Fagin calls split. In this case we decompose a relation by splitting, and recreate it by unioning the decomposed fragments. Projection and split can be used together on the same relation, perhaps repeatedly, creating small 'normalised' fragments. Smith (1978) has pointed out some of its advantages and suggested a possible definition of a 'projection-split-join-union' normal form, as a starting point for further investigation.

The most important contribution of the normalisation theory seems to be on data analysis (Ullman, 1980). The third normal form provides a real basis for disentangling the cobwebs of relationships among data by allowing data to be isolated and disjointly grouped around candidate keys. The fourth normal form, and even the fifth, can be used for further refinement. However, the more recent advances in normalisation theory appear to have less relevance to most database designers.

Exercises

7.1 Consider a university department which offers a set of courses where each course (C) is taught by *one* tutor and is taken by a number of students, and has a set of recommended textbooks. A student (S) might take more than one course, a given textbook (B) might be recommended for more than one course, and a tutor (T) might teach more than one course, although the same course is *not* taught by more than one tutor. A relation T (C S T B) can be used to hold all this information. An example of the extension of this relation is given show below.

```
R ( C   S   T   B )
    C1  S1  T1  B1
    C1  S1  T1  B2
    C1  S2  T1  B1
    C1  S2  T1  B2
    C2  S1  T1  B1
    C2  S1  T1  B3
    C2  S3  T1  B1
    C2  S3  T1  B3
    C3  S1  T2  B6
```

Now, in the sequence given:
(a) Define third (Boyce–Codd) and fourth normal forms.
(b) Explain, using your definition, why relation R given above is not in 3NF.
(c) Express relation R in 3NF by breaking it into two relations.
(d) If any of the resulting relations is not in 4NF, explain the reason for it in terms of your definition of 4NF.
(e) Resolve the offending relation into 4NF.

Note that, in your answers, you are required to write only the intention rather than the extension of the relations.

7.2 Explain, with examples, the situation where an implied independent repeating group is separated into a different relation by 3NF.

7.3 Define the term fourth normal form. Explain the terms multideterminant and multi-valued dependency, referring, for illustration, to the following scenario.

A project uses parts, each supplied by a different supplier. Each supplier can have a number of warehouses. If a supplier supplies a part to a project, all warehouses of that supplier supply that part.

7.4 Consider the following two relations
(a) EMP (ENO SKILL LANGUAGE)
(b) PART (ITEM COLOUR SUPPLIER)

Discuss the circumstances in which these two relations will in 3NF but not in 4NF.

7.5 Consider a relation SIP for supplier (S), item (I) and project (P). Discuss the conditions in which this relation will be in 4NF but not in 5NF.

7.6 Explain the following with examples:

(a) Irreducible relation.
(b) When a binary relation is not irreducible.
(c) When a binary relation is not in 4NF.
(d) The distinction between irreducible relations and relations in 5NF.

7.7 Discuss why and under what circumstances 5NF is the ultimate normal form, and comment on its impact on data analysis.

References

Biller, H. (1979). On the notion of irreducible relations. *Data Base Architecture*, edited by G. Bracchi and G. M. Nijssen, North-Holland, p. 277

Deen, S. M. (1980). A canonical schema for a generalised data model with local interfaces. *Computer Journal*, Vol. (23:3), August, p. 201

Fagin, R. (1977). Multivalued dependencies and a new normal form for relational databases. *ACM TODS*, Vol. (2:3), September, p. 262

Fagin, R. (1979). Normal form and relational database operators. *Proceedings ACM SIGMOD Conference 1979*, p. 153

Kent, W. (1983). A simple guide to five normal forms in relational database theory. *Communications of the ACM*, Vol. (26:2), February, p. 120

Smith, J. M. (1978). A normal form for abstract syntax. *Proceedings of the 4th VLDB Conference, 1978*

Ullman, J. D. (1980). *Principles of Database Systems*, Pitman, chapter 5

8 Relational Languages

One of the outstanding contributions of the relational model is the powerful relational languages, introduced in chapter 6. In this chapter, we shall present two implemented languages: SQL (Chamberlin *et al.*, 1976; Chamberlin, 1980; Date, 1981) and QBE (Zloof, 1975, 1977; Date, 1981), based on tuple calculus and domain calculus respectively. The differences between the domain and tuple calculus are discussed in section 8.3, followed by a description of some implementation techniques in section 8.4.

Both SQL (Structured Query Language) and QBE (Query By Example) are well-known IBM products. QBE has a special feature of two-dimensional syntaxes. Another well-known relational language is QUEL, described in chapter 6, as an implementation closest to Codd's Alpha. The power of SQL and that of QBE are the same, not only on queries but also on updates and built-in functions; there are also some differences which we shall point out. Again, the closeness between SQL and QBE is coincidental rather than by design (both of them, of course, draw from DSL Alpha).

It would therefore be interesting to bring out the relative strengths and weaknesses of the two languages by answering the same set of questions in each language. We have selected 17 queries and several updates to be formulated by both the languages. The list includes a number of queries which are very similar in SQL, but not so in QBE. Some built-in functions and other types of commands are also illustrated. Apart from the relations STD, CSL and CRS of figure 6.13, we shall also use the following two relations: (i) relations TUTOR containing tutor number (TNO), tutor's name (TNAME), tutor's department number (TDN), the number of tutor's head of department (HNO) and salary (SAL) in units of 1000; (ii) relation DEPT containing department number (DNO), department name (DNAME) and departmental budget in units of 1000. The contents of these two relations are given in figure 8.1 (aside: relation TUTOR is not in 3NF, but we use it as a convenience).

8.1 Structured Query Language (SQL)

Structured English Query Language or SEQUEL was developed by Chamberlain *et al.* of IBM as part of the SYSTEM R research project. The name SEQUEL was subsequently changed to SQL (Structured Query Language) when the acronym SEQUEL was found to have been used previously by someone else. Although called

TUTOR (TNO	TNAME	TDN	HNO	SAL)
T0	SMITH	D20	T4	20
T4	SMITH	D20	T4	18
T6	PITT	D20	T4	10
T7	CLARK	D15	T2	18
T2	TAYLOR	D15	T2	20
T3	CURRY	D15	T2	15
T5	WATT	D15	T2	21
T1	HARTLY	D25	T1	23
T8	KEITH	D25	T1	16
T9	BAKER	D32	T9	13

DEPT (DNO	DNAME	BUDGET)
D15	COMPSC	600
D20	PHYSICS	800
D22	MATHS	500
D25	STATISTICS	400
D30	GENETICS	700
D32	ECOLOGY	100

Figure 8.1

a query language, SQL permits updates, and even data definitions. It can be used both as a stand-alone language and also as a data sublanguage embedded in PL/I and Cobol. It is available in SYSTEM R, SQL/DS and DB2. While SYSTEM R is a research prototype, SQL/DS and DB2 are commercial products based on SYSTEM R. SQL is currently being standardised by ANSI X3H2 as a standard language for the relational model (section 11.2).

The most basic operation in SQL is called *mapping*, which implies transformation of values from the database to user requirements. This operation is syntactically represented by a

```
SELECT ...
FROM   ...
WHERE  ...
```

block. In general, a mapping returns a collection of SELECTED attribute values of tuples FROM the specified relation(s), optionally subject to conditions stated in the WHERE clause. For example

Get the tutor numbers and tutor names for department D15.

```
SELECT  TNO, TNAME
FROM    TUTOR
WHERE   TDN = 'D15'
```

(SQL uses single quotes for literals.) The use of the keyword SELECT is unfortunate since it corresponds to the projection rather than the selection operation of the relational algebra. However, the PAL equivalent of the above query is

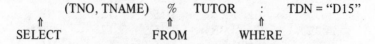

$$(\text{TNO, TNAME}) \quad \% \quad \text{TUTOR} \quad : \quad \text{TDN} = \text{``D15''}$$

$$\underset{\text{SELECT}}{\Uparrow} \qquad\qquad \underset{\text{FROM}}{\Uparrow} \qquad \underset{\text{WHERE}}{\Uparrow}$$

The % sign is equivalent to the SELECT FROM, and the : sign to the WHERE clause.

The SELECT clause may contain one or more attribute names, or SQL functions involving one or more attribute names or permitted arithmetical expressions with one or more attribute names. The attribute names must be drawn from the relations specified in the FROM clause. The permitted arithmetical expressions include addition (+), subtraction (−), multiplication (∗) and division (/) (see also below). The FROM clause may contain one or more relation names and optional labels (see later) of relation names.

The WHERE clause contains a predicate which allows logical operators (NOT, AND, OR), standard comparison operators, IN, ALL and some other operators (symbol ⌐ = is used for ≠). Most of these operations will be illustrated later. The attributes in the predicate of the WHERE clause must be drawn from the relations of an appropriate FROM clause. Consider the following query:

Find the tutor names of physics tutors

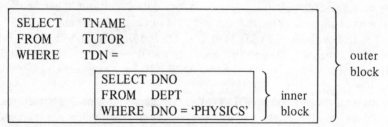

Its equivalent in PAL is

TNAME % TUTOR: TDN = DNO % DEPT: DNO = "PHYSICS".

As in PAL, this query has two blocks; the inner SELECT. . .FROM. . .WHERE block returns the DNO value of the physics department which is used in the WHERE clause of the outer block which yields tutor names. SQL permits such nested blocks to an arbitrary depth. The attributes in a WHERE clause of an inner block can come from relations specified in the FROM clause of any outer block (see Q11 below).

8.1.1 SQL queries

We answer below 17 queries Q1 to Q17 to be compared with QBE later.

Q1. Get the department tuples from the DEPT relation

> SELECT *
> FROM DEPT

* implies tuples, that, is SELECT * stands for SELECT tuples.

Q2. Get the department names from the DEPT relation

> SELECT DNAME
> FROM DEPT

Answer:

DNAME
COMPSC
PHYSICS
MATHS
STATISTICS
GENETICS
ECOLOGY

Q3. Get the different department numbers from the TUTOR relation

> SELECT UNIQUE TDN
> FROM TUTOR

The clause SELECT UNIQUE is equivalent to project unique of the relational algebra.

Answer:

TDN
D20
D15
D25
D32

Q4. Get the tutor names from department D25.

> SELECT TNAME
> FROM TUTOR
> WHERE TDN = 'D25'

Answer:

TNAME
HARTLY
KEITH

Q5. Get the tutor names and department numbers for department D15, D22 and D32 from relation TUTOR.

> SELECT TNAME, TDN
> FROM TUTOR
> WHERE TDN = 'D5' OR TDN = 'D22' or TDN = 'D32'

Answer:

TNAME	TDN
CLARK	D15
TAYLOR	D15
CURRY	D15
WATT	D15
BAKER	D32

(Note that there is no department D22.)

The WHERE clause above can be written more compactly as WHERE TDN IN ('D5', 'D22', 'D32').

Q6. Get the tutor names in department D20 for salary higher than 16K.

> SELECT TNAME
> FROM TUTOR
> WHERE TDN = 'D20' AND SAL > 16

Answer:

TNAME
SMITH
SMITH

If only different teacher names are wanted, then SELECT UNIQUE should be used, in which case the answer will be only one SMITH.

Q7. Get the names of tutors in department D15 and D20 with salary greater than 15K but less than 20K.

> SELECT TNAME
> FROM TUTOR
> WHERE TDN IN ('D15', 'D20') AND SAL > 15 AND SAL < 20

IN is used in place of = when the right-hand side has a set of objects to choose from. Readers' attention is also drawn to the QBE formulations of Q7 to Q9.

Answer:

TNAME
SMITH
CLARK

Q8. Get the names of tutors in department D15 and D20 with salary either less than 15K or greater than 20K.

> SELECT TNAME
> FROM TUTOR
> WHERE TDN IN ('D15', 'D20') AND (SAL < 15 OR SAL > 20)

Answer:

TNAME
PITT
WATT

Q9. Get the names of tutors in department D15 whose salary is higher than 17K
and who are not the head of the department.

```
SELECT TNAME
FROM TUTOR
WHERE TDN = 'D15' AND SAL > 17 AND TNO ⌐ = HNO
```

Answer:

TNAME
CLARK
WATT

Q10. Get Clark and his colleagues in the same department.

```
SELECT TNAME
FROM TUTOR
WHERE TDN =
    SELECT TDN
    FROM TUTOR
    WHERE TNAME = 'CLARK'
```

Answer:

TNAME
CLARK
TAYLOR
CURRY
WATT

Q11. Get the colleagues of Clark in the same department who get a higher salary
than Clark.

```
SELECT X.TNAME
FROM TUTOR X
WHERE TDN =
    SELECT TDN
    FROM TUTOR
    WHERE TNAME = 'CLARK' AND SAL < X.SAL
```

Answer:

TNAME
TAYLOR
WATT

We have here a nested query where the inner block selects Clark whose
salary has to be compared with the tuples of the relation in the outer block.
Since both are the same relation TUTOR, we differentiate between them by
declaring X as a label (which is a counterpart of a range variable in DSL Alpha
and QBE). A label is valid only in the block where it is defined, and in all its

inner blocks. In the query, no qualifier is required for TDN, TNAME and SAL in the inner block, as they by default refer to TUTOR in the same block. Likewise a qualifier is not needed for TNAME and TDN of the outer block either, as they refer to X by default. However, a qualifier X is essential in X.SAL, to resolve the conflict between the variable SAL of the outer and inner blocks appearing in the same predicate. As there is no such conflict in Q10, we did not declare any range variable there.

Q12. Get the tutor names and heads' names for tutors earning more than their heads of department.

> SELECT X.TNAME, Y.TNAME
> FROM TUTOR X, TUTOR Y
> WHERE X.HNO = Y.TNO
>   AND X.SAL > Y.SAL

Answer:

X.TNAME	Y.TNAME
SMITH	SMITH
WATT	TAYLOR

This is an example of self-join, the same relation TUTOR being joined with itself, over the common columns HNO and TNO. As there are no inner or outer blocks to separate the two TUTORS, we use range variable X and Y. The result of the self-join is

X.TNO	X.TNAME	X.TDN	X.HNO	X.SAL	Y.TNAME	Y.TDN	Y.HNO	Y.SAL
T0	SMITH	D20	T4	20	SMITH	D20	T4	18
T4	SMITH	D20	T4	18	SMITH	D20	T4	18
T6	PITT	D20	T4	10	SMITH	D20	T4	18
T7	CLARK	D15	T2	18	TAYLOR	D15	T2	20
T2	TAYLOR	D15	T2	20	TAYLOR	D15	T2	20
T3	CURRY	D15	T2	15	TAYLOR	D15	T2	20
T5	WATT	D15	T2	21	TAYLOR	D15	T2	20
T1	HARTLY	D25	T1	23	HARTLY	D25	T1	23
T8	KEITH	D25	T1	16	HARTLY	D25	T1	23
T9	BAKER	D32	T9	13	BAKER	D32	T9	13

The predicate X.SAL > Y.SAL may be assumed to operate on the result of this join. The qualifiers X and Y are required to avoid ambiguity. Thus a natural join in SQL is defined in the WHERE clause by an equality sign between the common columns. To take another example of a join: find department name and tutor names from DEPT and TUTOR.

> SELECT DNAME, TNAME
> FROM DEPT, TUTOR
> WHERE DNO = TDN

Some people seem to prefer the implicit join operation of SQL while others criticise SQL for the absence of an explicit join operation. If the WHERE clause is omitted, the FROM clause would yield a quadratic join of DEPT and TUTOR.

Q13. Get the names of physics tutors who earn more than 19K.

        SELECT TNAME
        FROM TUTOR
        WHERE SAL > 19 AND TDN =
          SELECT DNO
          FROM DEPT
          WHERE DNAME = 'PHYSICS'

Alternatively

        SELECT TNAME
        FROM TUTOR
        WHERE (TDN =
          SELECT DNO
          FROM DEPT
          WHERE DNAME = 'PHYSICS')
        AND SAL > 19

Answer:

TNAME
SMITH

Q14. Get the tutor names and departmental budgets for tutors earning more than 20K.

        SELECT TNAME, BUDGET
        FROM TUTOR, DEPT
        WHERE TDN = DNO
          AND SAL > 20

Answer:

TUTOR	BUDGET
WATT	600
HARTLY	400

This is another example of a join and a selection.

Q15. Get the names of students in STD relation who took all the courses C1, C2, C3 (the same as Query 8 of section 6.3.1).

        SELECT SN
        FROM STD, CSL
        WHERE S# = SS AND CC = ALL ('C1', 'C2', 'C3')

Answer:

SN
WARD

Q16. Get the names of students in STD who took all the courses in CRS (same as Query 7 of section 6.3.1).

SELECT SN
FROM STD, CSL
WHERE S# = SS AND CC = ALL
SELECT C#
FROM CRS

The answer is the same as in Q15.

Q17. Get the departments without tutors.

SELECT DNO
FROM DEPT
MINUS
SELECT TDN
FROM TUTOR

Answer:

DNO
D22
D30

8.1.2 SQL updates

To give a flavour of the update facilities in SQL, we illustrate here the use of the basic commands:

U1.   Insert a new department tuple {D36 ECON 400} in DEPT relation.

INSERT INTO DEPT:
< 'D36' 'ECONOMICS' 400>

U2.   Delete a department tuple DNO = "D15".

DELETE DEPT
WHERE DNO = 'D15'

U3.   Increase the budget of department D15 by 20K.

UPDATE DEPT
SET BUDGET = BUDGET + 20
WHERE DNO = 'D15'

The SET option in SQL acts like assignment of values for updates.

U4.   Give all tutors of department D7 a rise of 10 per cent.

UPDATE TUTOR
SET SAL = SAL * 1.1
WHERE TDN = 'D7'

SAL in the WHERE clause refers to the salary before the update.

An assignment command can be used to create a new relation from one or more relations and to store the new relation in the database as shown here. Create a new relation REL (with suitably defined attributes) to store tutor number and salary from the TUTOR relation for salary higher than 15K.

> ASSIGN TO REL (TNUM, SALARY):
> SELECT TNO, SAL
> FROM TUTOR
> WHERE SAL > 15

8.1.3 SQL functions

SQL supports the following five statistical functions:

COUNT (x)   to count the values in column x
SUM (x)   to sum the values of column x
AVG (x)   to find the average value of column x
MAX (x)   to find the maximum value in column x
MIN (x)   to find the minimum value in column x

In addition, there are also an ORDER BY, a GROUP BY and a HAVING clause, as will be explained with examples later. The COUNT function has also two other forms, as shown here. To count the number of salary values (including duplicates) in relation TUTOR we may write

> SELECT COUNT (SAL)
> FROM TUTOR

which will yield 10. Alternatively we can write

> SELECT COUNT (∗)
> FROM TUTOR

where COUNT (∗) counts tuples, with the same result. However, to count the salary values without duplicates, we must write

> SELECT COUNT (UNIQUE SAL)
> FROM TUTOR

For any of the other statistical functions we may write

> SELECT f (SAL)
> FROM TUTOR

where f is SUM, AVG, MAX or MIN. These functions can also be used directly in the WHERE clause, for instance

> SELECT TNAME
> FROM TUTOR
> WHERE SAL = MAX (SAL)

will find the tutors earning the maximum salary. We present below some further queries which will be repeated in QBE later.

F1. Get the total number of different departments in TUTOR relation.

> SELECT COUNT (UNIQUE TDN)
> FROM TUTOR

F2. Get the number of DEPT tuples.

> SELECT COUNT (∗)
> FROM DEPT

F3. Get the average departmental salaries in their value order.

> SELECT AVG (SAL)
> FROM TUTOR
> GROUP BY TDN
> ORDER BY AVG (SAL)

The GROUP BY operation ensures that the average is calculated for each department. In its absence the average will be calculated for the whole relation, irrespective of departments. However, when a GROUP BY clause is used, each item in the SELECT clause must be a unique property of a group, rather than of an individual tuple.

F4. Get the average weekly budget of departments.

> SELECT AVG (SAL)/52
> FROM DEPT

Thus the SELECT clause permits not only functions, but also arithmetical expressions.

F5. Get the department numbers and the average salary of each department except 'D15'.

> SELECT TDN, AVG (SAL)
> FROM TUTOR
> WHERE TDN ⌐ = 'D15'
> GROUP BY TDN

A condition on the evaluation of a GROUP BY is stipulated by a HAVING clause, as shown in the next query.

F6. Get the departments other than D15 with more than two tutors.

> SELECT TDN
> FROM TUTOR
> WHERE TDN ⌐ = 'D15'
> GROUP BY TDN
> HAVING COUNT (∗) > 2

The WHERE clause contains conditions for the SELECT operation, whereas the HAVING clause applies to the GROUP BY operation, with the following precedence: first the WHERE clause is applied to qualify tuples in the relations of the FROM clause, then the groups are formed and then the HAVING clause is applied to qualify groups; finally the SELECT clause is used on those groups. However, there can be only one GROUP BY clause (and hence one HAVING clause) for each SELECT. . .FROM. . .WHERE block.

8.1.4 SQL data definitions

As pointed out earlier, SQL provides both data manipulation and data definition facility, the latter permitting definitions of relations, addition of new relations, deletion of old relations, creation of indexes, definitions of views, and the specifications of privacy and integrity constraints – all in one language. Some of these functions will be illustrated below.

A *view* in SQL is a virtual relation that is derived from one or more other relations. This is the counterpart of the data definition facility of PAL. To define a view, say V30, for tutor numbers and salaries for departments other than D20 and D32

> DEFINE VIEW V30 AS
> SELECT TNO, SAL
> FROM TUTOR
> WHERE TDN ⌐ IN (D20, D32)

The PAL equivalent is

$$V30 = = (TNO, SAL) \% \text{ TUTOR} : TDN \neq D20 \text{ AND } TDN \neq D32$$

Once defined, a view can be treated like any other relation, except for certain restrictions on updates. SQL allows authorisation to be granted to other users by a GRANT statement selectively for Read, Insert, Delete, Update (optionally restricted to named columns), and Revoke (to revoke an authorisation granted earlier). For instance, to grant Read, Insert and Update permission to Bilbo and Frodo for relation TUTOR

> GRANT READ, INSERT, UPDATE ON TUTOR TO BILBO, FRODO
> WITH GRANT OPTION

The phrase WITH GRANT OPTION permits Bilbo and Frodo also to grant these privileges to others.

Integrity assertion

Integrity constraints can be specified by an Assertion command, as shown below.

(1) Assert that no tutor can have a salary more than 30K.

$$\text{ASSERT A1 ON TUTOR} : \text{SAL} \leqslant 30$$

Each assertion is given a name such as A1 above. Any operation that violates the truth value of such an assertion is rejected.

(2) Assert that no row in TUTOR relation can have a TNO value which is not present in the department record.

ASSERT A2
(SELECT TNO FROM TUTOR
IS IN
SELECT DNO FROM DEPT)

(3) Assert that the new salary of a tutor cannot be smaller than his old salary.

$$\text{ASSERT A3 ON UPDATE OF TUTOR (SAL) NEW SAL} \geqslant \text{OLD SAL}$$

Some comments on the implementation and optimisation of SQL are made in connection with SYSTEM R (section 13.1).

8.2 Query-By-Example

Query-By-Example (QBE) was developed by M. M. Zloof at the IBM Yorktown Heights Laboratory. Like SQL, it is both a data manipulation and definition language, providing parallel facilities.

A special feature of the QBE language is its two-dimensional syntax which requires the specification of a query in the form of an example — and hence the name Query-By-Example. It is a screen language since all requests are expressed by filling tables on the VDU screen; the answer also appears on the screen. The tables can be drawn on the screen by the user with the help of a special *function key* provided with the key board of the VDU. For instance, for a query to print the department names for department with budgets greater than 300K, we write

DEPT	DNO	DNAME	BUDGET
		P.$\underline{X}$	> 300

The user will first draw a skeleton of the Department relation (as a table) by the function key and then type in P.$\underline{X}$ and > 300 in the appropriate columns. P. stands for print, $\underline{X}$ is called an *example element* and 300 a *constant element*. The query can be paraphrased as: "Print department names, such as $\underline{X}$ where the budget is greater than 300K". $\underline{X}$ is a user-defined example of a possible answer, and 300 is an actual value. An example element can be any value, fictitious or actual, but must be underlined. A constant element must be an actual value and is *not* underlined. The result of this query is

DNAME
COMPSC
PHYSICS
GENETICS

Before we proceed further, we summarise some of the general rules.

1. Each constant represents a condition.
2. The conditions in the same row of the query table are 'AND'ed together (see Q6).
3. A query can spread over several rows, and in that case
   (a) the ordering of the rows is immaterial (see Q5)
   (b) the separate rows are 'OR'ed together unless they are linked through a common example element (see Q7, Q8).
4. There must be a distinct and appropriate name for each relation involved in a query, the relations being linked together by a common example element (see Q13).
5. If the resultant columns come from more than one relation, then a new table must be created for the result (again with the help of the function key) (see Q12, Q14).
6. If some conditions cannot be expressed within the framework of the specified relations, then a special purpose table can be created for these conditions (see Q9).
7. If a column is too narrow to write the conditions, it can be widened by the function key (see F2).
8. The comparison operators allowed are the same as in SQL.

8.2.1 QBE queries

We give below the QBE formulations of 17 queries given earlier in section 8.1.2.

Q1. Get the department tuples from the DEPT relation

DEPT	DNO	DNAME	BUDGET
	P.$\underline{X}$	P.$\underline{Y}$	P.$\underline{Z}$

or

DEPT	DNO	DNAME	BUDGET
P.			

P.$\underline{X}$ in a column causes column value X to be retrieved, whereas P. under the relation name (DEPT here) causes the whole tuple to be retrieved (no example element needed).

Q2.   Get the department names from the DEPT relation

DEPT	DNO	DNAME	BUDGET
		P.DT	

In QBE, unlike PAL and SQL, duplicates are always removed from the result unless the qualifier ALL – such as P.ALL.DT in place of P.DT – is used.

Q3.   Get the different department numbers from the TUTOR relation

TUTOR	TNO	TNAME	TDN	HNO	SAL
			P.X		

Since duplicates are automatically removed, there is no need to put UNIQUE anywhere.

Q4.   Get the tutor names from department D25.

TUTOR	TNO	TNAME	TDN	HNO	SAL
		P.N	D25		

Q5.   Get the tutor names and department numbers for department D15, D22 and D32 from relation TUTOR.

TUTOR	TNO	TNAME	TDN	HNO	SAL
		P.K	D15		
		P.L	D21		
		P.M	D25		

In terms of QBE, we have here three unconnected subqueries, tutors of D15 or tutors of D21 or tutors of D25. Therefore they are shown as three separate subqueries (implicitly connected by OR), each with its independent example and constant elements.

Q6.   Get the tutor names in department D20 for salary higher than 16K.

TUTOR	TNO	TNAME	TDN	HNO	SAL
		P.ALL.X	D20		> 16

Without *ALL*, only one Smith will be output.

Q7.   Get the names of tutors in department D15 and D20 with salary greater than 15K but less than 20K.

TUTOR	TNO	TNAME	TDN	HNO	SAL
		P.M	D15		> 15
		M	D15		< 20
		P.N	D20		> 15
		N	D20		< 20

We need a separate line for each condition on the same attribute, in this case SAL. This query is equivalent to finding tutors in either department D15, *or* department D20, the salary in each department being in the specified range. The presence of the same example element $\underline{M}$ in the first and second lines implies an AND operation; and likewise $\underline{N}$ in the 3rd and 4th lines. The use of different example elements $\underline{M}$ and $\underline{N}$ indicates an OR operation between the subquery for department D15 and D20 (see also the query below).

Q8. Get the names of tutors in department D15 and D20 with salary either less than 15K or greater than 20K.

TUTOR	TNO	TNAME	TDN	HNO	SAL
		P.M1	D15		<15
		P.M2	D15		>20
		P.N1	D20		<15
		P.N2	D20		>20

This is equivalent to four separate subqueries, connected by OR operators, since the example elements are different.

Q9. Get the names of tutors in department D15 whose salary is higher than 17K and who are not the head of the department.

TUTOR	TNO	TNAME	TDN	HNO	SAL	CONDITIONS
	Y	P.X	D15	Z	>17	Y ¬ = Z

In this query we need to assert that $\underline{Y} \neq \underline{Z}$, for which no convenient column exists. QBE allows additional tables (with the help of the function key) to be created on the screen for such conditions, as shown by our CONDITIONS box above.

Q10. Get Clark and his colleagues in the same department.

TUTOR	TNO	TNAME	TDN	HNO	SAL
		P.X	Y		
		CLARK	Y		

The presence of the same example element $\underline{Y}$ indicates that $\underline{X}$ is to be printed if it belongs to the department of Clark. The two lines may be assumed to be ANDed together.

Q11. Get the colleagues of Clark in the same department who get a higher salary than Clark.

TUTOR	TNO	TNAME	TDN	HNO	SAL
		P.X	Y		Z
		CLARK	Y		<Z

Note how easily the salary condition is shown.

Q12. Get the tutor names and heads' names for tutors earning more than their heads of department.

TUTOR	TNO	TNAME	TDN	HNO	SAL
	$\underline{X}$	$\underline{T1}$		$\underline{Y}$	$>\underline{Z}$
	$\underline{Y}$	T2			$\underline{Z}$

The TUTOR table shows that the head of $\underline{X}$ is $\underline{Y}$ and that the salary of $\underline{X}$ (the first line) $> \underline{Z}$ where $\underline{Z}$ = salary of $\underline{Y}$ (the second line). However, we need a new table to print the name of tutors ($\underline{T1}$) and their heads ($\underline{T2}$) side by side since the Tutor relation does not provide this facility. We therefore create such a table, with user-defined column name X.TNAME and Y.TNAME for the result, as shown below.

RESULT	X.TNAME	Y.TNAME
	P.$\underline{T1}$	P.$\underline{T2}$

If we wanted to print only the tutor name ($\underline{T1}$) without the names of their heads ($\underline{T2}$), then we could have done it by writing P.$\underline{T1}$ in place of $\underline{T1}$ in the TUTOR table, without creating a new table.

Q13. Get the names of physics tutors who earn more than 19K.

DEPT	DNO	DNAME	BUDGET
	$\underline{Y}$	PHYSICS	

TUTOR	TNO	TNAME	TDN	HNO	SAL
		P.$\underline{X}$	$\underline{Y}$		>19

This query involves two relations, DEPT and TUTOR, and both must be created by the function key. The relations are linked by the common example element $\underline{Y}$.

Q14. Get the tutor names and departmental budgets for tutors earning more than 20K.

DEPT	DNO	DNAME	BUDGET
	$\underline{D}$		$\underline{Z}$

TUTOR	TNO	TNAME	TDN	HNO	SAL
		$\underline{X}$	$\underline{D}$		>20

RESULT	TNAME	BUDGET
	P.$\underline{X}$	P.$\underline{Z}$

Here again we need two relations for the query, with a third relation RESULT for the answer. If, instead of creating the result relation, we write P.$\underline{X}$ in TUTOR table and P.$\underline{Z}$ in DEPT table, then the output will be two separate lists, one containing department budgets and the other containing tutor numbers, without showing which tutor corresponds to which budget.

Q15. Get the names of students in STD relation who took all the courses C1, C2, C3.

STD	S#	SN	AGE	CSL	SS	CC	MK
	$\underline{X}$	P.$\underline{N}$			$\underline{X}$	C1	
					$\underline{X}$	C2	
					$\underline{X}$	C3	

Q16. Get the names of students in STD who took all the courses in CRS.

STD	S#	SN	AGE	CSL	SS	CC	MK
	$\underline{X}$	P.$\underline{N}$			$\underline{X}$	ALL.$\underline{Y}$	

CRS	C#	CN	YR	MX
	ALL.$\underline{Y}$			

Q17. Get the departments without tutors

DEPT	DNO	DNAME	BUDGET
	P.$\underline{X}$		

TUTOR	TNO	TNAME	TDN	HNO	SAL
			$\neg\underline{X}$		

It is also possible to include arithmetic expression and statistical functions in any of the columns, paralleling SQL.

8.2.2 QBE updates

In the previous section, we have used P in each query for printing the result. By replacing P with I, D or U, we can insert, delete or amend (update) tuples. We give below the QBE formulations of the update transactions given in section 8.1.2.

U1. Insert a new department tuple {D36 ECON 400} in DEPT relation.

DEPT	DNO	DNAME	BUDGET
I.	D36	ECON	40

U2. Delete a department tuple DNO = "D15".

DEPT	DNO	DNAME	BUDGET
D.	D15		

U3. Increase the budget of department D15 by 20K.

DEPT	DNO	DNAME	BUDGET
	D15		$\underline{B}$
U.	D15		$\underline{B}$ + 20

U4. Give all tutors of department D7 a rise of 10 per cent.

TUTOR	TNO	TNAME	TDN	HNO	SAL
	$\underline{Y}$		D7		$\underline{X}$
U.	$\underline{Y}$				1.1 * $\underline{X}$

A new result relation from a query can be saved in the database if P. is replaced by I.

8.2.3 QBE functions

The five statistical functions listed under SQL are also supported in QBE, except that the term CNT replaces COUNT, and that the word ALL *must* always be appended in each function. This is to ensure that duplicate values are not removed in the evaluation of the QBE functions. Ascending order is indicated by AO, descending order by DO, and the Group By of SQL by G, but there is no equivalent of the HAVING clause. We give below the QBE formulations of functions F1 to F6 given in section 8.1.3.

F1. Get the total number of different departments in TUTOR relation.

TUTOR	TNO	TNAME	TDN	HNO	SAL
			P.CNT.UNQ.ALL.$\underline{X}$		

The presence of both UNQ and ALL is required to remove duplicates; UNQ indicates Unique.

F2. Get the number of DEPT tuples.

DEPT	DNO	DNAME	BUDGET
	P.CNT.ALL.$\underline{X}$		

F3. Get the average departmental salaries in their value order.

TUTOR	TNO	TNAME	TDN	HNO	SAL
			G.X̱		P.AO.AVG.ALL.Y̱

F4. Get the average weekly budget of departments.

DEPT	DNO	DNAME	BUDGET
			P.(AVG.ALL.X̱)/52

F5. Get the department numbers and the average salary of each department except D15.

TUTOR	TNO	TNAME	TDN	HNO	SAL
	Ẕ		P.G.X̱		P.AVG.ALL.Y̱
	Ẕ		⌐D15		

F6. Get the departments other than D15, with more than two tutors.

TUTOR	TNO	TNAME	TDN	HNO	SAL	CONDITIONS
	X̱		P.G.Y̱			CNT.ALL.X̱ > 2
	X̱		⌐D15			

A superset version of QBE called Office procedures By Example (OBE) has also been specified by M. M. Zloof for office users (Zloof, 1981).

8.3 Tuple versus domain calculus

As mentioned earlier, there are two types of calculus – tuple calculus and domain calculus. In tuple calculus we basically process tuples of one or more relations, whereas in domain calculus we process domains (not to be confused with attributes) spanning over one or more relations. Codd's orginal calculus, along with DSL Alpha and QUEL, belongs to the former category, as they use tuple variables irrespective of whether the variables are relation names or range variables. SQL is basically tuple oriented, using relation names and labels as tuple variables. For instance, in Q4 of SQL (section 8.1.1), relation name TUTOR is the tuple variable where each tutor tuple is retrieved in turn during the processing of the query; the content of the tuple in TUTOR corresponding to the TDN field is tested for match with 'D25' and if it matches the TNAME field is projected (selected in the SQL term). In more complex SQL queries such as Q11 and Q12, labels are also used in place of tuple variables.

Domain calculus is a later innovation due to Lacroix and Pirotte (1977). In this calculus, the user declares domain variables (as against attribute names) which can hold a value of a domain which may span over the same or different attribute names of the same or different relations. The user processes the values of a domain, rather than the tuples of a relation. Although it pre-dates the paper of Lacroix and Pirotte, QBE is nevertheless a domain oriented language. The example elements there are domain variables. For instance, in Q12, Y is a domain variable of tutor numbers (for both TNO and HNO). Likewise in Q14, the domain variable D for department numbers appears under TDN of TUTOR and DNO of DEPT.

Domain oriented languages are sometimes claimed to be easier for naive users (Pirotte, 1979). A number of studies have been made on user experience of QBE, SQL and a relational algebra (Greenblatt and Waxman, 1978). According to these studies the naive users find QBE to be the easiest and algebra the most difficult to learn and use — although the statistical errors are too wide to reach a definitive conclusion. As regards the experienced users, it is doubtful if they would find QBE very attractive, particularly because of the need to create tables and fill-in columns. Moreover, large and complex queries involving many relations and many conditions are likely to fill up the screen too quickly, making QBE less useful in those cases. Comparison between SQL and an algebra depends partly on the syntax of the algebra. If the choice is between SQL and a PAL-like language, the advantage of SQL over algebra may be less significant. It is relatively easier to carry out optimisation in an algebra than in a calculus-based language, since an algebraic query specifies the actual operations. Despite this inherent disadvantage of a calculus-based language, the SQL implementation on SYSTEM R supports a powerful optimiser (see section 13.1).

Although SQL and QUEL are tuple oriented, they are very different structurally. In SQL the level of nesting (SELECT. . .FROM. . .WHERE. . . block) increases with the complexity of the query, which makes query expressions easier for simple queries and complex for complex queries. In contrast, in QUEL (and also in DSL Alpha) the structure of the query remains unaltered; the complexity does not produce more nesting but increases the size of the predicate. It is difficult to judge which one is better — there seem to be strong adherents for each side.

In this chapter we have seen the power and the variations of some relational languages. The power of such languages is usually measured in terms of what Codd (1972) has defined as *'relational completeness'*. Basically the expressive (or selective) power of a data manipulation language is complete if it allows the formulation of any conceivable user query (excluding deduction) without any programming loop or branched execution, ideally by a single statement. Codd postulates a language to be *relationally complete* if its expressiveness is equal to that of his original calculus (now called tuple calculus), which is a *first order predicate calculus*, and can retrieve from the database any value or any set of values that can be defined by a predicate. According to Codd, a language should — besides being relationally complete — support statistical functions such as those listed in DSL Alpha (section 6.3.3). He has shown both DSL Alpha and relational algebra to be relationally complete. Although a particular implementation of a relational algebra might not permit a complex query to be expressed by a single instruction for other considerations, but this does not affect the relational completeness of Codd's original relational algebra. There are five basic relational operations, namely, Union, Difference, Selection, Projection and Quadratic join (natural join is a subset of quadratic join). Intersection (!) and Division can also be created from these. For instance, A ! B = A $-$ $-$ (A $-$ $-$ B) where $-$ $-$ implies the difference operation (see also exercise 8.5 at the end of this chapter). Any language that permits these basic operations can be assumed to be relationally complete. QUEL, SQL, QBE, and indeed the whole of domain calculus, are considered to be relationally complete; although we have not always discussed it, they permit quadratic join.

Finally, is relational completeness the ultimate glory of a data manipulation language, or are there other issues which we should be aware of? These questions are considered in chapter 14.

8.4 Implementation of relational operators

We shall present here some basic implementation techniques of the main relational operators — namely union, difference, intersection, projection, selection, join and division — to provide an understanding of the relevant issues. Although expressed in terms of the relational algebra, these operations and the associated query optimisation techniques are used in the implementation of the calculus-based languages as well. In the discussions below we shall assume A and B to be the input relations (only A for projection and selection) and R to be the resultant relation. Relation I has Pi number of pages, each page having an average Ni number of tuples, where I can be A, B or R. Let us also suppose that Si is the number of page accesses needed to sort relation I by an external sort using disc. (We shall ignore the time needed for sorting in the memory, that is, internal sort.) In the estimates given we shall not include the cost of writing Pr pages to the output relation R, and assume a page access to be equivalent to a disc access.

8.4.1 Union, difference, intersection

To union A and B, copy A to R and then append B to R; the total number of pages scanned will be $Pa + Pb$. However, if union unique (that is, without duplicate tuples) is required, then first sort A and B separately and then merge them, removing duplicates during the merge. Generally $Sr > (Sa + Sb)$ and therefore it is more efficient to sort A and B separately, rather than to sort R to remove duplicates. The page accesses required for union unique are $Pa + Pb + Sa + Sb$. However, if at least one of the relations, say B, is in the memory, then instead of sorting, B can be scanned once for every tuple of A to find a duplicate. Preferably B should be sorted in the memory to avoid repeated scanning. The cost is then $Pa + Pb$ (Pb to read B into the memory), the cost of scanning or sorting in the memory being ignored.

The difference operation A − − B can be evaluated as follows. Produce a list of primary key values of B, either by scanning B or preferably from the primary key index of B if it exists. Then extract the tuples from A whose primary key values do not match those in the list. The total cost is Pa + Pb, if B does not have a primary key index. However, this method is not very general, since many relations, particularly temporary relations, may not have known primary keys. Therefore, the general technique will involve sorting A and B, and then removing rather than adding B tuples in a subsequent merge of A and B. If B has tuples not in A, then they can be ignored. The total cost is Pa + Pb + Sa + Sb, as in union. Again if one of them, say B, is in the memory, then the disc sorting of A and B will be unnecessary.

The intersection operation A ! B can be implemented by extracting and sorting the primary key values of A and B into two separate lists; and then selecting the common key values which can be used to extract the common tuples from the smaller of the two relations. The total cost is Pa + Pb + min [Pa, Pb] page accesses, ignoring the time for sorting the primary key values. However, as in the difference operation the primary key values may not be easily recognisable. In that case proceed as in the second method for the difference operation − sorting A and B, and then merging them − except that in the merging process extract only the common tuples. The cost of the operation is again (Pa + Pb + Sa + Sb). As before, if at least one of the relations is small enough to be held in the memory, then sorting of either is unnecessary; the cost of the operation is then (Pa + Pb) page accesses.

Therefore the general implementation techniques of union, difference and intersection operation are very similar, with the same cost formula.

8.4.2 Projection and selection

For a projection, scan the input relation A, tuple by tuple, and then write out the desired attribute values of each tuple in the specified order. Therefore the cost is Pa page accesses. However, for the project unique operation, resultant relation R must be sorted so that the duplicate tuples are clustered together. The additional cost is Sr page accesses for sorting and Pr page accesses for scanning R to remove duplicates. Thus total cost for project unique is Pa + Pr + Sr page accesses. However, if R can be held in the memory, then disc sorting is unnecessary and hence Sr = 0 and Pr = 0.

In a selection we may scan the input relation A, writing out only the qualifying tuples. This will take Pa page accesses. However, depending on the tuple placement technique used and indexes implemented, the search area for selection can be reduced drastically. For instance, if tuples are stored in primary key order, or if there is a primary key index, then the selection of a tuple matching a primary key value can be accomplished by a random access (1 page access, ignoring the index overhead). Likewise selection by secondary key values will require less than Pa page accesses. In general, the presence of indexes, pointers and the placement technique should be taken into account in the implementation of a selection operation. During the compilation of a selection operation (or possibly later, depending on the time of binding), the DBCS can ascertain the best strategy for its evaluation.

8.4.3 Join

Both join and division are expensive operations, but division is less so, as it reduces the number of tuples in the resultant relation. At a primitive level, both can be implemented by first sorting the operand relations in the common domain order, and then carrying out the join/division operation. However, external sorting can be expensive, particularly for large relations, and hence is avoided if possible.

In the basic join technique, we scan the tuples of relation A, and for each A-tuple we scan the whole of relation B, extracting each B-tuple that matches the A-tuple on the common domain. During the extraction of the B-tuples, the A-tuple concerned is concatenated with each qualifying B-tuple, thus creating a joined tuple which is written out in relation R as the result. In discussing the implementation techniques, we shall first examine different scenarios and then present what are called good implementation techniques.

Scenario (1): At least one of the relations A or B is small enough to be held in the memory. Then read this relation into the memory as B. Scan relation A, and for each A-tuple scan the whole of relation B, as in the basic technique above; but since B is in the memory, its scanning cost can be ignored. Thus the cost of join is $(Pa + Pb)$ — that is, the time to read A and B.

Scenario (2): Both A and B are large (that is, too large to be held in the memory) and unsorted. The basic technique given above can be used, scanning relation A once, and scanning relation B once for each tuple of A. Thus the maximum cost is $(Pa + Na \times Pa \times Pb)$. Alternatively, if B is made the first relation and A the second relation, then the cost is $(Pb + Nb \times Pb \times Pa)$. In either case, the join will probably be too expensive; the sort should be done as discussed later.

Scenario (3): Both relations A and B are large, but at least one of them has a suitable index on the common domain. Use the relation with index as relation B. Scan A and, for each tuple of A, find the qualifying B-tuples from the index on B. This will require one disc access to B for each A-tuple (assuming for simplicity that if more than one B-tuple matches the same A-tuple, they are on the same page, and that each A-tuple has a matching B-tuple). Then the cost of join is $(Pa + \text{cardinality of } A) = (Pa + Na \times Pa) = Pa(1 + Na)$. However, if only U per cent of A-tuples qualifies and if on average each of these qualifying A-tuples concatenates, on average with V number of B-tuples (assuming that each such B-tuple is on a different page), then the cost is $(Pa + U \times Na \times Pa \times V) = Pa(1 + UVNa)$ disc accesses. In this calculation, we have ignored the cost of processing the index itself.

Scenario (4): Both A and B are large, but are sorted in common domain order. Then *join A and B by merging.* Scan A, and for each A-tuple read the matching B-tuples, concatenating them in the process. Also hold the original B-tuples just concatenated in the memory, until the next A-tuple with a different value on the common domain is found. Thus if several A-tuples have the same value in the common domain, the corresponding B-tuples are retrieved only once. The cost of the join is (Pa + Pb) page accesses if the relations are already sorted; but if they are sorted specifically for this join, then the cost is Pa + Pb + Sa + Sb disc accesses.

The following techniques should be good in most situations.

(i) If one of the relations is small enough to be held in the memory, then use it as relation B, preferably after sorting it in common domain order, by an *internal* sort (sorting is generally faster than repeated scanning in scenario (1)). Scan relation A; for each A-tuple, find the matching B-tuples in the memory by applying a *binary chop* method (section 3.3.1). The cost is Pa + Pb disc accesses.

(ii) If both are small enough to be in the memory, then read them both in the memory, sort them internally (in common domain order), and join them by merging on the common domain. The cost is again Pa + Pb, but the internal sorting might save some CPU time.

(iii) If both A and B are large but if one of them has a suitable index on the common domain, then use it as relation B, and apply scenario (3). If both of them have suitable indexes, then one of them can be selected as relation B on the basis of cost figures given in scenario (3). Note that one relation (relation A in our assumption) has to be scanned even if it has an index, since accessing by index may take up to Na × Pa disc accesses (one access for each A-tuple) which will generally be higher than Pa disc accesses.

(iv) If both A and B are large and if no suitable index on common domain exists on either, then sort both of them (using external sort) and apply scenario (4). The cost is (Pa + Pb + Sa + Sb) disc accesses.

Blasgen and Eswaran (1976) of the SYSTEM R group have studied ten different techniques for join, and found (iii) and (iv) given above as the best (or near best) for most situations, except that if a suitable index is available in (iii), then they normally, but not always, use this index. (If the tuples are randomly scattered, then technique (iv) can be faster than the use of an index.) Technique (iv) is used in the absence of a suitable index on either relation. If more than two relations are joined successively, then more complex techniques based on the separation of (internal identifier, common column) from each relation can be employed, but this is beyond the scope of this book.

8.4.4 Division

The division algorithm can be implemented efficiently with the help of a set of bit maps, maximally one such bit map for each result attribute value. Each bit map, initially set to zero, will contain one bit position for each attribute value of the divisor column. To illustrate the principle, consider the division R:= DT (S#|C#)/ (C#)DJ given in section 6.3.1. Since DJ contains two values C1 and C2, we set up a two-bit bit map, prefixed by a location for a S# value, the bit map being initially set to zero − the bit positions reflect the order of DJ tuples, that is, C1 followed by C2.

S#	C1	C2		R	S#
	0	0			

The first DT tuple has S# = S1 and C# = C1; hence modify the bit map as

S#	C1	C2
S1	1	0

indicating a match for S1 at C1. The second DT tuple has S1 and C2, again matching for C2 in DJ. Hence the bit map is altered as

S#	C1	C2
S1	1	1

R	S#		S#	C1	C2
	S1			0	0

since the bit map is full, S1 is copied to result relation R and the bit map is set to zero again, as shown in the diagrams above. The next tuple is S1 but, since S1 is already in the result relation, we ignore this tuple. After skipping another S1, we get S2 and C1. We can now set these in the bit map as

S#	C1	C2		R	S#
S2	1	0			S1

We continue scanning DT. The next two S2 tuples do not have any matching C# values in DJ and hence are ignored. We then encounter S3 C1, requiring another new bit map which we set up as

S#	C1	C2		R	S#
S2	1	0			S1
S3	1	0			

By the way, we cannot re-use the incomplete bit map of S2 until the end of relation DT, since in general there could be some S2 tuples later in the relation.

The next tuple is S3 C2, again matching in C# of DJ. So we modify the S3 bit map as

S#	C1	C2		R	S#		S#	C1	C2
S2	1	0	$\Rightarrow$		S1		S2	1	0
S3	1	1			S3				

Since the S3 bit map is full, S3 goes to the result, and the S3 bit map is set to zero as shown in the diagrams above. Now we have exhausted the relation. The result is S1 S3 without any contribution from S2, as its bit map is incomplete.

This technique, implemented in PAL, uses a minimal memory and does not require any sorting of the dividend relation. The total cost is the scanning of Pa + Pb pages for division of A by B.

8.4.5 Relative efficiency of operations

Among the selection, division and join operations, selection is the least expensive, and join is the most expensive operation. Since the cost of join or division depends on the number of tuples involved, it is preferable to carry out selection whenever possible before join/division, as selection reduces the number of tuples. Projection should be done as late as possible in order to avoid unnecessary intermediate projections (Smith and Chang, 1975; Todd and Verhofstad, 1978). The PAL precedence of operations given in section 6.3.1 reflects these considerations.

We list below some of these considerations as a rule of thumb (the term select used below is the selection operation of an algebra – not SELECT of SQL).

(1) Select as early as possible.
(2) Project as late as possible.
(3) Use selection in place of join and division whenever possible.
(4) Use join only when attributes in the final result relation are drawn from more than one relation.
(5) Use projection in place of project unique whenever possible.

These rules are useful in most relational languages directly implemented on a relational database, but may not be so in other cases. For instance, if a relational algebra is implemented on a Codasyl database by Codasyl DM commands, then the operational efficiency could depend on other factors, such as the mapping between the Codasyl and the relational data structure, Codasyl storage structure, and the efficiency of Codasyl DM commands. These factors could outweigh any advantages to be gained from the rules.

An optimiser for query expression can be used to reformulate queries in an optimal fashion during the pre-processing of the queries, further improvement being done by selecting an optimal execution strategy and access paths. Finally, although we have used the term optimisation, the process is one of amelioration, the resultant queries strictly being ameliorated rather than optimised.

8.4.6 Query amelioration

It is possible to formulate a relational expression in many different ways, some being more efficient than others (Smith and Chang, 1975; Todd and Verhofstad, 1978). Consider the following example for instance. Find the names and marks of all first year students who scored more than 60 marks in course C1. This can be rewritten in PAL as

$$((SN, MK) \% (STD(S\#) * (SS) CSL)) : CN = \text{``C1''} \text{ AND } MK > 60 \tag{8.1}$$

Here we first join, then project, and finally select. This is inefficient. We should first select so that the number of tuples in the join is reduced, and then join and finally project; thus

$$(SN, MK) \% STD (S\#) * (SS) CSL : CN = \text{``C1''} \text{ AND } MK > 60 \tag{8.2}$$

Alternatively we could have projected columns S#, SN of STD, and (SS, MK) of CSL before joining. For simplicity, we will show this in several steps:

(a) V1 = = (S#, SN) % STD
(b) V2 = = (SS, MK) % CSL
(c) (SN, MK) % V1 (S#) * (SS) V2 : CN = "C1" AND MK > 60

We have done three projections instead of one; this is also inefficient. However, in the derivation of V1 and V2 we have used "%" since project unique is unnecessary. The best solution is expression (8.2) given above. Sometimes special optimisation techniques are used during compilation to make the query expression efficient. As indicated earlier, these considerations are important in the optimisation of all relational languages, irrespective of whether they are algebra or calculus based.

Exercises

8.1 Answer the following queries in SQL and QBE from the relations given below:

   (a) Find the employee name and the salary of all clerks in Aberdeen.
   (b) Find the departmental average salary of all clerks earning between 10K and 20K.
   (c) Find the employee name and manager name of employees earning more than their managers.
   (d) Count, for each department, the employees whose salaries are more than their departmental average.

(e) Find the employees whose individual salaries are more than 25 per cent of their departmental total.

Relations
   (i) EMP (ENO ENAME MNO JOB SAL EDN), consisting of employee number (ENO), employee name (ENAME), manager number (MNO), job title (JOB), salary (SAL) and employee's department number. Note that MNO contains employee number of the manager.
  (ii) DEPT (DNO DNAME TOTSAL LOC), consisting of department number (DNO), department name (DNAME), total departmental salary (TOTSAL) and location (LOC).

8.2 Answer the queries of 6.8 and 6.9 of chapter 6 in SQL.
8.3 Describe and evaluate the implementation techniques of the join and division operations.
8.4 Discuss the issues and trade-offs in query optimisation.
8.5 Express the division operation in terms of the five basic relational algebraic operations.
8.6 Discuss the difference between tuple and domain calculus and their respective impact on queries.
8.7 Design a relational schema on the attached case study on a bakery, by listing the relations and their basic contents. The database is expected to be used for the following purpose:

   (1) to accept customers' orders and to invoice them as described in the case study
   (2) to produce van loading schedule
   (3) to generate sales reports.

Using the schema you have designed, answer the following queries in PAL and SQL.

   (i) Find the names and addresses of those customers who are due to be invoiced on a day number held in data name DAYN.
  (ii) Find the details of the customer orders (item codes and quantities each day) for these customers.
 (iii) Find the prices of the items as needed for invoicing these customers.

CASE STUDY ON A BAKERY

A bakery accepts daily orders from its regular customers for a month at a time, up to a month in advance with a minimum of a fortnight's notice. Each order contains a customer number, item codes and quantities for each item type for up to 31 days. The customers are divided into 28 invoicing groups, each group being invoiced monthly on different days, 1 to 28, of a month for the previous 28 to 31 days, as the case may be. Each invoice contains an invoice number, date, customer number, quantity in each item type in the invoicing period, cost per item and the total value.

The company has a fleet of vans to deliver the goods to the customer, but not all customers use this service; a route number (depending on the delivery point) is, however, allocated to each customer in case any of them uses the service. Delivery is free only for goods exceeding a certain total value in the invoicing period, which can be checked when the invoices are produced. A small charge per delivery is made for the customer whose total invoice value falls short of the minimum required. Information on the total number of times that the delivery service was used in the invoicing period is maintained for each customer, but the actual dates are not recorded. A van loading schedule is prepared daily, one or more vans being allocated to a route, depending on the sizes of the vans and the demand of a route on that particular day.

The company also keeps monthly sales data on each item type for the previous 24 months, for sales analysis.

8.8 Design a relational schema for the attached case study on a Car Rental Company. Write PAL and SQL expressions for the following queries, given that the customer number and order number are held in data items CNUM and ONUM respectively:

(i) Find the cars of the next more expensive model.
(ii) Find the cars of the next cheaper model.
(iii) Find the mileage charge and daily fixed charge for the customer invoice
   (note that the customer may not have used the model originally asked for).

CASE STUDY ON CAR RENTAL COMPANY

A Car Rental Company owns fleets of cars, each fleet being a different model and each having a fixed hiring charge per day plus an additional charge per mile. Cars may be booked for whole days from 1 day to 28 days, three months in advance. If no car of the requested model is available, the firm quotes the next more expensive (based on the fixed daily charge) model. If subsequently a car of the booked model is not available, owing to breakdown or other reasons, the customer is given a car of the next more expensive model at the price of the originally booked model, or alternatively, if the customer prefers, a car of the next cheaper model at its usual cheaper price.

Every car is serviced regularly, but servicing does not take more than one day at a time. The firm prefers the service intervals not to be exceeded by more than 15 per cent. Occasionally a car needs repair lasting up to a week. All cars are sold off after one year, all information on the sold cars being subsequently destroyed.

The firm wishes to use a relational database for the following activities:

(1) To respond to booking requests quickly.
(2) To provide the after-booking service (such as a car of a different model if a car of the original model is not available), as described earlier.

(3) To invoice the customers monthly for the bookings that end in the month, each invoice containing the customer number, the order number, the start and finish dates, the model and cost of each booking, the year to date (YTD) sales, the amount paid and the amount outstanding. (Assume that the order numbers are unique only within a given customer number, and that there is a separate order number for every car booked.)

(4) To produce quarterly reports on the age and mileage of every car, model by model.

8.9 Read the attached case study on an Electronics Component Company and design a relational schema for a database to hold information on components, raw materials and suppliers, so that the need of the company, as described, can be met efficiently. Answer also the following query by PAL and SQL for a component code held in data item COMPC:

Find the detailed information (component code, description, re-order level, quantity in stock and price) of all its immediately subordinate and immediately superior components.

CASE STUDY ON ELECTRONICS COMPONENT COMPANY

An Electronic Component Manufacturing Company produces 2000 types of components, each component containing up to 10 levels of hierarchy and 50 subordinate components. The company maintains 100,000 items of components and 3000 items of raw materials in stock. When an order is received, the inventory is searched, first for the ordered items themselves (the top level components), or failing this, their successive lower level components. All the available components are then withdrawn from stock and the top level components are assembled from the lower components if necessary. If some lowest level components are out of stock, they are fabricated from raw materials and, if raw materials in stock are insufficient, they are quickly ordered from the suppliers. A basic component may use more than one item of raw material, and the same raw material may be needed in more than one basic component. The company does not employ two suppliers for the same raw material but any one supplier usually supplies more than one raw material.

Owing to rapidly advancing technology, components become obsolete fairly fast, being replaced by new products. Since the same component may appear as a subordinate component of some components, and as a superior component of some others, the change of one component usually affects many others. To respond effectively to such changes, the company needs to know quickly about all the affected superior and subordinate components.

References

Blasgen, M. W. and Eswaran, K. A. (1976). On the evaluation of queries on a relational database system. *IBM Research Report RJ1745*, April

Chamberlin, D. D. (1980). A summary of user experience with SQL data sub-language. *Proceedings International Conference on Databases, Aberdeen, 1980*, edited by S. M. Deen and P. Hammersley, Heyden

Chamberlin, D. D. *et al.* (1976). SEQUEL2: a unified approach to data definition, manipulation and control. *IBM Journal R and D*, Vol. (20:6), November

Codd, E. F. (1972). Relational completeness in relational database systems. *IBM Research Report RJ 987*, March; see also Date (1981), p. 215

Date, C. J. (1981). *Introduction to Database Systems, Vol. 1*, 3rd edition, Addison-Wesley

Greenblatt, D. and Waxman, J. (1978). A study of three database query languages. *Databases: Improving Usability and Responsiveness*, edited by B. Schneiderman, Academic Press, New York

Lacroix, M. and Pirotte, A. (1977). Domain oriented relational languages. *Proceedings of the 3rd VLDB Conference, 1977*

Pirotte, A. (1979). Fundamental and secondary issues in the design of non-procedural relational languages. *Proceedings of the 5th VLDB Conference, 1979*, p. 239

Smith, J. M. and Chang, P. Y. T. (1975). Optimising the performance of a relational algebra database interface. *Communications of the ACM*, Vol. (18:16), October, p. 568

Todd, S. J. P. and Verhofstad, J. S. M. (1978). *An optimiser for a relational database system − description and evaluation*, IBM UK Scientific Centre, Peterlee, U.K., October

Zloof, M. M. (1975). Query-by-example: the invocation and definition of tables and forms. *Proceedings of the 1st VLDB Conference, September 1975*

Zloof, M. M. (1977). Query-by-example: a database language. *IBM System Journal*, Vol. (16:4), p. 324

Zloof, M. M. (1981). QBE/OBE . . . . *IEEE Computer*, May, p. 13

9 Codasyl Model

The Codasyl model is a proposed specification of a database management system by Codasyl and is intended as a common database facility for all users. Its data structure is based on what is increasingly referred to as the network structure and hence the alternative name of network model. As mentioned in chapter 1, the model enjoys the active support of most manufacturers, software houses, user organisations and professional bodies. Because of its importance, ANSI has produced a standard for this model under the name of the network structured data model, as described in chapter 11.

The first draft of the Codasyl model appeared in 1971, with a two-level architecture, a schema providing the system view and a subschema providing the user view. The system view was later modified into a logical view (still called a schema) and a storage view called a storage schema. A draft specification of a storage schema was released in 1978, but no final version has ever been approved. In 1983 the main Codasyl committee dealing with the model was disbanded, presumably because it achieved its objective in creating a successful model which ANSI undertook to standardise.

In this chapter we shall describe the principal features of the Codasyl schema, subschema and DM facilities, deferring the proposed storage schema, past changes, Fortran facilities and the evaluation of the model to the next chapter. We shall begin in section 9.1 with a history of Codasyl activities on databases, followed by some relevant concepts in section 9.2. The data description language for the schema is covered in section 9.3 and the Cobol subschema facility in section 9.4, with Cobol DML in section 9.5. Some further characteristics are discussed in section 9.6.

9.1 Codasyl

On 8 April 1959 a small group of computer users and manufacturers met in the University of Pennsylvania, in order to review language developments for business applications. At their request, the U.S. Defense Department, a major computer user, convened a meeting of over 40 representatives from users, manufacturers and other interested parties at the Pentagon on 28 May 1959, to discuss the feasibility of a Common Business Oriented Language (COBOL). The meeting decided to press ahead with the development of COBOL, referred to here as Cobol, and agreed on the concept of the Conference on Data Systems Languages (CODASYL), referred to here as Codasyl, as an informal and voluntary organisation of interested individuals, supported by their institutions, with the objective of designing and developing techniques and languages to assist in data systems analysis, design and implementation.

After its great success with Cobol, Codasyl decided to extend its activities to all developments that could be useful to Cobol. Accordingly, in June 1965, the Cobol Language Subcommittee of Codasyl created a List Processing Task Force to develop list processing capabilities for Cobol. Two years later this was renamed as DataBase Task Group (DBTG) whose activities were greatly inspired by three individuals, namely W. G. Simmons of the United States Steel Corporation, C. W. Bachman, the pioneer of the IDS (then General Electric, later Honeywell) and his co-worker, G. G. Dodd of General Motors.

In August 1968, Codasyl was reorganised to produce three standing committees.

Systems Committee: to develop advanced languages and techniques for data processing, with the aim of automating the process of systems analysis, design and implementation.

Planning Committee: to assist in planning by collecting information from the users and implementors pertaining to the goal of Codasyl.

Programming Language Committee (PLC): to develop programming language specifications to facilitate compatible and uniform source programs and object results, and to minimise the changes necessary for conversion or interchange of source program and data.

The PLC assumed all the functions of the former Cobol Language Subcommittee, including the responsibility for all database activities. In October 1969, the DBTG submitted its first report to the PLC, proposing a Data Description Language (DDL) to describe a database and a Data Manipulation Language (DML) to be used as an extension to a host language to manipulate the data of the database. The report produced a great deal of interest, discussion and criticism. A revised report was produced in April 1971, suggesting for the first time two data description languages, one for the schema and the other for the subschema. This report, usually referred to as the 1971 DBTG report, was accepted by the PLC despite objections from the IBM and the RCA corporation members.

Late in 1971 a new standing committee called the Data Description Language Committee (DDLC) was formed in order to finalise the specification of the schema DDL based on the 1971 DBTG report. Two years later, in April 1973, the DDLC published its proposal for the schema DDL in a *Journal of Development* (to be referred to in this book as the 1973 DDLC JoD), recognising that the process of development in database languages should be evolutionary, as in Cobol. In 1973 the DDLC chartered a British Computer Society (BCS) working group called the Database Administration Working Group (DBAWG) for the development of tools for the use of the database administrator. A major contribution of the DBAWG to the Codasyl model is its Data Storage Description Language (DSDL) for the storage schema. The DDLC published its JoD subsequently in 1978 and in 1981, before its dissolution in 1983.

From the original DBTG of the PLC a Database Language Task Group (DBLTG) was later formed to develop subschema DDL and DML. In May 1973 it produced a draft based on the 1971 DBTG report for the Cobol subschema and DML, the final specification being published in 1975 as the Cobol database facility, in the *Cobol Journal of Development*, to be referred to in this book as the Cobol JoD, subsequently updated in 1978 and in 1981. Codasyl also set up a Fortran DML committee which published its JoDs – largely based on the earlier Cobol JoDs – in 1976 and 1980.

It should be emphasised that although it specifies common user languages, Codasyl has no charter to standardise. The responsibility for standardisation lies with national organisations such as ANSI in the U.S.A. As a general rule, standards organisations do not innovate, but develop standards based on existing facilities; thus there is an ANSI standard for the Codasyl model.

9.2 Basic concepts

The schema in the Codasyl model is described by a free-standing declarative data description language (DDL) but the subschema is host language dependent, each subschema describing a logical subset of schema data (not necessarily disjoint) in a subschema DDL. Only Cobol and Fortran subschema DDL have been specified, the Fortran facility being largely drawn from the Cobol facility. The Codasyl model does not include any non-procedural language or a data dictionary facility, but both can be added by the implementors. The operational concepts of the Codasyl model are similar to those described in section 5.6.3.

Over the years the Codasyl model has undergone many changes, but the presentations in this book are based on the latest version of the model, except where indicated otherwise. Since two separate Codasyl committees (DDLC and Cobol DBLTG) have produced the Codasyl specifications, the 1981 DDLC JoD (DDLC, 1981) and the 1981 Cobol JoD (Cobol, 1981) are incompatible in some aspects, as described in the next chapter. In these cases we have drawn on material from the previous JoDs for a uniform picture. The decisions as to what should or should not be included were also partly influenced by the ANSI specification on network model.

9.2.1 Records

The Codasyl model uses record types and set types for data representation. A record may contain data items and data aggregates, commonly referred to here as components. An entry for a record in the schema constitutes a record type which represents all the records of that type. A record is the basic unit of access.

In the earlier version of the Codasyl model, each record in the database was given a unique internal identifier called a *database key*. A database key was perman-

ent and was available for fast direct access. The term database key is also retained in
the latest version, but it is no longer a permanent identifier. It is only a conceptual
pointer to a record, and its value is valid only during the lifetime of the same run-
unit (see section 9.5.2 for details).

9.2.2 Sets

Associations in the Codasyl model are basically represented by disjoint A-sets and
A-set types (section 2.5.4) called *sets* and *set types* respectively, except that sets and
set types allow members from more than one record type. A set type is defined as
a named logical collection of one owner record type and one or more member
record types, a set or set occurrence being characterised by an owner record from
the owner record type of the set type and none, one, or more member records from
the member record types. The name given to a set type is its *set name* which represents a unique identifier for the set type; a set is identified by the set name plus
the owner record identifier. (To avoid confusion with mathematical sets, some
experts prefer the term *Coset* for Codasyl set).

Sets are considered to be the basic building block of a Codasyl type database.
Since its parallel concept A-set has been explained earlier (sections 2.5, 4.3 and 4.4)
at length, we shall discuss here only the main points of departure, that is, the set
types with multiple member record types. Consider the three record types and their
occurrences, denoted by their respective keys, as shown in figure 9.1.

Record Type	Record occurrences
Doctor Records	D1, D2, D3, D4
Nurse Records	N1, N2, N3, N4, N5
Patient Records	P1, P2, P3, P4, P5, P6, P7, P8

Figure 9.1

We construct a set type named, say, DOCNP with record type Doctor as the
owner and the other two record types as the members, as shown in figure 9.2. We
may represent set type DOCNP in a modified Bachman diagram (figure 9.3).

Set name	:	DOCNP
Owner name	:	DOCTOR
Member name	:	NURSE and PATIENT

Figure 9.2

Such a set type is called a multimembered set type. This set type will represent as
many sets as there are owner records, each set being owned by a specific owner

record; some of its instances are shown in figure 9.4. Set 1 does not have any
member and is therefore known as an *empty set*. Owing to subsequent update by
an application program, the number of sets in the set type and their memberships
may change. Although each occurrence of an owner record type has a set, be it
empty or not, some occurrences of member record type(s) need not belong to any
set type. In this example, N5 and P8 do not belong to any doctor set; they could
be nurses and patients who have nothing to do with the doctors of record type
DOCTOR.

The 1:*n* association restriction rule stated in section 4.3.2 applies to the Codasyl
sets as well. Thus the same record could be owner and member of the same set type,
and even in the same set. As in A-set types, the same record can participate in many
set types, subject to this rule. The direct representation of *m:n* associations is not
possible in the Codasyl model, they must be resolved into 1:*n* association types for
representation by set types as in figure 4.4. In general, any network can be represented in the Codasyl model by using several − though not a single − set types.
This is why the Codasyl model is called a *network data model*. It may be observed
here that some models, such as the hierarchical model (section 13.2), do not permit
the use of networks, except in a limited fashion.

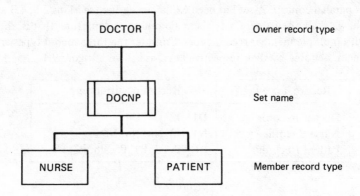

Figure 9.3 Multimembered set type

Sets	Owner	Members
Set 1	D1	
Set 2	D2	P2, P3
Set 3	D3	N1, N3, P1, P4
Set 4	D4	N2, P5, P6, N4, P7

Figure 9.4

Sometimes it is necessary to group a logical subset of records of a given type as a set for special processing. Such a group could be the employees on sales commission, as against other employees. In this case we can create a special set type in the Codasyl model, by declaring a dummy record type called SYSTEM as the owner, and the employee record type as the member with a user-defined set name. Such a set type has only one set occurrence, containing, in the above example, all the employees on sales commission, and it is referred to as a *singular set* or SYSTEM set (see its use in exercise 9.10 at the end of this chapter).

9.2.3 Access paths

All access paths discussed in section 4.4.5 are permitted in the Codasyl model. The members of a set can be processed in both a forward and a backward direction with an additional facility for finding the owner from the member records. The members of a set can also be accessed directly. Since the members can be processed both forward and backward, the logical order in which the members of a set appear is important. This logical order can be supported in several different ways, as discussed later.

9.3 Codasyl schema model

Many of the clauses presented in this section will be illustrated with examples from the schema of the education database given in subsection 9.3.5; the reader is therefore advised to browse through the introductory part of that subsection before moving to subsection 9.3.2. We begin with the skeleton entries of the schema.

9.3.1 Schema skeleton

The schema contains the following four entries.

1. Schema name entry: one for the whole schema.
2. Record entry: one entry for each record type.
3. Set entry: one entry for each set type.
4. End schema: to indicate end of the schema.

Both record and set entries have subentries, as shown in figure 9.5. There are two KEY clauses, one in the record entry, and the other in the member subentry of set entry. To distinguish between them, we shall refer to the former as record key and to the latter as member key. Record name, set name and key names must be unique in the schema. As we cannot have a Codasyl database without records, there has to be at least one record entry in a Codasyl schema. But we could have a database without sets, and hence set entries *should not* be

SCHEMA NAME IS name
    [CALL procedure name   ]
    [ACCESS CONTROL LOCK _ _ _]

RECORD NAME IS name
    [KEY keyname is {ASCENDING/DESCENDING} data identifier
        DUPLICATES ARE { SYSTEM DEFAULT/NOT ALLOWED}]

[CHECK IS _ _ _]
[CALL procedure name]
[ACCESS CONTROL LOCK _ _ _]

[Level number] data name
    [TYPE _ _ _]
    [OCCURS _ _ _]
    [SOURCE _ _ _]
    [RESULT _ _ _]
    [CHECK IS _ _ _]
    [CALL _ _ _]
    [ACCESS CONTROL LOCK _ _ _]

SET NAME IS name
    OWNER IS   {record name/SYSTEM}
    ORDER FOR INSERTION IS
        {FIRST/LAST/NEXT/PRIOR/SYSTEM DEFAULT/
        SORTED BY DEFINED KEYS/
        SORTED BY DEFINED KEYS RECORD TYPE _ _ _/
        SORTED WITHIN RECORD TYPE}
    [CALL procedure name]
    [ACCESS CONTROL LOCK _ _ _]
    MEMBER IS record name
        INSERTION IS {AUTOMATIC/MANUAL}
        RETENTION IS {FIXED/MANDATORY/OPTIONAL}
    [KEY IS {ASCENDING/DESCENDING} {RECORD TYPE/data identifier } . . .
    [DUPLICATES ARE { NOT ALLOWED/SYSTEM DEFAULT}]

Figure 9.5

[CHECK IS condition   ]
[STRUCTURAL CONSTRAINT IS member-data identifier
        EQUAL TO owner-data-identifier   ]
  SET SELECTION IS
        {[THRU set-name OWNER IDENTIFIED BY
        {SYSTEM/APPLICATION}]/[BY STRUCTURAL CONSTRAINT]}

[CALL _ _ _   ]
[ACCESS CONTROL LOCK _ _ _   ]

END SCHEMA

Figure 9.5 (continued)

compulsory. However, 1981 JoD is somewhat unclear on this point, and hence variations could be expected in implementation.

Notations used in the syntaxes are:

 (i) Upper case underlined: key words that must be present
 (ii) Upper case but not underlined: optional words
 (iii) Lower case entries: to be supplied by the user
 (iv) Clauses separated by /: alternative clauses
 (v) Clauses enclosed [ ]: optional facilities
 (vi) A clause enclosed { }: the clause must be present
 (vii) Clauses enclosed { }: only one of the clauses (separated by /)
                    must be present
(viii) Clauses enclosed ‖ ‖: at least one of them (separated by /)
                    must be used
 (ix) _ _ _: incomplete syntax
 (x) ... after an enclosure: the enclosed item(s) may be repeated.

9.3.2 Schema name entry

The schema name entry is the first entry of a schema and is used to name the schema and to associate two optional facilities through a CALL and an ACCESS CONTROL clause.

The CALL clause allows a user-defined procedure to be called for special action in the event of errors or other specified conditions. The ACCESS CONTROL clause allows the specification of privacy locks. Both the CALL and ACCESS CONTROL lock can be specified not only in the schema name entry, but also for each entry and subentry in the rest of the schema.

A locked object can be accessed by a key specified in the subschema or in the user program or in an interactive manner, depending on implementation. The lock itself can be specified as a constant, as the value of a variable or as the result of a named procedure. The key could be a value or the function of a value which matches the lock; the action of the named procedure is implementor-defined.

The schema of the education database described in section 9.3.5 can be accessed (line 020) either by a matching key value for the lock SCH-LOCK or by the user-defined procedure called SECURITY. The key value for the lock can be either specified in the subschema which is unwise, or entered interactively by the user. The procedure SECURITY could carry out various identification checks (for example, user id, password, name) before granting access, depending on implementations.

9.3.3 Record entry

There is one record entry for each record type, each entry being composed of one record subentry, followed by one or more data subentries. There must be at least one record entry in the schema.

A record key, made up of components of the record type, can be declared in the record subentry for sequential access by record selection format 1 (section 9.5.4). This key is known as the *record order key*. The term *data identifier* used in the syntax implies one or more component names of the record type. If the key is to be unique, then the option DUPLICATES ARE NOT ALLOWED must be specified for the key. If it is not unique, then duplicates can be ordered in several different ways, but we have given here only the SYSTEM DEFAULT option, which means that the DBCS arranges the order in any way it prefers. In discussing member keys later, we shall likewise restrict to the SYSTEM DEFAULT option for non-unique keys.

The examples of record order keys are given in the sample schema of section 9.3.5, but this is an area where the Codasyl 1981 schema and subschema are incompatible; for details see section 10.3.

Data subentry

One data subentry is required for each component of the record type, and a component is described in a manner similar to Cobol, except that a TYPE clause replaces the Cobol PICTURE clause. (The PICTURE clause was a valid descriptor in the earlier Codasyl model.) However, level numbers can be omitted, in which case all the components are assumed to be at the same level. (The component description in the 1981 JoD is closer to PL/I than to Cobol).

The subentries on lines 150, 345 and 480 of the sample schema represent data aggregates, the others are data items. The use of the OCCUR clauses parallels that in Cobol. TYPE FIXED DECIMAL n implies a decimal integer of n digits, whereas

TYPE FIXED DECIMAL n, m implies a decimal fixed point number with n places before the decimal point and m places after it.

A CHECK clause can be specified as a condition in the record, data and member subentries for data validation. Conditions in the Codasyl schema are expressed like the predicates of the relational languages, using the logical operators (NOT, AND, OR) and comparison operators ($< \leqslant = \neq \geqslant >$). An example of the CHECK clause for the record subentry of the Tutor record could be

CHECK IS (SALARY $>$ 10000 AND SALARY $\leqslant$ 20000
AND TNO $<$ 1000) OR (SALARY $>$ 20000
AND TNO $\leqslant$ 1000)

The function of the CALL clause, which can also be specified at this subentry, is different; it invokes a user procedure on specified execution condition. Its basic format for record subentries gives the flavour:

CALL procedure name || BEFORE/ON ERROR DURING/AFTER||
||DELETE/INSERT/MODIFY/. . . ||

Some of the options are different for different subentries. The action of the ACCESS CONTROL clause is similar to that in the schema name entry.

The SOURCE and RESULT clauses are used to avoid direct and indirect data redundancy respectively, but the former can be used only on a member record of a set. Its basic format is

Level number data item
SOURCE IS source data item OF OWNER OF set name

If a member record type and the owner record type of a set type have a common data item, then the data item in the member record (called subject record) can be declared as a copy of the corresponding value of the owner record. The subject data item takes the TYPE of the source data item and hence TYPE declaration is not needed. An example of its use is given in line 470 of section 9.3.5.

The basic format of the RESULT clause is

Level number data item TYPE
RESULT OF {condition/PROCEDURE procedure name . . .}

This clause allows a data item (called target data item but not subject data item) to be derived from one or more other data items in accordance with a specified Boolean condition or a named procedure. The details are beyond the scope of this book.

The formats of the SOURCE and RESULT clauses have been changed almost continuously since their first introduction in the 1971 DBTG report, indicating an unsatisfactory state of affairs. The basic idea behind them — a need to reduce data redundancy — is good, but the benefit seems to have been overshadowed by their processing overhead. For instance, the SOURCE clause implies extra disc accesses to retrieve the owner record whenever the subject data item is needed. The target data items in the RESULT clause need to be re-evaluated in a complex fashion when any source data item changes. No wonder that most Codasyl implementors have ignored these clauses.

To summarise the record entries, we have one record subentry for each record type, which allows specification of record order keys for sequential access to the records by record selection format 1 (section 9.5.4). There is one data subentry for each component, described with level numbers as in Cobol, but using a TYPE (instead of a PICTURE) clause. A data item can be a copy of another, or derived from others. A data validation facility is provided by a CHECK clause. Database procedures can be called for special action during the execution of the database. Privacy constraints can be specified for every subentry.

9.3.4 Set entry

There is one set entry for every set type in the schema, each entry consisting of one set subentry for the set type and one member subentry for each member record type.

In the set subentry we must specify set name and owner name; the latter can be SYSTEM (for singular set type as explained earlier) or a record name. The functions of the optional CALL and ACCESS CONTROL clauses are similar to those discussed earlier. The ORDER clause specifies the *set order criteria* and is compulsory. Its function is to insert members in each set of the set type in a specified sequence in which the members can be accessed by record selection format 4 (section 9.5.4). There can be only one such sequence for a set type. There are three main options in the order clause:

Positional — relative to other members
System default — don't care order
Sorted — in order of member keys.

In the system default option, the order is defined by the system. The positional insertion has four suboptions: FIRST, LAST, PRIOR and NEXT. The option LAST makes the most recently stored member last in the queue, thus inserting in the increasing time sequence, as shown in figure 9.6.

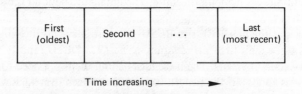

Figure 9.6 Member insertion: option LAST

Option FIRST makes the most recent member first in the queue, thus giving an insertion in reverse time sequence. As mentioned in chapter 4, the option FIRST/ LAST can be made to yield a given order by sorting the initial members in that order, although the future insertions may not necessarily arrive in that order. The PRIOR/NEXT options can be used to insert a member prior to or next to another member record. Some examples of these options are given in the sample schema in lines 615, 675, 735, 865 and 925.

In the SORTED option the member records of each set of a set type are maintained in a sorted order of a key, usually implemented by a B-tree (chapter 3). The key itself is the member key specified in the member subentry given later. This option has three suboptions as follows:

(i) SORTED BY DEFINED KEYS
(ii) SORTED BY DEFINED KEYS RECORD TYPE member record names
(iii) SORTED WITHIN RECORD TYPE.

The first suboption maintains the member records of each set in order of the member key. If this option is used for a multimembered set type, then the members are ordered irrespective of their record type, strictly by the member key values. The other two suboptions are only for multimembered set types, and will be explained after the introduction of the member key clause.

Member subentry

Each member subentry begins with a member name. In addition to the standard CHECK, CALL and ACCESS CONTROL clauses, the other major options are: Membership class, Member KEY and SET SELECTION clauses, as explained below.

Membership class

The membership clause specifies conditions under which a record can be a member (INSERTION condition) and also the conditions under which it may cease to be a member (RETENTION condition). These conditions define the membership class of the member record type and may be viewed as integrity constraints that set out the relevant assertions. Their formats are:

INSERTION IS {AUTOMATIC/MANUAL}
RETENTION IS {FIXED/MANDATORY/OPTIONAL}

A record can be inserted to a set either automatically or manually. If a record type is declared AUTOMATIC in the member subentry, then as soon as a record of this type is stored in the database, the DBCS automatically makes it a member of the appropriate set occurrence of the set type concerned, the set being selected on the basis of the specified SET SELECTION criteria (see below).

If membership is MANUAL, then a record is made a member of a set by a DM command issued from an application program. Consider, for instance, an organisation having Department records and Employee records, each department having a number of employees, some of whom are entitled to commission. We may construct a set type COMMISSION owned by the Department records with the employees on commission as the members. Here the membership class of the record type Employee should be MANUAL so that the application programmer can choose only the employees on commission for membership.

Once a record is made a member of a set it may or may not be removable, depending on the option specified. If the Retention is OPTIONAL the record concerned can be terminated from the membership without any restriction; on the other hand, if it is MANDATORY, the record must remain a member of the set type although its membership may be switched from one set to another of the same set type. Finally, if Retention is FIXED, a member record cannot be disconnected from its set occurrence at all, unless of course it is deleted from the database.

Combining these options, we have six membership classes to which a member record may belong: MANDATORY AUTOMATIC, OPTIONAL AUTOMATIC, MANDATORY MANUAL, OPTIONAL MANUAL, FIXED AUTOMATIC or FIXED MANUAL. Examples of these can be seen in the set types specified in the sample schema (lines 535, 565, 635, and so on).

The STRUCTURAL CONSTRAINT clause can be specified if the member record type shares some common component(s) with the owner record type, as implied by the condition 'member-data-identifier EQUAL TO owner-data-identifier'. The clause will prevent records without the matching values for the common components from becoming a member. If the owner-data-identifier is a unique identifier of the owner record type, then in terms of the relational model we may call it a primary key, and the member-data-identifier the corresponding foreign key. Thus the STRUCTURAL CONSTRAINT clause may be assumed to enforce the referential integrity constraint of the relational model. Examples of the use of this clause are given on lines 640 and 950 of the sample schema.

Set selection criteria

During the processing of the database, it is often necessary to select a particular set out of all the occurrences in a given set type. The programmer can locate the wanted set by first finding the owner or via a known member, as we shall show later. However, there are also occasions when the DBCS has to find a correct set automatically; for instance, to insert a record as set number when the membership class is AUTOMATIC. Similarly an automatic set selection is also needed for the execution of set update commands CONNECT and RECONNECT and also the record selection format 7 of the FIND command, as explained in sections 9.5.3 and 9.5.4. The set selection clause specifies the rules for the selection of the correct set; its format is rather complex, but we present here three important (and relatively simpler) options:

SET SELECTION IS {{THRU setname OWNER IDENTIFIED BY
    {SYSTEM/APPLICATION}}/{BY STRUCTURAL CONSTRAINTS}}

The SYSTEM option is used for SYSTEM set; since it is a singular set, the selection is nominal. The APPLICATION option selects the set currently available to the run-unit (see section 9.5.2 for further explanation and the sample schema for its use).

The STRUCTURAL CONSTRAINT option can be used for set selection only if the STRUCTURAL CONSTRAINT clause has been specified earlier under the member subentry, and if the owner-data-identifier is a unique identifier of the owner. It is used in line 645 of the sample schema.

Member key clause

There can be only one member key in each member subentry, and it does not have any key name. Its basic format is

> KEY IS {[ASCENDING/DESCENDING] component name}...
> DUPLICATES ARE {SYSTEM DEFAULT/NOT ALLOWED}

The key may contain one or more data items of the member record type, the duplicate values being handled by the DUPLICATES clause as in record keys. The first item in the KEY clause must be the member record name instead of a component name if the sorted set order suboption (ii) is used (see below). Some examples of the use of the KEY clause are given on lines 540, 570, 820 of the sample schema.

Member keys are never directly used by a programmer and hence are not named. The objective of the member key is only to define the sort order criterion of the member records which are accessed in that order by the record selection format 4 of the Codasyl FIND command. If the SORTED option is not used in set order criteria, then this key clause is not required.

Sorted set order option

To discuss the sorted option, we shall consider a multimembered set type DES-SET where DEPT record type is the owner and EMP and STUDENT record types are members, all three record types being taken from the sample schema. Assume the following as the appropriate entry.

Line no.
```
10    SET NAME DES-SET
15        OWNER IS DEPT
20            ORDER IS SORTED BY DEFINED KEYS

30        MEMBER IS EMP
35        INSERTION MANUAL OPTIONAL
40        KEY IS ASCENDING ENO
45            DUPLICATES ARE NOT ALLOWED
50        SET SELECTION THRU DES-SET APPLICATION

60        MEMBER IS STUDENT
65        INSERTION MANUAL OPTIONAL
```

70   KEY IS ASCENDING SNO
75   DUPLICATES ARE NOT ALLOWED
80   SET SELECTION THRU DES-SET APPLICATION

As pointed out earlier, the member records of each set occurrence in the above example will be sorted in the key order, irrespective of their record types. Of course it is possible, for instance, for all SNO values to be higher than all ENO values, and as such student member records will be grouped together, but this will be coincidental. It is also possible to have identical SNO and ENO values in a given set; but the current Codasyl specification does not say what will happen in that case and therefore we assume it will be implementor-defined.

If we wish to sort the member records of different types of a given set separately, we can use their record names as part of the member key. To do so, we use the sorted suboption (ii), and modify the member key clause to include member record name in it. If we do this the line numbers 20, 40 and 70 given above will be changed as follows:

20   ORDER IS SORTED BY DEFINED KEYS
            RECORD TYPE EMP STUDENT
40   KEY IS ASCENDING EMP ENO
70   KEY IS ASCENDING STUDENT SNO

By permitting record names to be used as major keys in the member key, this suboption effectively separates member records of different types. Note that a member key can and must have its member record name as first item in the key if and only if the sorted suboption (ii) is used.

In the third sorted suboption, the member records of different types are sorted separately for the same set, but the member record name is *not* specified as part of the member key. In this case line 20, 40 and 70 will be

20   ORDER IS SORTED WITHIN RECORD TYPE
40   KEY IS ASCENDING ENO
70   KEY IS ASCENDING SNO

An implementor could use the record name as part of the sort key, but the schema specification does not demand it. This third sorted suboption seems unnecessary, as its difference with suboption (ii) is trivial. Separate syntaxes to permit such trivial differences often make the Codasyl model unnecessarily complex. The ANSI proposal has dropped this third option (see section 11.1.1).

9.3.5 Sample schema

In this subsection, we present an example of a Codasyl schema for a more comprehensive understanding of the schema DDL. The reader is advised to look at this example before proceeding to the next section. The line numbers given in the example are for ease of referencing and do not form part of the Codasyl schema. We assume an education database made up of six record types and seven set types (figure 9.7). The record types are

1. DEPT records for department
2. TUTOR records for teachers
3. EMP records for employees other than tutors
4. COURSE records for courses offered
5. STUDENT records for students
6. CSL records for course student links.

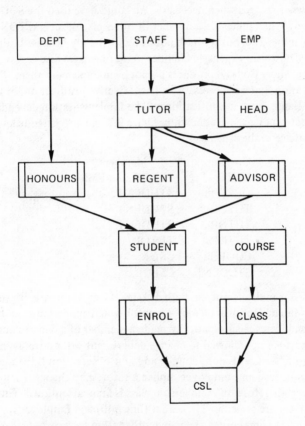

Figure 9.7 Set types of the sample chosen

In record type DEPT, DNO is department number and DNAME is department name, both DNO and DNAME being the unique identifier of Department records. In Tutor records TDN is tutors' department number and TNO is tutor numbers. We assume TNO to be unique only within a department and hence TDN and TNO concatenated together can act as the unique key. Alternatively social security number SSN (National Insurance Number in the U.K.) can also act as unique key. The unique identifier of the Employee record is employee number ENO, as well as social security number (SSN). Unlike TNO, ENO is assumed to be unique, irrespective of departments.

Courses and students have many to many relationships, resolved by introducing CSL (Course-Student Link) records where CN is the course numbers and SN the student numbers, corresponding to CNO and SNO in the COURSE and STUDENT record respectively. We have used the SOURCE clause in line 470 to show that the value of CN in a CSL record is a copy of the CNO value of its owner record in the set type CLASS (see below). Therefore CN values will not be stored, but brought in from the owner records when necessary. We could have used the SOURCE clause for SN in line 475, and indeed in a number of other places, such as TDN (from set type STAFF) in line 210; but we have not done so, mainly because both SOURCE and RESULT clauses are expensive facilities, requiring extra disc accesses to get the required values. Many Codasyl products do not even implement them. The line 470 gives an illustration, but not necessarily a cost-effective justification, of the use of the SOURCE clause. Such a justification will be implementation dependent.

The seven set types given are shown in figure 9.7 and also listed below in order of their appearance in the schema.

Set name	Owner	Member
1. STAFF	DEPT	TUTOR and EMP
2. HONOURS	DEPT	STUDENT
3. ADVISOR	TUTOR	STUDENT
4. REGENT	TUTOR	STUDENT
5. HEAD	TUTOR	TUTOR
6. CLASS	COURSE	CSL
7. ENROL	STUDENT	CSL

Set type STAFF is multimembered, with TUTOR as an Automatic Fixed Member, and EMP as a Manual Optional Member. A tutor, when appointed must belong to a Department, and is hence automatically made a member of a department. Once appointed, tutors are not allowed to change department without resigning (that is, interdepartmental transfer is not allowed) and hence Retention is Fixed. On the other hand, a non-academic employee, unlike a tutor, may change from one department to another; therefore his membership class is Manual Optional. Tutor records of each STAFF set are sorted in TNO order (line 540) and Employee records in ENAME (employee name) order, independently within each record type. Since the TNO values are unique in each department (and hence in each STAFF set), we have disallowed duplicates in the Member Key clause of TUTOR. However employee names can be duplicates and, if they are, the system will order them in a manner convenient to itself (SYSTEM DEFAULT option).

It is assumed that each student must belong to a department — the department of his Honours subject ('major' in the U.S.A.). The department is chosen at the time of registration, and cannot subsequently be changed. Hence students are Automatic Fixed Members in set type HONOURS. We also assume the university tutors to act as both regents and advisors of students, and hence we have two further set types: REGENT and ADVISOR (see also section 2.5.4), both being owned by TUTOR and membered by STUDENT. It is further assumed that regents and advisors are allocated after the registration and can be changed but, once allocated, a student must always have a regent and an advisor. Therefore the membership class is MANUAL MANDATORY.

Set type HEAD is recursive in the sense that a tutor as Head owns other tutors and also himself as the members of that department. We could have made, but did not make it also a multimember set type with both TUTOR and EMP as member record types. We have used the Defined key option in set type HEAD for sorted ordering, and positional (FIRST/NEXT) and SYSTEM DEFAULT options in several others for no special reason.

```
010   SCHEMA NAME IS EDUCATION-DATABASE.
020       ACCESS CONTROL LOCK IS SCH-LOCK OR PROCEDURE SECURITY.
100   RECORD NAME DEPT
105       KEY DKEY ASCENDING DNO
110           DUPLICATES ARE NOT ALLOWED.
130   03 DNO                TYPE CHARACTER 4.
135   03 DNAME              TYPE CHARACTER 20.
140   03 DBUDGET            TYPE FIXED DECIMAL 7, 2.
145   03 NO-OF-COURSES      TYPE FIXED DECIMAL 2.
150   03 INTAKE-LIMIT       OCCURS NO-OF-COURSES TIMES.
155       05 COURSE-NO      TYPE CHARACTER 6.
160       05 LIMIT          TYPE FIXED DECIMAL 2.
180   RECORD NAME TUTOR
185       KEY TKEY ASCENDING TDN TNO
190           DUPLICATES ARE NOT ALLOWED.
210   03 TDN                TYPE CHARACTER 4.
215   03 SSN                TYPE CHARACTER 10.
220   03 TNO                TYPE FIXED DECIMAL 3.
225   03 TNAME              TYPE CHARACTER 30.
230   03 SALARY             TYPE FIXED DECIMAL 5, 2.
235   03 TENURE             TYPE CHARACTER 1.
250   RECORD NAME EMP.
255   03 ENO                TYPE CHARACTER 6.
260   03 SSN                TYPE CHARACTER 10.
265   03 ENAME              TYPE CHARACTER 30.
270   03 JOB-TITLE          TYPE CHARACTER 10.
275   03 SALARY             TYPE FIXED DECIMAL 5, 2.
280   03 HNO                TYPE CHARACTER 7.
```

```
300   RECORD NAME STUDENT
305       KEY SKEY ASCENDING SNO
310           DUPLICATES ARE NOT ALLOWED.
335   03 SNO                TYPE CHARACTER 5.
340   03 SNAME              TYPE CHARACTER 20.
345   03 DATE-OF-BIRTH.
350          05 DD          TYPE FIXED DECIMAL 2.
355          05 MM          TYPE FIXED DECIMAL 2.  ·
360          05 YY          TYPE FIXED DECIMAL 2.
370   03 YEAR-OF-STUDY      TYPE FIXED DECIMAL 1.
375   03 SADDRESS           TYPE CHARACTER 40.
410   RECORD NAME COURSE
415       KEY CKEY ASCENDING CNO
420           DUPLICATES ARE NOT ALLOWED.
430   03 CNO                TYPE CHARACTER 6.
435   03 CNAME              TYPE CHARACTER 20.
440   03 DNO                TYPE CHARACTER 4.
460   RECORD NAME CSL.
470   03 CN                 SOURCE CNO OF OWNER OF CLASS.
475   03 SN                 TYPE CHARACTER 5.
480   03 EXAM-MARKS         TYPE FIXED DECIMAL 2 OCCURS 3 TIMES.
500   SET NAME IS STAFF
510       OWNER IS DEPT
515           ORDER IS SORTED BY DEFINED KEYS RECORD TYPE TUTOR
              EMP.
530   MEMBER IS TUTOR
535       INSERTION AUTOMATIC FIXED
540       KEY IS ASCENDING TUTOR TNO
545           DUPLICATES ARE NOT ALLOWED
550       SET SELECTION THRU APPLICATION.
560   MEMBER IS EMP
565       INSERTION MANUAL OPTIONAL
570       KEY IS ASCENDING EMP ENAME
575           DUPLICATES ARE SYSTEM DEFAULT
580       SET SELECTION THRU STAFF APPLICATION.
600   SET NAME IS HONOURS
610       OWNER IS DEPT
615           ORDER IS LAST.
630   MEMBER IS STUDENT
635       INSERTION AUTOMATIC FIXED
640       STRUCTURAL CONSTRAINT IS SDEPT EQUAL TO DNO
645       SET SELECTION BY STRUCTURAL CONSTRAINT.
660   SET NAME ADVISOR
670       OWNER IS TUTOR
```

```
675          ORDER IS FIRST.
690       MEMBER IS STUDENT
695          INSERTION MANUAL MANDATORY
700          SET SELECTION THRU ADVISOR APPLICATION.
720   SET NAME REGENT
730       OWNER IS TUTOR
735          ORDER IS LAST.
750       MEMBER IS STUDENT
755          INSERTION MANUAL MANDATORY
760          SET SELECTION THRU REGENT APPLICATION.
780   SET NAME HEAD
790       OWNER IS TUTOR
795          ORDER IS SORTED BY DEFINED KEYS.
810       MEMBER IS TUTOR
815          INSERTION MANUAL MANDATORY
820          KEY IS ASCENDING TDN TNO
825             DUPLICATES ARE NOT ALLOWED
830          SET SELECTION THRU HEAD APPLICATION.
850   SET NAME CLASS
860       OWNER COURSE
865          ORDER IS SYSTEM DEFAULT.
880       MEMBER IS CSL
885          INSERTION AUTOMATIC FIXED
890          SET SELECTION THRU CRS-SET APPLICATION.
910   SET NAME ENROL
920       OWNER STUDENT
925          ORDER IS SYSTEM DEFAULT.
940       MEMBER IS CSL
945          INSERTION AUTOMATIC FIXED
950          STRUCTURAL CONSTRAINT IS SN EQUAL TO SNO
955          SET SELECTION THRU ENROL APPLICATION.
990   END SCHEMA.
```

9.4 Cobol subschema model

The Codasyl Cobol facilities include a subschema Data Description Language (DDL) and a corresponding Cobol Data Manipulation Language (DML); both, in this book, are drawn from the *Codasyl Cobol Journal of Development 1981* (to be referred to as the 1981 Cobol JoD), except where stated otherwise.

9.4.1 Subschema characteristics

The Cobol subschema proposed consists of entries in a DDL and is divided into three Divisions: Title, Mapping and Structure (figure 9.8). The subschema is named in the Title Division. The Mapping Division provides the facility to define logical relationships between the schema and the subschema definitions, and contains an Alias Section where the schema data names can be renamed for the subschema. Such renaming is essential if the schema data names are illegal in the host language.

The Structure Division has four sections: Realm, Record, Set and Working-storage, of which the last two are optional. A realm may be viewed as a user-defined logical file, made up of one or more record types (see its syntax), which can be opened and closed by DM commands in Exclusive, Protected or Shared mode for update or retrieval (see later). It thus provides data protection in a concurrent environment. The Record Section describes records, with record names and their data subentries. Each subentry, as in the schema, describes a component with level numbers, but using Cobol PICTURE(PIC) clauses and conventions. Each data subentry can also include a Check clause (as in the schema) for additional data validation. All data and record names must be those of the schema unless renamed in the Alias Section.

TITLE DIVISION
SS subschema-name WITHIN schemaname

[MAPPING DIVISION
  [ALIAS SECTION
    {AD {SET setname/RECORD recordname/dataname} IS newname}...]]

STRUCTURE DIVISION
  REALM SECTION
  {RD realmname CONTAINS {ALL/{recordname}...} RECORDS}...
  RECORD SECTION
  {01 recordname

      [ACCESS CONTROL LOCK _ _ _]
      {data-subentries ...}
      [SET SECTION
      SD setname
          [SET SELECTION FOR member-record name IS VIA setname
          BY STRUCTURAL CONSTRAINT/CURRENT/
              VALUE OF owner-identifier IS alternate-data-item}...]...]
  [WORKING-STORAGE SECTION
    {01 dataname ALTERNATE FOR identifier} ...]

Figure 9.8 Subschema skeleton entries

The set entries specify set names and an optional subschema set selection clauses which over-ride those in the schema. It has several options of which three are shown in the subschema entries (figure 9.8). The STRUCTURAL CONSTRAINT option is the same as that of the schema, and is subject to the same pre-conditions. The CURRENT option is equivalent to the APPLICATION option of the schema and chooses the set identified by the current of the set type (see later). In the third option the set is selected by identifying the owner through an owner identifier (made up of one or more of owner's data items) whose value can identify the owner record uniquely. The value itself is supplied by the user in what is called an *alternate data* item which brings us to the working-storage section.

This working-storage section is a special section for the subschema to describe working data items to be used by the DBCS, except that each of these data items can be an alternate of a database item, to be accessed and updated by the programmer. The DBCS uses it only if specified in the third set selection option described above, but the DBCS cannot change its value. (See also the sample subschema given below.)

If the reader is looking for record keys, and additional access control facilities, as were in the 1978 Cobol JoD, then the search will be in vain. These were withdrawn from the 1981 Cobol JoD, so creating an anomalous situation, particularly with respect to the record keys in the schema (see section 10.3).

9.4.2 Subschema independence

The Codasyl model allows the following major variations between the schema and the subschema.

(a) *Data items*. The format of a data item in the subschema can be different from that in the schema. A group of data items can be selected from the schema, grouped in a different order and given a new groupname in the subschema.
(b) *Record*. A subschema record can be constructed from a subset of the data items of a given schema record, and the data items can be reordered. The unnecessary record types can also be omitted.
(c) *Set*. Unnecessary set types and member record types can be excluded from the subschema, and the new set selection criteria can be specified, as mentioned earlier.

All access paths specified in the storage schema are transparent to the application programmer who accesses the database following the standard DM commands. A subschema is independently compiled and stored, to be subsequently invoked by an application program. Although a schema can support an unlimited number of subschemas with two or more subschemas sharing the same part of the database if necessary, an application program can use only one subschema, the binding between the subschema and the database being implementor-dependent.

9.4.3 Sample subschema

The sample subschema given in figure 9.9 is based on the schema of section 9.5, but contains only record types STUDENT, TUTOR, DEPT, COURSE and CSL, with set types ADVISOR, REGENT, HONOURS, ENROL and CLASS. Record type CSL is renamed as LINK-REC and data item EXAM-MARK as MARKS, as declared in the Alias Section. Only some schema data items are included in the record types, which form three realms REALM1, REALM2 and REALM3.

In set types ADVISOR and REGENT, the sets (in fact, the set owners) are identified by matching social security number SSN. The value supplied by the programmer is held in ASN which must be declared in the subschema Working-storage section as an alternative data item for SSN. Likewise HONOURS sets are identified by DNO values held by the programmer in SDN, which must also be an alternative data item.

Although subschema set selection criteria are optional they, if specified, over-ride those in the schema. For instance, the set selection for HONOURS in the schema is by Structural Constraint, whereas in the subschema it is by alternate data items. Likewise the set selection for ENROL is by Application in the schema, and by Structural Constraint in the subschema. We can specify the Structural Constraint option for set type ENROL in the subschema only because two pre-conditions are met:

 (i) Structural Constraint is specified in the schema in the member subentry for common data items (SN and SNO).

(ii) Owner-data-identifier (SNO) is a unique identifier of the student records which are the owners.

```
            TITLE DIVISION.
            SS STUDENT-DATA WITHIN EDUCATION-DATABASE.

            MAPPING DIVISION.
            ALIAS SECTION.
            AD RECORD CSL IS LINK-REC.
            AD EXAM-MARKS IS MARKS.

            STRUCTURE DIVISION.
            RD REALM1 CONTAINS TUTOR.
            RD REALM2 CONTAINS STUDENT, DEPT.
            RD REALM3 CONTAINS COURSE, LINK-REC.

            RECORD SECTION.
            01 STUDENT.
               03  SNO              PIC X(5).
               03  SNAME            PIC X(20).
```

```
    03  DATE-OF-BIRTH      PIC X(6).
    03  YEAR-OF-STUDY      PIC 9.
    03  SADDRESS           PIC X(40).

01 DEPT.
    03  DNO                PIC X(4).
    03  DNAME              PIC X(20).

01 TUTOR.
    03  TDN        PIC X(4).
    03  SSN        PIC X(10).
    03  TNO        PIC 9(3).
    03  TNAME      PIC X(30).
    03  SALARY     PIC 9(5)V99.

01 COURSE.
    03  CNO        PIC X(6).
    03  CNAME      PIC X(20).

01 LINK-REC.
    03  CN         PIC X(6).
    03  SN         PIC X(5).
    03  MARKS      PIC 99 OCCURS 3 TIMES.

SET SECTION.
SD ADVISOR.
SET SELECTION FOR STUDENT IS VIA ADVISOR
        VALUE OF SSN IS ASN.
SD REGENT.
SET SELECTION FOR STUDENT IS VIA REGENT
        VALUE OF SSN IS ASN.
SD HONOURS.
SET SELECTION FOR STUDENT IS VIA HONOURS
        VALUE OF DNO IS SDN.
SD ENROL.
SET SELECTION BY STRUCTURAL CONSTRAINT.
SD CLASS.
SET SELECTION FOR LINK-REC IS VIA CLASS CURRENT.
WORKING-STORAGE SECTION.
01  ASN    ALTERNATE FOR SSN.
01  SDN    ALTERNATE FOR DNO.
```

Figure 9.9 A sample subschema

9.5 Cobol data manipulation facilities

We present here the data manipulation facilities available to a Cobol programmer, the first two subsections introducing the Cobol application environment and the third subsection the DM statements (alternatively called DM commands). The record selection formats are explained in subsection 9.5.4, followed by a sample program in subsection 9.5.5. Since most words in the syntaxes of the DM commands are key words, we shall not underline them in our presentation here.

9.5.1 Structure of a Cobol database program

A Cobol program wishing to use a database must contain a subschema section in its Data Division as shown below:

```
DATA DIVISION
SUBSCHEMA SECTION
DB Subschemaname WITHIN Schemaname
LD KLIST1   LIMIT 10 ⎫        see the KEEP
LD KLIST2   LIMIT 5  ⎭        command in the next section
FILE SECTION
(Cobol file description, if any)
. . . . .
. . . . .
WORKING-STORAGE SECTION
(Cobol data description, if any)
. . . . .
. . . . .
PROCEDURE DIVISION
(Cobol host language and Cobol DML statements)
. . . . .
. . . . .
```

Every Cobol application program is given an exclusive User Work Area (UWA) for the subschema data and system communication locations. The latter include, among other things, a special register called DB-STATUS which holds codes for database exception conditions (that is, error codes flagged during the execution of a DM statement). These codes are called status indicators. If the execution of a DM statement fails, then DB-STATUS is updated with appropriate status indicator. If DB-STATUS = 0, then the command is executed successfully. Application programmers are expected to check DB-STATUS after every DML command and to take appropriate action in the event of errors. This checking is done by the Cobol IF statement (see the sample program). There is a long list of exception conditions published in the 1981 Cobol JoD.

By using DM statements an application program can transfer data between the database and the UWA which then can be accessed by the host language statements.

9.5.2 Database keys and currencies

A database key is defined as a conceptual entity having a value that identifies
uniquely a record within a run-unit. The value cannot be accessed as data by a host
language program, but can only be referenced by DM commands, such as to keep
it in a database buffer (called keeplist) and subsequently to use it in the *same*
run-unit for referencing that record. Two concurrent run-units could be given
different database key values for the same record.

The data manipulation facilities of the Codasyl model are centred on a concept
of what are called *currencies* or *currency indicators*. In a conventional file processing, the latest record of a file read by the program may be assumed to be the
current record of that file as it is available to the program for processing. This concept is extended in the Codasyl model as follows:

(i) Current of a record type: the record of the record type currently available to
the run-unit for processing.
(ii) Current of a set type: the *tenant* of the set type (irrespective of set occurrences)
currently available to the run-unit to be processed as a tenant of that set type.
A *tenant* is either member or owner of a set. The set occurrence to which
current of the set type belongs is called the *current set* of the set type. Since
the same record can be the tenant of many different set types, it can thus be
the current of many set types at the same time.
(iii) Current of realm: the record of the realm currently available to the run-unit
for processing.
(iv) Current of the run-unit: although there are many current records of different
types at the same time, only one of them can be processed by the run-unit at a
given time. This record is the current of the run-unit.

Basically when a record is selected from the database by a DM command or
stored in the database by a DM command, then it becomes the current record of
the record type, set type(s) and realm concerned. The latest current record (irrespective of record types) is the current of the run-unit (more details later). Currency
indicators are special indicators to hold unique identifiers of these records. These
unique identifiers are implementor-defined, and can be − but are not necessarily −
the database key values. At the start of a run-unit, all currencies are set to null
values by the DBCS which automatically updates them at the successful execution
of a relevant DM command; but in some cases their updates can be suppressed by
the programmer. Many of these currencies may point to the same record; for
instance, the current of the run-unit, barring null values, will be the same as the
current of the record type, set type(s) and the realm to which it belongs. Therefore
if the run-unit currency changes, some record, set and realm currencies will be
affected in accordance with elaborate rules. Non-observance of these rules can cause
programming problems (see later).

9.5.3 DM statements

The Codasyl DM statements are fairly complex, each with many options, but here we shall give only the basic formats, stressing the main functions. Some of the statements have been used in the sample program of section 9.5.5, and hence their use has not been illustrated by examples in this subsection.

For convenience we shall group the DM statements as follows:

(1) Open/Close

READY }   to open and
FINISH }   close realms

(2) Record retrieval statements

FIND   to select a record from the database
GET   to retrieve a record or its data

(3) Record update statements

STORE   to insert a record
ERASE   to delete a record
MODIFY   to modify a record

(4) Set update statements

CONNECT   to insert a member to a set
DISCONNECT   to remove a member from a set
RECONNECT   to change a member from one to another set

(5) Database currency and condition statements

KEEP   to hold a database key value in a buffer
FREE   to release a database key value from the buffer

Database condition (see later)

(6) Miscellaneous commands

COMMIT   to release locks
ROLLBACK   to return to a previous quiet point
ORDER   to reorder set membership
USE   to specify procedures to be executed on database exception condition

We shall describe these commands below more fully.

(1) READY and FINISH statements
The format of the **READY** and FINISH commands is used to open/close realms, like the Open/Close verbs for Cobol files.

<u>READY</u> {realm name} . . .
    [USAGE-MODE EXCLUSIVE/<u>PROTECTED</u>/<u>SHARED</u>]
      {<u>RETRIEVAL</u>/<u>UPDATE</u>}]
<u>FINISH</u> {realm name} . . .

The usage mode Retrieval/Update indicates the intended usage. If the usage mode is Shared, then other run-units can update it, but if it is Protected, then this realm (or an overlapping realm) cannot be opened for Update by a concurrent run-unit, though it can be opened for Retrieval; on the other hand, the usage mode Exclusive forbids opening of this realm by a concurrent run-unit even for Retrieval. The record and set update statements cannot operate unless the realm is opened in Update mode. Some examples of these commands are given in the sample program.

(2) Record retrieval statements

In the Codasyl model a record is first selected by a FIND command, and then it (or some of its data items) is retrieved by a GET command. There are seven different ways of selecting a record by a FIND command as described in subsection 9.4.5. The FIND command itself has the following structure:

  <u>FIND</u> [FOR <u>UPDATE</u>] record selection format [; <u>RETAINING</u> ||
    <u>RECORD</u> / <u>REALM</u> / {set name} . . . || CURRENCY]

The object record of a successful FIND command becomes the current record of the record type, set type(s) and realm concerned, unless the updating of the relevant currency indicators is suppressed by the **RETAINING CURRENCY** clause. The RECORD or REALM options suppress currency updates for the current record type or the current realms respectively. The set name option can be used to suppress the currency indicators of the named set types; an example of its use is given in exercise 9.12(b) at the end of this chapter. The option FOR UPDATE can be used only if the realm is opened in Update mode; its effect is to lock the object record found. The format of the GET command is

    GET record name or GET {identifier}. . .

where identifier is the one or more attributes of the record concerned. The GET command operates only on a current of the run-unit, and does not change any currency. Some examples of the GET command are

    GET STUDENT
    GET SNAME
    GET SNAME, DATE-OF-BIRTH, SADDRESS

There is a FETCH command which is FIND and GET combined.

(3) Record update statements

There are three record update statements, STORE, ERASE and MODIFY for insertions, deletion and amendments respectively. Their basic formats are

STORE record name [RETAINING ‖ <u>RECORD</u> / <u>REALM</u> / {setname} . . . ‖
        CURRENCY]
<u>ERASE</u> [record name]
<u>MODIFY</u> record name, or <u>MODIFY</u> identifier . . .

The STORE command operates on any record that the user wishes to insert into
the database and, after the successful execution of the store command, this record
becomes the current of the run-unit, record type, realm and set-type(s) concerned,
unless it is suppressed by the RETAINING clause, as in the case of the FIND command. Examples of the STORE commands are

> STORE   STUDENT
> or, STORE   STUDENT, RETAINING FOR RECORD ADVISOR

Assuming that these commands operate on the subschema of figure 9.9, the first
command would make the stored student record the current of the run-unit, record
type STUDENT, realm REALM2 and all the relevant set types. The second STORE
command would also make this record the current of all these, except record type
STUDENT and set type ADVISOR.

If the record name is specified, both ERASE and MODIFY statements would
operate on the current of the specified record type; however, MODIFY would make
this record the current of the run-unit but would not change other currencies. If
record name is not specified, then both ERASE and MODIFY would act on the
current of the run-unit, but MODIFY would not change any currency, since the
record is already the current of the run-unit. ERASE always sets the current of the
run-unit to null, even if the record erased was not the current of the run-unit. It
also sets some other currencies to null (not discussed here). The MODIFY command can be used to modify either a whole record or only one or more of its
named identifiers.

Some examples of these commands are

> ERASE TUTOR
> MOVE "SMITH" TO SNAME,
> MODIFY STUDENT (or alternatively MODIFY SNAME)

(4) Set update statements
The Codasyl Model permits insertion, deletion and modification of the set membership by the CONNECT, DISCONNECT and RECONNECT statements which have
the following formats

> <u>CONNECT</u> [recordname] <u>TO</u> setname
> <u>DISCONNECT</u> [recordname] <u>FROM</u> setname
> <u>RECONNECT</u> [recordname] <u>WITHIN</u> setname

All three commands operate on the current of the record type if record name is
specified and make it the current of the run-unit. If the record name is not speci-

fied, then they operate on the current of the run-unit. For both CONNECT and RECONNECT, the set to be updated is selected by the set selection criteria.

The CONNECT command makes the object record a member of the named set type(s) and also their current record. This command is used if Membership is MANUAL. If it is AUTOMATIC the DBCS will automatically make the relevant record a member when it is stored in the database, selecting the set through the set selection criteria. An example of its use can be seen in lines 780 and 810 of the sample program. The DISCONNECT operation removes the object record from membership of the set(s) of the set type(s) to which it belonged, and changes the currencies of the involved set type(s) to null if this record was their current record. A set with Retention Fixed or Mandatory cannot be Disconnected. Since the object record itself identifies the set to which it belongs, set selection criteria are not needed for the DISCONNECT operation.

The RECONNECT command changes a set number from its present set to another set of the same set type, the new set being selected by the set selection criteria: its effect on set currencies is too complex to discuss here. RECON-NECT cannot change set membership if Retention is Fixed. (Aside: the set selection criteria are used to find the set to be connected to, but not for the set from which the member is removed, since this set is already identified by the member.)

(5) Database key statements and condition

The Codasyl model allows the users to declare special system buffers called *Keeplists* in the Subschema Section under LD, each keeplist to hold a specified maximum number of database key values. In section 9.5.2 we have declared two keeplists KLIST1 and KLIST2, KLIST1 for 10 database key values and KLIST2 for 5 database key values. The contents of the keeplists cannot be accessed by host language statements, and are available only to KEEP, FREE and FIND statements. The KEEP statement is used to insert the database key value of the current of the run-unit to a keeplist, and FREE to free the keeplist. Their formats are

KEEP CURRENT USING keeplist
FREE ALL FROM keeplistname

There are three types of *Database Conditions* — tenancy, member and database key conditions — whose truth value can be ascertained by Condition statements to be used with an IF instruction (see line 620 of the sample program for an example). The basic format of the tenancy condition is

setname {OWNER / MEMBER / TENANT } . . .

which is true if the current of the run-unit is owner, or member or either in any set of this set type. The member condition

setname IS [NOT] EMPTY

is used to determine if the current of that set type is empty (that is, does not contain a member record) or non-empty. The third condition can be used to check if a database key is null:

$$\{\text{database-key-identifier}\} \text{ IS [NOT] NULL}$$

The following database-key-identifiers are available

(i) CURRENT   [for current of run-unit]
(ii) CURRENT {recordname}   [for current of record type]
(iii) CURRENT {setname/realm}   [for current of set type or realm]

These database key identifiers can also be used as parameters of the KEEP and FREE statements; for example

> KEEP database-key-identifier USING keeplist
> FREE database-key identifier

Finally, {KEEP database-key-identifier WITHIN keeplist} is itself also a database-key-identifier (note the change: USING is replaced by WITHIN), and therefore can be used in a KEEP statement!

The commit statement COMMIT releases all locks and makes the currency indicators and keeplists null. Every record that has been the object of a successful FIND FOR UPDATE or any record update or set update statement is automatically locked to other concurrent run-units by this run-unit unless released by the Commit statement. The execution of a Commit statement signifies a new consistent state of the database, sometimes called a *quiet-point* (see its use in the sample program). The Rollback command ROLLBACK returns the database to the previous quiet-point, nullifying updates done since then.

The Order statement 'ORDER setname [LOCALLY] ON key' allows reordering of set member on a specified key. If LOCALLY is specified, this order remains valid only within this run-unit, otherwise it is permanent. There is also a USE statement which can be used to invoke procedures on specific exception conditions.

Finally we summarise below the impact of DM statements on currencies.

(i) FIND and STORE commands can act on any record, make the record current of the run-unit, and update all currencies unless suppressed.
(ii) GET command acts only on the current of the run-unit (the reason for this restriction is not clear — see section 11.1.3 for ANSI proposal).
(iii) MODIFY, ERASE and set update commands act on either the current of the run-unit or the current of the named record type, and they make the object record the current of the run-unit (if it is not so already), except in the ERASE command which sets run-unit currency to null. The effects of these commands on other currencies are more elaborate.
(iv) The KEEP commands act on the current of run-unit, record type, set type or realm as specified, and do not change any currency.

Since the rules governing the changes of currencies are generally complex, it is advisable to steer clear of them in programming whenever possible.

9.5.4 Record selection expressions

A record in the Codasyl model can be selected by the FIND statement using any one of seven different selection formats, each format having several options. We shall list the formats below and explain their main options. The term *identifier* used in these formats means one or more components of the record type concerned.

Format 1: sequential access by the record order key

{FIRST/NEXT} record name [USING identifier]

This format delivers records in order of the record order key specified in the schema (see also section 10.3.2). To get the first student record we must write

FIND   FIRST   STUDENT

To find the next student in that key order, write

FIND   NEXT   STUDENT

The FIND NEXT command can be repeated until the end of the record type is reached, but cannot be used for the very first record. There are perhaps two main reasons why FIND NEXT cannot act as default for FIND FIRST. The first reason is the implementation problem, the FIND FIRST has to initialise many tables, process many routines and search through many indexes before the first record is located. The FIND NEXT command is much simpler to implement. The second reason relates to integrity protection, requiring the user to make a deliberate attempt for the very first record, rather than get it by a default of a Next.

In the USING option the record selected is the one matching the specified identifier values. For instance, to get the first student with name SMITH (when there are several students, all called Smith)

MOVE "SMITH" TO SNAME
FIND FIRST STUDENT USING SNAME

and for the next Smith

FIND NEXT STUDENT USING SNAME

The order in both cases is defined by the record order key in the schema. The USING option can have components which are part of the record order key; for instance, to find the first Tutor in department D123

MOVE "D123" TO TDN
FIND FIRST TUTOR USING TDN

and for the next tutor of the same department

FIND NEXT TUTOR USING TDN

Format 2: Random access by identifier

{ANY/DUPLICATE} record name USING {identifier} . . .

This format finds a record *directly* by the values of the specified identifier(s) of the record (see also section 10.3). The reader should note the distinction in the USING clause of formats 1 and 2. To find a student record of student number SN240 by format 2, we may write

MOVE "SN240" TO SNO
FIND ANY STUDENT USING SNO

This can be done also by format 1, where after moving SN240 to SNO, we may write

FIND FIRST STUDENT USING SNO

In this case the DBCS searches sequentially rather than randomly. To find a student named Smith by format 2

MOVE "SMITH" TO SNAME
FIND ANY STUDENT USING SMITH

Again this record can also be found by format 1; the DBCS will search sequentially in format 1 and randomly in format 2. Therefore, there may be some efficiency consideration here. If we want to find the next student having the same name Smith by format 2

FIND DUPLICATE STUDENT USING SMITH

FIND DUPLICATE can be repeated until the end; each time it yields the next matching record in the record order key sequence. Once the first Smith is found randomly (format 2), the subsequent Smiths will be accessed in record order key sequence.

Format 3: Access by searching set with an identifier

DUPLICATE WITHIN set name USING identifier

is used to find a member record through the current record of the set type if both records belong to the same record type and have identical value of the specified identifier. The DBCS searches for the wanted record from the current record in the order specified by the set ordering criteria.

Format 4: Access by position within a set or a realm

{FIRST/NEXT/n/PRIOR/LAST} [record name] WITHIN
{set name/realmname}

is used to access the FIRST, LAST, nth, PRIOR or NEXT record of a set, in set order criteria, the set being selected by the current of the set type. If the record name is specified, all other record types are ignored in evaluating the position. If the set name is replaced by a realm name the record retrieved belongs to the realm with an implementor-defined order. In contrast to format 4, format 1 allows only FIRST/NEXT but not nth, PRIOR or LAST. The Codasyl model has many such inconsistencies.

To use format 4 for a set type we first have to find (to make it current) the desired set, say by selecting the owner record through format 1

FIND FIRST TUTOR

Now we can use format 4 for any set type owned by TUTOR, the set occurrence concerned being owned by that first TUTOR selected by format 1. So we can write

FIND FIRST STUDENT WITHIN ADVISOR
FIND FIRST STUDENT WITHIN REGENT

After we find the first student within Advisor, this student *may* make a Regent set not owned by the original tutor as current, and hence the command FIND FIRST STUDENT WITHIN REGENT may give the student of a different tutor. As explained in connection with format 1, FIND NEXT can be used only after FIND FIRST. Further examples of the use of format 4 are given in lines 410 and 460 of the sample program.

Format 5: Selection by database key

{FIRST/LAST} <u>WITHIN</u> keeplist name or database-key-identifier

is used to find the FIRST or the LAST (but not the NEXT or the PRIOR — yet another example of an inconsistency) database key value held in a keeplist by the KEEP command, or from the database-key-identifier given earlier. Examples are

FIND FIRST WITHIN KLIST
FIND CURRENT STUDENT
FIND CURRENT ADVISOR

Format 6: Access to owner record

OWNER <u>WITHIN</u> set name

is used to find the owner record of a set from a member record, provided that the member record is the current record of the wanted set type. Assume that we have selected a Student record by a previous FIND command or stored it in the database by a STORE command; this Student record will now be the current of set type

ADVISOR, REGENT and HONOURS. If we wish to find the owners of that Student in any of these set types, we can write

```
FIND    OWNER    WITHIN HONOURS
GET     DEPT     [to retrieve the owner department]
FIND    OWNER    WITHIN ADVISOR
GET     TUTOR    [to retrieve advisor]
FIND    OWNER    WITHIN REGENT
GET     TUTOR    [to retrieve regent]
```

But beware of the currency problem between Advisor and Regent mentioned earlier.

Format 7: Access to set member by an identifier

Recordname **WITHIN** setname [**CURRENT**] [**USING** identifier]

is used to find a member of the named record type in a set type. If CURRENT is specified, the set selected is the current set of the set type, otherwise the DBCS uses the specified set selection clause to find the set. The value of the identifier in the USING option identifies the wanted record in the selected set. If the USING option is not specified, the first record (in set order criteria) of the named record type in the selected set will be identified.

9.5.5 A sample program

We present here some examples of the uses of DM commands in a Cobol program based on the subschema of section 9.4.3. The program shows only a PROCEDURE DIVISION and parts of a DATA DIVISION. Strictly speaking, the status indicators (DB-STATUS) should be checked after every DM command, but for the sake of simplicity we have refrained from doing so. The logic is deliberately kept simple for ease of understanding.

In the first part of the program we list (using the Cobol DISPLAY verb) the name of every student in student number order, each name being followed by the list of courses that the student has taken. In the second part of the program, the student records are updated from data supplied by an input file (INFILE) in two record types, INREC1 and INREC2, with RT = A and I respectively. INREC1 contains corrected student address (SADD) for amendment, and Advisor's social security number (ASN1) to make the student a member of the set type ADVISOR, unless the student is already a member. Alternate data items have been used in this example.

INREC2 contains new student record (SREC) for insertion, plus student's department number (SDNUM), his advisor's social security number (ASN2) and his regent's social security number (RSN2). The values of SDN, ASN2 and RSN2 are used to initialise the appropriate key values of the owner records in the set types HONOURS, ADVISOR and REGENT. Since a student is an Automatic Member of his department, the DBCS will automatically make it a member of the correct HONOURS set (with the help of the subschema set selection criteria) but in the case of ADVISOR and REGENT which are manual set types, the programmer must use the CONNECT statement. We assume that each student is assigned to an advisor, but not necessarily to a regent; in that case the value of RSN2 is space and the student concerned cannot be connected to a regent.

```
010   DATA DIVISION.
020   SUBSCHEMA SECTION.
030   DB STUDENT-DATA WITHIN EDUCATION-DATABASE.
050   FILE SECTION.
060   FD INFILE.
070         LABEL RECORDS STANDARD.
080   01   INREC1.
090         02   RT        PIC X.          [value "A" for amendment]
100         02   ASN1      PIC X(10).      [Advisor's social security number]
110         02   SN1       PIC X(5).       [Student number]
120         02   SADD      PIC X(40).      [Student's address]
130   01   INREC2.
140         02   RT        PIC X.          [Value "I" for insertion]
150         02   SDNUM     PIC X(4).       [Student's department number]
160         02   ASN2      PIC X(10).      [Advisor's social security number]
170         02   RSN2      PIC X(10).      [Regent's social security number]
180         02   SREC.                     [Student record to be inserted]
190              04   SN2   PIC X(5).      [Student number]
200              04   REST  PIC X(67).     [rest of the student's data]
300   PROCEDURE DIVISION.
310   PARA-10.
320   READY REALM1 REALM3
330         USAGE-MODE IS PROTECTED RETRIEVAL.
340   READY REALM2
350         USAGE-MODE IS PROTECTED UPDATE.
360   PARA-20.
370         FIND FIRST STUDENT.       [format 1]
380   PARA-30.
390         GET SNAME.
400         DISPLAY SNAME.
410         FIND FIRST LINK-REC WITHIN ENROL          [format 4]
420   PARA-40.
430         FIND OWNER WITHIN CLASS.                  [format 6]
440         GET CNAME.
450         DISPLAY CNAME.
460         FIND NEXT LINK-REC WITHIN ENROL.          [format 4]
```

```
470       IF DB-STATUS = 0, GO TO PARA-40.
480       FIND NEXT STUDENT.                          [format 1]
490       IF DB-STATUS = 0, GO TO PARA-30.
500   PARA-50.
510       OPEN INPUT INFILE.
520   PARA-60.
530       READ INFILE AT END GO TO PARA-80.
540       IF RT NOT = "A" GO TO PARA-70.
550       MOVE SN1 to SNO.
560       FIND FOR UPDATE ANY STUDENT USING SNO.     [format 2]
570       IF DB-STATUS NOT = 0,
580           DISPLAY "ERROR ON UPDATE", INREC1
590           GO TO PARA-60.
600       MOVE SADD TO SADDRESS.
610       MODIFY STUDENT.
620       IF ADVISOR MEMBER          [Database condition]
630           GO TO PARA-60,
640       ELSE MOVE ASN1 TO ASN
650           CONNECT STUDENT TO ADVISOR
660           GO TO PARA-60.
700   PARA-70.
710       IF RT NOT = "I"
720           DISPLAY "ERROR ON UPDATE" INREC 2
730           GO TO PARA-60.
740       MOVE SREC TO STUDENT.
750       MOVE SDNUM TO SDN.
760       STORE STUDENT.
770       MOVE ASN2 TO ASN.
780       CONNECT STUDENT TO ADVISOR.
790       IF RSN2 = SPACE, GO TO PARA-80,
800           ELSE MOVE RSN2 TO ASN
810           CONNECT STUDENT TO REGENT
820           GO TO PARA-60.
880   PARA-80.
890       COMMIT
900       FINISH REALM1, REALM2, REALM3
910       CLOSE INFILE.
920       STOP RUN.
```

Some comments and record selection formats are indicated on the right-hand side of the codes. In PARA-10, the relevant realms are opened in the appropriate modes. In PARA-20, the first Student record (in order of the schema record order key SKEY) is selected by format 1, the student name extracted and printed. In PARA-30 the first Link record of set type ENROL owned by the first student is selected by format 4. In PARA-40, the owner (Course record) of the current Link record in set type CLASS is selected by format 6. The course name is then retrieved and displayed. We have used DB-STATUS $\neq 0$ as an indicator for the end of records in a record type and the end of a set in a set type.

In PARA-60, line 560, the appropriate Student record with SNO = SN1 is selected by format 2. Line 610 could be equivalently replaced by MODIFY SADDRESS rather than MODIFY STUDENT. In line 620, we check if the current Student record is a member of set type ADVISOR. If it is a member we return to PARA-60, else we initialise ASN as required by the set selection criteria of ADVISOR in the subschema. The DBCS will then select the correct set for the subsequent Connect statement. We then connect the Student record to the set before returning to PARA-60. We did not use the command NOT (tenancy condition), as it is not available in the Codasyl model.

In PARA-70, line 750, we initialise SDN as required for the set selection criteria of set type HONOURS in the subschema. Since STUDENT is Automatic Member of set type HONOURS, the DBCS will make each Student record the member of the selected set as soon as the Student record is stored. Therefore the initialisation of SDN must precede the STORE STUDENT command, as we have done. If the set selection for set type HONOURS in the schema was instead

SET SELECTION THRU HONOURS APPLICATION

or if we equivalently specified in the subschema under SD HONOURS

SET SELECTION FOR STUDENT IS VIA HONOURS CURRENT

then the set would have been selected by the current of set type. In that case, in our program we must write

MOVE SDNUM TO SNO
FIND ANY DEPT USING DNO

in place of line 750. This would have made the HONOURS set owned by this department as the current of set type. Observe also the use of FIND command without a GET command. To connect student to ADVISOR and REGENT, we initialised the same ASN on line 770 and 800 as necessary.

9.6 Other characteristics

Data independence is provided in the Codasyl model by a three-level architecture, mentioned earlier. The model provides a framework for concurrent usage by allowing locking facilities on realms and on records, backed by the COMMIT and ROLL-BACK statements. A run-unit holds the *update locks* of each record that has been the object of FIND FOR UPDATE, record update (STORE, ERASE or MODIFY) and set update (CONNECT, DISCONNECT or RECONNECT) statements, the locks being released by COMMIT, ROLLBACK or STOP RUN statements or by an abnormal termination. The changes made into the database are available to other concurrent run-units only after the COMMIT statements.

A run-unit also holds what are called *selection locks*, one for each record identified by either any of the currency indicators or any of the keeplists. A selection lock is released by the FREE statement or any DM statement that updates currencies. They are also released automatically when update locks are released. The holding of a selection lock prevents the ERASE, MODIFY, CONNECT, DISCONNECT and RECONNECT statements being executed on the object record by any concurrent run-unit. The mechanisms for the prevention, detection and resolution of deadlocks are implementor-defined.

Data validation facility is provided by the CHECK and CALL clauses, more so than in most other models. Privacy protection can be enforced by the ACCESS CONTROL clauses in the schema.

Exercises

9.1   Describe the entries and the major subentries of the Codasyl schema, and explain briefly why the Codasyl schema does not fulfil the requirements of a conceptual schema.

9.2   Explain the concept of the Codasyl set type, with an example, and discuss all the access paths (ordering, pointers and keys) that can be specified for it.

9.3   List and explain the basic contents of a Codasyl subschema and discuss the variations that can be permitted between a Codasyl schema and its subschema.

9.4   Give the syntaxes of record selection formats 1, 2, 4 and 6 of the Codasyl model and explain them with examples.

9.5   Discuss the Codasyl DM commands and their effects on currency indicators.

9.6   Write a critical assessment of the merits and demerits of the concept of currency in the Codasyl model.

9.7   Write an essay on data independence in the Codasyl model with particular emphasis on the schema/subschema independence.

9.8   Explain the following terms, stating where they are used.

   (i) Database key
   (ii) Database conditions
   (iii) Update and selection locks
   (iv) Set membership class
   (v) Set selection criteria
   (vi) Set order criteria.

9.9   (a)   Design a Codasyl schema, following the guide lines given below, for the case study of exercise 8.7 of chapter 8.

Guide lines for schema design

In this design, you are required to list the record types, record contents, record order keys (if any), set types, set name, owner name, member name and set order criteria. You need not bother about the actual syntaxes and other schema entries such as Access Control, Check clause, Type clause and so on. Use only single member set types.

(b) Assuming that the schema you have designed also represents a subschema, show, by writing down the DM commands, how invoices can be produced from this database for a particular day number of a month, held in data item DAYN.

9.10 (a) Design a Codasyl schema for the case study of exercise 8.8 of chapter 8, using the design guidelines given above.

(b) Assuming that the schema you have designed also represents a subschema, answer the following questions:

(i) Write the DM commands to update the total mileage of a car after it has been returned by the customer. Assume that the customer number and the order number are held in data items CNUM and ONUM.

(ii) Supposing that a booked car is broken down, and has to be replaced, write down the DM commands necessary to search for a car of the same model, failing that a car of the next more expensive model and failing that a car of the next cheaper model. Assume that the registration number of the broken down car is held in a data name OLDRN.

9.11 (a) Design a Codasyl schema for the case study of exercise 8.9 of chapter 8, in accordance with the guidelines given earlier.

(b) Assuming that the schema you have designed also represents a subschema, answer the following query for a component code held in a data item COMPC:

Find by the Codasyl DM commands the detailed information (component code, description, reorder level, quantity in stock, standard manufacturing time and price) of all its immediately subordinate and immediately superior components.

9.12 In a sheep database, information about farms, sheep and breeding is maintained. The sheep are grouped into farms, but can move from one farm to another (that is, the current farm can change). It is important to maintain the information about the parentage of all sheep born. Other information recorded includes birth farm, year of birth and weight at birth. A sheep is uniquely identified by the sheep name made up of its birth farm and year of birth appended by a number. For each pregnancy, the litter size and the number born alive are recorded (the litter size includes still-born lambs).

(a) Design a Codasyl schema for this database in accordance with the guidelines given earlier.

(b) Assume this schema also represents a subschema. Answer the following query in Codasyl DML (warning: beware of currency indicators).

Find the litter size and the number born alive from a group of mother ewes selected by given current farm and year of birth (of these mothers).

For each lamb born of these pregnancies, find its birth weight and father.

References

Cobol (1978). *Codasyl Cobol Journal of Development 1978*
Cobol (1981). *Codasyl Cobol Journal of Development 1981*
DDLC (1978). *Codasyl DDLC Journal of Development 1978*
DDLC (1981). *Codasyl DDLC Journal of Development 1981*

10 Codasyl Model Revisited

This chapter is mainly concerned with the enhancements and past changes to the basic Codasyl model. The most important change is the division of the old schema into a new schema and a storage schema, the storage schema containing storage dependent clauses. Although the Codasyl DDLC has been dissolved, the proposed Data Storage Description Language (DSDL) for the storage schema nevertheless provides a glimpse of a possible storage schema for the Codasyl model. Therefore an overview of the storage schema entries has been included in this chapter, along with the Fortran database facility, the past changes and a critical evaluation.

10.1 Storage schema

The DSDL was published both in the 1978 (DDLC, 1978) and 1981 (DDLC, 1981) DDLC JoD — as a proposed draft language to specify a new storage schema and to modify an existing one. However, the overview presented here will be restricted to the former, focusing on the principal clauses. We begin with some basic concepts.

10.1.1 Basic concepts and skeleton entries

The physical database is assumed to be divided into a number of *storage areas*, each storage area occupying a physical portion of the storage medium, usually discs. A storage area may contain a collection of *storage records* and/or their indexes and could be viewed as a file. The storage schema permits both horizontal and vertical fragmentations (section 4.5.3) of schema records to go into one or more storage records (possibly overlapping), in order to improve efficiency. An example of fragmentation, where a record type is broken into four other record types F1, F2, F3 and F4, by a 'where' condition is shown in figure 10.1. All storage records of the same schema record are linked by what are called *record pointers*.

$$F1 \text{ (ENO, ENAME) where } E21 \leqslant ENO \leqslant E65$$
$$F2 \text{ (ENO, ENAME) where } E65 < ENO \leqslant E85$$
$$F3 \text{ (ENO, SAL, TAX, AGE) where } E21 \leqslant ENO \leqslant E75$$
$$F4 \text{ (ENO, SAL, TAX, AGE) where } E75 < ENO \leqslant E85$$

ENO	ENAME	SAL	TAX CODE	AGE
E21	SMITH	20	X15	32
E55	JONES	25	X20	29
E62	CONTI	32	X18	40
		28	X21	30
E75	SMITH			
E80	COOK	45	X15	28
E82	SIMS	38	X18	32
E85	TAFT	22	X15	28

Figure 10.1 Fragmentation

A storage area is divided into a number of pages, each page containing one or more storage records. A page is typically a unit of I/O transfer, but need not be so. A storage schema consists of the following entries

(1) storage schema entry
(2) {Mapping description entry} . . .
(3) {storage area entry} . . .
(4) {storage record entry} . . .
(5) {set entry} . . .
(6) {Index entry} . . .

The first entry is used to name the storage schema as STORAGE SCHEMA name.

10.1.2 Mapping and storage area entries

In the mapping description entry, a schema record type is mapped to a storage record type, optionally subject to a condition, as shown in the basic format below.

MAPPING FOR schema record name
[IF condition] STORAGE {storage record name} . . .

where the condition contains components of the schema record type. The storage area entry is used to declare storage areas with their sizes, in the following form

STORAGE AREA name
INITIAL SIZE – – – –
EXPANDABLE TO – – – –
PAGE SIZE – – – –

10.1.3 Storage record entry

This entry has three subentries, the first to specify a linkage for the storage record types of the same schema record type, the second for the placement of storage records in storage areas and the third to describe the record components. The first subentry has the form

> STORAGE RECORD (this storage record type)
> LINK TO (another storage record type of the same schema record type)

The Placement clause in the second subentry is a revised version of the Location Mode clause in the older Codasyl schemas. It is specified as

> [IF condition]
>   PLACEMENT IS
>   {{CALC [procedure name] USING Calc key   }/
>   {CLUSTERED VIA SET schema-set-name [NEAR OWNER]   }/
>   {SEQUENTIAL {ASCENDING/DESCENDING} identifier   }}
>
>   WITHIN storage area name

The condition is described in terms of data items of the schema record type, and it allows occurrences of the same storage record type to be stored with different placement clauses in different storage area, but the same storage area can have records of different types.

If the CALC mode is chosen, then the records are placed by applying a hashing algorithm (either user-defined or system-default) on a Calc key, which is a name given to the stipulated data item(s) of the schema record type concerned. In the clustered option the DBCS attempts to store the member records of the same set type together, optionally near the owner, whereas in the sequential modes the records are placed in order of the specified identifier (data items). Placement techniques have been discussed in detail in section 4.4.1 (see also section 10.3.1).

In the third subentry, physical characteristics of the data items of the storage records are described. If data item description is to be copied without change from the schema, then a DATA ALL option is stipulated.

10.1.4 Set entry

Although a schema record may be divided into a number of storage records, a set is always defined in terms of the schema records. In a set entry, pointers (including indexes) can be specified to support sorted set order criteria and to provide fast access to tenants. Pointers can also be supported for owner records (owner pointer) and member records separately. The basic format is

```
SET schema-set-name
[[OWNER STORAGE RECORD {storage record names}
    POINTER FOR – – – –     ]
{MEMBER RECORD schema record
    STORAGE RECORD {its storage record name}
    POINTER FOR – - –     } . . .]
```

The first pointer clause permits the schema owner record to be chained to the first and last schema member record (irrespective of schema member record types), and also stipulates the indexes, if any, to be specified for all schema member records. This index can be specified as an additional storage schema facility, or to support the sorted option of the schema set order. Note that no specific storage schema construct is necessary to support the positional (FIRST/LAST/NEXT/PRIOR) or the SYSTEM DEFAULT options of the schema set order criteria, since they define order of insertion rather than any pointers.

The second pointer clause allows each member record of a given type to be chained directly to its owner, and also to the Next/Prior member of the same record type. Additionally, indexes can be created for the members of the same type, independently of the member records of other types; the key for this index (referred to as *the search key*) is defined in the index entry. This search key, when it coincides with the identifier in the USING option of record selection format 7, should provide faster access.

10.1.5 Index entry

This entry is used to describe indexes for

(i)   record key of schema records
(ii) set owner and set member indexes.

The two corresponding formats are

(i)   INDEX NAME IS name
      USED FOR RECORD schema-record-name
(ii) INDEX NAME IS name
      USED FOR SET schema-set-name

There can be two types of schema record key in the storage schema: (a) those that are declared in the schema, and (b) those that are not. The first format above supports both (a) and (b), with appropriate subclauses. The second format is to specify indexes declared in the set entry of the previous subsection.

10.2 Fortran database facility

The 1980 Fortran JoD is based on the 1978 Cobol JoD, and corresponds quite closely to that database facility. Most of the Codasyl terms such as Subschema, Alias, Access-control, Duplicate, Current, Retaining, Invoke, and so on, are retained in the Fortran version which uses BNF notations in the presentation of its syntaxes. The Fortran subschema is divided into five parts, for SUBSCHEMA, ALIAS, REALM, RECORD and SET statements, with a facility to declare privacy locks for the subschema. The subschema statement gives the subschema name, and Alias statements define Alias names. Realms are defined by realm statements, and subschema set selection criteria by the set statement. The record statement names a record and describes its data item using Fortran-like declaration facilities, without any level numbers. However, unlike the 1981 Cobol JoD but like the 1978 Cobol JoD, the record statement (record section in the Cobol JoD) allows the declaration of record keys and record order keys. There is no equivalent of the subschema Working-storage Section, nor are there any Alternate identifiers in the Fortran facility. The set selection clauses are defined in a traditional way.

The concepts of status indicators, currency indicators, database keys, and database conditions are naturally retained, and so are most of the Cobol DM statements, including the following limitations of the DML in the 1978 Cobol JoD.

(i) There are no FIND FOR UPDATE, COMMIT, ROLLBACK, KEEP or FREE statements.

(ii) There is no RECONNECT statement, MODIFY being used for both changing record contents and set memberships.

(iii) GET, ERASE, MODIFY, CONNECT and DISCONNECT statements operate only on the current of the run-unit, but not on the current of record type. This makes programming tedious and cumbersome.

The allowed DM statements are

ACCEPT	to extract a database key value from a currency indicator, or to find a realm name from a current record (or from a database key value) — this was a facility in the 1975 Cobol JoD
CONNECT	
DISCONNECT	
ERASE	
FETCH	(FIND and GET combined, as in the 1981 Cobol JoD)
FIND	

FINISH
GET
INVOKE   equivalent to the DB subschema name entry in a Cobol program
MODIFY
PRIVACY   to supply key values to satisfy schema locks from a Fortran program
              – this command is executed prior to the DM command as it needs a
              privacy key
READY
STORE
USE

The PRIVACY statement is a useful addition, but the absence of COMMIT and
ROLLBACK is a shortcoming. The Fortran subschema permits 8 record selection
formats as follows.

Format 1:   Direct access to a record by database key value – this used to be a
            facility in the earlier Cobol JoDs.
Format 2:   The same as the Cobol format 2 of the previous chapter, except
            that like the 1978 Cobol JoD, record key names rather than data
            item names of the record type (see format 2 in section 10.3.2) are
            used.
Formats 3–7: They are the same as those of the Cobol format 3–7 of the previous
            chapter, except that Fortran formats are less powerful in some cases.
Format 8:   The same as Cobol format 1 of the previous chapter.

As indicated earlier, Fortran syntaxes are different for both DDL and DML,
including record selection formats. The absence of FIND FOR UPDATE, COMMIT,
and ROLLBACK commands makes concurrent usage facilities poorer.

10.3 Past changes

We wish to chart here the major changes of the Codasyl schema, and the Cobol database facility since the 1971 DBTG report. The separation of the storage dependent
clauses from the schema to the storage schema had some direct impact on the
schema, and some indirect impacts on the subschema and DML. There were also
other changes, some major and some minor.

10.3.1 Changes in schema DDL

The principal schema items affected by the removal of storage dependent clauses
are: database keys, areas, location modes, some set entries, and in a curious way
record keys. There are also some other changes of dubious nature.

In the 1971 DBTG report, a database key is defined as a unique internal identifier of records — an identifier which is permanent and available to the application programmer for fast access. Although the model did not suggest any implementation technique, it was generally implemented as consisting of area number, page number and a page offset value. In later implementations, more flexibility was introduced by replacing the page offset value with a fixed location on the page which held the offset value (section 4.4.2). In the latest version of the Codasyl model, the database key has become a conceptual entity for referencing a record, valid only for the duration of a given run-unit, as discussed in the previous chapter.

Originally the term 'area' was used to mean a physical portion of storage medium, to be specified in the schema. It is now called a storage area, to be specified in the storage schema. Corresponding to the PLACEMENT clauses of the storage areas, there were LOCATION MODEs in the schema to specify placements of records in areas, and to determine their database keys. The Location mode clause had the following options.

(i) DIRECT: records were placed in named areas in accordance with a direct key
    made up of one or more data items of the record type concerned.
(ii) CALC: the same as the CALC mode of the storage schema.
(iii) VIA set name: the same as the CLUSTERED mode of the storage schema.
(iv) SYSTEM: left to the DBCS to decide.

Records placed in an area used to have a contiguous sequence of database key values. Today, the implementors of the storage schema may still use permanent internal identifiers of records like the old database keys, except that these identifiers will no longer be called database keys.

In the 1978 DDLC JoD the concept of record keys was introduced, with the basic format

KEY keyname IS [{ASCENDING/DESCENDING}] data identifier
DUPLICATES ARE {SYSTEM DEFAULT/NOT ALLOWED}

It was possible to specify one or more such record keys for a given record type. If the option ASCENDING/DESCENDING was included in a record key, then this key — called record order key — defined the sequential order of access to this record type by record selection format 1 (as in the previous chapter), but all record keys, including the record order keys, permitted random access by record selection format 2. Record key of owner record was also used in defining set order criteria. These record key facilities were supported by the 1978 Cobol JoD, and remained unchanged in the 1981 DDLC JoD.

The 1971 DBTG report specified several set implementation techniques which included what it called Pointer Arrays for linking set members, later replaced by the Defined Keys option. Pointer Array implied non-embedded member pointers or indexes for random access to member records, whereas the Defined Keys option defines only the set order. The 1971 DBTG report also allowed owner pointers (LINK TO OWNER clause), backward processing of member records

(PRIOR PROCESSIBLE clause) and search keys (SEARCH KEY clause). Most of these storage dependent clauses, including search keys (section 10.1.4), can now be specified in the storage schema, although under different names.

The Structural Constraint clause in the set entry was first introduced in the 1978 DDLC JoD, but was withdrawn from the 1981 JoD; while absent in the 1978 Cobol JoD, it appeared in the 1981 Cobol JoD — just when it was dropped from the DDLC JoD! Since this clause cannot be used in the subschema set selection criteria unless specified in the member subentry of the schema, the present situation shows yet again the problem of defining a database model by two different committees. We have included this clause in section 9.3.4 because it is supported by the ANSI model (as a membership clause) and because it brings out the close correspondence of the Codasyl and the relational model.

These apart, a number of schema terms have undergone cosmetic surgery, not necessarily enhancing the elegance.

Old terms	*New terms*
PRIVACY	ACCESS CONTROL
ON specified condition	CALL procedure ON
CALL procedure	specified condition
PICTURE and TYPE	TYPE (only)

The new additions to the schema include record keys, Fixed option in the set membership class and recursive set type, although the Cobol subschema does not permit recursive set types.

10.3.2 Changes in the Cobol database facility

Since the Cobol database facility is dependent on the DDLC's specification, there is understandably a time lag before a new schema enhancement works its way through the Cobol JoD. In addition, there may also be genuine disagreement on a specific enhancement, between the two groups and/or the DBLTG (the committee responsible for the Cobol database facility — see section 9.1) which may find some enhancement unworkable. This may be a reason why recursive set types, around for a long time, were never included in the Cobol JoD. One of the interesting implementation questions of the recursive set type is which record determines the current of a set, the owner or the member? This is important since both owner and member belong to the same record type. Any decision taken can have side effects on other set types (see the ANSI solution in section 11.1).

In the earlier Cobol JoDs there was provision for the specification of additional (on top of those in the schema) privacy clauses in the subschema in all the main entries — namely, subschema-name, realm, record and set. As with the schema, the term privacy was subsequently changed to ACCESS CONTROL, but this subschema facility remained in the book until the 1981 Cobol JoD. The reason for their removal is not clear except that the ANSI subschema (section 11.1.2) does not have them either. Perhaps both these committees believe them now to be less useful.

The term realm, although used, was never clearly defined in the earlier sub-schema DDL; everyone assumed it to be the subschema term for the 'area' concept of the schema. However, when the area was dropped from the schema, realm found its distinctive individuality as a user-defined, logical collection of records of one or more types, which could be opened and closed in various usage modes. But realm seems to be a redundant concept; we could open/close individual record types, so why realm? This is a view taken up also by ANSI, who have dropped the term altogether.

In the 1975 Cobol JoD the record selection format 1 permitted direct access by database keys, provided that the record placement was defined by Location Mode Direct. Likewise, format 2 permitted direct access by the Calc key. When the concept of record keys was introduced and Areas/Location-mode/user-visible-database-keys were removed, these two formats were redefined for sequential access by record order key, and for direct access by any *named* record key (including record order key), as specified in the 1978 Cobol JoD.

The 1978 Cobol JoD permitted schema record keys to be copied on to the sub-schema, under Record Section as follows

> 01 record name
> [RECORD [ORDER] KEY keyname IS {identifier} . . .] . . .

where the ORDER option was used to indicate record order keys. A number of record keys, including at most one record order key, was permitted to be copied from the schema for each subschema record type. Corresponding to record order and record keys, the old record selection formats 1 and 2 were redefined as

Format 1: {FIRST/NEXT} record name [USING {identifier} . . .]
(this is same as given in section 9.4.4)
Format 2: {ANY/DUPLICATE} record name USING keyname

However, the 1981 Cobol JoD made the following changes:

(i) All record keys were dropped from the subschema, which makes nonsense of schema record keys since they cannot be used any more.
(ii) Format 1 was dropped as well, although format 1 can be supported in the absence of record order keys by an implementor-defined order (as done in the ANSI proposal -- chapter 11).
(iii) Since record keys are dropped, the keyname in format 2 is replaced by identifier in the 1981 Cobol JoD (as given in section 9.4.4). This enhances the user facility, which is welcome, but makes the model incompatible with the schema.

We have included format 1 in the previous chapter for two reasons:

(i) Its absence makes the record selection capability incompatible with the schema, the Fortran facility and the 1978 Cobol facility.

(ii) It is an important facility – indeed the power of this format should ideally be extended to allow sequential processing in both forward and backward directions in any user-defined order, rather than restricting it to a schema/subschema defined key order.

In order to deviate only minimally from the 1981 Cobol JoD, we have included in the previous chapter only format 1 from the 1978 Cobol JoD, ignoring the associated subschema facility. Our format 2 in the previous chapter uses identifier rather than keyname, again to conform with the latest Cobol JoD. We have now seven record selection formats in section 9.4.4 (as in the 1978 version) whereas the 1981 Cobol JoD has only six We shall, however, continue to assume seven formats in our discussion of the Codasyl model. Since the format 2 with record keys is withdrawn, we have not described any record keys in the previous chapter, except for record order keys (section 9.3.3), to be used with format 1. The withdrawal of record keys has also made the schema set selection criterion with owner record key unusable – since, in the absence of record keys in the sub-schema, the programmer cannot initialise the key value for the correct owner.

On the positive side, the 1981 Cobol JoD has enhanced the capability of the Cobol DML by extending the power of ERASE, MODIFY, CONNECT , DISCON-NECT and RECONNECT statements to operate on the current of record types. This simplifies programming. It is not clear why this power is not extended also to the GET command.

In the earlier Cobol JoDs, the MODIFY command was used to change both record values and set membership. The separation of these two functions into the new MODIFY and RECONNECT commands is a welcome feature of the 1981 Cobol JoD. The FIND FOR UPDATE command is also new in this JoD, and it improves the concurrent usage facility. Although the FETCH command as a combination of FIND and GET was around for a while, its formal inclusion in a Cobol JoD is also relatively recent.

10.4 Evaluation of the Codasyl model

The Codasyl model is large, with many facilities for its specification. It supports a three-level schema architecture, although these levels do not correspond precisely to the ANSI/SPARC definitions. (The Codasyl schema still has some storage dependent clauses left in it.) The model also lacks a query language and a data dictionary facility. It is nevertheless a leading data model, and is likely to be used for a long time to come, in the same way as Cobol and Fortran will be used. In our evaluation of this model we shall consider the following

> Schema
> Subschema
> Storage schema
> Functional issues

10.4.1 Schema

The Codasyl schema represents a network data model based on records and sets, but the model lacks a theoretical foundation, which has given rise to inconsistent and lopsided developments. Since it was specified by a committee, alterations/ enhancements were introduced by individual *ad hoc* proposals submitted to the committee rather than by a requirement of a sound formal model. *Ad hoc* facilities and pragmatism are good in small doses, but too much of either can lead to chaos.

The proposal for record keys was passed by the Codasyl DDLC because the proposer convinced the committee of their need, showing many examples of possible use (the author was present at some of these meetings), rather than through a realisation that, in principle, records exist outside set types, and hence they should have access paths that are independent of set types. On the other hand, the presence of storage dependent record keys is an anachronism, besides being restrictive. Ideally, record keys should be declared in the storage schema, but not in the schema, so allowing the user to define any record order (for sequential access) that he wants in his program, and also permitting him to have random access by data item values, as is done in the record selection format 2 of the 1981 Cobol JoD. The introduction of record keys in the 1978 DDLC JoD was all the more surprising, since by then the DDLC had abolished Search keys from the schema, so making it less storage dependent. However, since the 1981 Cobol JoD and ANSI do not permit record keys, they are less likely to be included in the future implementations of the Codasyl model.

The set order criterion is a debatable facility of the Codasyl model. This criterion defines the order in which members can be processed sequentially by record selection format 4, and therefore it can be treated as an access path which should not be in the schema. However, it is sometimes argued that this order can contain essential information which may otherwise be inconvenient to hold in the database (see also section 11.3.1 for information-bearing repeating group).

However, assuming for the time being that we need set order criteria for 'essential information', we should drop such criteria where they do not represent essential information. One such case is the sorted option of the set order criteria; since this option is defined by a key made up of data items of the member records, the information is already present in the database. In other words, a programmer can order the member records in his program by that key, and hence there is no need to specify that order in the schema. Indeed by moving the Order clause from the schema, a greater freedom can be given to the programmer by allowing him to specify in his program any order of interest. Such an order can be defined by the DM statement ORDER (section 9.5.3).

Since the SYSTEM DEFAULT option is the absence of a specific order, the only other candidate for holding 'essential information' is the positional set order criterion. This order can be subdivided into two types: chronological (FIRST/LAST) and adjacent (PRIOR/NEXT); but we dismiss the chronological order, as it is not a general facility for holding/updating essential information since it does not permit future insertions, if needed, in the middle of the queue. To examine the adjacent option, let us consider airline records (ALR) containing airline name (AL) and flight route number (RN); and airport records (APR) containing airport name (AP), number of runways (NR) and standard landing charge (LC). We may define flight routes as an ordered collection of airport records associated with each airline. So we define a set type ROUTES as follows

set name	ROUTES
owner	ALR
member	APR
order	NEXT (or PRIOR)

The order represents an essential piece of information – the new airports can be inserted in a route knowing, say, its next airport. However, this set order can alternatively be stored in a record type say, RTS (RN, AP, SN) for routes where RN is the route number, AP is the airport name and SN is the sequence number in the route. We have thus transformed the ordering information from the set order criteria to explicit records. This shows that it is not necessary to use set order criteria to hold essential information

As it stands, most of the options in set order criteria represent access paths. The schema can be made simpler and cleaner by removing this criterion without any loss of modelling capability. The set selection criterion is quite unnecessary in the schema; it should be left to the subschema where the user can specify the selection path that he needs.

The support of the multimembered set type has attracted much criticism of the Codasyl model. The single member set type seems neat and theoretically attractive, whereas the concept of the multimembered set type is, at best, a cumbersome aberration since the same information can be represented by two separate set types. The advantages of multimembered set type appear marginal, but their programming is tedious since they can cause havoc with currency indicators. Additionally, their presence makes the Codasyl set construct complex. However, there are some strong supporters of multimembered set types. In fact, the criticism of these set types led Charles Bachman to propose his Role model, which permits not only multimembered, but also multi-owned set types (section 14.1.2).

10.4.2 Subschema

The subschema facility provides a reasonable service to the Cobol and Fortran users, but the absence of high level query language is a serious drawback. We have voiced some criticism of the currency indicators earlier on. There is a strong case for their abolition in favour of the user-defined and user-controlled cursor proposed in 1975 by R. W. Engles of IBM (Engles, 1975).

10.4.3 Storage schema

The Codasyl storage schema is designed to provide the following facilities:

(i) Independence from the schema
(ii) Independence from the operating system and physical storage
(iii) Reorganisation facility
(iv) Efficiency in operations.

The independence from the schema facilitates easy reorganisation which the present storage schema is meant to achieve. The independence from the operating system and physical storage permits the same storage schema to be used in different environments. This independence is secured in the storage schema with a user-defined page size as the unit of disc access, but arbitrary page sizes (unless they are a multiple of the unit of disc access) can be quite expensive. The DSDL also provides a number of facilities for running and reorganising the database, but their implementation may not be easy.

Finally we must turn to efficiency. The design of an efficient storage system depends not only on the storage schema but also on its interactions with the particular facilities of an operating system and the characteristics of physical devices. Therefore independence is expensive. The DSDL is very elaborate, and it is difficult to see clearly the overall impact of choosing one or the other facility in a design. Perhaps the DBAWG, the committee that designed the DSDL (the author was a member at the time), has gone too far on details, and a simpler language might have been more successful.

10.4.4 Supporting features

The Codasyl model permits concurrent usage where locks can be established both on realms and pages, supported by the COMMIT/ROLLBACK facilities. Both the schema and subschema permit integrity controls through the CALL and CHECK clauses. The set memberships clause may be regarded as an integrity constraint on set types. Compared to other models, the Codasyl model is excellent in these respects, although it is still far from satisfying the integrity requirements advocated in a modern conceptual schema. The model also provides many facilities (better than most) for access control.

Although the need for a data dictionary is recognised, it is not seen as part of the model, but rather as something to be supported by the implementors. A specification for a data dictionary facility that permitted queries on the semantic description of schema items would have been useful. This could support facilities for higher level meaningful groupings of record types, set types, data items and so on. Finally, the Codasyl model is too complex for small users — a simpler subset would have been more attractive to them. The small user market is an expanding territory where TOTAL has prospered, and the relational model will be sure to flourish although it has escaped, probably forever, from the grasp of the Codasyl model.

Exercises

10.1 Discuss the main techniques of representing records and sets in DSDL.
10.2 Explain the concept of Location Mode with examples and discuss some implementation techniques.
10.3 Explain the following:
      Record fragmentation
      Storage records and storage areas.
10.4 Compare the Codasyl Fortran facilities with those of its Cobol.
10.5 Describe the evolution of the Codasyl models from 1971, with comments on the changes.
10.6 Evaluate the Codasyl model critically with respect to schema, subschema and DM facility.

References

Cobol (1975). *Codasyl Cobol Journal of Development 1975*
Cobol (1978). *Codasyl Cobol Journal of Development 1978*
Cobol (1981). *Codasyl Cobol Journal of Development 1981*
DBTG (1971). *Codasyl DBTG Report April 1971*
DDLC (1978). *Codasyl DDLC Journal of Development 1978*
DDLC (1981). *Codasyl DDLC Journal of Development 1981*
Engles, R. W. (1975). Currency and Concurrency in Cobol Database Facility. *IFIP TC-2 Working Conference on Modelling in DBMS*
Fortran (1980). *Codasyl Fortran Database Facility 1980*

11 Standards and Equivalence

As indicated in chapter 1, technical committee X3H2 of ANSI has started to standardise the network and the relational models from 1978 and 1982 respectively. The work on the network model (ANSI, 1984a, b, c, d), based on the Codasyl model, is nearly complete, whereas that of the relational model (ANSI/SPARC, 1984) is still at an early stage (Gallagher, 1984). In this chapter we shall discuss the proposed network model in some detail, with a short section on the relational model. The remainder of this chapter will be devoted to an examination of the network (both Codasyl and ANSI) and relational facilities, with a view to identifying the equivalent features of the two models.

11.1 ANSI network model

ANSI X3H2 has proposed what it calls a Network Database Language (NDL) which includes a schema definition language, a subschema definition language and a host-language independent DML. The NDL follows the Codasyl specifications fairly closely, and therefore in this section we shall discuss only the main differences, ignoring some of the details. For the sake of compatibility, the presentation will be made in Codasyl-like syntaxes rather than in the BNF notation of ANSI, and will cover the following topics: schema, subschema, DM statements, DBCS interfaces and the Cobol database facility.

11.1.1 ANSI schema

The structure and the content of the ANSI schema are similar to those of the Codasyl schema, with the following main exceptions.

(i) ACCESS CONTROL clauses are withdrawn on the grounds that the old lock and key facility is outdated, and it should be replaced by something better (but no replacement is proposed by ANSI).

(ii) CALL clause is dropped.

(iii) Record key clauses are removed and an optional record uniqueness clause is introduced (to define unique keys).

(iv) Components allowed in a record type are data items and fixed length (optionally multidimensional) arrays, but not repeating groups.

(v) Complex data description clauses, such as RESULT and SOURCE clauses, are dropped.

(vi) Level numbers of components are replaced by the term ITEM.

(vii) An optional DEFAULT clause is introduced to initialise components values.

(viii) A new STRUCTURAL clause is introduced for set membership class.

(ix) Set selection clauses are withdrawn, even from the subschema.

The ANSI schema definition consists of

> SCHEMA schemaname
> [{record definition/
>   set definition}] . . .

Each record is subdivided into components: a component being a data item value or a vector. A record definition contains

> record name clause
>   [record uniqueness clause]
>   [record check clause]
>   {component definition} . . .

A component definition contains

> component name clause
>   Type clause
>   [Occur clause]
>   [Default clause]

The record uniqueness clause is specified as

> UNIQUE {components identifier . . .}

which specifies components of the record type which cannot have duplicate values. A component is defined as

> ITEM component name

whereas a Default clause is specified as

> DEFAULT initial value

The syntaxes for other entries, such as record name, check, type and occur clauses, are largely identical with those of the Codasyl model (section 9.3.3), except that OCCURS DEPENDING ON is not permitted, the allowed format of the Occur clause being:

> OCCUR n TIMES

where n is an unsigned integer greater than zero.

The set definition is given as

> set name clause
>   owner clause

order clause
{member clause} . . .

with a member clause having

member record name
insertion clause
retention clause
[member key clause]
[member check clause]
[member uniqueness clause]

The member uniqueness clause is similar to the record uniqueness clause. The singular, recursive and multimembered set types are retained, along with all the options of the set order criteria, but the sorted option is now simplified to

SORTED RECORD TYPE

which requires a member key to be defined in the member subentry. Therefore this clause is semantically equivalent to SORTED BY DEFINED KEY [RECORD TYPE. . .] of the Codasyl model.

All the old set membership classes (AUTOMATIC, MANUAL, OPTIONAL, MANDATORY, FIXED) are retained, along with a new one called STRUCTURAL, which has the format

INSERTION STRUCTURAL member-data-identifier = owner-data-identifier

If the STRUCTURAL clause is specified, the member record is made a member when it is stored, but the set is selected through the matching values of the member and owner data identifiers. On the other hand, if insertion is AUTOMATIC or MANDATORY, then the set is selected from the current of the set type.

11.1.2 ANSI subschema

There have been some structural changes in the proposed ANSI subschema, the major ones being as follows.

(i) Divisions and Sections are withdrawn.
(ii) Alias declarations are removed to the respective record, component and set entries with a RENAMED clause.
(iii) Realms are dropped.
(iv) As in the schema, each component declaration uses the term ITEM in place of level numbers, but there is no Type declaration for the components.
(v) There is no Check or Access control clause in the subschema.
(vi) Set selection clause, Alternate clause and Subschema Working-storage Section are dropped.

A subschema is defined as

> SUBSCHEMA subschemaname OF schemaname
> {record view clause/
>   set view clause} . . .

A record view clause is specified as

> RECORD [schema record name RENAMED] record view name
>   {component view clause} . . . /ALL}

The component view clause is

> ITEM [schema component name RENAMED] component view name

Record view names and component view names are the subschema names of the record types and component types concerned, and they must be identical with their names in the schema unless RENAMED in the respective entries. If ALL is specified, all the schema components are assumed.

The specification of the set view clause is

> SET [schema set name RENAMED] set view name

As before, a set view name is the subschema name, and must be identical with the schema name of the set type, unless RENAMED in the set entry. An example of a subschema is given in section 11.1.4.

11.1.3 ANSI DM facility

As indicated earlier, the DM statements in the ANSI model are host language independent, and this is achieved by separating all the DM statements of a particular application into a database program called a DBCS module (or a database module), which consists of a set of database procedures. A host language dependent application program, referred to as an *external program*, invokes the module by calling the appropriate procedures of the module, with relevant parameters. An example of the process will be given later, but first the concepts.

A DBCS module is defined as

> MODULE modulename
>   LANGUAGE {COBOL/FORTRAN/PASCAL/PLI}
>   SUBSCHEMA subschemaname OF schemaname
>   [{temporary set specification} . . .]
>   [{procedure} . . .]

The LANGUAGE clause specifies the intended host language for the module which, therefore, is not host language independent. The main reason for this language dependence is the need to match the data types of the parameters in the procedures both in the external program and the module. If a procedure in a module is called by an external program written in a host language for which the module is not intended, then the outcome would be uncertain, since that host language may not cater for the required data types.

Cursors and temporary set types

NDL supports database keys and currencies. There is one current record of the session (the same as the current of the run-unit), one current record for each record type in the subschema and one current owner record and one current member record of each set type in the subschema. The currency indicators, called cursors, hold the database key values of these current records; in contrast, contents of the currency indicators in the Codasyl model are implementor-defined and hence not necessarily the database key values. A set cursor contains the database key values of both the current owner and the current member record of a set type (whereas the Codasyl model retains only the current tenant); this facility resolves the currency problem of a recursive set type, as mentioned in section 10.3.2. The cursors are updated by the FIND, STORE and some other DM commands, roughly in the same way as in the Codasyl model. A *database-key-identifier* is defined as

{SESSION/record view name/OWNER set view name/MEMBER set view name}

and it yields the database key value of the corresponding current record.

NDL has replaced the Keeplist of the Codasyl model by what is called the *temporary set type*. A user can declare any number of temporary set types (which are singular sets) in a module, and can insert (by the Connect statement) the desired set of records as members, with a system-defined ORDER LAST. The user can then access these records as set members by the FIND command, using an appropriate record selection clause. This is considered to be a better facility than the one provided by Keeplists. A temporary set type is defined as

SET set view name

A declaration such as

SET SET1

for a temporary set type SET1 is treated by the DBCS as being equivalent to

SET SET1
OWNER SYSTEM
ORDER LAST
MEMBER R1 INSERTION MANUAL RETENTION OPTIONAL
MEMBER R2 INSERTION MANUAL RETENTION OPTIONAL

. . .

MEMBER Rn INSERTION MANUAL RETENTION OPTIONAL

where R1 . . . Rn are the record view names (that is, record types) in the subschema.

Procedures and DM commands

Each procedure is a collection of DM statements, sometimes referred to as DBCS statements or DBCS functions. A procedure is defined as

PROCEDURE procedure name [{parameter} . . .]
{statements} . . .

The parameters may include external program variables, but not any *subschema variables* (such as set view name, record view name, component view name). This is because the subschema variables are not visible to the external program, which must define its own variables and pass them as parameters, to which the relevant database values from subschema variables are transferred in the DBCS module by appropriate commands (further explanation is given later). However, the parameter list may include three special DBCS parameters: RECORD (to pass the name of a wanted record type), STATUS (to pass exception condition – equivalent to the DB-STATUS of the Codasyl model) and TEST (to pass the result of test conditions – see later).

NDL supports most of the Codasyl DM statements (notable exceptions are the ORDER and USE commands), along with a few additional commands, as given below. For economy we shall use record name and set name rather than record view name and set view name below.

(1) *Open statements*

READY recordname {EXCLUSIVE/PROTECTED/SHARED}
{RETRIEVE/UPDATE}

There is no separate FINISH statement, it is included in the COMMIT and ROLL-BACK statements below. Instead of realms, here record types are opened or closed.

(2) *Record retrieval statements*

(i)   FIND record-selection-format [FOR {RETRIEVE/UPDATE}]
[{AS MEMBER set name/RETAIN ALL/
RETAIN { [RECORD] [SET {set name . . .}]}}]

The record selection formats are discussed later. The FOR and RETAIN options are functionally unchanged from the Codasyl model. The AS MEMBER clause is new and it affects the set-cursor update in recursive set types. In the absence of a RETAIN clause (RETAIN ALL or RETAIN clause for the set type), the update of the set cursor of a set type is governed by the following rules:

(a) If the selected record is *only* a member record in this set type, then this record is made the current member in the set cursor of this set type and the owner of this record in this set type is made the current owner in that set cursor.

(b) If the selected record is *only* an owner record in this set type, then this record is made the current owner of this set type, setting the set cursor position for the current member to null.

(c) If the selected record is both owner and member in this set type (as in a recursive set type), then this record is made the current member if the AS MEMBER clause is specified; in this case, the owner of this record is made the current owner. If the AS MEMBER clause is not specified, then the selected record is made the current owner and the corresponding set cursor position for the current member is set to null.

Rules (a) and (b) are relevant to all set types, whereas rule (c) is relevant only to the recursive set type.

(ii)   GET recordname {SET {parameter TO component name}} . . .

where parameter is a parameter declared in the DBCS procedure and component name is the subschema component name (that is, a subschema variable). The GET command retrieves the current of the named record type and copies its content, by the SET clause, from the component name(s) to the parameter(s) — thereby transferring the record component value(s) from the subschema variables to the variables in the external program. A reverse process takes place in the STORE and MODIFY commands described below.

(3)   *Record update statements*

(i)   STORE recordname SET {component name TO parameter} . . .
         {RETAIN ALL/RETAIN {[RECORD] [SET {set name . . .}] }}

This command stores a record whose values are supplied in the parameters by the external program. However, before storing, these parameter values are transferred to the subschema variables by the SET clause. The RETAIN clause is the same as in the FIND command.

(ii)   ERASE {SESSION/record name}

The SESSION option implies the current of the session. This command has further clauses, stipulating whether other database records affected by this deletion should also be deleted.

(iii)   MODIFY recordname SET {component name TO parameter} . . .

The SET clause is the same as in the STORE command.

(4)   *Set update statements*

 (i) CONNECT {SESSION/recordname} TO {setname} . . .
 (ii) DISCONNECT {SESSION/ recordname} FROM {setname} . . .
 (iii) RECONNECT {SESSION/recordname} IN {setname} . . .

(5)   *Database currency and condition statements*

(i)   NULLIFY {SESSION /recordname/{OWNER/MEMBER} setname

This is used to set the named cursor(s) to null.
(ii)   TEST
This is an extended form of Codasyl database condition statement.

(6)   *Miscellaneous commands*
 (i)   COMMIT [FINISH]
(ii)   ROLLBACK [FINISH]
The FINISH option, if specified, will terminate READY.

In contrast to the Codasyl DM commands, the NDL commands do not operate on session cursors (currents of the run-units in Codasyl terms) by default, they must be specified explicitly.

Record selection format

The record selection formats are

(i) By database key identifier

SESSION/recordname/OWNER setname/MEMBER setname

The FIND command with this record selection format can retrieve the current of the session, the current of a named record type and the current owner and current member of a named set type.
(ii) By search specification

{FIRST/LAST/NEXT/PRIOR} {recordname/
[recordname IN] setname/ SUBSCHEMA RECORD}
[WHERE condition]

Specification (ii) combines the Codasyl record selection formats 1, 2, 3, 4 and 7. The sequential order of records in record type (equivalent to Codasyl format 1) is implementor-defined, but the order of set members is defined by the schema set order criteria. The condition in the WHERE clause permits not only comparison operations but also logical operators NOT, OR and AND. It is therefore equivalent to the predicate of the selection operator in the relational model and is obviously more powerful than the record selection formats of the Codasyl model (section 9.5.4). We present below some examples in NDL.

FIND FIRST STUDENT
(the order is implementor-defined)
FIND FIRST STUDENT WHERE SNAME = "SMITH"
Its Codasyl equivalent requires two statements
MOVE "SMITH" TO SNAME
FIND ANY STUDENT USING SNAME
(or FIND FIRST STUDENT USING SNAME)

To show a more powerful query

> FIND FIRST TUTOR WHERE TDN = "D123" OR
>   SALARY > 10 AND SALARY < 20

To take another example

> FIND FIRST STUDENT WITHIN HONOURS WHERE SNO > 500

This is not possible in Codasyl formats 3 or 4.

11.1.4 ANSI DBCS interface

A *session state* is an emphemeral object associated with the execution of a module. A session is created prior to the first execution of any procedure in a module and destroyed after the last execution. The physical representation of a session state is implementor-defined, but it contains cursors, temporary sets and a so-called ready list. The cursors hold the database key values of the various current records, and the temporary sets maintain the content of each temporary set. The ready list holds record names, usage modes and so on, associated with the execution of the READY command for each record type.

Since the database module is an independent program, all its communications with the external program are handled by procedure calls, while its interface to the database is provided by DM statements (figure 11.1).

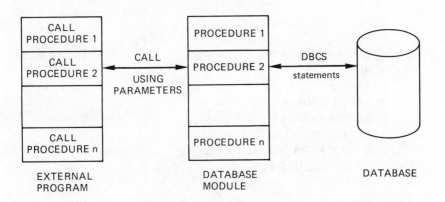

Figure 11.1

To show this process more clearly we shall consider below a small example, with a subschema (figure 11.2) taken from the Codasyl schema of section 9.3.5.

We shall insert in the database some department and student records described in a Cobol external program (figure 11.3) as DREC and SREC, each DREC containing department number (DTNO) and department name (DTDEPT) and each SREC containing student's name (STNAME) and year of study (STYY). Assume

```
SUBSCHEMA ADMISSION OF SCHEMA EDUCATION-DATABASE
     RECORD DEPT
          ITEM DNO
          ITEM DNAME
     RECORD STUDENT
          ITEM SNO
          ITEM SNAME
          ITEM YEAR-OF-STUDY RENAMED YR
     SET HONOURS
```

Figure 11.2 ANSI subschema

```
DATA DIVISION
WORKING-STORAGE SECTION.
01   DREC.
     03   DTNO        PIC X(4).
     88   EOB1        HIGH-VALUE.
     03   DTNAME      PIC X (20).
01   SREC.
     03   STDEPT      PIC X(4).
     03   STNO        PIC X(5).
     88   EOB2        HIGH-VALUE.
     03   STNAME      PIC X(20).
     03   STYY        PIC X(90)
PROCEDURE DIVISION.
PARA-10.
     CALL RDS.
     ACCEPT DREC.
     PERFORM PARA-20 UNTIL EOB1.
     ACCEPT SREC.
     PERFORM PARA-30 UNTIL EOB2.
     CALL PROCEDURE FIN.
     END RUN.
PARA-20.
     CALL PROCEDURE DINS USING DTNO DTNAME.
     ACCEPT DREC.
PARA-30.
     CALL PROCEDURE SINS USING STNO STNAME STYY STDEPT.
     ACCEPT SREC.
```

Figure 11.3 ANSI external program

that we first input the batch of DREC records, terminated by a HIGH-VALUE for DTNO, and then the batch of SREC records, terminated by a HIGH-VALUE for STNO (note the use of condition names of Cobol; EOB1 (end of batch 1) will be True if DTNO = HIGH-VALUE and likewise EOB2 will be True if STNO = HIGH-VALUE). The relevant DBCS module with three procedures is shown in figure 11.4.

```
MODULE
        LANGUAGE COBOL
        SUBSCHEMA ADMISSION OF EDUCATION-DATABASE
PROCEDURE RDS
        READY DEPT PROTECTED UPDATE
        READY STUDENT PROTECTED UPDATE
PROCEDURE DINS DTN CHARACTER 4, DNA CHARACTER 20
        STORE DEPT
                SET DNO TO DTN
                SET DNAME TO DNA
PROCEDURE SINS NUM CHARACTER 5 NAME CHARACTER 20 YY NUMERIC 1
        SDT CHARACTER 4
        FIND FIRST DEPT WHERE DNO = SDT
        STORE STUDENT
                SET SNO TO NUM
                SET SNAME TO NAME
                SET YR TO YY
                SET SDT TO SDN
        END PROCEDURE
PROCEDURE FIN
        COMMIT FINISH
        END MODULE
```

Figure 11.4 ANSI DBCS module with three procedures

The Cobol external program begins by invoking procedure RDS of the DBCS module to open the DEPT and STUDENT record types. It then reads by the ACCEPT verb a DREC record and performs PARA-20 until the end of the DREC batch. Then, the program reads an SREC record and inserts it in the database by invoking procedure SINS in PARA-30, which also reads the next SREC record; PARA-30 is repeated until the end of the batch. Thus the Cobol program calls PROCEDURE DINS with parameters DTNO and DTNAME successively, each time to insert a DEPT record; and likewise the STUDENT records are inserted by calling PROCEDURE SINS, with parameters STNO, STNAME, STYY and STDEPT, successively. As STUDENT records are AUTOMATIC members (as described in the schema of section 9.3.5) of set type HONOURS, we need to make the appropriate set the current of the set type before storing the student record. This is done by the instruction FIND DEPT WHERE DNO = SDT. However, if instead of AUTOMATIC, the member subentry in the schema contained INSERTION STRUCTURAL DNO = SNO, then we would not have needed to write FIND DEPT WHERE DNO = SDT, since the DBCS would have found the correct owner from the STRUCTURAL clause. On the other hand, if STUDENT records were MANDATORY members, then we would have needed the extra line

CONNECT STUDENT TO HONOURS

in the program, after the STORE STUDENT line in the PROCEDURE SINS. The final call to the PROCEDURE FIN is used to commit the update and to close the DEPT and STUDENT record types.

The interfacing technique described above is called *explicit subroutine calls*. The advantage of such an interface is that no change is required in the host language compiler, provided that

(i) it can declare the DBCS data types adequately, and
(ii) it can call a pre-compiled procedure written in a different language, in a manner analogous to calling, say, a Fortran subroutine from a Cobol program.

The disadvantage is that programming in this way requires two programs (external program and the module) instead of one, thus making the task of programming harder. There are two other ways of interfacing the host language with the DML, namely *implicit subroutine calls* and the *native syntax* approach. In implicit subroutine calls, the user writes only one program, the external program, but in an extended form – replacing each "Call procedure" statement by the DM statements of the intended procedure in the DBCS module. This extended external program is then processed by a pre-compiler which generates the purer external program and the corresponding module. Thus the user does not need to write two separate programs, and also no change is required in the host language compiler provided that the two conditions stated above are also met.

The third option corresponds to the one used in the current Codasyl Cobol database facility, where the host language is extended to include native (that is host language dependent) DM commands. An extended host language compiler can then generate the pure external program and a DBCS module, as necessary. In fact the host language dependent DM commands could be designed to be syntactically nearidentical with the DBCS statements, if so desired. Needless to say, among the three interfacing techniques the native syntax approach is the easiest for the users, but most difficult for the compiler, as it involves the extension of the host language compiler, thus requiring the modification of the compiler each time that a new version of the ANSI standard is produced.

11.1.5 ANSI Cobol database facility

ANSI X3H2 describes these three techniques as illustrations, leaving it to the host language designers to choose the one they prefer. The responsibility for standardising host language interfaces lies with the relevant host language committees of ANSI. The Cobol committee (ANSI X3J4) has already begun its work on a standard Cobol interface for network databases. It has opted for the native syntax approach, and produced a preliminary draft, containing specifications for

(1) subschema entry in the Cobol DATA DIVISION which includes the subschema name and the declaration of temporary sets and Cobol names for the special DBCS parameters STATUS, RECORD and TEST
(2) database conditions
(3) database-key identifier
(4) DM commands
(5) data types (to match those in the schema component entries so that they can be used for the parameters in the procedure calls).

The syntaxes suggested for this Cobol facility lie somewhere between NDL and the Codasyl Cobol DML (for instance, the term CURRENT rather than SESSION is preferred in the proposed Cobol DM commands). In general, the function of a Cobol DM command corresponds to the execution of a DBCS procedure, preceded or followed by some additional processing as defined by the general rules for the command. The external program, which might resemble a Cobol application program for a Codasyl database, may be translated by a pre-processor into a DBCS module and another Cobol external program where the DM statements are replaced by Cobol procedure calls to the DBCS module, with appropriate parameters. The programs can then be compiled by the relevant compilers. Other alternatives are also possible; however, it is too early to make any comments on this draft.

The ANSI network model appears to be neater and clearer than the Codasyl model, with some of its excesses trimmed. However, the use of explicit or implicit subroutine calls is likely to make the task of programming harder, at a time when the ease of programming, leading to a higher programmer productivity, is considered to be an important virtue. Therefore the native syntax approach, as adopted by the Cobol committee, appears to be the only realistic alternative.

The X3H2 committee is aware of some of the shortcomings of the proposed NDL, including the need to support a query language, interface to a data dictionary, authorisation controls, further integrity controls and utilities.

11.2 ANSI relational model

The ANSI X3H2 has produced a preliminary draft for what it calls a Relational Database Language (RDL). It is in fact a standardised version of SQL, extended by the module concept of the ANSI network model. The alterations in the SQL syntaxes have been minor (for instance, DISTINCT in place of UNIQUE in the SELECT clause). It defines a schema consisting of base tables, views, authorisation clauses, and some uniqueness constraints (as in the ANSI network model for record uniqueness). The entries are described in syntaxes which in most parts are identical with those of SQL. No subschema has been proposed. An external program (based on a host language) can interact with the database only by procedure calls to a module, as in NDL. The draft is aimed at host language based application programs, and does not cover stand alone SQL which might not use a module. A module consists of

> MODULE module name
>   LANGUAGE {COBOL/FORTRAN/PASCAL/PLI}
>   AUTHORISATION to control permission for Retrieve,
>   Delete, Insert and Update operations
>   [{cursor declaration} . . .]
>   {procedure} . . .

A cursor permits sequential processing of tuples in a defined relation, which can be optionally ordered. When a cursor points to a tuple, this tuple becomes the current row of the table. A cursor is declared as

> CURSOR cursorname CURSOR FOR query-expression
>   [FOR UPDATE OF column list] [ORDER BY . . .]

A cursor can be used for retrieval, amendment and deletion of current rows but not for insertion of new rows. The query expression in the cursor definition is typically a SELECT . . . FROM . . . WHERE block of SQL, which defines a relation on which the cursor will act. A procedure may contain the following types of DM command

  (i) Relational queries
 (ii) Insert/Delete/Update commands } (as in section 8.1)
(iii) Open/Close cursor
(iv) Fetch — (to retrieve sequentially by named cursors)
 (v) Update/Delete by a named cursor
(vi) Commit/Rollback

These cursor operations are not new; they are available in SQL embedded in a host language (such as PL/I), though they are not discussed in this book. It would be premature to make any comment on this RDL.

11.3 Equivalence of the two models

In any attempt to establish equivalence between the relational and network models (Kay, 1975; Deen, 1980, 1984), perhaps the most fruitful areas of examination are schemas and data manipulation facilities, since there is a wide divergence between the two models on other areas such as external schema, storage schema, data protection, concurrency, recovery and so on. We shall therefore restrict ourselves to the following areas:

Records and keys
Set types
DM commands

and conclude with a discussion on the implementation issues of a relational subschema on a network model. By network model, we shall imply both the Codasyl and ANSI models, except where indicated otherwise.

11.3.1 Records and keys

The relational model demands all relations to be at least in first normal form and therefore records with data aggregates are not acceptable. If we agree to resolve all records into first normal form (to be referred to as normalised record type, interchangeably with normalised relations), then we can establish an equivalence between the two models. We discuss below how normalised record types can be created without any loss of information in the Codasyl model.

A repeating group in a record represents a natural sequence which would be destroyed if it is separated into an independent record type. In most cases, sequencing is required only to provide fast access, such as a sequential file to access all employee records in employee number order. This type of sequencing does not carry any essential information, since employee numbers which define the order are present in the records. A counter-example is queueing where this is not true, for instance, in the definition of bus routes consisting of route number (RN), stop name (SN) and frequency (FR) of arrival at that stop (assume the frequencies of arrivals vary from stop to stop). The information given above cannot define a bus route unless we specify the sequence in which the bus stops are to be visited. This sequencing information, which cannot be obtained from RN, SN or FR, is an essential piece of information, and can be represented by records containing route number, the stop names and frequencies, appearing in the correct order. Alternatively, we can introduce an extra field of stop sequence (SS), thus each record contains (RN, SS, SN, FR). A set of these records will then represent a bus route. Thus, we can convert the sequencing information from a repeating group to a sequence number, implying that a repeating group can be dropped, if we are prepared to introduce an extra field. Therefore, normalised record types can be used, without any loss of information, as the common basis of data representation in the relational, ANSI network and Codasyl models. (Note: the ANSI network model does not permit repeating groups anyway).

The relational model demands each record type to have at least one unique key, to be called a primary key; in addition, no attribute of a primary key can be null valued. In the network model there is no equivalent concept, although there can be unique keys. On the other hand, primary keys appear to be expendable in practice, even in the relational model (purists will not agree); for instance, SQL does not use any primary keys.

Relations by definition cannot have duplicate tuples (this is ensured by the primary key), but some intermediate relations (results of some projections or unions) can in practice have duplicates, unless they are removed. In the network model, there is no conceptual requirement for not having duplicate records in a record type, although in practice there do not seem to be any grounds for keeping duplicate records. Therefore, we may assume that primary keys and duplicate records do not pose any serious problem of incompatibility between the two approaches.

The Codasyl schema allows explicit key definitions in the schema to facilitate faster access. Such keys are non-essential and restrictive, as discussed earlier. However, since the Codasyl subschema, ANSI network and the relational model do not support such keys, we can also drop them from consideration.

11.3.2 Set types

Relations in the relational model are related by foreign keys, and record types in the network model by set types. There is an equivalence between these two approaches. Consider, for instance, a record type DER having department number (DNO), department name (DNAME), total number of employees (NEMP), and for each employee the employee number (ENO), employee name (ENAME) and employee salary (ESAL), written as DER (DNO, DNAME, NEMP, ENO(1), ENAME(1), ESAL(1), ENO(2), ENAME(2), ESAL(2) . . . . . . ENO(NEMP), ENAME(NEMP), ESAL(NEMP)). We can resolve this record type into

> R1 (DNO DNAME NEMP)
> R2 (ENO ENAME ESAL EDN)

where EDN is a foreign key holding employee's department number. From the relational point of view, a $1:n$ relationship is established between R1 and R2 via the foreign key. If in place of R2 we assume R2' (ENO ENAME ESAL) in the network model, then we can construct a set type EDN to give the $1:n$ relationship.

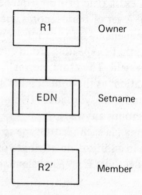

Clearly the foreign key name is equivalent to the set name, and therefore we can interchange them in the two models as necessary. However, there are two further points of interest.

(i) We have used R2′ rather than R2 as the member record in the network model. We can in fact use R2, in which case EDN would be both an attribute and set name — the difference would be clear from the context of use. However, if R2 replaces R2′, then the construction of a set type may not be essential in the Codasyl model, since employees can be identified with their department by EDN; but the use of foreign keys in the member records allows the Structural clause to be specified in the Insertion clause of the ANSI network model or the set selection criteria of the Codasyl model.

(ii) If the repeating group contained essential ordering information, then we must build an extra data item in R2 to yield that sequence.

In DER discussed above, there is no essential ordering information, since the ENO defines the order; but in the bus route example given earlier, there is. On the other hand, we have only one record type (RN, SS, SN, FR) in the bus route example, and hence there is no need for a set type. But, if we expand the example to contain bus company (BC) then we shall have two normalised record types (BC, RN) and (RN SS SN FR) to be linked by a set type RN.

There are two further characteristics of network set types — set order criteria and set selection criteria — neither of which has any relational equivalence. However, if we assume set order to be user-defined, then an equivalence can be established there. Set selection is withdrawn from the ANSI network model, and is irrelevant in the relational model since the owner can always be identified by the foreign key in the member record. An equivalence can be established if the Codasyl set selection is restricted to the STRUCTURAL CONSTRAINT or the APPLICATION option. We can now postulate the following conversion rules between the two models.

(i) A record type with repeating groups can be resolved into one or more normalised record types, without any loss of information, provided that the essential sequencing information, if any, is retained by creating an additional data item in the appropriate record type. Set types can be created to link the normalised record types.

(ii) If we have two normalised record types X (owner) and Y (member) linked by a set type S (set name), then we can equivalently, without any loss of information, represent them by two relations X and Y, provided that S is included in Y as the foreign key name for the primary key of X.

Conversely, if we have two relations X and Y, linked by a foreign key S in Y, then we can represent this relationship by a set type S, with X as the owner and Y as the member. The member record type Y in the set type S may optionally contain S as a data item.

11.3.3 DM facilities

The relational model permits an original unnormalised relation, such as DER to be created by a natural join operation:

$$DER : = R1 (DNO) * (EDN) R2$$

in PAL notation. There is no equivalent of this in the network DML. However, the selection operation has an equivalent as shown below.

(i) To find the employee tuples/records of Department D5 and salary 15.

Relational	R2: EDN = "D5" AND SAL = 15
ANSI Network	FIND FIRST R2 WHERE EDN = "D5" AND SAL = 15
	GET R2
Codasyl	MOVE "D5" TO EDN
	MOVE 15 TO SAL
	FETCH ANY R2 USING EDN SAL

(ii) To find employees of department D5 with salaries less than 15 or employees with salaries greater than 25.

Relational	R2: (EDN = "D5" AND ESAL < 15) OR ESAL > 25
ANSI Network	FIND FIRST R2 WHERE (EDN = "D5" AND ESAL < 15)
	OR ESAL > 25
	GET R2

Only the first qualifying employee will be delivered, unless repeated with FIND NEXT as shown in the next query

Codasyl	MOVE "D5" TO EDN
	FETCH ANY R2 USING EDN

But the check on salary cannot be made since the Codasyl model cannot deal with inequality conditions or any Boolean conditions.

(iii) To find the employees of department PERSONNEL with salary less than 20 (processing with set type).

Relational	R2: ESAL < 20 AND EDN = DNO % R1 : DNAME =
	"PERSONNEL"
ANSI Network	FIND FIRST R1 WHERE DNAME = "PERSONNEL"
	FIND FIRST R2 IN EDN WHERE ESAL < 20
	GET R2

FIND NEXT R2 IN EDN WHERE ESAL < 20

(continue until end of set)

Codasyl   MOVE "PERSONNEL" TO DNAME
           FIND ANY R2 USING DNAME
           FIND FIRST R2 WITHIN EDN

the condition ESAL < 20 cannot be specified by Codasyl DM commands, and hence

GET R2

Apply the condition ESAL < 20 by host language. Then

FIND NEXT R2 WITHIN EDN

(continue until end of set).

These examples also show that, while the relational DML delivers all the qualifying records, the network DML delivers one record at a time. Compared to the Codasyl DML, the ANSI DML is closer to the relational DML as it permits complex condition on the FIND command.

11.3.4 Relational subschema on a network database

Since the network model is low level (more detailed) compared to the relational model, it is relatively easier to support a relational interface on a network model rather than the converse (see also section 6.4). Such an interface will permit relational queries on a network database via a relational subschema where

 (i) all data aggregates should be resolved into separate record types, and
 (ii) set names should be treated as foreign keys of the member records.

It will also be necessary to

(iii) ignore all access control/integrity constraints or make special provision for them, and
(iv) convert efficiently, with an optimiser, all relational commands into the network DML.

Multimembered set types should be treated as two separate single member set types, the set name appearing in all member record types as a foreign key (Kay, 1975; Mercz, 1979; Zaniolo, 1979; Deen, 1980, 1984; Esslemont and Gray, 1982; Gray, 1984).

A network subschema can be used on a relational model only if a selected set of network constructs are allowed. The PRECI system (Deen, 1980, 1984) provides such a facility.

Exercises

11.1 Explain the concept of a module in NDL and evaluate the different interfacing techniques proposed.
11.2 Compare the ANSI network model with the Codasyl model, with comments on their relative merits.
11.3 Show how the functions provided by the seven record selection formats of the Codasyl model are covered by the record selection format of ANSI.
11.4 Compare the network and the relational models with respect to

Entity record representation
Association representation
Access paths.

References

ANSI (1984a). *Draft proposed ANS Database Language NDL*, ANSI, 1430 Broadway, New York, New York 10018, August
ANSI (1984b). *Evolution of the Draft proposed ANS Database Language NDL. ANSI X3H2 Database*, August (this provides a rationale for the changes from the original Codasyl model)
ANSI (1984c). *Procedure language access to Draft Proposed ANS Database Language NDL. ANSI X3H2 Database*, August
ANSI (1984d). Preliminary draft proposed ANS network database interfall, doc. no. X3J4/W-389 ANSI X3. *Cobol Information Bulletin, no. 22*, July
ANSI/SPARC (1984). *Working draft ANS database language SQL*, October document number X3H2-84-117, ANSI/SPARC project 363D, October
Deen, S. M. (1980). A canonical schema for a generalised data model with local interfaces. *Computer Journal*, Vol. (23:3), August p. 201
Deen, S. M. (1984). ANSI/SPARC architecture and its implementation in PRECI. *Database – Role and Structure* (CREST Advanced Course), edited by P. M. Stocker *et al.*, Cambridge University Press, p. 93
Esslemont, P. E. and Gray, P. M. D. (1982). The performance of a relational interface to a Codasyl Database. *Proceedings of the Second British National Conference on Databases (BNCOD-2)*, edited by S. M. Deen and P. Hammersley, BCS
Gallagher, L. J. (1984). Procedure language access to proposed ANS DBMS. *Computer Network*, Vol. 8 pp. 31–42 (North-Holland)
Gray, P. M. D. (1984). Implementing the Join operation on Codasyl DBMS. *Database – Role and Structure* (CREST Advanced Course), edited by P. M. Stocker *et al.*, Cambridge University Press, p. 185
Kay, M. H. (1975). *Data Base Description*, edited by B. Douque and G. M. Nijssen, North-Holland, p. 199

Mercz, I. (1979). Issues in building a relational interface on a Codasyl DBMS. *Data Base Architecture*, edited by G. Bracchi and G. M. Nijssen, North-Holland, p. 191

Zaniolo, C. (1979). Design of relational views over network schemes. *Proceedings ACM SIGMOD Conference, 1979*

PART IV: THE STATE OF THE ART

12 User Issues in Implementation

Over the past decade, databases have been accepted as an essential part of the data-processing facility by most large organisations, just as computers were accepted two decades ago. Today many small organisations are also using databases; we even have databases on microcomputers. The advent of databases has also changed the attitude towards data, which is now regarded as a resource in its own right — a resource to be cared for and protected. This attitude has given rise to new breeds of experts such as data analysts and database administrators (DBA). In this chapter we wish to present some of these user issues, with overviews of the database environment in section 12.1 and product selection in section 12.2.

12.1 Database environment

The introduction of a database affects the user organisation in a number of ways: it changes the organisation's attitude to data requirements and management, it creates new authorities and it brings in new skills. It also demands greater co-ordination between the various user departments and it requires stricter adherence to standards. A good implementation scheme includes adequate provision to tackle these problems, in addition to the plans for system developments and scheduling of resources. Much of this is planned and controlled by the DBA on whose ability largely depends the success of the venture, provided that the right DBMS is selected in the first place. In this section we shall consider some of the implementation issues and the role of a DBA.

12.1.1 Implementation issues

A database offers many advantages to the users, as discussed in chapter 1, but it is an expensive investment and without careful plans and extensive preparation its success is likely to be elusive. The groundwork usually commences as soon as a decision to implement a database system is taken. This decision is a difficult one, being dependent on a complex set of factors, many of which are hard to assess. It is often said that a database does not save money but it can make more money. The extent to which it is able to make more money by improving the company performance is dependent on the present and future requirements and anticipated growth. The upper management is usually in a better position to make the decision; but once the decision is taken, the data-processing department should begin preparations in earnest.

The first task is to produce a set of selection criteria based on the assessment of the organisation's present and future needs. Freedom to select a DBMS is often constrained by the hardware availability — this is particularly true for the DBMSs supplied by the manufacturers, since the DBMSs vended by the software houses are usually more flexible and can be implemented on a range of computers. The computer independent DBMSs are obviously preferable as they allow change of the computer if need be, without having to change the DBMS as well.

Databases should be developed gradually with an evolutionary approach, permitting the user to learn from past mistakes. A sudden changeover of all the relevant systems from conventional files to a database is risky and hence inadvisable. Ideally only one system should be added to the database at a time, and only when this is performing satisfactorily should another be added. The first system is the most difficult one as the user cannot normally rely on previous experience, and therefore its implementation should be regarded as exploratory, with adequate provision being made for mistakes and surprises.

There appears to exist a fallacy in the minds of some people that, since a database is supposed to provide data independence, the old conventional programs will not require rewriting when they are changed over to a database environment. This is wrong. Firstly the data independence available varies from nothing to a great deal, depending on the DBMS, and secondly data independence attempts to provide immunity only to the application programs of a database from the changes in the same database, as discussed earlier in this book. All conventional programs will generally require redesign and rewriting, optionally to take advantage of the database facilities, and compulsorily to meet the database requirements with regard to data validation, data manipulation, integrity controls, privacy codes and so on. In addition, as the old input and output files will not be available any longer, the processing requirements of a program will also be affected. It is difficult, in these circumstances, to see how the rewriting of the programs can be avoided, except in so far as program converters or program generators can be used.

The most underestimated task in implementation is that of the conversion of the conventional files to the database, mainly owing to the presence of duplicate and inconsistent data. It appears deceptively easy at first sight, but as the work progresses the magnitude of the problem gradually unfolds. The user experience singles this out as a main cause for late implementation (Palmer, 1973; Davis, 1975).

Another major task is the analysis of the data, typically carried out by a data analyst who examines the data, their interrelationships and their usage constraints, and eventually designs the database schema. He has to identify

(i) What are entities and what are attributes.

(ii) How these can be grouped and classified.

(iii) Their interrelationships and how they can be best formalised

(iv) What integrity and privacy constraints there are and how they can be described.

None of these decisions are easy. For instance, if we have data about persons, then person, parent, male person, female person, employee and salesman could also be the entities. Which one should we choose? Each choice leads to a different combination of attributes and different record relationships. Indeed the analyst has to work in cycles, going over the same data many times until he reaches a satisfactory overall decision. The analyst must also take into consideration the missing data, likely additions, changes and growth, including the consequences of the present decision on future usage. A data dictionary is a very useful aid in data analysis. Once the analysis is complete, the model dependent database schema is designed with the help of schema design tools where available. There is a wide variety of techniques that are used by data analysts, but most of them are *ad hoc* rather than formal (Davenport, 1978; Proceedings of the 4th VLDB Conference, 1978; Shave, 1981). However, since human decision is pivotal in each phase of data analysis, the usefulness of all these techniques is somewhat limited.

To administer the database it is often necessary to employ a database administrator. He is normally an experienced person who is preferably involved from the beginning of the database selection process. In a database environment, there is also a need for a co-ordination committee formed with representatives of the user departments to co-ordinate all activities and to resolve the conflicting needs of the users. The details of the functions of the DBA are discussed in the next subsection.

Attention also needs to be paid to the training requirements of the staff including the DBA, data analysts, systems designers, programmers and operators. Any slip here might show up later as implementation delay. It is likely that the vendor of the DBMS would assist in providing some reorientation course.

The reorientation course should be designed not only to teach the staff new skills, but also to reorient their outlooks as dictated by the needs of the database. It particularly affects the systems designers and the programmers whose traditional roles are significantly altered by a database. For instance, in a database environment the systems designer need not concern himself with the design of files and allocation of storage space, but instead he has to concentrate on choosing the right data structure with appropriate access paths and the most convenient host language (if several are available). He has to pay attention to a number of new problems such as additional data validation, integrity control, privacy control, concurrent usage and so on, and learn to take advantage of the multiplicity of access paths available. His task would be more arduous if subschema independence is lacking.

The programming task is often claimed to be simpler in a database environment, since sorting, multiple updates and collating information from multiple files become unnecessary. However, the programmer needs to adhere to stringent controls as regards coding, data validation, and program testing.

12.1.2 Database administrator

In a conventional system, files belong to the relevant user departments. It is they who are responsible for the accuracy, consistency and up-to-dateness of data in the file, although regular maintenance on their behalf is normally carried out by the data-processing staff. In a database where all company data is centrally held, no single user department being responsible for it, this responsibility is usually exercised by the database administrator on behalf of the whole company with a view to preserving the interests of both the current and the future users. In addition, the DBA is also responsible for creating, expanding and improving the database and for providing user facilities. For a small database the function of the DBA can be performed by an individual as a part-time job, but for a large database the function can require the full-time services of a team, often involving many people. To be effective the DBA has to represent a senior position with sufficient authority to arbitrate disputes between the user departments as regards database usage, and to impose decisions in the case of deadlocks. He may also act as the final authority in all matters relating to the management of the database. The function of the DBA should include the following activities:

Creation of the database
Performance optimisation
Data protection
Specification and enforcement of standards
Co-ordination and the provision of the user facilities.

Creation

To create a database the DBA has to analyse and assess the data requirements of the users. He must examine the existing data, their representation and usage statistics, and from these determine the logical datasets required and the access paths needed for each dataset. He has to design, with the help of a data analyst, a schema and a storage schema. It is a demanding job that needs all the skills and the knowledge of the DBA. When the storage schema is ready, the DBA loads it with data as the final act of creation.

Performance optimisation

The DBA needs to carry out regular clean-up operations to release space occupied by the deleted data, and reorganise the existing data in the primary and overflow areas to increase effectiveness by taking advantage of the free space made available. His responsibility also includes the analysis of the usage statistics collected, and their interpretation, with an eventual reorganisation of the storage schema for optimal performance. However, this is easier said than done (Deen, 1981).

Data protection

The specifications of privacy locks, data validation requirements, backup files and so on have to be provided by the DBA. For the purpose of privacy locks the DBA might define data ownership, the owner department being responsible for access authorisation. The owner department could stipulate the level of privacy protection required and supply the list of authorised users to the DBA.

The DBA is clearly responsible for recovering the database after failure. Some of the recoveries may be automatic, while others may require human intervention. The DBA has to ensure that the necessary backup files are maintained.

Standards

The specification and enforcement of standards is a major responsibility of the DBA. Some of the areas where standards are required are

Data validation
Update
Program testing
Privacy codes
Subschema specification
Documentation.

As mentioned in section 5.2.1, data validation is the key to integrity control. To ensure the validity of data, the DBA may specify detailed checks and incorporate them into standards for strict compliance. For more common types of data validation he could develop database procedures, wherever possible, for the use of the application programmers. Ideally all validation requirements, along with database procedures to be invoked, if any, should be stipulated in a data dictionary.

Program testing has to be thorough and must be rigidly controlled to a standard. The DBA may create a test database – particularly for update programs. Allocation of privacy locks and access code should be standardised as well. There is also a clear need for establishing standardised procedures for subschema specification and generation. Finally all user programs, systems, subschemas and so on must be properly documented so that, in case of errors or subsequent modification, the user can easily find the required information.

Co-ordination and user facilities

The DBA normally acts as the controlling element between the database and the users. The user departments and the systems designers will need to communicate with him frequently. In order to ensure smoother operations amidst conflicting user needs, it is advisable, as suggested earlier, to form a co-ordination committee, with the user departments as the members. In it the users can vent their grievances, suggest improvements and approve future plans. The DBA is, of course, responsible for all user facilities, some of which have already been mentioned. All aspects of a database should be properly documented for the benefit of the users, such aspects preferably being held in a data dictionary.

12.2 Database selection

We shall first present a brief overview of the major commercial database management systems that are available today, and then outline some aspects of the selection process.

12.2.1 Major commercial products

At present the following major types of products are marketed.

Codasyl systems   (DMS 1100, IDS-II, DBMS-10, PHOLAS, SIBAS, IDMS
                    and many more)
Relational systems (SQL/DS, DB2 and many others)
Hierarchical systems (IMS, DL/1)
Inverted structured systems (ADABAS, SYSTEM 2000)
Net structured systems (TOTAL)
Microcomputer-based DBMS (DBASE II).

There are a large number of Codasyl implementations available today, some by manufacturers and some by software houses. Although none has implemented the full Codasyl specification, most have included all the major features, such as record type, set type and most DM commands, including almost all the record selection formats. Variations arise in the support of data validation (Check and Call clauses), access control clauses, some set order and set selection clauses, subschema independence, concurrency facility and the like. Many of the implementations also have some additional features outside the Codasyl model. The past changes in the Codasyl model itself, often with incompatibility between the DDLC and Cobol database specifications, have also contributed to this variation. Further variations exist in the implementation techniques, which make some of the products more efficient for some types of processing than for others.

Of the Codasyl implementations listed above, DMS 1100 of Univac is one of the earliest, originally being designed for the Univac 1100 series of computers. The first version, released in late 1971, was based on the 1971 DBTG report and it allowed Cobol, Fortran and PL/I as the host languages. Since then it has been continually improved with newer Codasyl facilities. IDS-II of Honeywell (as successor to pre-Codasyl IDS-I) was launched in 1976 for Honeywell machines, and it permits Cobol, Fortran and PL/I as host language. DBMS-10, originally for DEC-10 computers, was released in 1973, while PHOLAS (for Phillips computers) and SIBAS (of Norksdata) came to the scene in the mid seventies.

IDMS (Integrated Data Management System) of Cullinane Corporation, is probably the most widely known Codasyl implementation, partly because of its machine independence, and partly because of its availability on IBM hardware. Launched in 1973, it quickly became very popular, so much so that a number of manufacturers, including ICL, acquired rights to develop their own versions of IDMS. The original product was developed in 1972 by Goodrich Chemical Company of Ohio which was a member of the Codasyl DBTG; a year later it was passed to the Cullinane Corporation for marketing, development and support responsibility.

Like most Codasyl products, IDMS supports both batch and online processing, but its main host language is Cobol, although it can also be accessed by Fortran, PL/I and Assembler. It uses a centralised data dictionary.

The relational model had been implemented in the past mostly as research proto-types, and only recently as commercial products. INGRES, originally a research prototype, is now marketed as a commercial product. IBM has developed SQL/DS and DB2 as commercial products based on SYSTEM R. SQL/DS (operating systems DOS/VSE and VM) can be used in conjunction with IMS, with some facility to transfer data between them. DB2 (operating systems MVS/XA and MVS/370) is more recent, and is considered to be the main IBM product on the relational model.

There are a number of other commercial products providing some relational facilities; RAPPORT of Logica in the U.K. – which supports a relational algebra and also a calculus based on SQL – is one of them. More recently, relational DBMSs on microcomputers have become very popular, but the available relational query facilities vary widely from nominal to substantial (INRIA, 1983). A well known microcomputer-based DBMS is DBASE II, which can be installed in most large microcomputers, including IBM PC. Although claimed to be relational, it does not support any relational language at all, but uses the equivalents of some relational operations (such as join) in a peculiar fashion. DBASE III is an improved version of DBASE II for 16-bit microcomputers.

IBM's IMS is built on a hierarchical data structure, often regarded by many as the third type of data model after the relational and network models. A subset of IMS facilities is also packaged as the DL/1 system. We shall return to IMS in the next chapter, where ADABAS and TOTAL will also be discussed, along with a note on SYSTEM 2000.

12.2.2 Selection process

It would seem that in many cases the primary motivation (Davis, 1975) for changing over to database system comes from the need to avoid data duplications which give rise to data inconsistency and require heavy maintenance. The inflexibility of the existing system to cope with the growing volume of data and increasing demand for information often play important roles in the decision. In some cases the need for integration of the related systems along with a desire to minimise program develop-ment and maintenance cost also act as the prime mover. Sometimes, the need to

provide better and speedier management information is given priority, the facility
to support online systems being also regarded as another important deciding factor.

Whatever the motivation, as a first step in a selection process, the user organisation needs a selection committee to carry out the technical evaluation of available
products and an assessment of the current and future requirements of the organisation. If the in-house expertise is not available, outside experts can be called in.
Having established the requirements, tenders can then be invited from the database
vendors. In the initial evaluation phase, most of the database management systems
are normally eliminated on the basis of the user requirements; this leaves two or
three products for detailed evaluation in the final phase, where a comparative study
of the characteristics, performance and support facilities of the products can be
made as regards the user requirements.

One of the most important factors in the selection is the expected processing
efficiency, since databases are notoriously slow, but this is the most difficult parameter to evaluate. The only available means is benchmark testing by creating a small
representative database for the purpose, but there are problems. Apart from the
difficulty of defining and creating a representative database, there is also an additional complication, owing to the dependence of the test performance on the size
of the database, user experience and so on. In general, the result of the processing-
cost evaluation has to be treated with caution. Because of these uncertainties, some
organisations are reluctant to estimate processing cost, but there are others who
believe it to be a useful exercise for reducing the margin of error.

Some DBMSs are easier to install than others, the ease in installation being a
reflection of the complexity of the DBMS. All sophisticated DBMSs are complex,
but all equally sophisticated DBMSs are not necessarily equally complex. Often
there is a choice; if there is, it should naturally be exploited. TOTAL, ADABAS and
SYSTEM 2000 are easier to install, but IMS and Codasyl type DBMSs are more
difficult and require greater skill. Relational DBMS should be easier to deal with.

The ease in systems design emanates partly from data independence and partly
from the access paths and data structures supported by the DBMS. Subschema
independence, the complexities of DM commands and the additional work required
by the programmer to ensure data integrity determine the ease of programming.
The binding procedures of a DBMS generally affects the frequency of compilations.
Adequate error diagnostics, not only in programming but also in all aspects of database operations, are essential for efficient performance of the system. Query and
host languages supported and the relative ease of their use are obviously crucial
factors in database selection. A data dictionary system and adequate utilities are
also essential prerequisites for a good database management system.

The size of the computer memory required to operate a database is an important
consideration and must clearly lie within a prescribed limit. The DBMS should
ideally be portable so that the user can change computers if necessary. Another
important feature is the compatibility of a DBMS, particularly with the existing
systems in the organisation, so that data can be transferred between them if needed.
For longer term development, network and relational systems, particularly those to
be built on expected ANSI standards, will be preferable.

The user should also examine the extent of the vendor's support and the documentation available for the product. The vendor is likely to provide pre-installation support quite readily as otherwise the user may not buy the product, and therefore attention should be directed to the post-installation supports, including the nature of the maintenance contracts offered. The level and the quality of documentation available should also be checked thoroughly, before a decision is made. User experience suggests that lack of adequate documentation is a major source of frustration. Depending on the aids available, the cost of changeover to the database can vary. The changeover cost should be taken into consideration before arriving at a final decision.

Lastly, in selecting a DBMS, it is better not to be a pioneer as the risk is great, and it is also advisable to check with other users of the product, preferably those with similar problems. This last exercise can reveal startling information on many unsuspected fronts.

Exercises

12.1 Describe the functions of a database administrator.
12.2 Discuss, giving reasons, the items that should be included in the technical evaluation of a database package.

References

Davenport, R. A. (1978). Data analysis — experience with a formal methodology. *Proceedings of Euro IFIP 79*, edited by P. Samet, North-Holland (this reference and Shave (1981) describe similar techniques but, generally speaking, there are not many formal methodologies available, although each practitioner seems to prefer his own)

Davis, B. (1975). *Data Base Management Systems: User Experience in the U.S.A.*, U.K. National Computing Centre Publication

Deen, S. M. (1981). The state of the art in database research. *Proceedings of the First British National Conference on Databases (BNCOD-1)*, edited by S. M. Deen and P. Hammersley, Pentech

INRIA (1983). *Workshop on Relational DBMS Design/Implementation/Use on Microcomputers, February 1983, Toulouse*, INRIA, B.P. 105, 78150 Le Chesnay, Cedex France (this volume describes many microprocessor-based relational DBMSs)

Palmer, I. (1973). *Data Base Management*, SCICON, London

Proceedings of the 4th VLDB Conference (1978). (This contains many articles on data analysis)

Shave, M. J. R. (1981). Entities, functions and binary relations . . . . *Computer Journal*, Vol. (24:1), February, p. 4

13 Prototypes and Earlier Models

This chapter is intended to cover some interesting research prototypes and to discuss the earlier database models. The systems included are

SYSTEM R   (relational)
IMS (hierarchical)
ADABAS, SYSTEM 2000 (inverted)
TOTAL (net).

13.1 SYSTEM R

In the seventies, a number of relational database systems were developed as experimental prototypes. Among them INGRES (Stonebraker *et al.*, 1976), PRTV (Todd, 1976) and SYSTEM R(Astrahan *et al.*, 1976; Chamberlin *et al.*, 1976; Chamberlin, 1980; Date, 1981) are well known. INGRES (Interactive Graphics and Retrieval System) was built by M. Stonebraker *et al.*, now of the University of California at Berkeley (originally at Carnegie-Mellon), on PDP 11 hardware under the Unix operating system in 1974 and has been used by many academic institutions both for teaching and for research purposes. More recently, it is being marketed as a commercial product. One of its outstanding contributions is the QUEL language (section 6.3.4). Stonebraker's group used INGRES also for research in distributed databases.

PRTV and SYSTEM R are both IBM research prototypes. PRTV (Peterlee Relational Test Vehicle) was designed by S. J. P. Todd *et al.* at Peterlee, England, and was at one point used by the Greater London Council and the World Health Organization on an experimental basis. It supported relational algebra and perfected some query optimisation techniques, but its update facility was rather poor and its storage structure primitive. However, all development on PRTV ceased some time ago and it is not now available to outsiders. SYSTEM R is the prize research product of IBM, designed and implemented at the San Jose Laboratory between 1974 and 1979. Although a number of relational DBMSs are now commercially available, SYSTEM R still remains the most elaborate implementation of a relational research prototype. In this section we shall give a brief account of this product and attempt to bring out some of its significant features.

13.1.1 Architecture

SYSTEM R is *not* based on the ANSI/SPARC architecture although there are some parallels. It basically has only one level of description consisting of

Views (or derived relations)
Base tables (or base relations)
Storage and indexes

all written in SQL. A *base table* is a basic relation which is physically stored in the database, and *views* are derived relations generated by SQL statements (as we have seen in section 8.1.4) from base tables and/or other derived relations. The tuples represented by a view are not generally physically stored, but derived during the run-time; however they can be stored, if desired, by the SQL assignment command. The entry for a base table also contains the description of its physical storage and indexes (B-trees), each tuple being stored as a storage record.

The description of the base table correspond to th? conceptual schema. A given user can interact with any number of base table and views. Therefore there is no external schema representing a subset of the conceptual schema. An SQL program can be stand alone or embedded in PL/I or Cobol. SYSTEM R supports an integrated data dictionary facility where all table descriptions, visible to the users, are held. User can include English text in the dictionary along with these descriptions.

13.1.2 System components

The SYSTEM R has two major subsystems, namely, Relational Data System (RDS) and Research Storage System (RSS), linked together by what is called Research Storage Interface (RSI). An interface called Relational Data Interface (RDI) supports the external user languages (SQL or embedded SQL) on RDS (figure 13.1).

RDI consists of a set of procedures (including one called SQL for SQL facilities) that can be invoked from a PL/I or a Cobol program. It can potentially support other user languages, and it sits on the top of RDS which consists of a pre-compiler and a run-time system. Stand alone SQL is supported by a simple program called User-Friendly Interface (UFI) which is implemented on the top of RDI to handle terminal communications.

RDS first pre-compiles SQL program using XPREP. If SQL is used under UFI (that is, as a stand alone language) then the pre-compiled program is immediately executed via XRDI. However, if a host language is used, the pre-compiled SQL program is replaced by Call XRDI statement in the host language program, which is then compiled by invoking the host language compiler. After this the fully compiled user program can be run.

The pre-compiled process itself begins with parsing, when the appropriate authorisation and relevant integrity checks are made. XPREP then invokes the optimiser which selects the optimal access paths for execution from the available

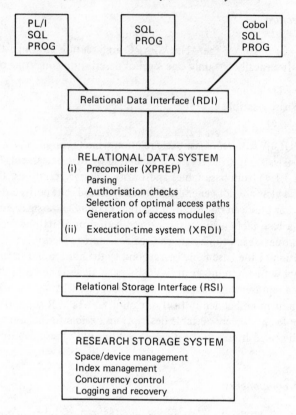

Figure 13.1 SYSTEM R architecture

indexes and from certain statistical information on the relations. The best access path is the one that is expected to incur least inout–output and CPU cost. Machine language codes embodying this access path, called *access modules*, are then generated for execution by XRDI which is called by the user program. On each first call by a user program, XRDI checks the authority of the current user, and the validity of the module before it proceeds further. The Access module operates on the database by making calls to RSS, and delivers the result to the user program.

Research Storage System (formerly Relational Storage System) manages the details of the physical level of SYSTEM R, and supports RSI which provides tuple-at-a-time operations on the base relations. All SQL statements (access modules) are converted into low level RSI calls which require the use of data areas called segments (see below) and indexes. Thus a SQL program is first optimally precompiled and then executed by tuple-at-a-time operators of RSI.

The basic objects supported by RSS are stored relations and B-tree indexes. Any number of indexes can be declared for the same relation during its creation or even later. No pointers or links, although advocated in some of the earlier publications (Blasgen *et al.*, 1979), are currently used. The storage is logically divided into a set of segments, each segment containing an integral number of 4096-byte pages. The number of pages in a segment can vary dynamically. A segment contains all the tuples of one or more relations, although the same page can have tuples of different relations. A page may contain either data or indexes, but not both.

SYSTEM R does not support any concept of primary keys; instead, each stored tuple is given an internal tuple identifier, called TID, made up of page number and page offset as in figure 4.11. When a tuple is inserted, the user can suggest a TID; but if no space is available on the suggested page, the tuple is stored on an adjacent page. SYSTEM R allows variable length attributes (thus permitting variable length tuples), and also the addition of new attributes dynamically (by SQL commands), both of which can lead to overflows. If a tuple thus expands and cannot be accommodated in the original page, it is moved to a new page, replacing the tuple in the original page by a pointer (tag) giving the new location; TID is not changed. If the tuple expands again, then the complete tuple will be moved, if necessary, to another page, and the tag in the original page is modified to give the new location. Thus a tuple can be retrieved by a TID in 1 and sometimes 2 disc accesses, but never more than 2 accesses. However, to find a TID from a B-tree of level n, an additional $(n-1)$ disc accesses are needed (the root being in the memory).

RSS is also responsible for storage and index management, concurrency control, logging and recovery.

13.1.3 Supporting facilities

Optimiser

SYSTEM R is well known for its comprehensive query optimisation facility (Blasgen *et al.*, 1979; Selinger *et al.*, 1979). The optimiser is designed to minimise the weighted sum of the predicted number of input/outputs and the predicted number of RSS calls in processing a SQL statement (RSS calls give the CPU cost). The relative weights of these two factors are also adjustable. Given a query, the system either scans the relations and applies the predicate on it, or uses a suitable index, if it exists, to extract the qualifying tuples. A further predicate may apply on the extracted tuples. For instance, to find the programmers of project P1 from an Employee relation, the system may do the following, assuming that a suitable index exists both for job title and project.

(i)   Use the index on job title to find programmer tuples and then examine their projects.
(ii)   Use index on project to find those who work in project P1, and then examine their job titles.

If no suitable index exists, the whole relation is scanned to select tuples satisfying both the conditions. The choice between (i) and (ii) is based on what are called *selectivity* and *clustering* properties of each index, both of which are stored as statistics in the data dictionary. Selectivity is the ratio of distinct key values to the total number of key values. Therefore the selectivity is 1 in the unique key index and more than 1 in indexes for non-unique keys. An index is clustered if the key order in the index reflects closely the physical storage order of tuples, that is if this key is the placement key. These two properties can be used to estimate the disc accesses needed to extract a tuple. The technique used in the join operation was described earlier in section 8.4.

Concurrency control

SYSTEM R allows a full range of concurrency facilities. The user can initiate a commit-unit by a BEGIN TRANSACTION and terminate it by an END TRANSACTION command. The system carries out locking (a hierarchy of locks ranging from individual records to segments are used) as necessary, using the pre-emption strategy. A deadlock is recognised from cycles in stategraphs and is resolved by backing out a transaction, usually the youngest one. Transaction recovery and checkpoint restart facilities are available. The recovery schema uses the DO/UNDO/REDO protocols of Gray (section 5.7) and comprises 10 per cent of the total SYSTEM R codes.

Modification facilities

SYSTEM R provides a number of database modification facilities which are carried out dynamically by SQL commands. They include

creation and destruction of base tables
creation and destruction of indexes on tables
addition of new attributes
changes of authorisation held by users
creation and deletion of views.

Some of these have been mentioned before, in section 8.1. In the IBM San Jose Laboratory, SYSTEM R is used as the vehicle for research in a number of areas, such as document retrieval, distributed databases and so on; however, it is reported to be somewhat inefficient in operations (although not confirmed by IBM). But this inefficiency is not surprising, since the primary objective of a research prototype is the provision of facilities to experiment with new ideas, rather than an efficient implementation needed in a production prototype. To achieve this research objective the system has to be designed very flexibly, often with redundant features, and it has to be implemented in a high level language such as PL/I so that changes can be incorporated easily. The overhead of design flexibility incurred by PL/I is usually very heavy, which makes the overall run-time operation inefficient. This is probably the case with SYSTEM r. However, from the research point of view this inefficiency does not matter so much, so long as it can be quantified and accounted for in the experimentation studies. A product prototype is usually designed in a more non-redundant fashion and written in a more efficient language, taking advantage of the operating system and often incorporating Assembler routines, particularly for input/output.

13.2 Hierarchical model (IMS)

The Information Management System of IBM (Date, 1981; IBM, 1982) was originally developed for the Rockwell International Corporation of California. Its first version IMS/1 was released in 1969, followed by another version called IMS/2. The system has been improved gradually over the years by the addition of new features, including a virtual storage (VS) version called IMS/VS. IMS can be operated in both batch and teleprocessing mode, and it is designed for the larger machines of IBM. The memory required just for the resident routines of IMS/VS is about 220K bytes; the minimum memory size required varies from 384K bytes to 768K bytes, depending on the option. An additional 256K bytes are needed to support the remote terminals.

IMS can be used by programs written in Assembler, Cobol and PL/I. Instead of a single database, it supports a number of what are called *physical 'databases'* which together constitute a database. Each *physical 'database'* consists of all the occurrences of a single tree structure whose description, together with its mapping into the storage device, is known as *Data Base Description* (DBD). *A logical 'database'* is a subset of a physical 'database' and is defined in a *Program Communication Block* (PCB) in accordance with user requirements. A PCB also includes the mapping of the logical into the physical 'database'. The set of all PCBs for one user is known as a *Program Specification Block* (PSB). This cannot be shared, although two PSBs may contain the same data. The DBD is equivalent to the database schema, and the PSB to the external schema (admittedly with a restrictive facility). A single language called *Data Language/One* (DL/1) is used as DDL and DML.

IMS is the principal IBM database product (apart from recent SQL/DS and DB2), and is widely used by large organisations. IBM has invested vast sums of money in the system and is naturally pleased with its success. This perhaps explains IBM's reluctance to implement the Codasyl proposal.

13.2.1 Architecture

In IMS the basic unit of access is a *segment*. This is defined as a collection of data items within a record and it can be of variable length. Data are represented in a tree showing one to many relationships between segment types. The segment at a node is called the *parent* and those at the branches the *children*. The occurrences of a segment type are known as *twin segments*. A tree may consist of 1–255 segment types with a maximum of 15 levels. One occurrence of the whole tree is known as a '*record*' and all the occurrences of a tree constitute a *physical 'database'*.

Physical data structure

To illustrate the IMS data structure, we consider a physical 'database' containing the data of health centres belonging to a health board. Each centre has a number of doctors and nurses, and each doctor has a number of patients. We may represent the data by a tree containing four segment types as shown in figure 13.2.

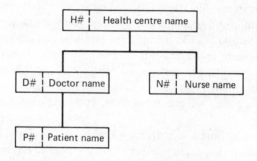

Figure 13.2 Tree structure for IMS

We have assumed that every segment type contains a *segment key* for the identification of the twins, represented here by H#, D#, P# and N#. Depending on its position in the tree, each segment type is given an exclusive type number by the system, which we have indicated here by T1, T2, T3 and T4. One occurrence of this tree for health centre number H1 is shown in figure 13.3(a). This 'record' is presented sequentially in figure 13.3(b), which demonstrates that an IMS 'record' is really a conventional record with a variable number of repeating groups. The physical 'database' consists of all such 'records' — one 'record' per health centre. The tree used for a physical 'database' is known as a *physical tree* to distinguish it from a *logical* tree, which is defined as a subset of a physical tree used in a PCB; all the occurrences of a logical tree constitute a *logical 'database'*.

If two physical trees share a common segment type, then data redundancy is avoided by including it physically (that is, as a *physical child*) in one tree, and by maintaining a *child pointer* to it from the appropriate parent in the other tree. This segment type is then said to be a *logical child* of a *logical parent* in the second tree. Any segment type, except the root, can be a logical child of another segment type. A physical tree can have as many logical children as

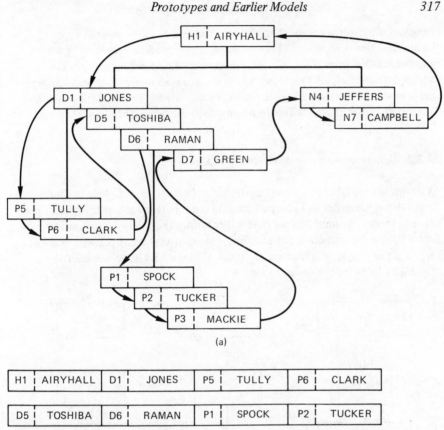

(a)

H1 ¦ AIRYHALL	D1 ¦ JONES	P5 ¦ TULLY	P6 ¦ CLARK

D5 ¦ TOSHIBA	D6 ¦ RAMAN	P1 ¦ SPOCK	P2 ¦ TUCKER

P3 ¦ MACKIE	D7 ¦ GREEN	N5 ¦ JEFFERS	N7 ¦ CAMPBELL

(b)

*Figure 13.3 (a) A physical 'record' (note: Dr Toshiba does not have a patient);
arrows show the hierarchical key order (see later). (b) Sequential
presentation of the physical 'record' (this is also in a hierarchical key
order)*

necessary, but all of them must be specified in the DBD. If a segment type is
included in a tree as a logical child then, subject to specification, only some or
all the subordinate segment types of this logical child can be included there.

Logical data structure

A PSB consists of a collection of logical trees, each representing a subset of the
physical tree and including the logical children of the physical tree, if any. It

is a subset only to the extent that we may omit one or more segment types of the physical tree — except the root segment, which must be present. If a segment type is excluded from a logical tree, all its subordinate segment types are also excluded. Conversely, if a segment type is included, all its superior segment types that provide the hierarchical sequence to the root segment must also be included. This sometimes restricts the freedom to exclude the unwanted segment types.

13.2.2 Data representation and network model

As shown above, IMS can support both tree and net structures. We consider below some further examples and compare its data representational capability with the network model. Assume that we have patient, drug and nurse records, where each doctor has a set of patients, and each nurse looks after a set of patients and also keeps a set of drugs, such that the set types of figure 13.4 are possible. The corresponding IMS tree is given in figure 13.5:

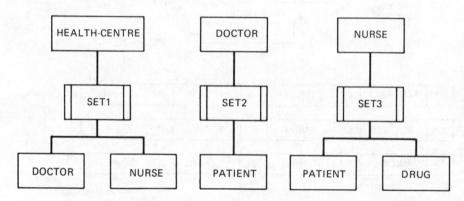

Figure 13.4 Network representation

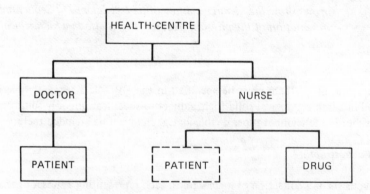

Figure 13.5 IMS representation

In the IMS representation, Patient is a physical child of Doctor and logical child of Nurse (we have used continuous lines for physical and dashed lines for logical children in the examples). To take another example, consider the part explosion problem whose network solution is shown in figure 4.8 of section 4.3.3; its IMS solution is given in figure 13.6(a) where the PLINK segment appears twice, once as physical and once as logical child segment, corresponding to the set type SUPSET and SUBSET of figure 4.8 respecitvely.

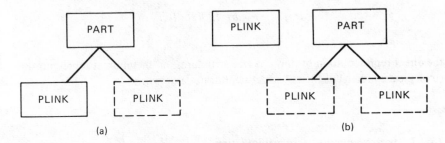

(a)   (b)

Figure 13.6 Part explosion problem in IMS

In figure 13.6(b), we have attempted an alternative technique by creating two independent IMS 'databases', one containing PLINK as the only segment (hence the root segment) and the other containing PART as the root segment but parenting the PLINK segment twice (again corresponding to the superior and subordinate part numbers), but both times as logical parent. This is not allowed in IMS for two reasons

(i) A root segment (PLINK segments in this example) cannot be a logical child of another segment.
(ii) The same segment type cannot appear more than once as logical child of the same parent segment type.

Because of (ii), a given child segment type can appear at most twice, once as physical child and once as logical child, of the same parent segment. So figure 13.6(a) is valid but 13.6(b) is not. There is, however, a further restriction: the same owner segment occurrence cannot own the same child segment occurrence more than once. Thus a given part segment of figure 13.6(a) cannot own the same PLINK segment twice (say once as logical and once as physical child). This does not matter here since the part explosion problem does not violate this restriction (see section 4.3.3). However, set type REGENT and ADVISOR of figure 2.17 would violate it if the same tutor is both regent and advisor of the same student; and if so, the database of figure 13.7 would be invalid.

There is no easy way of solving this network relationship in IMS, although the network and relational models do not present any problems here. Thus IMS does not permit a network representation, even indirectly. Summarising, IMS permits

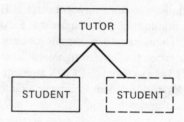

Figure 13.7

the direct representation of only the tree structure, and the indirect representation (by logical children) of the net structure, but not a network.

13.2.3 Access paths and data manipulation

In IMS a segment can be accessed by following the hierarchical path embedded in the tree, which we shall define here in terms of a hierarchical key (not an IMS term) consisting of the segment type numbers and the successive parent keys. For patient TUCKER of our example, the hierarchical key is T1H1T2D6T3P2, where Ts identify the segment types and H1 and D6 are the segment keys of the successive parents, as explained earlier. In figure 13.3(a) the arrows link segments in the hierarchical key order, while in figure 13.3(b) the segments are physically stored in that key order. We can access an individual 'record' occurrence of the 'database' − that is, the root segment − sequentially in order of the hierarchical key by scanning or directly, the direct access being provided either through an index or by hashing. From each parent a child can also be accessed either sequentially or through special pointers. Taken together, the following access facilities are available in IMS:

(i)   sequential or direct access to root segments
(ii) sequential access to subordinate segments either in hierarchical key order or in segment key order within each segment type under a given parent
(iii) secondary key index for subordinate segments in a specified secondary key order, but by-passing the hierarchical sequence.

The first two techniques constitute the primary facilities of IMS and are implemented by the following four access methods within the hierarchical framework:

HSAM: Hierarchical Sequential Access Method
HISAM: Hierarchical Indexed Sequential Access Method
HIDAM: Hierarchical Indexed Direct Access Method
HDAM: Hierarchical Direct Access Method.

In HSAM, 'records' and segments within 'records' are stored sequentially in the hierarchical key order, typically on magnetic tapes, as shown in figure 13.3(b). For the other three access methods, 'records' must be stored on disc.

In HISAM, each root segment is accessed by an index, but the segments within a 'record' are accessed sequentially as in HSAM. All segments of a 'record' are stored in physical blocks chained in hierarchical key order, thus requiring reorganisation of storage in the event of insertion of new segments. In HIDAM, like HISAM, the root segments are accessed through an index, but access to the subordinate segments is provided by pointers in two ways as follows.

(1) *By hierarchical pointers*. All occurrences of a given segment type within a 'record' can be linked in the ascending and, optionally, the descending order of the hierarchical key (figure 13.3(a)). If such linkages are specified for a segment type, its last occurrence is automatically given a pointer to the first occurrence of the next segment type, unless the end of the 'record' is reached. Unlike HISAM, the segments here need not be stored in the physical device in order of the hierarchical key, since hierarchical sequence is determined by the pointers.

(2) *By parent-child-twin pointers*. All the twins of a given segment type under the same parent can be linked by one or two-way chains; each parent has a compulsory pointer to the first and an optional pointer to the last occurrence of every child segment type under it. In addition, a pointer from the child to the parent segment type can also be specified (figure 13.8). Note that in the case of hierarchical pointers (figure 13.3(a)), Jones is not directly linked with Toshiba.

Only one of these two options can be specified for a given segment type, but the different segment types of the same tree can have different options. In figure 13.8 we have shown the access paths for only three out of four segment types of the tree.

In HDAM, the root segments can be accessed by using a hashing algorithm and the subordinate segments can be accessed through pointers, as in HIDAM. In both HIDAM and HDAM, the root segments are also connected by one or two-way chains. IMS/VS (and not the other versions) provides Virtual Storage Access Method (VSAM), in which a device independent approach is used for HISAM, HIDAM and HDAM.

At this point it might be useful to make another comparison with the network model where a set, and not a tree, is the basic building block. Thus, for a set of patients owned by Dr Jones, we can provide in the network model (figure 13.9)

(i) forward and backward links between members
(ii) direct links from the owner to each member
(iii) direct link from each member to the owner
(iv) direct access to each member irrespective of member record types

not to speak of additional access by user-defined identifiers. In contrast, IMS permits only hierarchical pointers or parent-child-twin pointers, but not both even on the

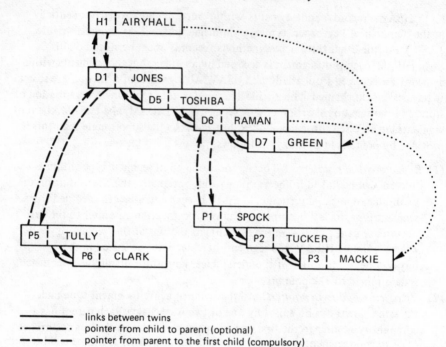

links between twins

pointer from child to parent (optional)

pointer from parent to the first child (compulsory)

pointer from parent to the last child (optional)

Figure 13.8 Parent–child twin pointers for Health centre, doctor and patient segments of the record in figure 13.3

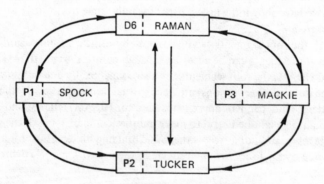

Figure 13.9 Access paths in the network model

same segment type. In the case of the network model, all access paths can be specified simultaneously. To access TUCKER, in the fastest IMS scheme we would need to traverse five preceding segments, compared to one in the case of the network model if owner record is used, and none if appropriate secondary keys are implemented in the internal schema. However, secondary keys are also possible in IMS.

The IMS access methods are transparent to the application programmer who is only concerned with the logical tree, and requests for segments as necessary, without specifying the retrieval mechanism. The system selects the access methods, which are mapped into a PSB during its compilation. The efficiency of access clearly varies, depending on the nature of the query. It is the task of the DBA to choose the right access methods for optimal performance with help of utilities available; however, the retrieval speed in IMS is known to be low. The inability to access every child directly from a parent, and the need to trace the whole hierarchical path for any subordinate segment, must be viewed as the major obstruction to speedy access.

Data Language/One

Apart from specifying various clauses necessary to describe DBD and PSB, DL/1 provides the following basic commands for data manipulation.

GET UNIQUE: to retrieve a unique segment directly.
GET NEXT   : to retrieve a segment sequentially.
GET NEXT WITHIN PARENT: to retrieve sequentially under current parent.
GET HOLD NEXT: to warn the system for REPLACE and DELETE.
REPLACE: to replace the data of an existing segment.
DELETE: to delete a segment — note that if a segment is deleted, its subordinate
         segments are also deleted.
INSERT: to insert a new segment to a pre-defined parent.

13.2.4 Other characteristics

Data independence and optimisation

IMS does not permit access to data item values, a segment being the smallest unit of access. If a programmer needs a new logical relationship among the segments of a tree, the physical tree must be redesigned to include them — through logical children if necessary. The physical 'database' has to be reloaded and all relevant PSBs recompiled. However, the existing application programs need not be changed.

The application programmer has no freedom in defining the access path, for instance, a new sequence for accessing child segments or twins. Modifications to block sizes, pointer options to access the subordinate segments in HIDAM and HDAM, and the hashing routines for HDAM are transparent to the application programs.

Subject to certain restrictions, it is possible to replace one access method by another, for example HISAM by HIDAM, without affecting the application programs Some utilities are provided to produce usage statistics for the purpose. IMS is very sensitive to tuning, and a number of tuning tools are available. Deleted segments in

HISAM are usually left in the 'database', to be removed subsequently by the appropriate utility; but in HDAM and HIDAM this removal is automatic. Although IMS is claimed to provide evolutionary facilities, its data structure (tree) is rather rigid, making it difficult to incorporate changes. This applies in particular to the insertion of new segment types, which often involves the recreation of the entire 'database', depending on their points of insertion in the tree. However, new data items can be added to an existing segment type.

Concurrency and data protection

IMS/VS provides facilities for concurrent usage through what it calls program isolation features. Four types of access are permitted – retrieve without lock, retrieve with lock, single update with lock and exclusive locks for multiple updates. Run-units are automatically queued and the system maintains state graphs for all exclusive locks. A detected deadlock is released by returning to a previous state through log files. Updates are consolidated into the database only when the log buffer is full, but separate protection exists against the copying of this inconsistent state into the backup files.

All changes are logged and the copies of both before and after changes are retained on backup files; checkpoints are maintained and detailed recovery procedures provided. In the event of a failure, a 'database' can be reconstructed in parts. The reliability of IMS is reported to be good.

Privacy control is available in the form of a password from a terminal, backed up by an authorised list of commands and transactions for each user number. In a PSB, segments can be given specific protection against retrieval, insertion, deletion and amendment.

Comments and criticism

IMS supports excellent teleprocessing facilities and it has its own native communication facility. User experience suggests that the running costs of the batch and teleprocessing modes are more or less the same, although the manual data preparation cost is substantially higher for the batch mode (Jardine, 1974). IMS also provides some query language and data dictionary facilities, but no database procedure is supported, except for the hashing routines.

IMS is a large and complex system. Its overheads are very high and its processing speed is low (Data Base Systems, 1975), particularly in the sequential processing for producing reports and dump. According to some users (Computer Weekly, 1975) up to 90 per cent of the CPU time can be taken up in executing the IMS routines, as against the processing of the actual data. Cost apart, IMS appears to be the best system for those organisations where online processing is the prime motivation; it is particularly unsuited to applications where frequent changes to the data structures are needed.

Owing partly to an early start and partly to the vigorous marketing policy of IBM, IMS is the most popular large DBMS. However, this secure position is now being gradually dented through the arrival of other products, particularly by IDMS. In a survey of 100 database users (Data Base Systems, 1975), IMS had the lowest rating on nearly all counts, the other products involved being ADABAS, TOTAL, IDMS, and SYSTEM 2000. However, despite many adverse predictions, the IMS has retained its relative position as a leading product throughout the past decade.

13.3 Inverted and net structure models

ADABAS and SYSTEM 2000 are the more well known products which utilise inverted structures for data organisations. We shall here describe mainly ADABAS, with a short note on SYSTEM 2000. The third system to be covered in this section is TOTAL which is based on a two-level net structure and forms a class of its own. It is most popular with the small users and has the largest number of installations.

13.3.1 ADABAS

Adaptable Data Base System, or ADABAS, was developed by Software AG of Darmstadt, West Germany. Its first version appeared in 1971, and by now it has many installations in Europe and the U.S.A.

ADABAS can be operated in both batch and teleprocessing mode, the host languages provided being Cobol, PL/I, Fortran and Assembler. It uses inverted filing technique and supports both a data manipulation language and a query language. The minimum memory required is about 160K bytes and it can be installed in a variety of computers.

Architecture

ADABAS uses record types, with repeating groups, if needed, to represent data. Multiple record keys, called *descriptors*, are supported — and hence the use of the term inverted files. A record key may contain a repeating group, and if this is so it is called a *super descriptor*. Records of different types are linked by what in the relational model would be called foreign keys, except that in ADABAS these foreign keys may contain repeating groups. Super descriptors can be used to support $m:n$ relationships directly without the so-called link records. For instance, the relationship between course and student records can be directly represented by including:

either (i) a repeating group of student numbers as a 'foreign key' in
         course record

or   (ii) a repeating group of course numbers as a 'foreign key' in
          student records
or   (iii) both (i) and (ii).

An ADABAS database consists of up to 255 ADABAS files, with one or
more record types in the same file. Each file is divided into two separate areas,
known as *Data Storage* and *Associator*. The data records are stored in the
Data Storage area, but their inverted index, mapping and linkages (showing
record relationships) are kept in the Associator.

Data records are stored in Data Storage as compressed variable-length records,
omitting blank fields, leading zeros in numeric fields and trailing blanks in alpha
numeric fields. The space saved in Data Storage owing to data compression is
claimed to be 50 per cent on average and is some cases up to 80 per cent. Each
record is given a unique internal identifier, called the Internal Sequence Number
(ISN). A single file can hold up to nearly 17 million records belonging to one or
more record types. A record type may contain up to 500 data items, 200 of which
can be descriptors.

Field definition entries and the inverted index tables are kept in the Associator
along with other control information. An Associator has the following four
components.

(1) The field description table: contains field definition entries in the form of
     data name and picture clauses for all the record types of the database.
(2) Storage management table: maintains the mapping of the Associator with
     Data Storage. Storage control blocks are also set up here.
(3) Address converter: holds the lookup table for ISN and the physical address.
(4) Association network: contains two types of indexes – (i) record key index,
     called *inverted index* and (ii) record relationship index called *file coupling*.
     The inverted index is a standard (Descriptor, ISN) index which holds the
     ISNs of the matching records for each descriptor value, whereas in file coupling,
     two indexes are maintained, one for each of the related files. For example, for
     the course and student relationship, one index will give the ISNs of the relevant
     student records for each course ISN, and the other index will give the ISNs of
     the relevant course records for each student ISN. A single ADABAS file can be
     related to up to 80 other files (a file optionally having more than one record
     type). The recursive relationship can be supported by explicit inverted index
     with appropriate descriptors.

Since the Associator is both logically and physically distinct from Data
Storage, its content can subsequently by changed without affecting the Data
Storage portions or the application programs. This ensures flexibility and data
independence. The technique used here is roughly equivalent to separating the

set entries (that is, record relationships) from the Codasyl schema and imposing them subsequently on the schema as an additional interface. However, unlike set descriptions, we cannot define new record relationships in ADABAS unless the relevant common descriptors are included in the records in Data Storage, although there is a utility which can be used for the purpose.

Data manipulation

An application program wishing to use an ADABAS database has to define its own User Work Area in a desired format where all database records for the program are held. Access to the database is gained by a call statement specifying the intended command, for example

CALL ADABAS (READ DATA)

whereupon the requested DATA will be placed in the UWA.

The basic commands supported by ADABAS are FIND, READ, UPDATE, ADD, DELETE, OPEN, CLOSE and CHECKPOINT. The FIND command (corresponding to the Codasyl Find command) is used for finding records, subject to some selection criteria which can be formulated in terms of descriptor values, using logical operators such as AND, OR and NOT. This command locates the record from the Associator network by automatically using the most effective search algorithm out of a number maintained by the system. A related record is obtained by a FIND COUPLED command which must stipulate the name of the related (that is, coupled) file and a descriptor value or a range of values.

An individual record of a file can be read directly by the READ command. A group of records in a file can be accessed in the stored order or in the order of a key (that is, in a specified set of descriptor values). New records can be added by the ADD command. If a substantial number of records needs insertion, a utility can be used to expedite the process. DELETE and UPDATE (to modify) commands are used as necessary. The CHECKPOINT command facilitates checkpoints during execution under program control. The OPEN/CLOSE commands signal the beginning or the end of an application. ADABAS uses a number of special procedures to support fast retrievals and updates.

The query language supported by ADABAS is called ADASCRIPT. It permits the formulation of queries using conditions in a form close to PAL predicates (section 6.3). Data can be retrieved from only one file by a query, although the descriptors used in the selection criteria can be taken from up to five files. A report generator, named ADAWRITER, is also provided to select, format and print information from the database.

An added attraction in ADABAS is its phonetic search capability, which permits retrieval of items on the basis of sound pattern rather than the actual spelling. By invoking this facility a program can find a record for MEYER even if the name is spelled as MEIER or MAYER. Naturally, this has an overhead.

Data independence and optimisation

ADABAS provides some data independence. An application programmer may define his record by only a subset of the original data items of the record. He may also change the format of the data items and reorder then as necessary. Data items are bound at execution time, thus reducing the need for program recompilation.

The isolation of the specification for record relationships into a separate interface (the Association network) permits storage reorganisation and alteration in the record relationships without requiring modification in the application program, unless the changes in the record relationships directly affect the program. However, in the absence of an external schema, the application program does not have an independent local view of the record relationships in the database, and if new relationships are required they have to be explicitly defined in the Association network.

A number of utilities are provided for the reorganisation of the database: new files can be created, the old ones deleted, or an existing file can be altered by the addition or deletion of data items. File couplings can be modified and descriptors can be inserted or deleted. New record relationships can also be created by first inserting the necessary common descriptors in the original records in Data Storage. The database can be expanded to accommodate more data without having to reload it. The space allocation is dynamic, the released space after deletions being automatically consolidated and reused.

Concurrency and data protection

ADABAS supports concurrent usage, as mentioned in section 5.1. The concurrent user can lock records in a pre-defined sequential order to avoid deadlocks, but a back-up facility to resolve deadlocks by rollback is also provided. A HOLD command is available for locking records. Unauthorised access and updates can be controlled separately at record type and data item levels. Facilities for encoding records are also supported. The system provides 15 levels of read and write protection along with a database auditing facility.

Apart from checkpoints, ADABAS permits the dumping of the database with the facility for subsequent reloading. Log files on all updates are kept for use during database re-creation and automatic restart. A number of system reports are generated, giving information on storage space utilisation, file descriptions, coupling, checkpoint and restarts.

Comments and criticism

ADABAS users appear to be fairly satisfied with their products. Their only major complaint concerns the inadequacy of documentation. The system is easy to install and use, and it requires minimal file conversions. It is an efficient and flexible system, and eminently suitable for medium-large users.

13.3.2 SYSTEM 2000

SYSTEM 2000 was developed by the MRI Systems Corporation of Austin, Texas in 1970. It is a host language system supporting Cobol, PL/I, Fortran and Assembler. It requires a minimum memory of about 160K bytes and can be installed in a variety of computers. It supports both batch and online processing.

As a product, SYSTEM 2000 is remarkably similar to ADABAS in data structures, capabilities and facilities, except that no data compression facility is available. It is based on inverted file structures like ADABAS, the major structural difference being in the representation of record (*repeating group* in the terminology of SYSTEM 2000) relationships. Whereas ADABAS employs a network-like structure, the SYSTEM 2000 employs a hierarchical tree structure. The more recent versions allow the DBA to change the hierarchical structure to optimise performance without affecting the application programs. Again, like ADABAS, SYSTEM 2000 supports a good query language, in addition to a data manipulation language. However, it is a retrieval-oriented system providing four methods of data manipulation. Basic access is used in batch mode for interrogation and maintenance where a group of user commands is analysed before making a single pass of the database. Immediate access is provided for interactive processing, with procedural access for the host languages and non-procedural access for report generation.

The Data independence in SYSTEM 2000 is similar to that in ADABAS. The latest version provides reorganisation facilities. Concurrent usage is allowed by locking the records of a given type. Privacy is controlled by a master password for entering the database, and a series of other passwords for retrieval, updates and so on, of data items. Checkpoints and restart facilities are also available. The choice between ADABAS and SYSTEM 2000 is often a difficult one.

13.3.3 TOTAL

TOTAL was developed by Cincom Systems Incorporated of Ohio, in early 1969. It is based on a relatively simple architecture and it can be installed in a large variety of computers (for example, IBM, Honeywell, Univac, NCR), requiring a minimum memory of 30K bytes for a fuller version. The database can be accessed by host language programs written in Cobol, PL/I, Fortran, RPG or Assembler. It is one of the most successful products and has a large number of installations. It permits both batch and online processing, and is able to support ENVIRON/1, which is a communication package developed by Cincom.

Data structure in TOTAL is based on one to many relationships between two sets of records. The database is described in Data Base Generation (DBGEN), which consists of entries made by a Data Base Definition Language (DBDL) for *elements* (defined as a collection of data items), records, files, linkage path and buffer. To access the database, an application program has to issue a call statement with parameters that invoke the necessary DM procedures. An element is the basic unit of access.

Database organisation

TOTAL permits two types of file, known as *datasets*. One of these is for *single entry* or *master* (that is owner) records, and the other is for *variable entry* or *subordinate* (that is, member) records. A variable entry record may belong to more than one master record, thus establishing a net structure. There is no index in TOTAL; the owner is chained (figure 13.10) with all its member records by a two-way ring called

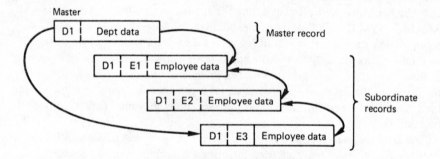

Figure 13.10 TOTAL data structure

the *linkage path*. No member pointers are provided, but each member must contain an owner identifier. A master record can be accessed directly, but the subordinate records can be accessed only through their linkage path. A variable entry dataset can support up to 2500 different record types, but all records of a *dataset*, irrespective of record types, must be of the same length. A master record cannot act as the subordinate record of another master record. This restricts multi-level data structure, which can be supported only by duplicating the master record as a subordinate record. This, of course, creates update problems.

The application program wishing to access the database requests the required service through a call statement, followed by a list of parameters which includes the DM command (such as read master record), system communication locations, master record name, elements wanted and input/output buffer. If a subordinate record is required, its linkage path must be given.

Other characteristics

Elements and record types can be added to or deleted from the database without affecting the application programs which are bound to the elements within a record at run-time. This reduces the need for recompilation. However, an application program cannot define new datasets or new linkages and, if such changes are required, the database has to be re-created. The application program is independent of the storage structure, but not of the logical structure, since the user has to specify the linkage path along with each DM command. Therefore, any modification of the logical structure requires recompilation of, if not changes to, the application program.

No statistics are kept, but the system does its own garbage collection. Concurrent usage is allowed, although no facility for the resolution of deadlock is provided. Run-units are limited to locking a file or 'a single record at a time' update. A report generator called SOCRATES is also available. Checkpoints and log files are employed for automatic restart. The system permits periodic dumping of the database, which can be used for its re-creation. No privacy protection is provided, but the user can invoke special database procedures for the selected elements.

In TOTAL the data structure is relatively rigid, data independence is poor, utilities are inadequate and optimisation facilities are lacking. It is a smaller package than the other systems described, and caters for relatively small applications where the more elaborate facilities are less important, as shown by its popularity and the relative absence of user complaints.

13.4 Summary and conclusion

The earlier models presented here might be regarded as endangered species, but their actual demise may not occur for a long time. The organisations which are currently using one of these earlier models will probably continue to do so for some time in the future and, at the same time, the vendors of these products will probably also increase their customer base since more people are using databases today. However, in the longer term, network and relational implementations are likely to be increasingly popular, although they may not necessarily drive other products out completely. In this context, the database scene has a close analogy with programming languages, where the introduction of Cobol and Pascal has not stopped people using RPG and Fortran, nor has it prevented newer languages such as BASIC, from cutting out a market share for themselves.

A new growth area of databases is microcomputer-based products, including what might be called personal databases. Since the capabilities of microcomputers are increasing continually, a distinction on the basis of size is not fruitful. What can be mounted on a mini today can be run on a micro tomorrow. The concept of a personal database, however, indicates a single user, easy-to-use system with easy maintenance. Such a system can be run on a large computer, but more often it is probably run on a micro. Most microcomputer/personal databases being designed today are based on the relational model, because of its simplicity and high level facilities.

Many large organisations usually have a number of databases, often of different types, either to cater for different requirements economically or as a hangover from the past unplanned growth. In either case there is a need to link them together for joint queries. This is achieved by distributed databases, as discussed in chapter 15. An associated growth area is an integrated office system where several small databases and word processors could be linked together over a local area network for office workers to use. This is a new developing area that is not covered in this book.

Exercises

13.1 Describe with a diagram, the architecture of SYSTEM R.

13.2 Describe the query optimisation facilities of SYSTEM R.

13.3 Describe the basic features of IMS under the following main headings:

Physical tree
Logical tree
Access path.

13.4 Describe a technique of representing an $m:n$ loop structure in IMS and comment on its limitations.

13.5 Compare the facilities of IMS with those of a network model under the following subheadings:

(1) Entity records
(2) Associations
(3) Usage constraints
(4) DM commands.

13.6 Describe the principal features of ADABAS and compare ADABAS with the relational model with respect to

Data representation
Query language
Keys and access paths.

13.7 Write an essay on the ADABAS system with the following major subheadings:

(a) Data representation
(b) Storage structure
(c) Access paths and indexes.

13.8 Describe the main features of TOTAL, and compare it with the network model with respect to the following features:

(i) Data records
(ii) Data relationships
(iii) Access paths
(iv) Data independence.

References

Astrahan, M. M. *et al.* (1976). SYSTEM R: A relational approach to database management. *ACM TODS*, Vol. (1:2), June p. 97

Blasgen, M. W. *et al.* (1979). SYSTEM R: An architectural update. *IBM Research Report RJ2581*, San Jose

Chamberlin, D. D. (1980). A summary of user experience with SQL data sub-languages. *Proceedings International Conference on Databases, Aberdeen, 1980*, edited by S. M. Deen and P. Hammersley, Heyden

Chamberlin, D. D. *et al.* (1976). SEQUEL2: A unified approach to data definition, manipulation and control. *IBM Journal R and D*, Vol. (20:6), November

Computer Weekly (1975). *Computer Weekly*, issue of 6 February, quoting Des Lee, secretary of IBM Computer Users Association

Data Base Systems (1975). *Infotec State of the Art Report*, pp. 139, 167–77

Date, C. J. (1981). *Introduction to Database Systems, Vol. 1*, 3rd edition, Addison-Wesley

IBM (1982). *Information Management System, General information manual GH20-1260*, San Jose

Jardine, D. A. (1974). *Data Base Management Systems*, North-Holland, p. 8

Selinger, P. G. *et al.* (1979). Access path selection in a relational DBMS. *Proceedings ACM SIGMOD Conference 1979*

Stonebraker, M. R. *et al.* (1976). Design and Implementation INGRES. *ACM TODS* Vol. (1:3), September

Todd, S. J. P. (1976). Peterlee Relational Test Vehicle – a system overview. *IBM System Journal*, Vol. (15:4), p.285

PART V: FUTURE DEVELOPMENTS

14 New Approaches

Research activities in databases began in the late sixties, at about the time when the Codasyl DBTG was formed. The first major contribution was the introduction of the relational model (Codd, 1970), which was followed by a number of other works, starting with the DIAM model of Senko (Senko et al., 1973; Senko, 1976). Today database research has spread on to many fronts, promising better databases for tomorrow. In this chapter we shall briefly review some of these new frontiers, particularly covering the areas of

Data modelling
End-user facilities
Database machines
New applications.

Distributed databases will be covered in the next chapter, as a separate subject.

14.1 Data modelling

Research in data modelling gained momentum after the publication of Codd's paper on the relational model, with a further impetus from Senko's DIAM model and ANSI/SPARC's conceptual schema. The great debate of the early seventies, on the relative merits of the Codasyl and relational models, also helped to develop a clearer understanding of their strengths and weaknesses. Bachman suggested an improvement of the Codasyl model by a Role model and Codd has proposed an extension of the relational model to capture more meaning. To overcome the limitation of the binary relational approach, we now have a new concept of 'irreducible relations', which permits use of relations of higher degress than binary only if absolutely necessary (section 7.1.2). Other workers adopted other approaches. Apart from the wide academic interest that the topic of data modelling has aroused, it has also caught the imagination of IFIP and ISO, both of which have set up working groups. The IFIP/WG2.6 deliberated on a conceptual schema for several years, and the ISO/TC97/SC5/WG3 (ISO, 1981) is studying data models with a view to future standardisation.

14.1.1 Universe of Discourse

In a database environment we deal with common data typically shared by many
users. This data refers to "things and happenings" outside, and these "things and
happenings" constitute a *Universe of Discourse* (UoD) (ISO, 1981). We may also
view a universe of discourse as a selected portion of the world that we are interested
in. This world of interest may be real like inventories, abstract like organisational
structures of an enterprise, or fictional like *Alice in Wonderland*. The content
of a universe of discourse can be divided into two parts: an *abstract system* and an
object system (figure 14.1). The abstract system refers to the rules and classifica-
tions, properties, constructs and so on, of the UoD, and its description is the conceptual schema. The rest of the UoD constitutes what is called the object system,
whose description is the information base. The abstract system changes more slowly
with time and governs the behaviour of the object system. The conceptual schema
and the information base together model the UoD; and the union of the conceptual
schema and the information base is the UoD description.

ISO defines a database as a concrete physical representation of the UoD description. In other words, a database includes data (the information base) and also its
'description' (the conceptual schema). However, the universe of discourse, as it
exists, is meaningful to us only through our own perception and therefore what we
model in the conceptual schema may vary, depending on our perception.

It is assumed that an ideal model of the abstract system would be able to support
not only more meaningful data description but also the user views of all other data
models as external schemas. This latter aspect, which Nijssen (1976) calls the *co-
existence approach*, is the primary objective of all *unified* or *canonical data models*.
The first aspect is however double-edged, since it is not clear how far we should
overload the structure of a model in order to make data more useful and meaningful, since too complex a structure, particularly if based on unfamiliar abstract concepts, is likely to be difficult for most users to handle. In any event, the improvement in data modelling is likely to be continuous and evolutionary.

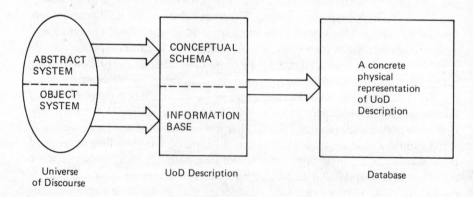

Figure 14.1

To understand the issues in data modelling, we need to study the content and characteristics of the UoD, but there are no universally agreed concepts. We shall therefore introduce some of our own, partly to provide a framework for the discussion of new ideas. We start with basic concepts: *entities* and *properties*. We then subdivide entities into four major types: *objects*, *classes*, *events* and *rules*, each of which can have properties, although sometimes the distinction between a property and an entity, particularly for object entities, can be perception dependent. An object is what was called an entity in chapter 4.

Entities and properties *can* be time dependent, an entity being in existence (or valid) for a given time, or a property being valid for a given time. Property salary changes with time, whereas property date of birth does not. Properties can also be *factual* or *deductive*. 'The name of an employee is Smith' and 'his grandfather is Walker' are examples of factual properties, but the statement that Walker is grandfather of Smith if Walker is the father of Baker and Baker is father of Smith represents a *deductive* property. We can say that a factual property is unconditional, whereas a deductive property is conditional, the property being true if the condition is true. They can also be viewed as 'physical'and 'logical', since a factual property is typically physically stored in a database, whereas a deductive property is derived (thus, logically stored) when needed. Traditional databases deal almost exclusively with factual properties while the deductive properties are largely new in concept — an outcome of the influence of artificial intelligence (see also later).

Entities can show hierarchies, but at the lowest level we have *elementary entities*. 'A person' is an *elementary object*, whereas 'a teacher' is a role of a person, and hence *non-elementary*. Similarly we may have *elementary events* and *elementary rules*. Elementary entities of the same type form *elementary classes*. An entity can belong to only one elementary class, but to many non-elementary classes. An event is something that happens in the UoD, and it may be made up of other events. An event *seat reservation* may trigger event *check* for flight number, date and empty seat, and subsequent update of data relating to seats and payments. An event creates/destroys/changes entities and properties at the abstract system, subject to *transformation* rules. These changes are carried out at the object system by transactions.

A rule entity may apply to other entities (including other rule entities) and properties, and may sometimes create other (higher level) entities and properties. We may subdivide a rule entity into the following subtypes:

(i) Abstraction
(ii) Deductive
(iii) Extraction
(iv) Transformation
(v) Structural

Abstraction rules can be of the following types:

Association
Categorisation

Aggregation
Role
Generalisation

each of which creates new classes. The concepts of aggregation and generalisation were first proposed by Smith and Smith (1977), the husband and wife pair of database research.

An *association* is formed when two sets of entities (not necessarily restricted to object entities) are related, as explained in chapter 4.

Categorisation is a special type of class, formed from objects showing some common properties of interest, typically expressed by a predicate, such as all employees with salary $> x$.

Aggregation creates higher level entities from several lower level entities, such as a superior part number from subordinate part numbers, entity car from entities car-door, car-engine, and so on. The inverse of aggregation is "components of . . ."; for example, car-door, car-engine are components of a car.

Role relates to the role that an entity can play. A person can be a parent, a child, an employee, an employer, a tax-payer, a car-owner and so on. The roles have $m:n$ relationships with entities, since the same role, such as car-owner or employer, can be played by both a person and an organisation. Roles can also show hierarchies, such as role university teacher is made up of role lecturers, readers and professors. However, a role is a time dependent behaviour of an entity; the same entity does not necessarily play the same role throughout its existence.

Generalisation raises an entity to a higher level, where it can share common properties with other entities, such as all persons and horses are mammals. Unlike a role, this is an intrinsic and permanent (time independent) characteristic – a person is a mammal and remains a mammal all his life. The inverse of this generalisation is "is always", such as a person is always a mammal. Some authors use the term generalisation to include role as well, but we have separated the concepts as they represent different types of behaviour with potentially different constraints on them.

All classes (including elementary classes) can have additional properties of their own and may be required to have some integrity constraints.

Deductive rules can be specified to deduce new properties from the existing database, as shown in section 14.4. *Extraction rules* include privacy constraints and specify what information can be extracted under what condition. *Transformation rules* control updates, and specify the rules of transforming the database from one valid state to the next. It thus incorporates all integrity constraints as well. Finally, *structural rules* are rules about rules, and also specify the valid description of an abstract system, and how this description can be changed.

A traditional database represents a state or snapshot of the UoD at time t. The collection of all these states from $t = 0$ constitutes the total content of the UoD. A number of researchers are interested in capturing the time dimensions (say, time dependent change of entities and properties) and in building databases which keep all past information; such databases are sometimes called *historical databases* (Jones and Mason, 1980; Dadam *et al.*, 1984).

The concepts discussed above are partly based on the ISO Report (ISO, 1981), and partly on the author's own research project on the Unified Data Model (UDM). We shall use them below in discussing a number of other data models, including the Role model of Bachman and the Entity-relation (E-R) model of Chen.

14.1.2 Role model

In the basic Codasyl model, data are described as record types which can be related to each other by set types, characterised by one owner record type and one or more member record types. Bachman (1980) has introduced in his Role model, as an extension of the Codasyl facilities, the concept of role and role records. A 'role' in Bachman's definition includes both role and generalisation.

An entity record in the Role model contains all the attribute values of an entity; but an entity may play one or more roles, and therefore the entity record should be logically subdivided into role records, one per role of that entity. Thus, if a person (entity) plays roles as an employee, as an employer and as a car owner, then in Bachman's schema we must describe three role records (with data redundancy where necessary), all of which can be collectively viewed as a person (entity) record. Since a role can be played by more than one entity type, a role employer can be played by both person and organisation; likewise a role vehicle can be played by car, bus, lorry and so on. A set type in the role model is defined between two role types, one as owner − such as customer − and the other as member − such as product (figure 14.2). Both owner and member roles in a given set type can belong to many different entity record types.

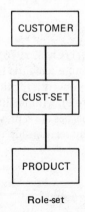

Role-set

Figure 14.2 Role model of Bochman

Entity Person
    Role: Parent, Child, Employer, Employee, Customer
Entity District-Council
    Role: Employer, Customer
Entity Car
    Role: Product, Person-carrier, Transport
Entity Truck
    Role: Product, Goods-carrier, Transport

One advantage of role sets is the meaningful grouping of data. For instance, if we are to make a set type family history between parent and child, then we have figure 14.3(a) in the Codasyl model and 14.3(b) in the Role model; 14.3(b) is semantically more meaningful.

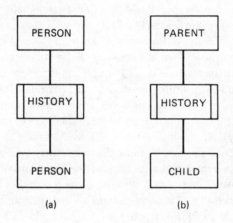

Figure 14.3

14.1.3 Entity relationship model

P. P. Chen's entity relationship model (Chen, 1976) may be viewed as an extension of the relational model, with some more semantic flavour. It recognises the concepts of entity (object), attribute (property), relationship (association), aggregation and generalisation (which includes role), with facilities for the representation of constraints. Entities with their properties are represented by entity relations, and relationships between entity types by relationship relations. Thus we have:

Entity relations
        DEPT(DNO   DNAME)
        EMP(ENO   ENAME   SAL)
        STUDENT(SNO   SNAME)
        COURSE(CNO   CNAME)

        PROJECT(PNO PNAME   PBUDGET)
        MACHINE(MNO MNAME)
Relationship relations
        EDN(DNO ENO)
        CSL(CNO SNO   EXAM-MARKS)
        EPM(ENO PNO   MNO   HOURS-WORKED)

Relation EDN represents a 1:n relationship, but the ER model specifies it as a
separate relation, and does not use DNO as a foreign key in the EMP relation.
This separation allows the 1:n relationship to evolve into m:n relationship, as
discussed in section 4.3.1. Relation CSL represents m:n relationships between two
entity relations, while EPM represents m:n relationships among three entity relations. The ER model thus unifies the 1:n and m:n representations into a single
structure.

   A relationship relation can be related to another entity relation, if the relationship is viewed as an aggregated entity. Generalisation can also be expressed by
other relations. The ER model, unlike the Role model, has received a wide acceptance by the database practitioners. There are, however, some similarities of ideas
between the two models, perhaps reflecting that Bachman and Chen were working
together when the ER model was first launched.

14.1.4 Other relational approaches

The original relational model as proposed by Codd is considered inadequate for
meaningful data description. We list its limitations as follows.

(i) Inability to support data meaningfully. Normalised relations are an abstraction
    of reality, but real entity records may have repeating groups and other charac-
    teristics, such as those mentioned in section 14.1.1, which the original relational
    model cannot represent directly.
(ii) Inability to support sequencing information directly. Consider the bus route
    example of section 11.3.1. We cannot represent a bus route just as a set of stop
    names, we must have stop sequence numbers, even if the bus company does
    not use them. We can represent the bus routes by a relation containing (RN,
    SS, SN, FR), as given in section 11.3.1; but if a stop is deleted or a new one
    added, then the SS values of all the subsequent tuples are affected, demon-
    strating that in real applications the tuples are not always independent of each
    other. Therefore, the assertion (in the relational model) that the tuples are
    independent of each other (that is, the ordering of tuples is immaterial) is a
    denial of reality, rather than a virtue. Because of this denial, the relational
    model cannot process tuples sequentially (Next or Prior) in any order, although
    in many cases this facility is essential (see exercise 8.8 of chapter 8 as an
    example).

(iii) Inability to define composite items (for example, to group day, month, year together as Date).

(iv) Difficulty in supporting semantic integrity among groups of tuples.

Codd has proposed an extended relational model (RM/T which stands for Relational Model/Tasmania — Tasmania being the place where he first proposed it) in which he subdivides normalised relations into meaningful subrelations (Codd, 1979; Date, 1981). Falkenberg's Object Role model (Breutmann *et al.*, 1979) is based on irreducible relations, where every object such as amount (for salary) has a role such as 'salary of' some other objects; an object person may play role 'has salary'. Thus the objects related by roles are collected together into what he calls associations, as shown below.

> *Association Type*   Salary
>   *Object type*   Person, *Role* has-salary
>   *Object type* Amount,   *Role* Is-salary
> *Object Type* Component
>   *Objects* Chassis, Tyre, Engine

Falkenberg's model is claimed to support rigorous integrity constraints and even time dimension. However the details are beyond the scope of this book.

Another important contribution to data modelling came from Hammer and McLeod (1978) who proposed a Semantic Data Model (SDM), which, although meant to be a model for an external schema, contains interesting notions that can be used for any conceptual schema. The SDM conceptualises a database as a collection of classes — made up of objects, events, attributes — and their descriptions. Classes can be related and organised into hierarchies and higher level entities; redundancies and derived objects are permitted. Although it produced many new ideas, this model is regarded by many as too complex for general implementation, but then this criticism is also valid for Codd's RM/T and Falkenberg's Object Role models. There are many other models, among them Nijssen's ENALIM model (Nijssen, 1976, 1977), which are too complex for presentation here.

14.2 End-user facilities

Although the need for end-user facilities has been recognised quite early in the evolution of the database facility, it is the advent of the relational model which has given the greatest impetus to the researchers in this area, notwithstanding the fact that non-procedural languages exist outside, and in some cases pre-date, the relational model. Therefore most of the interesting developments in this area are relation based. We wish to review these under the following headings.

Language characteristics
Relational languages
Application oriented languages
Functional languages.

14.2.1 Language characteristics

There is probably a limit, even if it is difficult to define, to the power of a non-procedural language, since non-procedurality depends on the extent to which the need can be generalised into high level constructs. Ideally the selection capability of a query language is complete if it allows the formulation of all possible user queries. In practice it depends on the formal model of information. As stated in section 8.3, Codd has defined relational completeness as a measure of completeness of a query language. The relationally complete languages should not need loops or branched executions, yet queries such as 'find the shortest route between two cities from a table of distances' or 'find all the superior parts in a part explosion problem' cannot be answered by traditional relational algebra/calculus. Therefore, the search for a more complete language must go on.

However the every-day ordinary English is unlikely to be better than structured English as a user interface. On the other hand, queries based on the understanding of the tabular form of information might not be the ideal for naive users. In particular relational approaches seem to suffer from at least the following two limitations (Pirotte, 1979):

(i) many queries that can be formulated are difficult to compose/comprehend
(ii) many queries that are very simple to state, such as "find the shortest distance" cannot be easily formulated.

Domain oriented query languages are claimed to be easier for naive users compared to the tuple oriented languages. Domains, as against tuples, are also used in constructs based on semantic nets, and functional languages (see later), and this domain orientation is considered to be one of their main attractions. The structure of a query can be orthogonal or layered. In an orthogonal structure (ALPHA, QUEL), each query construct is based on a major concept, and hence all queries, simple or complex, have similar looking expressions. In the layered style (QBE, SQL) additional constructs are added as the complexity of the query increases. This makes simple queries easier to understand, but complex queries more difficult. However the user's notion of a simple query does not always coincide with that of the language, and this leads to disenchantment. The 'form' of the language can be textual (ALPHA, QUEL, SQL), two-dimensional (QBE), and probably others. This 'form' perhaps makes QBE easier for naive users, and tedious for experienced users.

Integrity constraints is an area where query languages are generally weak. There also appears to be a need to support syntactical redundancy in query languages so that errors can be easily checked. Splitting of a relational query into several subexpressions is regarded as a trivial problem. Update facilities and relational view definitions are not considered to be linguistically difficult, although there is an implementation problem.

In general, views transfer information from DML to DDL and as such views are DML oriented. For some applications, the relational languages are not suitable, and hence different and more complex types of views are needed. Schneiderman

(1978) has identified some of the user needs, and the BCS Query Language Group (1981) has produced an outline of the content of a generalised query view.

14.2.2 Relational languages

The main thrust of the relational languages at the moment seems to be on the calculus based rather than algebra based languages. As we have discussed the better-known languages earlier, we shall consider here some less well-known but interesting developments.

Schmidt (1977) has extended the data type facilities of Pascal, and introduced three new constructs: (i) a loop to be controlled by a relation, (ii) a predicate facility and (iii) a construct to create new relations. Amble *et al.* (1976) have developed a DDL/DML called ASTRAL, with SQL-like queries. It is based on Pascal with extended data types, and was at one time considered for implementation on special hardware. Another language called DEAL has been proposed as an extension of PAL (section 6.3) and SQL. It permits relational functions and recursive queries; for instance, ancestors can be defined recursively, and questions on part explosion problems can be answered without looping or branching (Deen, 1985).

A 'natural language' interface with three user modes has been specified by Longstaff (Longstaff *et al.*, 1981). The user is meant to progress from mode 1 (naive user) to mode 3 as he gains experience. In mode 1, queries are specified using a system-initiated dialogue with menu selection from alternative 'natural language' statements. In the middle a query language based on ALPHA is available. The user can update, and can take recourse to 'natural language' if needed. The highest mode is the system-supported query language.

14.2.3 Application oriented languages

There is a need for application oriented languages which can be used to describe and manipulate special purpose databases under a general purpose DBMS. Some examples of these applications are: medical, inventory control, accounting, stock control, airline reservation, document retrieval and so on. The TAXIS programming language represents one such development.

TAXIS was designed by Mylopoulos, Bernstein and Wong (Mylopoulos *et al.*, 1980) for application oriented interactive information systems characterised by a large volume of transactions that are short, of predictable structures, and update-intensive. It can be used both to design and manipulate interactive systems — such as credit card, student registration and airline reservation — within a relational DBMS. The language integrates data and procedure as a combined DDL/DML in a SIMULA-like fashion, borrowing concepts from semantic network (for data and procedure), abstract data type, exception handling and the relational approach.

Data and transactions can be described, classified and grouped into hierarchies of abstract data types. The DML can act at the various levels of abstractions (hierarchies) rather than only at the tuple level. The semantic structures include data (in the relational form), procedures, integrity constraints and exceptions.

TAXIS is a very interesting language which will no doubt inspire further work in application areas, particularly for the design of application oriented user schemas based on abstract data types.

14.2.4 Functional languages

A stimulating development in the language scene is the promotion of the functional approach where a database operation is regarded as a collection of functions over data types (for example, Employee, Department) and basic types (for example, character-string, Boolean). Data type Employee may map over the types character-string, number, Boolean and Department — through the functions EMPNAME, SALARY, MARRIED and OWNER-DEPT respectively. We mention here two functional languages: Buneman's FQL (Buneman *et al.*, 1979) and Shipman's DAPLEX (Shipman, 1981). In FQL, a *stream* is a virtual sequence of objects obtained by an inverse function, for example, the inverse of EMPNAME on entity Department would give the list of entity employees for that department; and hence Codasyl sets can be supported. It is a domain oriented but layered language, in which new functions are created by using four special functions. A query is a function. The language permits complex queries to be specified very simply.

However, FQL is not easy for end-users — Shipman's DAPLEX seems better suited for that purpose, as it uses calculus-like expressions. DAPLEX is more developed, providing more extensive user facilities. But the two models are so compatible that FQL can probably be used as an internal form of DAPLEX (see also chapter 15).

14.3 Database machines

In a general purpose computer the hardware supported instruction set provides only a limited number of low level instructions accessible through the CPU. The instructions dealing with input/output provide a CPU-based low level interface to the secondary storage, and permit at best (in case of disc storage) one disc track at a time. Complex data manipulation commands must be built upon this low level interface by programming on the CPU. This is inefficient. A database machine (DBM) is meant to be a special purpose computer whose hardware supports directly high level data manipulation functions needed for database management. This is done by raising the level of input/output interface from the CPU to the storage and by distributing the processing power closer to the devices on which data are stored (Langdon, 1979; Maryanski, 1980). Some of the data management tasks are

File Level Tasks	*Record Level Tasks*
AUTHORISE	INSERT
TRANSFER	RETRIEVE
COPY	MODIFY
DESTROY	DELETE
LOCK/UNLOCK	SEARCH
ALLOCATE SPACE	SORT
COLLECT GARBAGE	MERGE

An ideal database machine should support functions such as these directly. In practice they might be resolved into a common set of DBM primitives to be implemented by hardware. The higher the level of the hardware supported primitives, the better should be the performance. These functions are useful for most non-numeric applications as well but, in the case of a DBM, they should also be executable in a concurrent and online environment as needed for a database.

Non-numeric processing is primarily input/output bound, and hence inefficient in general purpose computers owing to the sequential nature of the Von Neumann architecture. To overcome this, a number of associative processors were developed in the sixties and early seventies. The more sophisticated versions of these prototypes use the logic-per-track concept, first proposed by Slotnick as a cheaper alternative to the more expensive fully-associated memories. In this approach some processing power is dedicated to each track, and hence it is very effective in parallel search. The advent of databases in a major way in the early seventies shifted the emphasis from parallel processors to database machines where parallel processing is one of several requirements. The availability of cheap LSI chips, and new secondary devices such as CCD (Charged Coupled Device) and bubble memory, have also contributed to the expectation of some researchers, but there are major problems to be overcome.

The academic researchers do not employ any generalised DBM architecture; each research group concentrates on its own area of interest — basically treating DBM as a backend processor. Individual design choices are often intuitive, with trade-offs based on expected applications.

An ambitious and general purpose project is the DBC (Database Computer) of Hsiao (Banerjee *et al.*, 1979) (figure 14.4). It uses a modified moving-head disc with logic-per-track facility. All tracks of a cylinder are searched simultaneously, with control information, including indexes, stored on a new-memory device which could be CCD or bubble memory. The data records are stored on those discs according to the primary and secondary clustering attributes of the records, but other keys can also be used for search. The user request first enters the general purpose computer which treats the DBC as a resource (backend processor). For a given request the DBC consults its control information for authorisation and the necessary cylinder numbers of the disc storage. A complete cylinder is read at

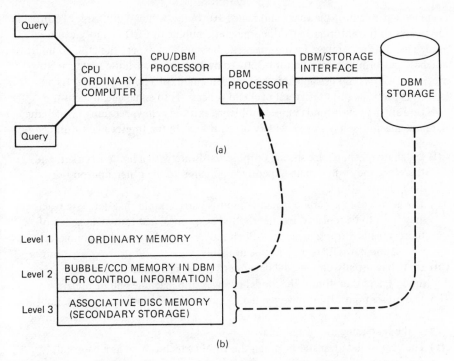

(a)

(b)

Figure 14.4 A conceptual diagram for a DBM: (a) DBM interfaces, (b) memory levels

each revolution, the information retrieved being processed on the fly by a set of Track Information Processors (TIP), one per track. The result is passed to the main computer (figure 14.5).

It is argued that for DBMs to be economically viable, the database should be large, typically 10^{10} bytes. In an ordinary database the index takes about 10-20 per cent of the space. In DBC the index is replaced by control information which

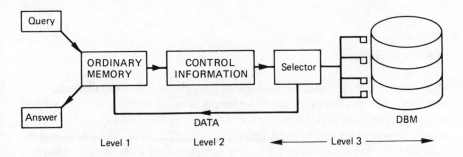

Figure 14.5

occupies 1 per cent of the space and hence 10^8 bytes, which is still large. To provide fast access to this information, either magnetic bubble or CCD memory can be used. The DBC researchers favour magnetic bubbles and expect the DBC to improve database performance by a factor of 20–40 over conventional disc systems. However, the DBC is only designed but not implemented. In a newer project, Hsiao (1983) is proposing to use several backend processors to enhance parallelism.

There are, however, fundamental problems, as listed below, because of which the database machines may not be widely used, at least in the foreseeable future:

(i) Database machines are special purpose hardware with a limited market, and therefore they will remain expensive compared to the general purpose computers.

(ii) The advances in general purpose computers are so rapid that database machines may have to be replaced frequently by better ones, just to remain ahead of those general purpose machines. Such replacement may not be economically viable, and new DBMs may not be available.

(iii) DBMs are usually data model dependent (most researchers use relational model), and therefore if the model changes, the machine will be useless.

(iv) The present day DBMs have tended to ignore the communications interface, which might become a significant cost factor in the future, particularly in view of the increasing use of terminals.

(v) The cost of data transfer between the DBM (which is used as a backend processor) and the general purpose machine is considered by some experts to be so high that even the most efficient DBM would turn out to be cost ineffective.

However, even if today's DBMs do not materialise as stand alone machines on special hardware, the ideas and concepts developed could still be incorporated in the general purpose machines of tomorrow, possibly within a new type of operating system which supports a variety of special functions, including DBM functions.

14.4 New applications

At an exotic level, databases may be regarded as extension of human memory on computers. As our memory is limited we keep additional information in books, in libraries, in files, and in various other forms (Sagan, 1977). One day in the future all such information could be on databases (Steel, 1982). If we take this extended view, then databases presented in this book represent only a beginning of what they can become in the future. We wish to explore here this area of new databases.

14.4.1 New types of databases

The new types of databases are that may be considered are

Numeric databases
Text databases
Image/picture databases
Speech databases.

In a numeric database, the main problem is the representation of vast, often sparse, matrices. In linear programming, we can have matrices having 16,000 columns and 1000 rows with many non-existing elements. There is clearly a need for compact storage and selective usage. Text databases deal with textual information, as in document retrieval systems and in word-processing environments. The logical structure of such information may be regarded as amorphous, since record types (assuming that we use record types there) are variable length, with potentially variable-length data items. A common document retrieval example is the information about books. There is no single entity which can act as primary key (some books do not have an ISBN), a book title may be long or short, it may have zero to many author names, each of different length, it may have zero to many editor names, each of different length, and so on. There are several hundred distinct pieces of information that can be stored about a book, but since every book does not have all that information (for instance, it may not have any editor), such book records have to be self-defined, with a self-identifier for each data item. Therefore there is no schema in the normal sense. Queries can also take different forms, sometimes matching part of a string within a given context. Now if we allow the contents of documents and books also to be stored in databases, then the problems of access and update will multiply. We might expect such a database to answer questions like: which Latin words are there in Shakespeare's Hamlet? But could it? Certainly the traditional databases discussed in this book cannot answer such a question — not easily at any rate.

Image or pictorial databases store images/pictures of objects using either graphics and/or digitisation. Facilities are required to construct three-dimensional images, and various cross-sections of such images. In computer aided designs (CAD), engineering designers often create new designs which are improved and stored in CAD databases. Once stored, such images can be used in manufacturing by an automated system. There are, however, many issues of image representation, reconstruction, creation, recognition, matching, storage and constraints which need solutions. In reconstruction, three-dimensional images may be produced from two-dimensional surfaces, and then a desired two-dimensional section may be produced. In creation, often some basic pieces are used. A typical example of matching is that of a thumb print. Image recognition is far more difficult. For instance, how can a computer find out by scanning a map if there is a bridge at a particular location.

In a speech database, sounds would be stored, analysed and selectively combined and reproduced. It should also allow operations, and conversion of sounds into text.

14.4.2 Intelligent databases

The query languages used in traditional databases are unintelligent in the sense that they do not have any deductive or inferential capabilities. If we have a database which has persons records and relates children and parents (say by having parents identifier as a foreign key in each person record), then our query languages will be able to find the parent of X but not X's grandparent, because the latter involves deductions. For a clearer understanding, let us assume the following facts and rules stored in a database.

Facts
All boys like cars
John is tall
Tim is father of Mary
Mary is mother of John
Jim owns a Rolls-Royce
Sara likes wine
Jane is pretty

Rules
If a person has a Rolls-Royce, he is rich
If X is a father or mother of Y, then X is a parent of Y
If X is a parent of Y, then X is an ancestor of Y
If X is an ancestor of Y and Y is an ancestor of Z, then X is an ancestor of Z
Sara likes anyone who is tall
John likes anyone who likes wine
Jane likes anyone who is rich

Note that facts describe unconditional information, while rules describe conditional information. We may now ask the following questions

Does John like cars?	Answer: Yes
Is Tim father of John?	Answer: No
Who are the ancestors of John?	Answer: Tim and Mary
Does Jane like John?	Answer: Not known
Does Jane like Jim?	Answer: Yes
Tell me all about Sara	Answer: She likes wine, she likes tall persons, she likes John, who likes her

These questions involve a certain amount of deductions or inferencing, and cannot be easily answered by traditional database query languages, but they can be answered by what is called an Intelligent Knowledge-Base System (IKBS), that is a sophisticated expert system. Prolog and LISP are commonly used languages for IKBS work.

The main differences between a DB and IKB system are:

(i) In a database, we organise information in a relatively stable data structure, each such structure, such as a record type, having a large number of instances. Database queries usually scan through a large amount of data.
(ii) In an IKB, data structures are basically less rigid, each query typically requiring a special data structure of its own. Therefore in an IKB query, the data structures are created, destroyed and processed dynamically, along with data, without much distinction. The amount of data instances involved is usually small, but there may be many data structures.
(iii) In addition to the data and structures, there are also numerous rules (to help in the deductions) which must be stored in an IKB.

Despite these differences, there are signs of convergence between the two approaches, perhaps because of two reasons.

(i) Present day IKB systems are usually toy systems. It is recognised that a large volume of information will be needed for practical IKB systems and therefore databases could be useful.
(ii) The database community recognises the need to include intelligent processing capability in databases.

As indicated in section 14.1, the facts and rules presented above can be represented in a database as factual and deductive properties. Intelligent query language, with some deductive capability, can be developed for databases (Deen, 1985). Alternatively, it should also be possible to interface an IKB to a database, through a suitable DML and external schema for either online or offline processing (figure 14.6). Either way, intelligent databases have become an interesting area of database research.

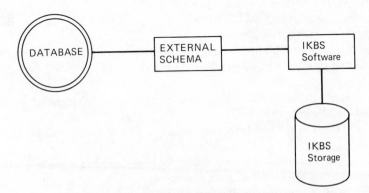

Figure 14.6

Exercises

14.1 (a) Describe the characteristics of the Universe of Discourse as understood
     in data modelling, and explain the functions of a conceptual schema.
   (b) Evaluate the relational data model as regards its ability to fulfil the
     requirements of a conceptual schema.

14.2 Explain the following concepts in data modelling:
   (i) object, event and role entities
   (ii) aggregation, role and generalisation
   (iii) extraction, transformation and structural rules
   (iv) factual and deductive information.

14.3 Write an essay on the new approaches to develop better end-user facilities.

14.4 Define the concept of a database machine and explain its functions. Describe,
   with a diagram, the basic components of a database machine and explain its
   search capability. Also comment on the potential impact of such a machine.

14.5 Explain the difference between traditional databases and knowledge bases
   and discuss how this difference will be lessened if databases are extended to
   include deductive information.

References

Amble *et al.* (1976). ASTRAL − . . . . *Modelling in DBMS*, edited by G. M. Nijssen,
   North-Holland, p. 257
Bachman, C. W. (1980). The role model approach to data structure. *Proceedings
   of International Conference on Databases*, edited by S. M. Deen and P.
   Hammersley, Heyden, p. 1
Banerjee, J. *et al.* (1979). DBC − a data base computer for large databases. *IEEE
   Transactions on Computers*, Vol. C-28, no. 6, p. 414
BCS Query Language Group (1981). *Query Languages − a uniform approach*, BCS
   monographs in Informatics, Heyden
Breutmann, B. *et al.* (1979). CSL − a language for defining conceptual schemas.
   Database Architecture, edited by G. Bracchi and G. M. Nijssen, North-Holland,
   p. 277
Buneman, P. *et al.* (1979). FQL − a functional query language. *Proceedings ACM
   SIGMOD Conference 1979*
Chen, P. P. (1976). The entity-relationship model . . . . *ACM TODS*, Vol. (1:1),
   March, p. 1
Codd, E. F. (1970). A relational model of data for large shared data banks. *Com-
   munications of the ACM*, Vol. (13:6), June
Codd, E. F. (1979). Extending the database relational model to capture more
   meaning. *ACM TODS*, Vol. (4:4), December, p. 397

Dadam, P. *et al.* (1984). Integration of time versions into relational database system. *Proceedings of the 10th VLDB Conference, August 1984*, p. 509

Date, C. J. (1981). *Introduction to Database Systems*, Vol. 1, 3rd edition, Addison-Wesley

Deen, S. M. (1985). *A relational algebra with some deductive capability*, Department of Computing Science, University of Aberdeen, Aberdeen, Scotland (to be published)

Engles, R. W. (1975). Currency and Concurrency in Cobol Database Facility. *IFIP TC-2 Working Conference on Modelling in DBMS*

Hammer, M. M. and McLeod, D. J. (1978). Semantic Data Model . . . . *Proceedings ACM SIGMOD Conference 1978*, p. 26

Hsiao, D. K. (editor) (1983). *Advanced Database Machine Architecture*, Prentice-Hall (this contains reports on several prototypes on database machines)

ISO (1981). *Concepts and Terminology for the Conceptual Schema*, edited by J. J. van Griethuysen *et al.* ISO Report ISO/TC97/SC5/WG3, February

Jones, S. and Mason, P. (1980). Handling the time dimension in database. *Proceedings of International Conference on Databases*, edited by S. M. Deen and P. Hammersley, Heyden, p. 65

Langdon, G. G. Jr, (1979). Database Machines: An introduction. *IEEE Transactions On Computers*, Vol. C-28, no. 6, p. 381 (this IEEE issue (Vol. C-28, no. 6) is devoted to database machines)

Longstaff, J. *et al.* (1982). ERQ: controlled inference and instruction techniques for DBMS query languages. *Proceedings ACM SIGMOD Conference 1982.*

Maryanski, F. J. (1980). Back-end database systems. *ACM Computing Surveys*, Vol. (12:1), March, p. 3

Mylopoulos, J. *et al.* (1980). A language facility for designing database intensive applications. *ACM TODS*, Vol (5:2), June, p. 185

Nijssen, G. M. (1976). Gross architecture for the next generation of DBMS. *Modelling in DBMS*, edited by G. M. Nijssen, North-Holland, p. 1

Nijssen, G. M. (1977). Current issues in conceptual schema concepts. *Architectures and Models in DBMS*, edited by G. M. Nijssen, North-Holland, p. 31

Pirotte, A. (1979). Fundamental and secondary issues in the design of non-procedural relational languages. *Proceedings of the 5th VLDB Conference, 1979*, p. 239

Sagan, C. (1977). *Dragons of Eden*, Random House

Schmidt, J. W. (1977). Some high level constructs for data type relation. *ACM TODS*, Vol. (2:3), September, p. 247

Schneiderman, B. (1978). Improving the human factor aspects of database interaction. *ACM TODS*, Vol. (3:4), December, p. 417

Senko, M. E. (1976). DIAM as a detailed example of the ANSI/SPARC Architecture. *Modelling in DBMS*, edited by G. M. Nijssen, North-Holland, p. 73

Senko, M. E. *et al.* (1973) *DIAM, IBM Systems Journal*, Vol. 12, p. 30

Shipman, D. W. (1981). The functional data model and data language. DAPLEX. *ACM TODS*, Vol. (6:1), March p. 140

Smith, J. M. and Smith, D. C. P. (1977). Database abstraction: aggregation and generalisation. *ACM TODS*, Vol. (2:2), p. 105, June

Steel, T. B. Jr (1982). International standardisation and distributed databases. *Distributed Data Bases*, edited by H. J. Schneider, North-Holland, p. 1

15 Distributed Databases

Over the last decade the database technology has established itself as a principal means of satisfying the information requirements of large and medium-sized organisations. As more and more databases are implemented, the need for inter-database communications will become very important, particularly to the corporate management. The prevailing spirit of decentralised management, with local control and at the same time co-operating at a higher level for greater good, makes distributed databases very desirable. With cheaper and more reliable hardware and communication links, this technology is expected to provide a real alternative to centralised processing. It is particularly attractive to multisite and multinational organisations with decentralised operations but requiring intersite information for integrated control at the corporate level.

A distributed database (DDB) is a facility to process data belonging to a number of linked databases, and it may be viewed as a database representing a *logical* collection of data from a number of interlinked databases (figure 15.1). The *logical site* of each such interlinked database is termed here as a *node*, each node holding the nodal database, its DBMS and all the necessary supporting facilities of the DDB. Nodes are normally, but not necessarily, geographically distributed over different physical sites linked by a data communications network. In some cases more than one node can reside in a large computer, and hence in the same physical site.

The primary objective of a DDB is to process data of several databases, irrespective of the nature of their communications links, and therefore the presence of a data communications network, although usual, is not essential in a DDB. However, in this chapter we shall generally assume the nodes to be geographically distributed and hence interlinked by a data communications network.

At this point, we shall also make a distinction between the purpose-built — to be referred to as the *closed* — and the more general purpose — to be referred to as the *open* — Distributed Database Management Systems (DDBMSs). In the former, the DDB is built from scratch, each nodal database being specifically designed to suit the requirement of the DDB within the constraints of the DDBMS. Therefore, incompatibilities or variations among the nodes are controlled, that is, nodal interfaces are closed and not open-ended. In contrast, an *open* DDBMS permits any data model at the nodes, including pre-existing databases. Therefore, *in theory*, there can be any amount of incompatibility or variation among the nodes in an open DDB.

In either case we may recognise two types of users (figure 15.1), the global user processing the data of the distributed database under the control of a DDBMS, and the local or nodal user processing the data of a particular node under the control of the NDBMS (Nodal Database Management System), ideally oblivious of the existence of the DDB. We shall use the term global database schema (GDS) to indicate the logical description of the data of a DDB, and correspondingly a nodal database schema (NDS) for the description of the data at a node, noting at the same time that the physical presence of a global database schema is not essential for a DDB.

In this chapter we shall examine the following issues of distributed databases:

(i) Multi-level control
(ii) Homogenisation of nodal models
(iii) User facilities
(iv) Privacy, integrity and reliability
(v) A general architecture.

In the last section we shall list some of the research prototypes and comment on future prospects.

15.1 Multi-level control

It is possible to have a single-level DBMS where data are distributed over several computers; some experts, but in decreasing numbers, also call them distributed databases. If we ignore these systems from our considerations, then we have two levels of controls in a DDB, the global and the nodal. If a node itself is a DDB, which is possible, then we would have many more levels but, within the context of a given DDB, we would still have only two levels, global and nodal, irrespective of whether one of its nodes is also a DDB. The global control (Deen, 1982) can basically be either of the following.

Centralised. All global processing is controlled by a central node through which all global transactions must be channelled. This creates bottlenecks and makes the system vulnerable to the breakdown of the centre and its communications links. Thus it is less stable. On the other hand, centralised controls make the task of preserving consistency during an update easier.

Decentralised. Each node keeps a copy of the DDBMS, each supervising the global transactions submitted from it (figure 15.2). The system is more stable, since there is no single centre whose breakdown can disable the whole DDB. However the exercise of controls and the preservation of consistency is more difficult, but the current trend is towards decentralisation.

As associated problem in a decentralised control system is the maintenance of a distributed directory/dictionary. Three possible options are (Mariella and Schreiber, 1980)

(i) a central directory copied at each node

(ii) a number of directories — each containing a subset of all entries (not necessarily disjoint) — at appropriate nodes

(iii) a selective directory, each node having only what it needs.

The autonomy enjoyed by a node in a distributed database can vary significantly from little to a great deal. In all DDBs an NDBMS controls the activities of each node, but the nodes are not necessarily fully autonomous; for instance, in some DDBs only global transactions are permitted (that is, transactions for purely nodal data are also treated as global transactions) whereas in others each node is fully autonomous, having its exclusive local users who need not be aware of the existence of the DDB. In the case of pre-existing databases as nodes, a full nodal autonomy is an essential prerequisite.

In some architectures all data belong to the DDB, while in others the data belong to the respective nodes, which may decide to contribute only some of their data to the DDB. In the latter case the node may retain the right to withdraw its data or to stipulate who can use the data and for what purpose. Ideally, it should also be possible for a node to join several DDBs.

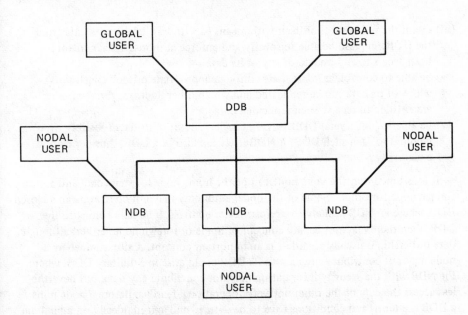

Figure 15.1 A distributed database, showing the hierarchical relationship

By nodal autonomy, we imply that an NDB should

(i) be allowed to have exclusive nodal users that are independent of the DDBMS

(ii) be able to join a DDB as a node by contributing only a logical subset of its own data, the subset containing none to all of its data

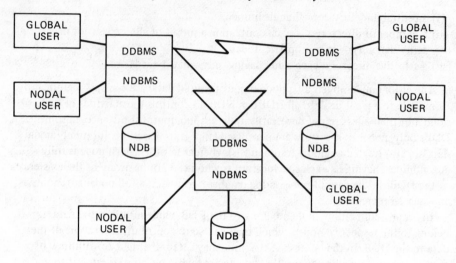

Figure 15.2 DDB with deeentralised control

(iii) retain the full control of itself with means to withdraw itself or its data from
the DDB; and also be able to specify and enforce authorisational control for
both access to and update of any of its data
(iv) be able to control, as *home node* (through appropriate privacy constraints),
which of its data can be replicated and which other nodes, as *foreign nodes*,
are entitled to receive such replicated data
(v) be able to join several DDBs, giving a logical subset of its data (possibly overlapping) to each such DDB. A NDB itself can also be a DDB, thus permitting
a hierarchy.

It is assumed that the same node can be the home node for some data and a
foreign node for others. Some of the nodal autonomy may not be relevant in a closed
DDB, where an NDB is likely to exercise fewer controls. If all data belong to the
DDB, then there may not be any concept of home or foreign nodes either, although
data ownership is usually regarded as an important concept. A situation where a
node may not contribute any data to its DDB could arise in a military DDB, where
the NDB with the security information may not contribute any data, but nevertheless access the data of the other nodes for operational reasons. Before a node joins
a DDB the terms and conditions have to be defined and agreed, ideally on a bilateral
basis with other nodes. It should be possible for a node in a DDB to be linked with
only some selected nodes, but not with all nodes.

We shall consider below only an open DDBMS – as it is the most flexible system
– with fully decentralised controls and full nodal autonomy, except where indicated otherwise. The global control system of such a DDB should support

(i) A decentralised control system with heterogeneous nodal data models.

(ii) Both retrieval and update facility for the global user by a high level language, without necessarily requiring the user to specify the nodes of interest (see location transparency — later).

(iii) Facility for a new node to join it at any time without necessarily affecting the other nodes.

(iv) Pre-existing databases as nodes.

 (v) Maximal nodal autonomy, and a node as a DDB.

(vi) Links to other independent DDBs (external DDB) at peer level for queries.

Point (vi) refers to a situation where independent DDBs wish to process joint queries, without one DDB becoming a node of another. In this case, all communications between them are at peer level (see also later).

In figure 15.2 we assumed each node to have a copy of the DDBMS, the global users accessing the DDB from any of these nodes. In an alternative architecture, the global user enters the DDB through what is called global transaction module (TM) which may be sited elsewhere in a different computer (Rothie *et al.*, 1980).

15.2 Nodal variations

Depending on the nodal data models, a distributed database can be either of the following.

Homogeneous: which allows only identical data models at each node. The DDB is fully homogeneous if all the nodes have identical machines as well, otherwise it is only partly homogeneous.

Heterogeneous: which permits different types of data models (such as network, relational, IMS) at the nodes. The problem of data conversion between incompatible models and the need for the preservation of model-specific privacy/integrity constraints make such systems complex.

If the DDB is homogeneous then there is no problem of intermodel conversion, but in a heterogeneous DDB there is. The presentation of data to a global user in a standard data model in spite of nodal variations, if any, is known as *homogenisation*. An additional problem, known as *data integration*, arises owing to variations in nodal data — for instance, if distance is expressed in kilometres in one node and in miles in another, or if one node gives net salary but the other only the gross salary and deductions (but not the net salary), or if one node expresses temperature in degrees and the other as cold, warm, hot and so on. Clearly the integration problem normally exists even in a homogeneous system, and it is compounded by the presence of different hardware and operating systems, including variations in codes (ASCII or EBCDIC etc.), in word length, in numerical accuracy and so on. Solutions to these problems vary with different implementations. The most difficult problem, however, is the homogenisation of heterogeneous data models, which includes the following intermodel conversion issues.

(i) *Data structure*

The usual practice is to define the global database schema in a standard or canonical data model into which all nodal data structures are converted. In the absence of the standard form, we would need $N * (N - 1)$ translators instead of $2 * N$ translators for N dissimilar nodes, as shown in figure 15.3(a) and (b) respectively. Figure 15.3(a) has $N * (N - 1) = 12$ translators (6 two-way links) as it does not use a standard form; the figure 15.3(b) has $2 * N = 8$ translators or 4 two-way links (node → standard, and standard → node, for each node).

(ii) *Assertion conversion*

Each nodal data model will have its own brand of privacy/integrity assertions which must be converted into a globally recognised form. This is not easy.

(iii) *Command conversion*

In a heterogeneous system, the global transaction language is likely to be different from its nodal equivalent. For instance, if the global language is relational and the local one the Codasyl DML, then not only the relational commands have to be translated into the Codasyl DML, but the Codasyl error messages must also be meaningfully transmitted back to the global user program.

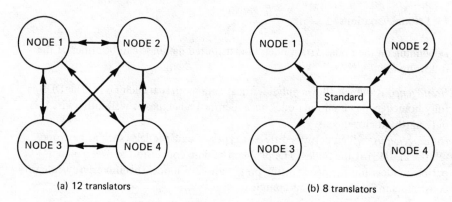

(a) 12 translators   (b) 8 translators

Figure 15.3

In most prototypes, relations are used as the standard data structures and a relational language as the standard user language; the reasons are

(i) Relations are simple to understand and can be mapped on to other structures with the fewest problems.
(ii) Relations are highly decomposable (Codd, 1982). A vertical, horizontal, or any fragment of a relation is still a relation, and the fragments can always be *joined* and *unioned* together to recreate the original relation.
(iii) Relational operations are closed, that is, the result of a relational operation is still a relation, which permits easier and repeated processing.

However, relational data structures are not the ideal in all situations, and hence newer and improved data structures could replace relations in the future.

15.3 User facilities

The most important facility for a global user is a high level language, such as SQL, that allows for both queries and updates. Navigational languages such as the Codasyl DML would involve unacceptably high data communications and global processing costs, and therefore they are not considered suitable for the bulk data transmission that is needed in a DDB. A high level language is, of course, also easier to learn. Given the existence of a suitable language, there are several associated issues, as discussed below.

15.3.1 Location transparency

Ideally a global user should be able to treat the DDB as a single database without concerning himself with nodes. In this case his query is expressed in terms of external-schema data names, but without specifying which data come from which nodes. Such a query is called a *location transparent query*, since the locations of data are not specified. This facility can be provided with the help of the global database schema and its supporting mappings.

Earlier works on distributed databases often assumed the provision of this location transparency to be a supreme goal. However, now we realise that, while the location transparency is an important facility, there is also a case for providing *location-dependent* facilities, particularly if we wish to provide a DDB facillity to hundreds of interlinked databases for occasional and selective use. In that case the implementation of a global database schema, which is essential for location transparency, may not be cost-effective. In a recent EEC project, the EEC explored the idea of linking European medical databases in a DDB, so that a medical doctor, say, at Aberdeen from the Aberdeen database, could extract information from a medical database, say, at Capri, where one of his patients was once treated. For such infrequent and location dependent queries, the construction of a global database schema for all EEC medical databases will be unnecessarily costly; what we need here is a location dependent facility for these medical doctors. Thus both location transparent and location dependent facilities are important in a DDB.

15.3.2 Fragmentation, replication, distribution

If a large relation is represented in the global schema, it may sometimes be more useful to resolve it into fragments (vertical, horizontal or both — see section 10.1) and to replicate and distribute them at selected nodes optimally, in order to improve the overall performance of the DDB. If we assume a closed distributed database, where the global schema is first designed and then the nodal databases are created for optimised performance, then there are likely to be many large relations at the global level which could be suitably fragmented for the nodes. On the other hand if the DDB is open, and contains a collection of pre-existing databases, then fragmentation is less important. However, data replication will still be relevant, since an entire relation can be replicated for faster queries. Again if the nodes are fully autonomous, then the DDBMS can fragment and replicate only if so permitted by the home node. In the case of a closed DDBMS, there may not be any such restriction.

15.3.3 Query processing

Another important topic in a DDB is global query optimisation where normal query optimisation (section 8.4) is compounded by the presence of several additional factors, such as fragmentation, nearest replicated copy and communications cost. Another important factor is the selection of an executions node, that is, the node where the query or part of the query should be executed for optimal processing. For instance, if node A wishes to get the result of the join of relation R1 from node B and relation R2 from node C (figure 15.4), then the following alternative actions could be possible

(a) send both R1 and R2 to A for the join
(b) send R1 to C for join with R2, and the result to A
(c) send R2 to B for join with R1, and the result to A
(d) send R1 and R2 to a third node, say D, for join and the result to A.

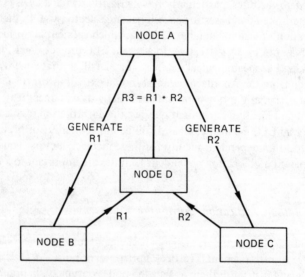

Figure 15.4 Use of an intermediate node D

One of these alternatives could be the best. If alternative (d) is most efficient, then it could involve the transfer of the following messages

(i) B and C acknowledge to A the receipt of the request
(ii) B and C inform A on the completion of their tasks and forward the intermediate result(s) to D
(iii) D acknowledges the receipt to B and C
(iv) D despatches the result of the join to A.

An optimiser must take into consideration all communications costs, as well as
other trade-offs. When a user transaction is submitted, the DDBMS may have to
decompose it optimally into subtransactions, with one or more subtransactions for
each relevant node, taking the replicated data into account. The aim would be to
reduce the total cost of the execution, including the cost of communications, but
true optimisation is not normally feasible, nor cost-effective. The techniques of such
a query decomposition and access path selection are implemented in some DDBs.
An associated issue is the minimisation of response time of a query, but much less
research has been done in this direction.

15.4 Privacy, integrity and reliability

Privacy is a very sensitive issue in a DDB, and most designers take this seriously.
Privacy checks can be made both at the compilation and at the execution time, as
necessary. However, as mentioned earlier, translation of nodal privacy assertions
into a standard global form for open DDBs is still an unresolved issue. As a result,
nodal data with unconvertible assertions cannot be accessed by global queries.

In section 5.2.1, we discussed three types of integrity controls and pointed out
that the internodal integrity is the specific concern of a DDB. However, as with
privacy, the translation of all semantic integrity assertions into a standard global
form for inclusion in the global database schema of an open DDB is not as yet
possible. Until this problem is solved, it will be difficult to support distributed
updates in open DDBs except in severely restricted cases; if an update fails owing to
a violation of an integrity constraint, the global user may not know why it has
failed or what he can do − through the global user language − to conform to the
requirements.

As indicated earlier, internodal integrity refers to the consistency of data among
the participating nodes. The sources of each inconsistency are two-fold:

(i) *Replicated data.* If data are replicated over several nodes, then the database will
be inconsistent if all the copies are not updated every time.
(ii) *Disperse update-unit.* If a set of data-units forming an update-unit is dispersed
over several nodes, then we have a *disperse update-unit.* Such a situation would
occur if the employee salary details are maintained in the branches (nodes) and
total salary expenditure at the head office (another node). However, in the
case of pre-existing databases as nodes, the instances of such update-units are
likely to be low.

Consistency can be *weak* or *strong.* In a *weak consistency*, the database can
remain in a *transient inconsistent state* without corrupting the data, whereas in a

strong consistency the database must be maintained in a consistent state at all time. A strong consistency must be enforced in the case of disperse update-units.

Data are generally replicated for ease of access when the frequency of retrievals exceeds that of updates. Sometimes in a retrieval, such as for a bank balance, a customer may ask for the *latest* piece of information (to be referred to as *mode L*), but at many other times retrieval requests can be satisfied by *any* consistent version of data (to be referred to as *mode A*). If the update and mode L rate together are low compared to the mode A rate, then weak consistency can be used effectively for the update of replicated data – if we accept the concept of home node (equivalently *master node, birth node* or *owner node*). In this case the latest version of data will be maintained at home nodes where all updates and mode L transactions will automatically be directed and queued by the DDBMS. Once an update is performed, the home node will transmit the update message to the relevant foreign nodes (equivalently *slave* or *subordinate* nodes) which will then copy the update to their databases – with the highest priority. The delay in effecting such updates in the foreign nodes is likely to be small. However, if there are too many updates and a high rate of mode L transactions, then there will be too long a queue in the home node, which will make the DDB inefficient.

There are a number of techniques for enforcing a strong consistency, with a varying degree of effectiveness, but the most general purpose technique is what is called a two-phase commit protocol or two-phase locking protocol (2PL). This uses the preclaim strategy (see section 5.1.3) where the DDBMS first sends a message (first phase) to all relevant nodes, indicating its wish to lock some of their data for update, thus preclaiming all the needed data. If all the nodes agree, the DDBMS locks them and commits the system to update (second phase). If any node disagrees or fails to respond within a pre-set time limit, then the transaction is aborted (Kohler, 1981). All locks are released after an update. Other techniques are also used (Bernstein and Goodman, 1981).

The need for database recovery arises owing to the following malfunctions.

 (i) User program failure
 (ii) Physical storage failure (in parts or whole)
(iii) Processor failure
(iv) DBMS failure
 (v) Communications link failure.

In the context of a DDB, we are particularly concerned with (v). The ISO (International Standards Organization) has specified a seven-layered protocol system – known as ISO/Open Systems Interconnection or ISO/OSI – for data communications networks. Its lower layers (layers 1–4) deal with physical networks while the upper layers, particularly layers 6 and 7, are relevant to distributed databases. These last two layers are intended to support functions such as data and command conversions between models, file transfers, query optimisation and so on. Typically, the DDBMS designers will consider the lower levels as a black box which either fails or succeeds in sending a message from one node to another. Backup and recovery facilities (including checkpoint, nodal rollback and global rollback facilities) are also required to guard against failure. Details are beyond the scope of this book.

For recovery purposes, each node can also maintain a set of mail boxes, one for each of the other nodes in the DDB, for holding messages sent out to those nodes, but not yet acknowledged. When a node starts a session or restarts after a breakdown, it must first take two recovery actions. It should read its mail boxes located at other nodes, and take action on the messages, such as the completion of lost updates. Secondly, it should broadcast all its outstanding messages to other nodes, including messages that were sent out earlier but for which acknowledgements were not received before the crash. It is possible that the other node received the message, acted on it, and despatched an acknowledgement, but that this node broke down before the acknowledgement arrived. In that case, this node would be retransmitting the message, possibly asking the other node to do something which it has already done. However, such a retransmission should not cause any update problem on replicated data if an update version number is maintained for each unit of data and if the requesting node transmits the update version number along with its request for an update. In this case, a node would check the update version number before each update, and thus avoid the repetition of the update. Other schemes are also possible.

15.5 Architectural issues

There is no general agreement as to the architectural framework of a DDB, each research group favouring its own ideas. However, to highlight some of the issues, we shall assume a general framework (figure 15.5) — a conceptual architecture, partly as an extension of the ANSI/SPARC model (as viewed by this author) (Deen *et al.*, 1985).

15.5.1 A general architecture

Figure 15.5 represents a generalised architecture in the sense that no distinction is made between centralised or decentralised control systems, or between homogeneous or heterogeneous classes. The DDB is a user of a node via a participation schema (PS), analogous to a nodal user via a nodal external schema. A nodal DB — homogeneous, heterogeneous or pre-existing — should be able to participate in a DDB via a participation schema, through which its data can be presented to the DDB. Although a given DDBMS designer may not implement a participation schema, conceptually it exists, just as the nodal and global external schemas can be assumed to have conceptual existence, irrespective of implementation.

This architecture allows for two types of nodes, *inner* nodes and *outer* nodes, the former contributing to the global database schema which can provide a loca-

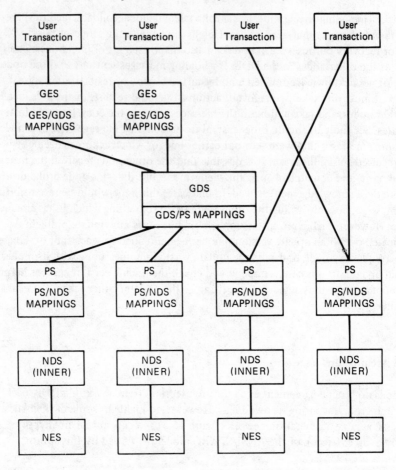

Figure 15.5 The general architecture of a DDB. Nodal databases are represented here by nodal database schema and nodal external schema

tion transparent transaction and the latter supporting only the location dependent transactions. We shall discuss these facilities below.

Global Database Scheme (GDS)

The GDS is formed by the participation schemas of the inner nodes, and in turn it supports global external schemas. The GDS should describe the following.

(i) *Nodal data*

Relations of the participation schemas (PSs), along with node names, fall under this category. Although a user can formulate location transparent queries via an appropriate external schema without node names, sometimes he might like to

know the home node of some data for some reasons, and hence the presence of
node names in the GDS is important.

(ii) *Integration data*

As indicated earlier, the same information can be presented at different nodes
in different forms. We therefore need additional data that gives units and conversion tables to carry out the integration. Although the GDS contains integration data, it does not provide an integrated view — this is done at the
global external schema.

(iii) *Meta data*

This is additional data that describes other data of interest — it is optional, and
depends on the facilities anticipated.

Associated with each GDS, we also need some GDS/PS mapping schema to give
information on fragmentation, replication and distribution of each relation, if
relevant.

The global external schema (GES) provides a transaction dependent, but integrated, view of data. If a user wants salaries in dollars, the GES will show the
salaries in dollars, the necessary conversion being done by the GES/GDS mapping
using the integration data of the GDS. The GES need not show the node numbers
of relations, unless a user transaction using this GES needs to display node numbers.

Participation schema

The participation schema (PS) should be specified in a canonical form. If we assume
relations as the standard data structures, then every nodal database, irrespective
of its data model or pre-existence, must support a relational participation schema,
and allow a suitable relational language to operate on its data; without this interface
the node will not be able to participate in an open DDB. Therefore, if a nodal
DBMS is of Codasyl type, it must support a relational interface before it can join
the DDB. This is, of course, a restriction, but all standards are restrictions; without
such a standard it would be very difficult to create an open DDB.

All nodal constraints, including privacy constraints, can be specified in the
participation schema.

Outer nodes

The outer nodes provide a mechanism to support location dependent transactions,
by permitting a user program to invoke one or more participation schemas directly,
instead of a global external schema. However, in the absence of a GDS, the outer
user cannot get data replication, integration or meta data facilities, as there will be
no place to describe them.

Subsidiary database

If we allow data replication in an open DDB, then there is an obvious question of
storage. Could we realistically expect to reorganise a pre-existing database, just
because we need to store there some foreign data? This is not a practicable propo-
sition; what we need is a *subsidiary database* (SDB) at each inner node, under the
control of the DDBMS, where we can store replicated data, integration data and
meta data, along with other directory data. Such an SDBMS could also support
extended query facility to the nodal DBMS. For instance, in figure 15.4 node D is
expected to join relations R1 and R2 received from outside; but the NDBMS at
D may not be able to join such external relations, that is, relations which are not
part of this database but received from outside. There are also other cases where an
SDBMS could be useful, such as to provide additional query functions that are not
available in the nodal DBMS. SDBs could be used also for outer nodes, with
restricted facilities.

   If we now modify figure 15.2 to include SDBs, then the resultant configuration
for a decentralised system would look like figure 15.6, where each inner node

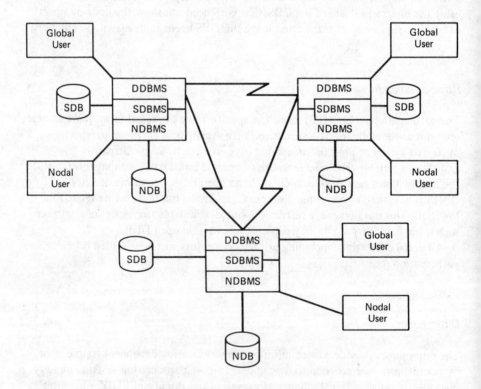

*Figure 15.6 Decentralised controls with subsidiary database. SDB is optional for
         outer modes*

contains GDS, GES, PS, SDB and a copy of DDBMS and SDBMS; but an outer node has PS, a copy of DDBMS and an optional SDB.

A DDB could support interactions to other DDBs in two ways.

(i) As a superior DDB: in this case the other DDB — to be called an internal DDB — must act as either inner or outer node and, as such, must have a copy of the DDBMS of the superior DDB.
(ii) As a peer: in this case the other DDB — to be called an external DDB — is independent of the first DDB, neither of them having a copy of the DDBMS of the other. Therefore, communications between the two are conducted via an accepted standard form, which provides the necessary conversion facilities.

In figure 15.5, we have also indicated where the relevant mappings should lie for maximal data independence, assuming that the nodal database schemas are paramount, that is, most stable. However, in a closed DDB, the GDS could be the most stable object, the global requirements subordinating the local requirements and dictating completely which data should be in which node. In this case, the mappings have to be placed differently.

The presence of so many levels in the architecture makes query processing quite complex. Some of the compilation (or translation) steps for inner nodes are given below.

1. Compile the user transactions against the global database schema via the global external schema. The user language commands may have to be converted into a standard form for the DDB.
2. The DDBMS may then resolve the global user transaction into a number of global subtransactions — one or more subtransactions for a given node which has the relevant data. If some data are replicated, then the least expensive node must be chosen for those data. The DDBMS then transmits the subtransactions to the relevant nodes. If a node (NDBMS and SDBMS together) is not powerful enough to perform the required query function, then the relevant relations from this node must be directed to a node which can.
3. Each node receiving a subtransaction may have to transform it into one or more nodal transactions, depending on the facility of the participation schema, and the underlying data model. For instance, if the data model supports SQL (via appropriate nodal external schemas) and the participation schema is also relational, then the global subtransaction must be converted into the nodal SQL form. No conversion will be needed if the global standard language is also SQL. In any case, the nodal transaction must then be compiled against the database, like any other nodal transaction.

In each step, privacy and integrity checks must be made, and error messages correctly transmitted. Once compiled, global transactions can then be executed, following the same steps.

15.5.2 Some prototypes

There are numerous prototypes of distributed databases, some of which have been implemented, while others are being developed. We mention here some of them, in no particular order.

   (i) SDD-1 (Computer Corporation of America). This represents a pioneering work on DDB, and contributed to many of our current ideas, particularly on concurrency control algorithm. It is a closed relational DDB (Rothnie *et al.*, 1980).

  (ii) POREL (University of Stuttgart). A closed homogeneous system, essentially single level (Neuhold and Walter, 1982).

 (iii) VDN (Technical University of Berlin). A closed homogeneous system, essentially single level (Munz, 1980).

 (iv) SIRIUS-DELTA (INRIA, France). This uses multi-level schemas but identical (relational) data models on dissimilar computers. Its architecture encompasses all the layers of figure 15.5, excluding outer nodes, although slightly differently (Litwin *et al.*, 1982). It is a closed DDB.

  (v) R* (IBM, San Jose). This allows SYSTEM R databases as nodes, but DDBMS and NDBMS are integrated into a single DBMS (special distributed versions of RDS and RSS replace those of figure 13.1 at each node). It does not support any global database schema or global external schemas (Daniels *et al.*, 1982; Williams *et al.*, 1982).

 (vi) MULTIBASE (Computer Corporation of America) to permit retrieval as an open DDB. In contrast to others, MULTIBASE uses DAPLEX constructs (section 14.2.4) rather than relations for conceptual schema (Landers and Rosenberg, 1982).

(vii) Multidatabase (INRIA, France) to permit retrievals using the equivalent of outer nodes (Litwin *et al.*, 1982).

(viii) PROTEUS (University of East Anglia). A centralised DDB linking pre-existing heterogeneous DDBs, primarily for queries (Atkinson *et al.*, 1984).

 (ix) DDM (Distributed Database Manager — by the Computer Corporation of America). This is a closed system permitting both updates and retrievals to purpose-built nodal databases, with Adaplex (DAPLEX embedded in ADA) as the user language both at the nodal and global levels. The system supports data replication, data distribution and a tuning facility for physical data distribution (Chen *et al.*, 1983).

  (x) PRECI* (University of Aberdeen). An open DDB to permit both updates and retrievals. The general architecture of figures 15.5 and 15.6 is used in PRECI* (Deen *et al.*, 1985).

In MULTIBASE there is no global database schema; its 'global schema' and 'local schema' correspond respectively to the global external schema and participation schema in our diagram. The users of R* (nodal or global) enter a node by SQL via derived and base relations. In the absence of global external and global database schemas in R∗, the user has to know what data are available from other sources (this is done partly to preserve confidentiality). In PROTEUS, the GDS is proposed as a standard internal form, the global users relying on external sources (probably as in R∗) to find what is available.

The distributed database discussed in this chapter uses 'traditional' databases as nodes, but future DDB must also permit text, numeric, image and speech databases as nodes, and may include distributed knowledge bases as well. It is possible to imagine a future world where every single database of any type everywhere on earth is interlinked, such that anyone from anywhere (with appropriate authorisation) is able to share easily the vast storehouse of information and knowledge that is available. This is a dream which will probably never be realised, but can only be aspired to.

Exercises

15.1 Explain the following concepts:
   (a) Open and closed distributed databases
   (b) Location transparency
   (c) External data
   (d) Fragmentation and replication
   (e) Nodes and sites.
15.2 Discuss the following issues in distributed databases:
   Multi-level controls
   Homogenisation and integration
   Integrity and recovery.
15.3 Explain, with a diagram, a general architecture of an open distributed database. Also describe the compilation and execution stages in query processing, as implied by this architecture.
15.4 Explain the function of the following:
   Global module
   Nodal module
   Subsidiary database
   Participation schema.

References

Atkinson, M. P. *et al.* (1984). The Proteus distributed database system. *Proceedings of the 3rd British National Conference on Databases (BNCOD-3)*, edited by J. J. Longstaff, Cambridge University Press, p. 225

Bernstein, P. A. and Goodman, N. (1981). Concurrency control in distributed database systems. *ACM Computing Surveys*, Vol. (13:2), June, p. 185

Chan, A. *et al.* (1983). Overview of an ADA∗ compatible distributed database manager. *Proceedings ACM SIGMOD Conference 1983*, p. 228

Codd, E. F. (1982). Relational database – a practical formulation for productivity. *Communications of the ACM*, Vol. (25:2), February (ACM Touring Award Lecture)

Daniels, D. *et al.* (1982). An introduction to distributed query compilation in R∗. *Distributed Databases*, edited by H. J. Schneider, North-Holland, p. 291

Deen, S. M. (1982). Distributed databases – an introduction. *Distributed Databases*, edited by H. J. Schneider, North-Holland, p. 239

Deen, S. M. *et al.* (1985). The architecture of a generalised distributed database system. *Computer Journal*, Vol (28:3), July

Kohler, W. H. (1981). A survey of techniques for synchronisation and recovery in decentralised computer systems. *ACM Computing Surveys*, Vol. (3:2), June, p. 149

Landers, T. and Rosenberg, R. L. (1982). An overview of Multibase. *Distributed Databases*, edited by H. J. Schneider, North-Holland, p. 153

Litwin, W. *et al.* (1982). SIRIUS systems for distributed data management. *Distributed Databases*, edited by H. J. Schneider, North-Holland, p. 311 (the second half of this article discusses Multidatabase)

Mariella, G. and Schreiber, F. (1980). A data dictionary for distributed databases. *Distributed Data Bases*, edited by C. Delobel and W. Litwin, North-Holland, p. 17

Munz, R. (1980). *Distributed Data Bases*, edited by C. Delobel and W. Litwin, North-Holland

Neuhold, E. J. and Walter, B. (1982). An overview of the architecture of DDBS POREL. *Distributed Databases*, edited by H. J. Schneider, North-Holland, p. 247

Rothnie, J. B. *et al.* (1980). Introduction to a system for distributed databases (SDD-1). *ACM TODS*, Vol. (5:1) March, p. 1, (the two following articles (p. 18 and p. 56) in the same issue of TODS are also on SDD-1)

Williams, R. *et al.* (1982). R∗ – an overview of the architecture. *Improving Database Usability and Responsiveness*, Academic Press

Hints and Answers to Selected Exercises

Chapter 4

4.6 Cousins can be best represented by two record types, person records and link records with one link record for each pair of cousins. The alternative technique will be the direct representation, with variable-length keys, as in ADABAS.

4.10 Non-disjoint A-set type will permit direct representation of $m:n$ relationships, whose implementation problems have been discussed in the text.

Chapter 6

6.5 Split relation R into EMP and COURSE, removing the repeating group

> WORK (ENO SECTION NI CNO SHN)
> COURSE (CNO TOPIC)

In relation WORK, SHN → SECTION, but SHN is not a candidate key and hence

> WORK1 (ENO NI CNO SHN), SECT (SHN SECTION)

However, in WORK1, ENO → NI, but ENO is not a candidate key (or ENO →→ CNO independent of SHN and NI, see chapter 7), and hence

> WORK2 (ENO NI SHN) and WORK3 (ENO CNO)

Note that relation (ENO NI CNO) is not in 3NF, since ENO → NI, but ENO is not a candidate key.

6.8 *PAL*

Let T = = BOOK : A# = A# % AUTHOR : AN = "DICKENS"
  (i) BN % T
 (ii) BN % BOOK : (B# = B# % LOAN) AND A# = A# % AUTHOR : AN = "DICKENS"
(iii) RN % READER : R# = R# % LOAN : B# = B# % T
 (iv) B# % BOOK - - B# % LOAN

In the first three queries, we have used T as a common subexpression.
QBE

> RANGE OF B IS BOOK ⎫
> RANGE OF A IS AUTHOR ⎪   Assume these ranges
> RANGE OF L IS LOAN   ⎬   have been declared
> RANGE OF R IS READER ⎭

   (i) RETRIEVE B.BN WHERE B.A# = A.A# and A.AN = 'DICKENS'
  (ii) RETRIEVE B.BN WHERE B.B# = L.B# and B.A# = A.A# and A.AN = 'DICKENS'
 (iii) RETRIEVE R.RN WHERE R.R# = L.R# AND L.B# = B.B# AND B.A# = A.A# AND A.AN = 'DICKENS'
 (iv) RETRIEVE B.B# WHERE NOT (B.B# = L.B#)

6.9   *PAL*

   (i) SNO % STUDENT : AGE > 21 AND REGENT = TNO % TUTOR : = "SMITH" OR TNAME = "MURRAY"
  (ii) SNO % STUDENT : NOT (REGENT = HNO % TUTOR)
Note that SNO % STUDENT : REGENT ≠ HNO % TUTOR will yield a different result

 (iii) SNO % STUDENT : REGENT = TNO % TUTOR: HNO = HDN % DEPT : DNO = SDN
       (This is a cyclic query)
 (iv) SNO % STUDENT : REGENT = TNO % TUTOR : HNO = HDN % DEPT : DNO = SDN % STUDENT
       (This is not a cyclic query)
  (v) TNAME % TUTOR : (HNO = HDN % DEPT : DNAME = "PHYSICS") AND NOT (TNO = REGENT % STUDENT)

QBE

> RANGE OF D IS DEPT
> RANGE OF T IS TUTOR
> RANGE OF S IS STUDENT
> RANGE OF X IS STUDENT

   (i) RETRIEVE S.SNO WHERE S.AGE > 21 AND REGENT = T.TNO AND (T.TNAME = 'SMITH' OR T.TNAME = 'MURRAY')
  (ii) RETRIEVE S.SNO WHERE NOT (S.REGENT = T.HNO)
 (iii) RETRIEVE S.SNO WHERE S.REGENT = T.TNO AND T.HNO = D.HDN AND D.DNO = S.SDN
 (iv) RETRIEVE S.SNO WHERE S.REGENT = T.TNO and T.HNO = D.HDN AND D.DNO = X.SDN
  (v) RETRIEVE T.TNAME WHERE T.HNO = D.HDN AND D.DNAME = 'PHYSICS' AND NOT (T.TNO = S.REGENT)

Chapter 7

7.1   C → T, but C is not a candidate key, hence

     R1 (T C)   R2 (C, S, B)

However C →→ S independent of B, but C is not a candidate key, hence

     R3 (C, S)   R4 (C B)

7.4   (a) If each employee has a set of skills and if each employee knows several
          languages, and if languages and skills are independent of each other.
     (b) If a supplier supplies many items, each of many different colours.

7.5   Consider the following rule: a supplier can supply an item to a project if
     he is the supplier of the item and if he is the supplier to that project and if
     the project needs that item. If this rule holds, then relation SIP is in 4NF
     but not in 5NF.

Chapter 8

8.1   *SQL*

(a)   SELECT ENAME, SAL
     FROM EMP
     WHERE JOB = 'CLERK' AND EDN =
          SELECT DNO
          FROM DEPT
          WHERE LOC = 'ABERDEEN'

(b)   SELECT AVG (SAL)
     FROM EMP
     WHERE SAL > 10 AND SAL < 20 AND JOB = 'CLERK'
     GROUP BY EDN

(c)   SELECT X.ENAME, Y.ENAME
     FROM EMP X, EMP Y
     WHERE X.MNO = Y.ENO
          AND X.SAL > Y.SAL

(d)   SELECT COUNT (∗)
     FROM EMP
     GROUP BY DEPT
     HAVING SAL > AVG (SAL)

(e)   SELECT ENO
       FROM EMP
       WHERE SAL >
            SELECT (0.25 * TOTSAL)
            FROM DEPT
            WHERE DNO = EDN

QBE

(a)

EMP	ENO	ENAME	MNO	JOB	SAL	EDN
		P.E		CLERK	P.S	X

DEPT	DNO	DNAME	TOTSAL	LOC
	X			ABERDEEN

(b)

EMP	ENO	ENAME	MNO	JOB	SAL	EDN
	X			CLERK	P.AVG.ALL.Z	G.Y
	X				> 10	
	X				< 20	

(c)

EMP	ENO	ENAME	MNO	JOB	SAL	EDN
	X	E1	Y		Z	
	Y	E2			<Z	

RESULT	X.ENAME	Y.ENAME
	P.E1	P.E2

(d)

EMP	ENO	ENAME	MNO	JOB	SAL	EDN
	P.CNT.ALL.X				> AVG.ALL.Z	G.Y

(e)

EMP	ENO	ENAME	MNO	JOB	SAL	EDN
	P.$\underline{X}$				$> 0.25*\underline{Z}$	$\underline{Y}$

DEPT	DNO	DNAME	TOTSAL	LOC
	$\underline{Y}$		$\underline{Z}$	

8.2   (i)   SELECT BN
          FROM BOOK
          WHERE A# =
            SELECT A#
            FROM AUTHOR
            WHERE AN = 'DICKENS'

   (ii)   SELECT BN
          FROM BOOK
          WHERE (B# IN
            SELECT B#
            FROM LOAN)
          AND A# =
            SELECT A#
            FROM AUTHOR
            WHERE AN = 'DICKENS'

   (iii)   SELECT RN
          FROM READER
          WHERE R# IN
            SELECT R#
            FROM LOAN
            WHERE B# IN
              SELECT B#
              FROM BOOK
              WHERE A# =
                SELECT A#
                FROM AUTHOR
                WHERE AN = 'DICKENS'

   (iv)   SELECT B#
          FROM BOOK
          MINUS
          SELECT B#
          FROM LOAN

8.5   Let U == (A, B) % R

V == C % R

Then R (A|B)/(C)S

= A % U −− A % ((A % U) ∗∗ V −− U)

8.7   *Schema*

(The capital letters in brackets in the relation descriptions below are attribute names used later in the queries.)

(1) Customer Order Relation (COR)

Customer no. (CN)/Item code (IC)/Daily quantities for 92 days.

(2) Item Detail Relation (IDR)

Item code (IC)/Description/Price (PR)/Weight/Size

(3) Sales Information Relation (SIR)

Item code/Monthly sales for 24 months.

(4) Van Information Relation (VIR)

Van no. (VN)/Van capacity.

(5) Customer Accounts Record (CAR)

Customer no. (CN)/Name and Address (NA)/Route no./
No. of times delivered/YTD sales/YTD payment/balance/
invoicing day number (DN).

Queries

PAL

(i) (CN, NA) % CAR : DN = DAYN

(ii) COR : CN = CN % CAR : DN = DAYN

(iii) (IC, PR) % IDR : IC = IC % COR : CN = CN % CAR : DN = DAYN

SQL

(i)   SELECT CN, NA
       FROM CAR
       WHERE DN = DAYN

(ii)   SELECT ∗
       FROM COR
       WHERE CN IN
          SELECT CN
          FROM CAR
          WHERE DN = DAYN

(iii) SELECT IC, PR
       FROM IDR
       WHERE IC IN
          SELECT IC
          FROM COR
          WHERE CN IN
             SELECT CN
             FROM CAR
             WHERE DN = DAYN

8.8 *Schema*

1. Car Charges Relation (CCR)
   Model (MD)/Fixed daily charge (DC)/Mileage charge (MC)/Next expensive model (NEXT)/Prior expensive model (PRIOR).

2. Car Detail Relation (CDR)
   Car registration no. (RN)/Model (MD)/Date purchased/Mileage (ML)/Daily bookings for 120 days, each containing the order number if booked.
   (Note that these 120 fields for bookings should be treated as a circular buffer to reduce updates.)

3. Customer Accounts Relation (CAR)
   Customer no. (CN)/Name and Address (NA)/YTD sales/YTD payment/Balance.

4. Order Completion Relation (OCR)
   Customer no. (CN)/Order no. (ON)/Miles driven/Fixed daily charge (DC)/ Mileage charge (MC)/Car registration no. (RN)/Start date/Finish date.
   (Daily and mileage charges or something in lieu of them are necessary for this record, since a customer can be charged at a rate which is different from that of the model actually used.)

This case study highlights one of the shortcomings of the relational model, as it requires the processing of car models sequentially in order of the daily charge. Since ordering is not supported in the relational model, we have added NEXT and PRIOR attributes (in daily charge order) in CCR. If the daily charge is updated, then not only this tuple, but also its Next and Prior tuples may have to be amended with new values for their Prior and Next fields. Therefore, the claim of the relational model that the ordering of the tuples is immaterial is not always true in practice. Instead of NEXT and PRIOR we could have used a sequence field in CCR as CCR (MD, DC, MC, SEQ) where SEQ will hold the sequential position of each tuple. In this case if a new tuple is inserted, all its subsequent tuples (in SEQ order) must also be updated in the SEQ field, again demonstrating that in real situations the tuples are not always independent of each other. In an alternative technique, a new inserted tuple is given a non-integer SEQ value between the two existing tuples; for instance, a new tuple falling between existing tuples 2 and 3 will get 2.5 in its SEQ field. This eliminates the need to update all subsequent tuples, but prevents the retrieval of a tuple by a relational query from its prior (next) tuple, since the SEQ value of this tuple cannot be deduced from its prior (next) tuple.

Queries

PAL

(i) Let M == MD % CDR : RN = RN % OCR : CN = CNUM AND ON = ONUM
    RN % CDR : MD = NEXT % CCR : MD = M

(ii) Using M defined above

    RN % CDR : MD = PRIOR % CCR : MD = M

(iii) (MC, DC) % OCR : RN = CNUM and ON = ONUM

The SQL formulation can be obtained directly from the PAL formulation, and hence we write it only for (i).

```
SELECT RN
FROM CDR
WHERE MD =
     SELECT NEXT
     FROM CCR
     WHERE MD =
          SELECT MD
          FROM CDR
          WHERE RN =
               SELECT RN
               FROM OCR
               WHERE CN = CNUM AND ON = ONUM
```

8.9   *Schema*

(1)   Component Information Relation (CIR)
      Component code (CC)/Quantity in stock/Reorder level/Standard manufacturing time/Price.
      (one record per component)

(2)   Component Link Relation (CLR)
      Superior component code (SUPC)/Subordinate component code (SUBC)/ Quantity of the SUBC in the SUPC.
      (one record per superior/subordinate pair — as in the PLINK records of figure 4.7)

(3)   Material Information Relation (MIR)
      Material code/Description/Quantity in stock/Reorder level/Lead time/Price supplier no.

(4)   Component Material Relation (CMR)
      Component code/Material code/Quantity of material required in the component.
      (one record per component code/material code pair)

(5)   Supplier Information Relation (SIR)
      Supplier code/Name and Address

Queries

To get superior components

```
CIR : SUBC = COMPC for superior components
CIR : SUPC = COMPC for subordinate components
```

The SQL version for one of them

```
SELECT *
FROM CIR
WHERE SUBC = COMPC
```

Chapter 9

9.9 (a) Use the relations in the answer to the exercise 8.7 of chapter 8 as record types, and then construct the following set types.

Set name	Owner	Member	Order
SET1	SIR	COR	Item code
SET2	CAR	COR	Item code

(b) B10.

    MOVE DAYN TO DN.

    FIND FIRST CAR USING DN.   [format 1]

  B20.

    GET CAR.

    FIND FIRST COR WITHIN SET2   [format 4]

    IF DB-STATUS > 0,

        DISPLAY "NO ORDER FOR CUSTOMER", CN;

        GO TO B40.

  B30.

    GET COR.

    MOVE IC IN COR TO IC IN IDR.

    FIND ANY IDR USING IC.   [format 2]

    GET IDR.

    (now process by Cobol as necessary and then get the next COR)

    FIND NEXT COR WITHIN SET2.   [format 4]

    IF DB-STATUS = 0, GO TO B30.

    DISPLAY "END OF ORDERS FOR CUSTOMER", CN.

  B40.

    FIND NEXT CAR USING DN.   [format 1]

    IF DB-STATUS = 0, GO TO B20.

    DISPLAY "END OF CUSTOMERS FOR DAY", DAYN.

9.10 (a) Assume the relations in the answer to exercise 8.8 of chapter 8 as record types, but drop NEXT and PRIOR attributes from CCR. The set types needed are

Set name	Owner	Member	Set Order
SET1	SYSTEM	CCR	Fixed daily charge
SET2	CCR	CDR	Registration number
SET3	CAR	OCR	Order number

Since the record selection format 1 does not permit finding of **PRIOR** record, we have to use SYSTEM set for CCR, so that we can get **PRIOR** record by the record selection format 4.

(b)

  (i) MOVE CNUM TO CN IN OCR.

    MOVE ONUM TO ON IN OCR.

FIND ANY OCR USING CN, ON.   [format 2]
GET OCR.
MOVE RN IN OCR TO RN IN CDR.
FIND ANY CDR USING RN.   [format 2]
GET CDR.
Update by Cobol and then,
MODIFY CDR.

(ii) We have used below the data NEWRN to hold the registration number
      of the newly selected car.

A10.

MOVE SPACES TO NEWRN.
MOVE OLDRN TO RN IN CDR.
FIND ANY CDR USING RN.   [format 2]
FIND OWNER WITHIN SET2.   [format 6]

A20.

PERFORM B-SEARCH SECTION.
IF NEWRN NOT = SPACE, GO TO A40-PROCESS.
FIND NEXT CCR WITHIN SET1.   [format 4]
IF DB-STATUS > 0,
   DISPLAY "NO NEXT CAR – END OF SET":
   GO TO A30.
PERFORM B-SEARCH SECTION.
IF NEWRN NOT = SPACE, GO TO A40 PROCESS.

A30.

(NOTE TWO PRIOR COMMANDS ARE NECESSARY.)
FIND PRIOR CCR WITHIN SET1.   [format 4]
FIND PRIOR CCR WITHIN SET1.   [format 4]
IF DB-STATUS > 0,
   DISPLAY "NO PRIOR CAR – END OF SET";
   GO TO A50.
PERFORM B-SEARCH SECTION.
IF NEWRN = SPACE, GO TO A50.

A40 – PROCESS
The desired car is found, and hence carry out further processings, if any.
A50.

EXIT
B-SEARCH SECTION.

B.10.

GET MD IN CCR.
FIND FIRST CDR WITHIN SET2.   [format 4]

B20.

> GET CDR.
> Now search for a free car by Cobol instruction; if found,
> MOVE RN IN CDR TO NEWRN. GO TO B40.
> If not found, continue as follows:
> FIND NEXT CDR WITHIN SET2.
> IF DB-STATUS = 0, GO TO B20.
> DISPLAY "NO FREE CAR, MODEL", MD.

B40.

> EXIT.

9.11 (a) Assume the relations in the answer to exercise 8.9 of chapter 8 as record types. The set types needed are

Set name	Owner	Member	Set Order
SUBSET	CIR	CLR	SUBC
SUPSET	CIR	CLR	SUPC

These two set types are similar to those of figure 4.7 (chapter 4); the other set types are

SET1	CIR	CMR
SET2	MIR	CMR
SET3	MIR	SIR

(b) Assume an array ARR of length 50 in the Working-storage section. To find the subordinate components

> MOVE 0 TO COUNT.
> MOVE COMPC TO CC IN CIR.
> FIND ANY CIR USING CC.   [format 2]
> GET CIR.
> FIND FIRST CLR WITHIN SUBSET.   [format 4]
> IF DB-STATUS > 0,
>   DISPLAY "NO SUBORDINATE COMPONENTS",
>   GO TO A50.

A20.

> GET SUBC IN CLR.
> ADD 1 TO COUNT.
> MOVE SUBC IN CLR TO ARR (COUNT).
> FIND NEXT CLR WITHIN SUBSET.   [format 4]
> IF DB-STATUS = 0, GO TO A20.
> PERFORM A40 VARYING I FROM 1 BY 1 UNTIL I > COUNT.
> GO TO A50.

A40.

> MOVE ARR (I) TO CC IN CIR.

FIND ANY CIR USING CC.   [format 2]
GET CIR.
Process as necessary by Cobol.

A50.

EXIT.

The superior components can be found if SUBSET is exchanged with SUPSET
and SUBC with SUPC everywhere. Change also the content of the DISPLAY
verb from SUBORDINATE to SUPERIOR.

9.12 (a) *Schema*

FARM RECORD
    Farm code   } Unique key
    Farm name
    Farm size
One record per farm.

SHEEP RECORD
    Farm at birth (BF) ⎫
    Year   (BYR) ⎬ Sheep name which is a unique key
    Number   (NO) ⎭
    Sex   (SEX)
    Weight at birth (BWT)
    Current farm or the last farm where it was disposed of (CF)
    Mother name (sheep name) (MUM)
    Father name (sheep name) (DAD)

One record for each sheep
    [Capital letters in brackets are the data names of the items used
    in the exercises later]

LAMBING RECORD
    Ewe name (EWE)
    Ram name (RAM)
    Number of lambs born (litter size) (LS)
    Number born alive (NL)

One record for each mating.
Unique keys can be

    (Ewe name + Ram name)

Set types needed are:

Set name	Owner	Member	Order
MUMSET	SHEEP	LAMBING	Ewe age
DADSET	SHEEP	LAMBING	Immaterial
OFFSPRING	LAMBING	SHEEP	Sheep name

9.12 (b) Assume that the necessary values are already moved to CF, BYR and SEX by Cobol and that a Keeplist LD INDIC LIMIT 1 is declared in the subschema.

A10.

FIND FIRST SHEEP USING CF, BYR, SEX. (format 1)

A20.

KEEP CURRENT USING INDIC. (retains the currency of this sheep
    record in Keeplist INDIC)
FIND FIRST LAMBING WITHIN MUMSET.

A30.

GET LAMBING.
DISPLAY LS, NL
FIND FIRST SHEEP WITHIN OFFSPRING;
      RETAINING MUMSET CURRENCY.

A50.

GET SHEEP.
DISPLAY BWT, DAD.
FIND NEXT SHEEP WITHIN OFFSPRING;
      RETAINING MUMSET CURRENCY.
IF DB-STATUS = 0, GO TO A50.
FIND NEXT LAMBING WITHIN MUMSET.
IF DB-STATUS = 0, GO TO A30.
FIND FIRST WITHIN INDIC. (format 5 to return to the starting
                             sheep (mother) record)
FREE ALL FROM INDIC.
FIND NEXT SHEEP USING CF, BYR, SEX.
IF DB-STATUS = 0, GO TO A20.

A80.

EXIT.
Warning: Beware of currency traps.

Index